D0457870

THEMES IN DRAMA

An annual publication
Edited by James Redmond

1

Editorial Advisory Board

DRAMA AND SOCIETY

CAMBRIDGE UNIVERSITY PRESS

CAMBRIDGE

LONDON · NEW YORK · MELBOURNE

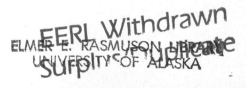

Published by the Syndics of the Cambridge University Press
The Pitt Building, Trumpington Street, Cambridge CB2 1RP
Bentley House, 200 Euston Road, London NW1 2DB
32 East 57th Street, New York, NY 10022, USA
296 Beaconsfield Parade, Middle Park, Melbourne 3206, Australia

© Cambridge University Press 1979

First published 1979

Printed in Great Britain by
Cox & Wyman Ltd, London, Fakenham and Reading

Library of Congress cataloguing in publication data
Main entry under title:

Drama and society.

(Themes in drama; no. 1)

1. Drama – History and criticism – Addresses, essays,
lectures. 2. Literature and society – Addresses, essays,
lectures. 3. Theater and society – Addresses, essays,
lectures. I. Redmond, James, M. A. II. Series.
PN1643.D67   792'.09   78–54723

ISBN 0 521 22076 9

Contents

REVIEW SECTION

Contributors

Nigel Alexander, *Professor of English, Queen Mary College, University of London*

John Allen, *sometime Principal of the Central School of Speech and Drama*

W. A. Armstrong, *Professor of English, Birkbeck College, University of London*

Harold C. Baldry, *sometime Professor of Classics, University of Southampton*

Michael R. Booth, *Professor of Theatre Studies, University of Warwick*

Hanne Castein, *Lecturer in German, Goldsmiths' College, University of London*

Bernard Crick, *Professor of Politics, Birkbeck College, University of London*

David Daniell, *Lecturer in English, University College, University of London*

Julie R. Dashwood, *Lecturer in Italian, University of Sussex*

Edwin Eigner, *Professor of English, University of California, at Riverside*

Istvan Eörsi, *Hungarian playwright and critic*

Inga-Stina Ewbank, *Hildred Carlile Professor of English, Bedford College, University of London*

Nicholas Grene, *Lecturer in English, University of Liverpool*

Elic Konigson, *Maître de Recherche, Recherches théâtrales et musicologiques, Centre national de la recherche scientifique, Paris*

James McFarlane, *Professor in the School of European Studies, University of East Anglia*

Brian Powell, *Lecturer in Japanese, St Antony's College, Oxford*

Donald Rayfield, *Lecturer in Russian, Queen Mary College, University of London*

J. E. Varey, *Professor of Spanish, Westfield College, University of London*

Illustrations

Editor's preface

This is the first volume of 'Themes in Drama', which will be published annually. Each volume will bring together reviews and articles on the dramatic and theatrical activity of a wide range of cultures and periods. The articles will offer original contributions to their own specialised fields, but they will be presented in such a way that their significance may be appreciated readily by non-specialists. The review section is especially important, since reviewers have much more than usual scope to give detailed critical accounts of drama in performance, and to discuss in depth the most significant contributions to dramatic scholarship and criticism.

Each volume will indicate connections between the various national traditions of theatre by bringing together studies of a theme of central and continuing importance. The present volume is concerned with the theme of 'Drama and Society'. There are studies of the various ways in which playwrights have reflected their own communities, and of the attempts by social classes, legislators, and bureaucracies to stimulate, monopolise, or stifle theatrical activity. Although the main periods of the dramatic tradition are examined in representative detail, with attention to Greek and Roman antiquity and the Middle Ages, the main emphasis in this volume is on Renaissance and modern drama.

In some communities drama has directly expressed the orthodox *mores* of the people, serving as an active support in the perpetuation of established religious, philosophical, and political beliefs. In other circumstances drama has emphasised divisive forces within society: for example, class divisions in medieval France and seventeenth-century Spain are analysed, as are ideological divisions in twentieth-century Germany and Japan. Separate papers examine some social aspects of Christianity, feudalism, communism, and fascism: there are papers on state subsidy of drama and on state suppression of drama in present-day Europe. In the past hundred years drama has very often had a negative relationship with the dominant ethos of its own society, and this is examined with reference to England, Ireland, Italy, Norway, and Russia. A political philosopher offers a detailed analysis of the political force in recent productions of the British National

Theatre and of the Royal Shakespeare Company, and an American critic considers the social policies and the social effects of British television drama.

The long review of drama in performance in this number is of the RSC productions of the three *Henry VI* plays: the unexpected success of this enterprise has rescued the trilogy from neglect and mutilation and extended the modern playgoer's awareness of Shakespeare as a playwright of social and political insight. The book reviews include a reassessment, after forty years, of L. C. Knights's classic study *Drama and Society in the Age of Jonson*; there is an authoritative response to a 'dissenting' view of Ibsen's plays, and a consideration of recent works on Marlowe and on the development of English drama over the past four and a half centuries.

The second volume in the series will be concerned with 'Drama and Mimesis' in the various ages of the theatre from the standpoints of the philosopher, literary critic, playwright, and theatrical practitioner.

Contributions are invited for the following volumes, and should be submitted before the indicated dates:

3. Drama, Dance and Music (1 June 1979)
4. Drama and Symbolism (1 March 1980)
5. Drama and Religion (1 March 1981)

Potential contributors should write to the editor for further information and a copy of the yearbook's style-sheet. The editor will also be pleased to receive books on all aspects of drama and theatre to be considered for review.

JAMES REDMOND

Westfield College,
University of London,
London, NW3 7ST

Theatre and society in Greek and Roman antiquity

HAROLD C. BALDRY

I must begin by stating the point of view from which this paper is written.

This congress is not a gathering of historians or antiquarians.* Our programme makes it clear that we are not primarily concerned with the past, but with the present and the future. For our purposes the past is relevant only in so far as we can extract from the earlier history of the theatre some clue to the basic question before us: the relation between the theatre, especially theatre buildings, and society.

It follows that there are certain things I shall not attempt. I shall not try to discuss the whole early history of the theatre – a feat which would, of course, be impossible in one short paper. I shall confine myself to the theatre as it existed in the ancient Greek and later in the Roman world. Even here there are vast controversial areas which I shall have to ignore: questions of evidence, for example, both literary and archaeological, although what I have to say will be based on the evidence as I understand it; or the notorious problem of the origins of drama, although I shall be following a generally accepted conception of the Greek theatre's beginnings and later development.

It seems essential to concentrate first on the one area where there is enough evidence to show the relation between a theatre and its community, Athens in the fifth century BC. From this time we have archaeological remains, although difficult to interpret, on the slopes below the Acropolis; we have over forty plays, although these are only a small fraction of those originally produced; and we know a good deal about the Athenian community and the place of drama in its life. Here, therefore, we can see a type of theatre – the basic model for theatre throughout antiquity – as it comes into being in a known social context. We can read some of the plays performed in that theatre, and ask what they imply about the methods and

*This paper was read in Munich at the Eighth World Congress of the International Federation for Theatre Research/La Fédération Internationale pour la Recherche Théâtrale, and published with other contributions to the congress in Heinz Huesmann (ed.), *Theatre Space/ Der Raum des Theaters* (Prestel-Verlag, Munich, 1977). The Editor wishes to express his gratitude to Heinz Huesmann for permission to reprint this article, and to James F. Arnott, Chairman of the Federation.

style of performance. We can discuss how the social context influenced the form of the theatre and the use made of it.

More dimly, we can look at the long and complicated sequel during which theatres derived ultimately from the Athenian prototype spread over the whole Mediterranean area and beyond. This development through the centuries down to the end of the Roman Empire in the West is a huge field where our knowledge is patchy and it is easy to get lost; but I shall pick out certain aspects of it which seem to me to throw some light on the situation in which the theatre finds itself today.

First, then, ancient Athens: the Athens of Aeschylus, Sophocles, Euripides, Aristophanes. Let us look briefly at the community before turning to the theatre which was such an important feature of its life.

Athens in the fifth century BC was no ordinary Greek city-state. Her successful leadership of Greece against the Persian invasion, commemorated by Aeschylus in the earliest of the extant plays, was transformed into imperial power under Sophocles's friend Pericles, culminating in the disastrous war against Sparta so often reflected in Euripides and Aristophanes. The temples on the Acropolis, the civic buildings in the market place and the theatre were evidence to all comers (as they still are today) of the city's wealth and prestige in this time of power and prosperity. But by modern standards this was not a large city. The population of Attica cannot have been much above three hundred thousand, and of these probably fewer than half lived in Athens itself. Why is it that whereas modern towns of this size pull their theatres down or must struggle to keep them going, in the theatre at Athens vast audiences, the majority of whom must have been native Athenians, watched the production of hundreds of new plays?

In my view the answer lies in the nature of the Athenian community. If we consider the population as a whole, Athens was no democracy. Something like half of the total were slaves; perhaps twenty or thirty thousand were non-Athenians without full citizenship. The adult male citizens to whom in any sense the term 'democracy' could apply numbered at most forty thousand, and even among them there were divisions based on birth and wealth which under stress could erupt into violence and even civil war. Yet it remains true (and all-important for the study of the Attic theatre) that Athens was a more compact, more integrated society than the democracies of today. Among its citizens there is little sign of the we–they antithesis which brings apathy to the life of so many modern communities. The decision-making parliament was no remote body, but a mass meeting in the heart of the city which all citizens could, and a large proportion did, attend. Of course there were means by which much of the real power was retained in certain hands; but the whole citizen body could feel that it participated directly in the running of its affairs. This was a place where what mattered was the spoken word, where articulate and effective use of the human voice was the central feature of both its politics and what we now misleadingly call its 'literature'. Most of the 'literary' genres practised at Athens were linked with open-air occasions involving speech or song: epic, with recitals at the city's greatest festival; oratory, with political debate in the assembly or with the law courts; the philosophic dialogue, with conversation in the market place or the wrestling school; drama, with festivals in the theatre. In London no one has yet thought of comparing the presentation of plays in the new National Theatre on one side of the Thames with what goes on in the Houses of Parliament on the other. But in ancient Athens there were obvious parallels between the meetings of the Assembly on the Pnyx and the performances in the theatre half a mile away: the involvement of the mass audience, the active participation of a large number of the citizens, the eloquence of the orators and of the actors.

One of the strongest bonds which held the citizen body of Athens together was religion: not so much a common faith, but participation in common rituals – above all, in the great religious festivals which marked the Athenian year and in honouring the gods brought the arts to the forefront of Athenian life. At the festival of Athena, with its procession represented on the frieze of the Parthenon, the mass audience listened to professional reciters of Homer and other epic poetry. In a Platonic dialogue one of these 'rhapsodes' described the effect of his performance on his hearers in a way which emphasises the power of the spoken word among the Greeks. 'Whenever I look down at them from the platform,' he says, 'I see them weeping, gazing wildly at me, marvelling at what they hear.' Although (or should one say because?) this is a response to narrative poetry, it brings us close to drama and the festivals of Dionysus, to which we must now turn.

Obviously I cannot deal here in detail with the problematic history of these festivals or the way in which dramatic competitions came to be their most important feature. Let us be content with the central point on which there is general agreement: that drama came into being when an actor was added to a chorus which danced and sang in honour of the god. The essential fact for understanding of the early Greek theatre is that the chorus was the basic element, the actor an addition. Perhaps the purpose of the change, and certainly its effect, was to make the performance more vivid and so increase the emotional involvement of the audience. A character previously only described in narrative was there, alive, speaking for himself. He could converse with the leader of the chorus. Later, when a second and then a third actor were added, dialogue between them became possible independent of the chorus; in short, a play.

With the details and uncertainties of this development we need not be concerned. What I want to stress is the involvement of the community. Because Attic drama seems strange to us, we do not easily realise how natural a part of life it was for the fifth-century Athenian. The playwrights' material, for example, which we find so remote, was drawn from the common experience and common knowledge of the thousands massed at the festival. The point is most obvious for comedy, with its topical jokes and its caricature of the personalities of the day. Aristophanes held up a mirror – admittedly, a distorting mirror – to the present. The tragic poets, on the other hand, were concerned with the past as it was seen by the community for which they wrote: occasionally, as in *Persians*, with recent events; more often, with stories from the common heritage of legend which was familiar from epic poetry, and which for them took the place of history.

Consider some other aspects of the occasion: the procedure on the days of performance; the numbers participating; the financial arrangements.

In Britain now one rarely hears the national anthem in the theatre. I cannot say that I regret its disappearance; but the fact heightens the contrast between our modern theatregoing, with its abrupt beginning of the play and the noise of latecomers scrambling into their seats, and what happened at the spring festival of Dionysus. On the first day of the festival the whole city was on holiday: even prisoners were released on bail. The proceedings opened with the full pomp and ceremony of a great procession through the streets. When the climax came with the dramatic contests, they began with items which to us, who see drama as a thing apart, seem a strange prelude to the presentation of plays. A sucking-pig was sacrificed to purify the theatre, and libations were poured. This was the time of year when the 'allies' brought their tribute to Athens; and now a line of young Athenians marched across in front of the audience, each carrying one silver talent in a jar to show the balance of tribute over expenditure for the past year. Announcements were made of honours conferred on citizens or strangers for services to the city. The sons of men who had died in battle for Athens paraded in armour given them by the state and listened to a short exhortation before going to the special seats allotted to them. Perhaps last came the completion of the selection of the judges: ten urns containing names were brought to the theatre and a name drawn from each, and the ten thus chosen swore to give an impartial verdict. Only after all this civic ceremony a trumpet sounded, and the first play began. Days later, when the contest was finished, a special Assembly was held at which the citizens reviewed the conduct of the festival and spoke their minds in awarding praise or blame.

If we turn to the people involved, we find a remarkable number of active participants, mostly drawn not from a separate professional class but from various points in the social spectrum. No doubt actors, musicians and trainers were specialised 'theatre people', and so in a sense were the poets;

but in the fifth century at any rate this cannot have been true of the chorus-members, who for all three contests – choral song, tragedy, and comedy – probably numbered nearly twelve hundred. Financial backing came from men of wealth and influence; ritual was in the hands of the priests; organisation and judging lay with ordinary citizens. If we add 'extras', stage-hands, wardrobe assistants and the like, the total actively concerned must have been not far short of fifteen hundred – apart from the many others who took part in ceremonies or processions. To these must be added the vast multitude of those who came to watch and listen: when the theatre was crowded, which seems to have been frequent, perhaps as many as seventeen thousand. Although many of these were foreigners and some were women or slaves, it is clear what a large proportion of the forty thousand citizens were involved, actively or as audience, in the presentation of the plays.

The financing of the theatre, important and significant then as now, points to the same conclusion. In ancient Greece no one imagined that the theatre could or should pay its way. Providing money for a production at the festival of Dionysus, like maintaining a warship for a year or paying for a delegation to another state, was seen as a service which the rich could be expected to give to the city. As for the audience, from the time of Pericles the state treasury paid for the seats of the citizens – a payment which has often been regarded as a form of 'dole', but which has another aspect: the assumption that drama is the community's concern, as we think education is today. It is difficult to estimate the total expenditure on the drama contests at a festival, but eleven talents is probably a reasonable guess. Some idea of the value of a talent may be gained from the rough calculation that it would keep fifteen or more families of four for a year, or would buy perhaps thirty slaves at average prices.

My aim so far has been to describe the place of drama in the life of fifth-century Athens: not the favourite pastime of a minority, but a great civic and religious occasion for the community as a whole, rich in pomp and ceremony, financed from the public treasury and from private wealth, involving hundreds of participants, attended by many thousands; a central event in the year, which not even the stresses of war and defeat at the end of the century could stop. It is not surprising that Plato assumed that dramatic and other poetry required treatment at length in a discussion of the ideal state, and believed that the writers of tragedy and comedy were such a powerful influence on the community that they must be expelled!

It is against this background that we can make sense of the theatre in which drama was performed. Its first essential characteristic, of course, was size. Although as time went on revivals of some plays already performed were permitted, there was never any possibility of a play having a 'run' in the modern sense. The performance was unique, like a football match, and the theatre auditorium, like a football stadium, had to be large enough to hold the vast crowd of those who wanted to take part in this one occasion and watch this single presentation of the play.

Size determined location. There is some evidence that at an early date performances were given in front of an audience seated in wooden stands, and that these may have been in the level market place north-west of the Acropolis. But if this interpretation of the evidence is right, it only confirms the inadequacy of early Greek technology for a task which the Romans later mastered – the building of a tiered auditorium on level ground. For the stands collapsed, and the disaster led to the adoption of the type of site which became the norm for Greek theatres in later centuries: a steep slope provided by nature, not by engineering. Such slopes were, of course, common in Greece. (If western theatre had started in the Netherlands, its history might have been different.) A slope of sufficient size lay beneath the Acropolis on its south-eastern side; and here rising terraces of earth were made to provide support for wooden benches and later (probably in the fourth century) for seats of stone. This natural amphitheatre, the use of which was extended and improved as time went on, would have been well described by the Latin word *auditorium*, a listening place, for the acoustics of such sites are naturally good; but the Greeks called it a *theatron*, a looking place, a place for thousands of spectators.

What did they see before them when they looked?

The general view, of course, was of familiar surroundings from which being in the theatre did not cut them off. (In later years a general theatre convention arose corresponding to what the Athenian audience could see: as the Piraeus and the Agora lay to their right, entrance from harbour or market place in the play must be on that side; entrance from open country, on the spectators' left.) But more immediately before them lay two things of which there are still slight traces on the site dating from the sixth century BC or earlier, a time well before the introduction of drama. One was a small temple of Dionysus: the theatre was a holy place. The other, closer to the foot of the slope, was a levelled circular area which perhaps once had been a threshing floor; at any rate it was like a large version of the round threshing floors which one can still see in the Greek countryside today. This circle was the *orchestra*, the dancing ground on which competing choruses had moved and sung before the days of drama, and which in the fifth century remained the most prominent feature of what the spectator saw. In the middle of its earthen floor there was a small altar, by which the flute-player stood who made music for the dancers.

This, then, is the picture before the coming of drama: thousands of spectators, mostly citizens of Athens, watched dancing and singing chor- uses drawn from among their number as they performed on the ancient circle near the temple of the god. But what happened when actors were added?

The archaeological evidence on this question is small although, as we shall see, it is significant. Inferences from the plays are debatable. But it is generally agreed that when one or more actors were included in the performance there must have been a tent or hut for the changing of masks or costumes, as there often is for an open-air production today. The Greek word for this was *skene* (Latin *scaena*), and the most likely place for it would be at the back of the dancing circle from the spectators' point of view. A slight addition, but one whose subsequent history is important for our purpose, for it played a large part in shaping the distinctive nature of the Greek theatre and of Greek drama itself.

The confusing remains of the theatre of Dionysus as we know them today include the bottom part of a long wall behind the site of the dancing circle, in which vertical grooves or slots have been cut in the face of the stone. These grooves, with their suggestion of heavy wooden posts now lost, are our one piece of material evidence for something clearly implied in most of the extant plays: the development of the *skene* into a structure more elaborate than the original tent or hut. The existing post-holes must have been for the

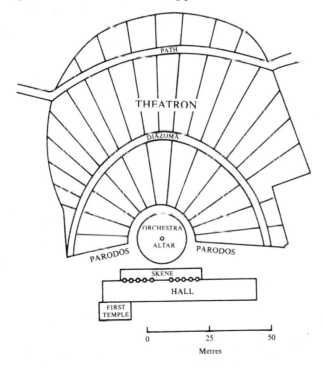

Sketch-plan of the theatre of Dionysus in the Periclean period

back of this structure, and imply other supports farther forward for its front. If all the grooves were used this enlarged *skene* would be over thirty metres long, but probably it was not more than four metres deep. Perhaps at either end it had projecting wings like the stone theatre buildings of later years, but this is a point on which there can be no certainty. Evidently it was made of wood, and it may well have been constructed afresh for each festival. But such a substantial erection could hardly be put up for single days, still less for particular plays: it must have been there throughout the dramatic contest.

A wooden façade behind the actors would be an effective sounding-board for their voices, as well as setting off their masks and colourful costumes; a great asset, in fact, just as background to the performances. But the *skene* had become more than this. Instead of a changing-tent or hut, an external accessory like a dressing-room in the modern theatre, it was now a place within the action of the drama. It had become part of the make-believe, part of the play, whether it stood in the audience's imagination for a palace or a temple or a general's tent or even a cave. Characters in the play could be regarded as living in it, and went in or came out. For the extant tragedies only one door is essential, but it has been argued that some of the comedies need at least two: probably by the closing years of the fifth century there were three entrances in the façade, a great central one perhaps four metres wide and smaller ones at either side.

The height of the *skene* is uncertain, though some have thought a scene in Euripides involved an actor's leap from roof to ground, and drawn the conclusion that it was no more than about three metres. It seems to have had a flat roof on which actors could appear, as the watchman does at the beginning of the *Oresteia*. Elevation to greater heights was achieved by the theatre crane, *mechane* (Latin *machina*). Euripides, of course, was notorious for ending his dramas with a *deus* (or *dea*) *ex machina*, and on occasion made more venturesome use of it: in the lost play called *Bellerophon* the hero was lifted skywards on his winged steed Pegasus (surely a dummy, not a live horse!). It is not surprising that Aristophanes saw the crane as a good subject for parody, or that the actor seems to have found his ride through the air a hazardous experience. The farmer-hero of *Peace* flies heavenwards on a giant dung-beetle like Bellerophon on Pegasus, and shouts 'Hi, crane-driver, take care of me!'

The actor could appear, then, on the *skene* roof, or be lifted even higher above it; but his normal place was the area in front of the wooden façade. These few square metres have become a scholars' battleground. Their relation to the dancing circle has been the most controversial of all the many problems of the fifth-century theatre. The issue most keenly contested has been the level of the acting area in relation to the dancing circle which separated it from the audience. Centuries later, writers on the Greek theatre assumed that it had a stage some three or four metres above the *orchestra*. But a number of the plays require intermingling of actors and chorus, and in some the chorus enter or leave through the *skene*, or actors come and go by the entrances at the sides of the dancing ground; in any case, an arrangement which put the actors on such a different level would scarcely be credible for the period when they were still a recent offshoot from the chorus. On the other hand, if the actors were on the same level as the chorus the sight-line difficulties are obvious, especially for the seats of honour in the front rows of the auditorium. Personally I am prepared, as are many others, to settle for a low platform in front of the *skene* at the back of the dancing circle. It may have been long, but it was certainly narrow: lack of depth was the most striking feature of this acting area in contrast with the modern stage.

Whether any scenery was used is a difficult and perhaps insoluble question. The interpretation of a key statement in Aristotle is disputed; and when the text of a play describes a scene, was the playwright referring to what was shown by material means in the theatre, or using verbal description all the more fully just because what he described was *not* visible to the eye? My own view is that the fifth-century theatre knew nothing of scenery in the modern sense. Whether the characters were supposed to be outside a temple or palace or encampment or in the country or on the shore, most of the action seen by the audience took place in front of the same façade with its door or doors, decorated perhaps with painting in perspective. It may well be that a simple wooden shape representing an altar or a tomb was sometimes placed at a little distance from the façade. Wooden statues of the gods, probably brightly coloured, are other likely theatre properties. But the essential point is that where the modern theatregoer looks for a 'set' designed for a particular play, his Athenian counterpart expected and found little or nothing more than a familiar structure used in all the plays. For the rest imagination, stimulated and guided by words, was enough. When Troy is set ablaze at the end of Euripides's *Trojan Women*, there was no spectacle such as modern stage mechanism and lighting can produce nothing more than the cries of the chorus or Hecuba:

> O horror, horror!
> Troy is aflame, the houses on the hill are burning,
> The city and the ramparts!

It was left to the Romans in Nero's time to burn a real house down on the stage.

Freedom of imagination, now returning to our theatres after a period of visual realism, has been the rule in the history of world drama, and ancient Greece was no exception. In the comedies of Aristophanes this freedom sometimes seems almost complete, transcending all limitations of place and time. It was greater in the tragedies of Aeschylus than in those of his

successors, especially Euripides. But we fail to grasp the distinctive character of the Greek theatre if we do not recognise those features of it which
tended to limit the free roving of the imagination, and to concentrate the
attention of the audience on a single place and a single time. This is the
essential point behind all the fuss over the theory of the 'unities' mistakenly
attributed to Aristotle. The presence of the chorus gave all fifth-century
Greek drama a continuity which Shakespeare lacks, and in the majority of
tragedies the imagined function of the *skene* and the space before it remained
the same. Whether it did duty for palace or temple or tent or cave, the *skene*
could and usually did provide a point of reference to which all the action of
the play was related. Here was the single focal point of the play, to which all
the characters must come to take their part in the action. But it is a focus in a
wider sense than this. The visible action performed here in front of the
audience is far from embracing all the events of the play. Many of them take
place elsewhere, and instead of a change of scene to show the event itself,
news of it is brought to this point by a messenger. What the Athenian
audience did expect to see was not the event, but its sequel. In a climax
prepared for by the messenger's speech, the result of the reported action is
often brought to the same focal point before the *skene* façade: Hippolytus is
carried in to die; deluded Queen Agave marches triumphantly in holding
her own son's head.

In tragedy, the same process of report followed by display of the result
was practised for action that took place 'within'. The Greeks never
developed the conception of an interior scene made visible to the audience
by the stage convention which we take for granted – the removal of one wall
of a room. Perception of events behind the *skene* façade was limited to what
was heard, not seen, and conveyed to the audience by the comments of
characters outside or the chorus: Medea's cries of anger and hatred at
Jason's new marriage; the death-shrieks of Clytemnestra; or – more subtle
use of the same device – Phaedra listening at the door as Hippolytus inside
the palace curses the nurse who has betrayed her secret. Otherwise what
occurred 'within' was treated in the same way as what happened on the
mountain or the seashore or in some other distant place. It could be related
by a messenger and its results could be brought out in front of the audience.
When Oedipus discovers the appalling truth about his past he rushes into
the palace and the door is closed. A slave comes out and tells how Jocasta
has hanged herself and Oedipus has destroyed his own sight. The audience
has watched the blinding in imagination through the messenger's report.
Now the door opens and the blinded king stands before them.

The re-entry of Oedipus presented no difficulty, only a change of mask;
and in Sophocles's play the dead Jocasta remained unseen. But it is clear
that in some tragedies the whole outcome of the catastrophe within was
made visible, including the dead. These scenes were not static tableaux:

they could involve speech and action, out of which flowed the further development of the play. How they were managed is one of the most controversial issues in the history of the Greek theatre. On the whole it seems best to accept the evidence that after the event its participants, dead or alive, were brought before the audience on a low wheeled cart pushed out through the central opening of the *skene*. If this platform on wheels with its burden of horror seems comic today, it is interesting that the Athenians were also prepared to find it so. The strongest reason for believing that it existed in the fifth century is that Aristophanes twice makes fun of it.

In later centuries the acting area acquired a name: in contrast with the *orchestra*, originally the dancing place of the chorus, it was the *logeion*, the speaking place. There is no evidence that the term was used in the fifth century BC, but it would have been apt. Many features of Greek theatrical practice point to the conclusion that the Greek actor was primarily a speaker rather than an actor in the modern sense. Admittedly, his appearance in the fifth century was less grotesque than in later times (a point which often seems unknown to contemporary theatre directors): vase paintings show that his mask had natural features boldly drawn, and he wore thin-soled boots in which movement was not difficult. But the wearing of a mask at all precluded changes of facial expression, which in any case would have been hardly visible to spectators sitting anything from twenty to eighty metres away on the other side of the *orchestra*. All the actors were men; and as (apart from silent 'extras') there were at most three actors in tragedy and four or perhaps five in comedy, and usually two or three times as many parts, a single actor often played – or rather spoke – a strange combination of roles. In Sophocles's *Antigone* the same actor is likely to have played both Antigone and Haemon: certainly the part of Ismene was combined with that of the Guard. In Euripides's *Bacchae* the deuteragonist probably 'doubled' King Pentheus and Agave, the King's mother who kills him. In his *Ion* and *Electra* one actor carried four parts, in *Orestes* at least five. In Sophocles's *Oedipus at Colonus* it seems simplest to suppose that one character, Theseus, was played by all three actors in turn. To these points must be added the nature and position of the main acting area. The new Olivier Theatre in London is in some ways like a miniature version of the Attic prototype I have been describing, but the actors do not make themselves heard from a narrow platform over an intervening group of dancers: they use the whole of the deep stage, and are at their most effective from a point near the front of it where every change of look is visible to every member of the audience.

The conclusion from all this is that in the fifth-century theatre of Dionysus the actor was mainly a voice, reaching out over the *orchestra* to the most remote rows of the vast auditorium. His voice was his greatest asset, which qualified him to become an actor and determined his prospects in the profession. To improve it he would go through meticulous training, fasting and dieting and seizing every chance of rehearsing. Strength of voice was the first essential, so that it could be heard throughout the theatre without shouting: there is no reason to suppose, as was once thought, that the mask did anything to enlarge it. But other qualities were equally necessary: clarity, correctness of diction (the comic playwrights never tired of making fun of one notorious mispronunciation), fineness of tone, adaptability to character and mood. The Greek actor had to be able to change his voice, as well as his mask, from young to old or from man to woman. On occasion, he must be able to sing, whether chanting in various rhythms or even breaking into a lyric solo. He had to show the same versatility in utterance as a modern actor displays in facial expression. He must be equally effective in argument and narrative, the two uses of the spoken word which counted most in the theatre, as in the public life of the city as a whole. Thus seen, the actor takes us back to the rhapsode reciting epic narrative to the excited crowd at the festival of Athena. He carries one's thoughts still further, out of the festivals altogether to the orators addressing the citizen assembly on the Pnyx. Like that assembly, a theatre performance in fifth-century Athens was a public event in a public place.

My purpose has been to show that drama flourished and rose to such heights of achievement in fifth-century Athens because it was not a fringe activity in a loosely knit society, but occupied a central place in the existence and the religious life – and the financial outlay – of a compact community. The nature of the plays and their performance, together with the size and location and lay-out of the theatre, were determined by the community's common life-style and experience and assumptions: an accepted ritual, the importance of the spoken word, familiarity with the epic tradition, the feeling for form and pattern in all art. It cannot be said that the plays moulded the theatre or the theatre shaped the plays: both were products of the same social background.

    May I digress for a moment from antiquity to look at the question whether the same kind of theatre–community relationship is possible in our very different situation today – our comparatively huge and complex societies, our vast range of available information, our diversities of belief and outlook and way of life? This is an issue much discussed in recent years in England: can we in the twentieth century really have a National Theatre? – a point we continue to debate even after we have built one. One of the most striking and, I think, admirable features of the great new building on the south bank of the Thames is the stress laid by both architect and director on the need to maintain a living relationship between the theatre building and the outside world. 'The building,' writes the architect, Sir Denys Lasdun, 'is an extension of the theatre into the everyday world from which it springs.' Or again: 'I feel that all the public areas of the building, the foyers and terraces, are in themselves a theatre with the city as a backdrop ... It is very important that the National Theatre becomes a part of the city. Any idea of a cultural ghetto has gone.'[1] Accordingly, the foyers, bars and restaurants of the theatre are open to anyone from morning to night, and there is nearly always something going on, whether it be folk music or kite-flying or an open-air scene from a medieval mystery play.

It will be interesting to see whether this bold effort to achieve some integration between theatre and modern society succeeds in a place where the audience is so diverse and the surroundings so dreary. One's belief that it is no easy matter, and that thought and experiment in this area are needed, is strengthened by the fate of the theatre in later antiquity. History does not repeat itself, but sometimes it has a warning to give.

Before considering the further development of the theatre we need to look at the general picture. The background is one of change from small scale to large, from comparative simplicity to diversity: the decline of Athenian wealth and strength, the ascendancy of Macedon and the conquests of Alexander, the spread of the Greek language and civilisation over the whole of the Middle East, the rise of Rome and her conquest of Greece but acceptance of Greek culture, the extension and eventual collapse of Rome's imperial power. What happened to drama through this complex history of nearly a thousand years during which not only kingdoms and empires rose and fell but cities of all sizes flourished, though never again with the arrogant sovereignty or the creative genius of Periclean Athens?

The theatre of Dionysus by the Acropolis continued in use of one sort or another until the fourth century AD, undergoing the various changes and reconstructions which have left their mark on the site as we know it today. But the most striking development after the fifth century is the expansion of theatre activity, more or less on the Athenian model, beyond Attica until in time it reached every corner of the Greek-speaking world. In the fourth century BC or later, as every Mediterranean tourist knows, scores of theatres were built – not only huge structures like those at Epidaurus or Megalopolis in the Peloponnese, or Pergamum near the Turkish coast, but others of various sizes to suit each community's needs. In these many theatres plays continued to be performed in their thousands in dramatic contests at local festivals – mostly in honour of Dionysus, but sometimes for Apollo or some other god. To the regular festivals of local communities were added others, often far more splendid, financed by great patrons or set up in honour of princes and kings. For centuries drama and music in the theatre were the chief entertainment and the most popular form of culture throughout the Greek world. The total aggregate of productions staged, of audiences reached, of money spent, was clearly greater than ever before.

The dramatic texts surviving from these later times are mainly comedy: the Greek Menander, from whom we now have one complete play and parts of several others; and derived from Menander or his contemporaries, the Latin plays of Plautus and Terence. These are not fantastic flights of imagination or topical satire in the style of Aristophanes, but comedies of manners which mirror the ups and downs of domestic life in fourth- or third-century Athens. Of their use of the theatre building I shall have more to say presently.

Because comedy predominates in our extant literature, however, it must not be supposed that the performance of tragedies had come to an end. It is true, and significant, that there was an increasing tendency to look back to the fifth-century masterpieces. When the Athenian statesman Lycurgus reconstructed the theatre of Dionysus in the second half of the fourth century with stone seating and a permanent stone *skene*, he ornamented it with statues of Aeschylus, Sophocles, and Euripides; while about the same time he established an authorised text of their plays. This canonisation of the three great tragic poets was reflected in the festival arrangements. The revival of earlier plays originally allowed as a compliment to Aeschylus was extended in the fourth century to Sophocles and Euripides as well, and the custom arose for a tragedy by one of the three masters to be presented at each year's spring festival of Dionysus as a prelude to the competition between new plays. It may fairly be said that the rigidity of Lycurgus's stonework was being matched by gradual ossification of the art of serious drama. Nevertheless, we know the names of many new tragic poets and titles of many of their works: the writing of tragedy, like the theatre, spread out from Athens and flourished at Alexandria and elsewhere. Eventually it reached Rome, and we have fragmentary remains of tragedy from several Latin playwrights of the Republican period. Even in the first century BC we hear that performances of tragedy – no doubt mostly revivals – were attended by eager crowds, who knew their stage classics well enough to prompt an actor whose memory failed him.

Of the new plays many seem to have been written for recital or reading rather than performance, and personally I would put the tragedies of Seneca in the first century AD also in this category. But the chief function of most of them (and of the revivals, too) was to provide material for the actor. His rising importance even in the fifth century BC is clear from the introduction of prizes for acting alongside the awards for plays. By Aristotle's time the actors' profession had far outstripped all others as the dominant element in the theatre, and we find the philosopher regretting that the actors now count for more than the playwrights. Leading actors toured the Greek world like the pop stars of today, receiving huge fees from states or wealthy patrons: Polus, the greatest star of the fourth century, is said to have been paid a talent for a two-day appearance. It does not surprise us to find that in time they consolidated their position by allying themselves together. From the third century BC, if not earlier, actors along with other professional groups – poets, musicians, reciters, choral singers and trainers – formed guilds of Artists of Dionysus, which enjoyed a position of power and privilege unparalleled in theatre history. A guild could operate almost like an independent state, receiving and sending ambassadors. The privileges of its members could include exemption from military service, freedom from arrest, security of person and property. They were honoured and feasted, and on ceremonial public occasions marched in processions robed in purple and gold. The most popular actors became such international figures that their statues were set up in many places and they were given the citizenship of many cities. Eventually, in the first century AD, a single association of Artists of Dionysus was organised throughout the Graeco-Roman world.

I have described this emergence of the acting profession on an international scale because it shows how far we have moved away from the participation of the citizens in the dramatic contests of fifth-century Athens. The same conclusion arises from the later organisation of the festivals, so imitative of the past yet also so different. After the fourth century BC the running of dramatic festivals at Athens or elsewhere was entrusted not to a leading citizen of the town, but to a festival organiser provided with funds by the state. (Modern parallels are not difficult to find.) We know little of how this official worked, but he must have gone beyond the local community to draw upon the general supply of professional talent no longer attached to any particular place; no doubt the guilds of the Artists of Dionysus had some part in the arrangements. The festival itself remained a great occasion, but with significant differences. After the Macedonian conquest the glory of the city could count for little, although much might be made of the glory of a royal patron. Ritual could continue as a formality, but had lost much of its earlier significance. The public came together for entertainment. It is interesting that, as far as we can judge, so little drama of any significance emerged out of so much theatrical activity.

The best surviving example of Greek theatre building from these later centuries is, of course, the great theatre at Epidaurus (see plate 1), constructed towards the end of the fourth century BC to the plan of a single architect, Polyclitus. This was regarded in antiquity, as well as by the modern visitor, as the peak achievement of its kind. Its symmetry is complete, its acoustics, as the custodians are ever ready to demonstrate, remarkable. Yet even here there are questions about the acting area; and if we turn to the scores of other remains of ancient theatres, each with its own problems of interpretation, the later development of the theatre building seems a subject of almost hopeless complexity.

1 The theatre at Epidaurus in the Peloponnese

Some theoretical guidance is provided by the Roman writer Vitruvius, whose Latin work *On Architecture*, published late in the first century BC, distinguishes 'the Greek theatre' from 'the Roman theatre' and devotes a chapter to each, describing its lay-out precisely in geometrical terms. He makes it clear that he is putting forward ideal blueprints, not dealing with any particular examples; and it is not surprising that among the extant remains we can find none which exactly corresponds to either of his plans. Nevertheless, his theorising at any rate divides these remains into two types, and tells us something about the general features of each. It is universally agreed now that by 'the Greek theatre' Vitruvius did not mean the Attic theatre of the fifth century BC, of which he must have known much less than we do, but the sort of theatre building practised by the Greeks nearer his own time. If we combine the archaeological evidence and the few surviving play-texts with what Vitruvius has to say, we can pick out certain trends as characteristic of the late Greek theatre, and draw a rather more definite picture of the Roman. Both, it seems to me, have implications about the relation between theatre and society which it is interesting to compare with fifth-century Athens.

The most important change has to do with the chorus. We have seen how the dancing and singing chorus, drawn from the local citizens, was the original stock from which drama grew, and its place, the *orchestra*, was the central feature which the fifth-century Athenian theatre audience had before them. The extreme example of that audience's involvement in the plays was the *parabasis* in Aristophanic comedy, when the chorus stepped out of the play, as it were, and directly addressed the massed spectators on political or other topics of the day. After the fifth century not only the *parabasis* goes, but the comic chorus itself becomes only an irrelevant interlude, and its performances are indicated, in our surviving texts, by no more than the heading 'Chorus' or 'Choral Song'. In tragedy as early as the beginning of the fourth century the playwright Agathon began the practice of writing choral songs which would do as well in one play as another. As the importance of the chorus in the plays diminished, this was bound to affect their place in the theatre: the original large dancing circle decreased in size and the stage building, successor to the early wooden *skene*, absorbed a segment of the circle as it advanced towards the auditorium.

We might have expected that the actors, now so dominant, would take over the *orchestra*; and there may have been a period when this was so – perhaps, for example, at Epidaurus. But possibly because in the frequent revivals of tragedy the chorus was still important and a place for them essential, a very different change occurred. Vitruvius states, and the archaeological evidence confirms, that the Greek theatre of which he is writing included a stage (Latin *pulpitum*) some three or three and a half metres high above the *orchestra*. As this was in front of the *skene* it was called the *proskenion* (Latin *proscaenium*). At the back of it was the *skene*, now increasing in grandeur and elaboration. While the chorus, if one was present, still moved on the *orchestra* below, the actors now performed on this upper level. In comedy it would probably represent a street with two or three houses opening on to it, whose inhabitants are the characters of the play. For tragedy we have no texts and know little about the settings portrayed; but painted scenery and other scenic devices seem more likely for this time than in the fifth century BC.

This raising of the acting area far above its earlier level made the actor more easily visible to the audience, but it also cut him off from them by a three-metre drop. We are on the way towards the proscenium arch with its dichotomy of brightly lit stage and darkened auditorium. Significantly, this change in the theatre building coincided with a gradual transformation of the tragic actor's appearance. Late in the fourth century BC a new type of tragic mask came into use with unnaturally high forehead covered by a tower of hair. Other modifications followed: the further distortion of the mask until it had an enormous forehead topped by close-packed ringlets, a gaping mouth, and staring eyes; the padding of chest and belly to swell the actor's bulk; the high-soled boot, eventually developed so far that it could raise him twenty-three centimetres or more above the ground. The tragic heroes and heroines, who once aroused pity and fear because for all their greatness they are somehow like ourselves, have become beings calculated to fill the audience with wonder and horror because they are so remote.

When we pass from Vitruvius's 'Greek theatre' to his 'Roman theatre', the difference from the fifth-century theatre of Dionysus becomes still more marked. At Rome the creation of a permanent theatre building was delayed for many years for a reason such as never obtained at Athens: the senate's objection to the people spending too much time at dramatic shows. At last in 55 BC a stone theatre was built in the Roman capital by Pompey. The displays presented at its dedication three years later included musical and gymnastic contests in the theatre, horse races and animal battles with lions and elephants in the hippodrome; and the Roman public's love of spectacle was further satisfied, we are told, by a performance of the *Clytemnestra* of the Latin playwright Accius in which a procession of the Greek victors returning from Troy included three thousand chariots, five hundred mules and countless elephants and giraffes, and took hours to pass across the stage. What a contrast with the entry of Agamemnon in Aeschylus's *Oresteia*, bringing Cassandra with him in his single chariot and showing his pride only by consenting to walk over a red carpet as he goes to his death!

About the same date the poet Lucretius wrote his great work *On the Nature of Things*. In the fourth book he explains his theory of vision, and gives an example of how colour is transmitted from surfaces to our sight. In Cyril Bailey's translation:

> And commonly is this done by awnings, yellow and red and purple, when stretched over great theatres they flap and flutter, spread everywhere on masts and beams. For there they tinge the assembly in the tiers beneath, and all the bravery of the stage and the gay-clad company of the elders, and constrain them to flutter in their colours. And the more closely are the hoardings of the theatre shut in all around, the more does all the scene within laugh, bathed in brightness, as the light of day is straitened.[2]

It is tempting to believe that the poet has Pompey's theatre in mind, although he may be referring to an earlier wooden structure or structures that preceded it. But in any case this rare glimpse from a contemporary source tells us several things about the Roman theatre which are confirmed and supplemented by Vitruvius and by remains of the same type of building elsewhere. The three elements which go back to the Athenian theatre of Dionysus – acting area, *orchestra* and *theatron* – were now brought together into a single unit which the Romans, with their engineering skill, could build on level ground without the assistance of a natural slope. The stage building, grandiose descendant of the wooden *skene*, equalled the auditorium in height, so that awnings such that Lucretius describes could be stretched across to form a partial roof and keep out the sun. The stage (*proscaenium*) was made low and deep, and not only the actors but all performers used it. The *orchestra* suffered its logical fate, and shrank to a semicircle which usually became the top class seating area. The ancient dancing circle, already encroached upon in the late Greek theatre, has now been completely devoured by the acting area and the auditorium, and we have arrived at the familiar modern situation of an audience facing a stage.

So was created the enclosed theatre shut off from the outside world: not a holy place or a place for ritual, although sometimes a shrine or shrines were attached, but a place for entertainment and above all for spectacle. In the fifth-century theatre at Athens audience, chorus, and sometimes actors had all come in by the same entrances; now the public were completely separate from the players, and entered by passageways of their own. Within the theatre the audience were divided according to rank and wealth. Senators, members of the city council and other dignitaries sat in the *orchestra*. Behind them fourteen rows were reserved for the *equites*, the wealthiest non-senatorial class. There were no special seats for priests. The change from community ritual to secular entertainment was complete.

This paper has concentrated on the changing history of the main type of theatre building known in antiquity, which after the rediscovery of Vitruvius in 1484 had so great an influence on the development of theatre in Europe. In this much abbreviated version of an extremely complex story many things of importance have inevitably been oversimplified or even ignored. One omission, however, must be repaired: to achieve anything like a balanced picture, brief reference must be made to another aspect which was probably at least as old as the performances in the Athenian theatre of Dionysus, and outlasted more formal drama when the Roman Empire declined in the West. I mean, of course, what the Greeks called mime – not the acting without speech which the word normally suggests today, but simple popular drama, put on by small groups of players and perhaps often improvised, with no connection with the gods except sometimes to make fun of them. A Latin growth of the same sort was the Atellan farce, with its stock characters Bucco, Dossennus, Maccus, Manducus, and Pappus.

At times the writing of such realistic scenes from ordinary life became a literary fashion, as among the learned poets of Alexandria about the end of the fourth century BC. But more relevant for a review of the use of theatre space are the South Italian vases of the fourth and third centuries BC which show such players of popular farce at work, burlesquing tragedy, ridiculing gods or heroes, or representing comic incidents from everyday life. The setting seems to be a wooden platform reached by a few steps, and bearing whatever simple structure was needed for the show – the sort of 'theatre' which could be erected and taken down again as it was needed. Some such wooden erection was probably used by Plautus for his comedies, which combine imitation of Greek comedy with popular farce, and perhaps it was from this that the lower stage in Roman theatre buildings was derived.

It is tempting to see in the mime and kindred forms of entertainment an ancient 'alternative theatre' which survived apart from the 'established' theatres and reappeared in the *jongleurs* of the Middle Ages or was even reincarnated in the *commedia dell' arte*. But history is never so simple as one would like it to be: in actuality the last phase in the story of the theatre in antiquity is the *invasion* of the main theatres, once the home of serious drama, by the mime and other popular entertainments despised by the upper classes. Unfortunately it is from this hostile source that nearly all our meagre evidence comes; but it seems clear that under the Roman Empire tragedy and comedy gave way to a variety of substitutes. Dramatic recitations (one-man shows, as we should now call them) replaced tragedy: that ambitious artist the Emperor Nero, we are told, 'sang' Orestes the Matricide, Oedipus Blinded, Hercules Mad. More important was 'pantomime', a solo performance by a masked dancer while a libretto was sung by a chorus – the nearest thing to ballet in the ancient world. Atellan farces seem to have been presented up to the end of the first century AD. Most popular of all was the mime itself, growing more and more 'realistic'. We read of sexual intercourse on the stage, even of executions carried out in reality when a condemned criminal was substituted for the actor. It is not surprising that the theatre building was sometimes modified so that it could be used for spectacles more usual in the arena. In the theatre at Athens as we now have it the semicircular *orchestra* is surrounded by a marble barrier probably erected to protect the spectators of gladiatorial shows after one of the fighters had been killed between the thrones of the priests; and other modifications seem to have had the object of making the area watertight for use in mock sea fights.

Whatever the truth about survival of the mime beyond the barbarian invasions of Italy, it is clear that one can legitimately speak of a rebirth of drama in the medieval church in the tenth century. History in this case did come near to repeating itself, for the dramatisation of an incident at a point in the liturgy strongly recalls the addition of an actor to a Greek choral performance, and both innovations must have had the same purpose: to make an episode in ritual more vivid for the people. Yet there were of course differences: not least, the use of multiple staging in medieval drama as against the concentration of Greek tragedy on a single focus. Behind these contrasting uses of theatre space in antiquity and the Middle Ages, there were differences in social and cultural background; complex, intricate differences which invite further exploration.

NOTES

1. *Architectural Review*, January 1977, pp. 11 and 25.
2. Titi Lucreti Cari, *De Rerum Natura*, edited with prolegomena, critical apparatus, translation and commentary by Cyril Bailey (Oxford: Clarendon Press, rev. ed. 1949) 1, 367.

Religious drama and urban society in France at the end of the Middle Ages

ELIE KONIGSON

In his *Essai de poétique médiévale*,[1] Paul Zumthor argues persuasively that a medieval play should be regarded as the expression of a *collective* experience. Naturally, there is no question of denying the existence of an individual author, but the medieval playwright, to a much greater extent than in most periods, may be regarded as just one of the links in a chain. And any particular play, far from having a rigidly fixed form, was freely reworked by subsequent writers and actors in accordance with current taste or to suit the wishes of those who were organising a particular performance. I would go further and say that even when the dramatic text remained unchanged, when it preserved the form and the limits originally imparted by an author, it was still the theatrical expression of a collective consciousness.

The force of the medieval religious play depended on its special functions in its society; and the play may best be regarded as a product not of one man's mind but of the community, or a section of the community, as a collectivity. Myths and legends must also have had original authors, but because they expressed in a special way the shared beliefs and values of a social group, they could not properly be attributed to any individual. This is precisely the case with medieval religious plays: through its religious drama, medieval French society revealed the image that it had of its own bases.

The original authors of the Miracle and Mystery plays gathered together the threads of tradition and legend, much as Charles Perrault and the brothers Grimm were later to do with folk-tales, and it is not by chance that so many of the subjects of the Miracle plays in the Cangé manuscript, written during the fourteenth century, appear again later in the Grimm collection, in the widely disseminated fascicles of the *Bibliothèque Bleue*, and in the oral tradition. Medieval religious theatre was a melting-pot into which the collective imagination poured its various ingredients based on texts (sacred, canonical or apocryphal), on the oral transmission of Christian legends, and on folk-tales.

Such a work, whether a Miracle or a Mystery play, was meaningful on more levels than the surface level of the simple development of the plot. But in order to grasp these varying levels of meaning, one must first try to define the 'collective voice' in the play. Was it the voice of the social group as a whole, or of just one section of society? A religious play acted out on a medieval stage had two distinct kinds of meaning: on the one hand, it had a general significance, common to the whole of society and reflecting the beliefs of all the people; and, on the other hand, it had a meaning that served the ideology of the particular social group which organised and patronised the performance.

I should like to stress the following two points. Firstly, religion was the cement binding together medieval French society and therefore any message conveyed by religion, whether or not it took a theatrical form, was understood and accepted by society as a whole. But, secondly, through the common fund of religion *particular* social groups could express their own sectional values, their own vision of the world, and their own conception of the social order. In other words, religion was indeed a common means of expression, a 'language' understood by the whole of society and, by virtue of its privileged position, it served to express this society in its various activities; but what was said by the different social groups using this common language was specific to each one of them.

The fact that in medieval society religion supplied an image of world order and also a 'language', explains why it should have served as both a *model* and a *medium* for different social groups. The staging of religious plays reflects this double function: although the performance may have a common religious reference, it is none the less used as a medium only by those able to participate in it, those who commissioned the texts, those who organised the performances, those taking part as actors and those who made up the audience. I should also like to stress that the various elements involved in a production form a united whole. If religion as such is a language, the language of a society, then so, in turn, is theatre: and this dramatic language only functions when all the different components combine, when the text is both acted and viewed. Analysis of such a complex structure can, of course, lead to a dissociation of the various levels represented by the text, the actor, the décor, and so on. But one must not lose sight of the fundamental unity of the whole, which is the very life-blood of the theatre and must be taken into account in any sociological study. In other words, if one is to define religious theatre in sociological terms, it is not enough simply to establish the relationship between the bare text and religion, for this leaves a number of questions unanswered. Who were the organisers of a production? Who were the actors? Who were in the audience? There remains the problem of who initially decided what role the dramatic text would play in relation to religion. What vitiated such an analytical approach for a long time was the evolutionary bias shown by those who studied the history of the drama. The tendency was to think of medieval religious theatre as a single, unique form of expression, part of a continuous process of evolution starting with the very first dramatised liturgy and continuing through to the last Mystery plays. And it was precisely the continuity of the referent, religion, which provided the theoretical basis for such an approach. However, the evolutionist school of thought was confronted by certain obvious facts which called into question the unity of religious theatre in the West (a theatre spanning nearly six centuries). On the one hand, the internal organisation and meaning of the texts and performances had undergone radical transformations. On the other hand, particular social groups had at times taken over complete control of the performances.

Within the framework of the dramatised liturgy, the text formed an integral part of the religious service. The spatial basis for the development of the dramatised liturgy was provided by the very architecture of the church. It was in terms of the symbolisation of the various parts of the church building that the dramatisation unfolded, just as it was as part of the service that the dramatisation developed. Finally, it was the clergy who officiated and were responsible for the dramatisation of the service. The situation is entirely different if we turn to the Miracle and Mystery plays. The event is no longer a ritual, but a play; the setting is no longer in the church but in the town; it is no longer organised and performed by members of the clergy, but by men who are, for the most part, members of the urban community. Finally, the audience is composed not of the faithful attending a religious service, but of the general public.[2] The striking differences between dramatised liturgies and performances of Miracle and Mystery plays can initially be reduced to one major opposition between social groups: on the one side stands the clergy and on the other the members of the urban community. From the thirteenth century, theatre became part of town life and this development gained strength throughout the fourteenth and fifteenth centuries with the growth of new religious dramatic forms.

Only the middle classes could claim full membership of the urban community. Middle-class status was defined in terms of rights and obligations: a number of conditions had to be satisfied, such as ownership of a town house of a specific value, residence in the city from All Saints to the Feast of St John, active participation in the major annual holy days, and so on.[3] The middle classes owned land which they either cultivated themselves or had others cultivate. Throughout the late Middle Ages, the class consolidated its power and wealth by controlling the trades, the distribution of goods, and finance, and also by the privileges that its members enjoyed from the Crown. It is not surprising, therefore, to find that documents in city archives also give evidence of the influence of the middle classes on the theatre. This urban theatre, divorced from its original ecclesiastical and liturgical framework – but retaining its religious nature – was the creation and the medium of those who had the money to patronise it. For some time it was to remain one of the privileged forms of expression of the rising bourgeoisie. Consequently, the collective message transmitted by the late medieval theatre was voiced exclusively by the middle classes, those representing the stable wealth of the city.

It is not so much in the Mystery play (about the organisation and production of which nothing is in fact known), but in the Miracle play that the domination of prosperous urban society first makes itself felt with some continuity. One must, however, remember that centres of theatrical activity dominated by bourgeois society can be found as early as the thirteenth century, Arras being one such example. But the fourteenth century offers us a rare example in the forty *Miracles de Notre-Dame par personnages* of the Cangé manuscript in the Bibliothèque Nationale in Paris. We now know with certainty, and particularly since the research carried out by Graham A. Runnalls,[4] that these Miracle plays were performed by and for the Guild of the Corporation of Parisian Goldsmiths. As heirs and successors of the *puys* in which the intellectual renaissance of the bourgeoisie found expression, producing works of literary and poetic value of which the Miracle plays were one example amongst many, the guilds of Parisian goldsmiths must have called on individual writers to give shape to the Miracle plays in their repertory. But what is important here is the nature of the 'collective message' transmitted. Since the majority of the Miracle plays in the Cangé manuscript drew their inspiration from legends, tales, romances, Latin lives, or Gautier de Coincy's poetical compilations, they consist of more than mere apologetic anecdotes about the compassion of the Virgin Mary. In fact they reveal a vision of the world through which the individual is seen in relation to the collectivity and to its conception of social morality. Erich Köhler drew attention to the fact that in courtly romances the hero gradually emerges from the fable and this, he claimed was due to an objective split between the individual and the collectivity.[5] It seems to me that a similar split, entailing comparable consequences, provides the point of departure for a definition of the dramatic structure of the Miracle plays. This split finds expression within the text, but emanates from a collectivity which is clearly defined when it is contrasted with the other strata of society.

The texts of Miracle plays are characterised by the fact that they were created outside the ecclesiastical sphere[6] within a sector of society, which was trying to show how the individual had emerged into a world deeply scarred by dualistic thought – by a philosophy which, according to Von Harnack,[7] is itself ultimately a mythology. The core of the Christian religion gives rise to a new mythology, and this, together with individualisation of the hero, seems to constitute the ideological axes of most of the Miracle plays in the Cangé manuscript. Certainly, as things stood in fourteenth-century France, there was still a long way to go before the philosophy of the individual was to become supreme; the impossibility of overcoming the contradictory attractions of a 'World of Virtue' and an 'Anti-World of Vice' could only be resolved by the merciful intervention of the Virgin. But the hero gradually emerging from these dramatisations can no longer be defined in terms of submission; this hero, who in many cases owes his origins to the courtly chivalric romances (Amiss and Amile, Robert le Diable, Berthe, *et al.*) appears first of all as a break with the collectivity. I should add that on the dramatic level the intrusion of mythology can just as easily take place here, through traditional religious channels which have been diverted from their normal course. It would often be futile to look for a difference in role between the Virgin in the Miracle plays and the fairies of oral tradition or of Courtly Romance. She is by definition the same 'beneficent adjuvant' as that about which Propp and Greimas have written.[8] In addition she is the only answer possible as yet for the individual hemmed in by opposing supernatural forces, for the wretched conscience in breach of contract with society or subject to a destiny which it cannot overcome unaided.

The ultimate theatrical image which the Middle Ages offer of this hero, victim of a determinism at odds with the dogma of free-will, is surely to be found in the character of Judas in the *Passion de Jean Michel*, performed in the last quarter of the fifteenth century and reappearing in part in the *Passion de Valenciennes* in 1547. This Judas, a reflection of the parricidal and incestuous Oedipus, is so crushed and overwhelmed by the forces of a world greater than himself that he betrays God.[9] It is not really surprising that this type of hero, born of a utopian vision of bygone chivalry, should be taken up again by the bourgeoisie; a hero presenting a very contradictory picture, appearing now as the victim, now as the guilty party, but always as the outsider cut off from the main body of society. In addition to the emergence of the social group there is also the individual affirmation of the judicial, economic and socio-cultural status of the middle class. It is precisely in the combination of these two forces, that of the group as a legal and economic entity, and that of the individual with legal rights, that one can see the rise of a social class growing increasingly conscious of its existence and projecting its own particular conception of economic, social and moral relations on to the rest of society. Now if a certain duality – which seems almost Manichaean at times – asserted itself in the last Miracle and Mystery plays to such an extent that a new mythology came to the fore which ranges wider than orthodox religious thought, drawing on apocryphal writings and on traditional tales and legends, it was because a section of the laity was in the process of replacing the clergy in the presentation of religious plays. At the same time the social emancipation, albeit on a limited scale, experienced by the middle classes in the closing centuries of the Middle Ages brought the

individual face to face with a world where the Church was no longer there to
act as a unique and privileged mediator. This individual owed it to himself
to reconstruct his own universe, complete with its own poles of morality, its
own set of rules and regulations. This is the only explanation possible of the
many varying examples of moral transgressions collated in the *Miracles de
Notre Dame par personnages* in the Cangé manuscript. Whether they be
transgressions inside the family (incest, adultery, deviation from
endogamy) or affecting the social order (such as the usurping of social
roles), they always point to a disruptive element existing within the group
which cannot be rooted out by means of the social apparatus alone (over
which middle classes did not as yet have control), but only by the intervention of the 'Fairy–Virgin', that beneficent intermediary from the Christian Otherworld. When any such intervention is impossible, as in the story
of Judas, the structure of the old world collapses.

Thus the texts comprising the repertory of urban religious theatre paint
rather a confused picture of the individual's still ambiguous status within
the group, simultaneously asserting himself and by-passing the religious
structures, using examples handed down from courtly, oral, or religious
tradition. And not the least paradoxical aspect of this theatre is the fact that
the author's anonymous immersion in the collective consciousness should
finally result in the emergence of an individual hero from within the
collectivity. The pendulum swings from the individual to the group and
from the group to the individual.

However, wherever the rising middle class can exert a more concrete
control, it does so, as in the area of artistic activity. The organisation of
theatrical productions from the fourteenth to the sixteenth centuries has
some interesting sociological implications. In the early stages, when the
middle classes first expressed themselves through the medium of the *puys*
and the guilds dedicated to the Virgin Mary or to other patron saints, the
material, if not the ideological structure of the spectacle, was still very
largely subordinated to the religious world. The statutes in a guild's charter
allied obligations of faith to the privileges of a legally defined association
which enjoyed certain economic influence. This influence underwent particular development throughout the fifteenth century and in the first half of
the sixteenth century. In so far as the production, financing and performance of the Mystery play were concerned, the traditional framework
represented by the guilds gave way more and more to groups of individuals
working to contract. And these, according to the archives, were *d'honorables
bourgeois de la cité*, members of the urban community, owners of property,
land, and wealth. Merchants, financiers, master-craftsmen, local magistrates and, occasionally, priests, were united in one group.

The legal statutes binding these temporary associations, which remained
together during the organisation of a play, were drawn up according to the

norms to be found in contemporary financial or labour contracts. These 'obligations' were essentially a defination of the duties and responsibilities incumbent on the organisers, actors, and others involved; they also established rehearsal times, seat-prices, the distribution of parts, and the fines payable for the infringement of rules, arriving late, and so on. There are a few of these contracts still extant from the first half of the sixteenth century, and some fragmentary evidence remains from the fifteenth century, telling us the names and indicating the social standing of the organisers and the actors in the Mystery plays.[10]

Apart from this contractual method of organising performances, the great innovation (if indeed, it is one, since the oldest documents remain silent on this topic) is the charging of an entry fee to watch a Miracle play. From the end of the fifteenth century, this seems to be more or less standard practice. The charging of entrance fees brought about two fundamental changes in the performance of religious plays, and these alone already define their social nature in urban society: firstly, the charge for admission limited the social range of the audience, and secondly the different prices for seats further divided the audience, which was already selected by class. The charging of entrance fees by theatres which, according to writings of the period, were built to celebrate and justify the Christian faith, has socio-economic implications which are not immediately obvious.

Why should entrance fees be charged by such theatres, for such performances? This question can be answered in a number of ways, some more satisfactory than others. Firstly, as stage décor and techniques became more sophisticated, the cost of staging a play increased proportionately, and the fact that productions were taken over by certain middle-class citizens, or by municipalities, indicates a desire to recoup expenses as much as possible. However, these performances (apart from such famous plays as those performed in Issoudun in 1535, Bourges in 1536, or Valenciennes in 1547) often ran at a loss, and so the 'privatisation' of Mystery plays is not sufficient explanation for the charging of entrance fees. It is of course true that, despite their religious nature, these plays often coincided with commercial fairs, or were simply part of the towns' attempts at economic development. This is not, however, always the case, and the different motives behind a production where religion and commercialism are found to be closely linked, do not provide a clear enough solution to the problem. But if, without overlooking the importance of the 'privatisation' of performances, we try to analyse urban society at the end of the Middle Ages in sociological terms (no matter how superficially), we can achieve some clarity.

Society at the time was torn apart and basically unstable. If this society allowed more freedom of movement in its higher echelons, if it allowed many wealthy middle-class citizens to join the nobility, and if it resulted in less of a gap than formerly between traditional orders with economic ties, or between the middle classes and royalty, which backed each other up, it nevertheless did establish a clear dividing line between those belonging to an order, a corporation or any formal body, and those who no longer belonged at all. At the end of the Middle Ages, examples of people wholly excluded from society were legion. Robert Fossier[11] claims that an average of one in three citizens was excluded from society. (Here I am not referring to rural society, where serfs were still numerous despite the many enfranchisements: the stabilisation of taxes had helped to bring about a slight improvement in the peasants' lot, though there still remained a certain category of peasants who had no rights whatsoever, and lived in the most dire poverty.[12]) It was in the towns, where the labourer had as yet no fixed conditions that an impoverished, increasingly numerous fringe employed by the week or by the day (after 'bidding' for jobs at public work auctions) created extreme social instability.[13] This sector of the population consisted of workers, criminals, and beggars – eighty thousand are estimated to have lived in Paris alone during the fifteenth century. As a result, alongside the middle class, who were men of property, wealth and stable employment, ranging from the merchant-financier to the master-craftsman and the modest shop-keeper, there existed an entire sector of the urban population which can initially be defined in terms of the potential threat which it posed to stable wealth, even to modest wealth. Thus one finds, to begin with, social unrest and instability, and society tended to close ranks, to become less flexible by rejecting an entire social stratum which in the past had been skilled in climbing the ladder of individual success. This particularly affected those apprentices who could no longer aspire to the position of master-craftsman, a position now reserved for the members of a master-craftsman's family. In this society, with its now totally rigid structure, which accentuated social and economic exclusion, the charging of theatre entrance fees represented something more than a means of helping to recover costs. Indeed the very fact that the prices charged tended to exclude a whole sector of society from attending performances acted as a guarantee of order and coherence. But that is not all. Even when one considers the wages paid to those who held the most permanent, most stable positions in society, one notices that the lowest theatre entrance charges corresponded to a third or a half of a day's pay,[14] and to more than a whole day's pay in the case of women (whose pay continued to decrease in relation to the male wage throughout the fifteenth and sixteenth centuries). One should also take into account the general rise in prices which began at the end of the fifteenth century, the economic crisis, and the fact that one wage often had to provide for a whole family. Obviously, we cannot say that this fraction of the working population was absent from *every* performance, but we can say that there was a very pronounced tendency in the fifteenth and the first half of the sixteenth century in France (much later in Germanic and Swiss societies) for theatre attendance to be limited to that sector of the urban population with wealth and middle-class status.

The second problem raised by the study of audience attendance at religious theatres charging entrance fees is that of the difference in seat prices. It would appear that upper and lower seat distribution reflected the standard of wealth, and that seat prices – depending on the performance and the town – could double or triple their original price, or even at times vary by a factor of twenty. Furthermore, boxes and upper tiers were generally hired out for the duration of the Mystery play which could last for several days, whereas lower seats were hired out by the day, or even half-day. In other words, and this is something clearly borne out by account-books kept at the time, attendance at performances was partial or total depending on the wealth of the spectators. The concrete manifestation of this difference in wealth was the separate arrangement of the theatre premises: boxes and upper galleries had different entrances and aisles from those of the less expensive seats. The lay-out of the space reserved for spectators marked the differences in wealth and social status to be found in the city.

If one views as a whole the various elements I have briefly summarised above, one can see that the general tendency at the end of the Middle Ages was to restrict entry on a class basis and also to segregate the different elements in the audience according to their degree of wealth. The most extreme example of this tendency is to be found in the performance of the Lucerne Mystery plays in the fifteenth and sixteenth centuries. The square in the Weinmarkt used for these plays is a particularly fine example of a structure where the spatial division defines the social division (see plate 2). The theatre site is completely enclosed by houses and erected stands, there being two doors on the east side and one on the west. On the two longest sides of the rectangle were window-recesses which served as boxes, for the magistrates, guests of honour and the local aristocracy. By contrast, those from the less wealthy ranks of society, but still within the regular income bracket, paid to watch the play from scaffolding stands, and were situated literally outside the theatre site, beyond the fountain to the west of the square. This part of the audience was outside the theatre and excluded from direct participation in the religious play, which it could only glimpse from afar.[15]

The limitations imposed on the audience confronted by a play organised by the dominating socio-economic forces of the city can also be seen in the actors, and here there is an added paradox which clearly shows up the nature of these limitations. Many of the documents about medieval religious theatre show that the actors came from the same background as the organisers: once again the majority were *d'honorables bourgeois* (honourable middle-class men). Very occasionally canons are found taking part,

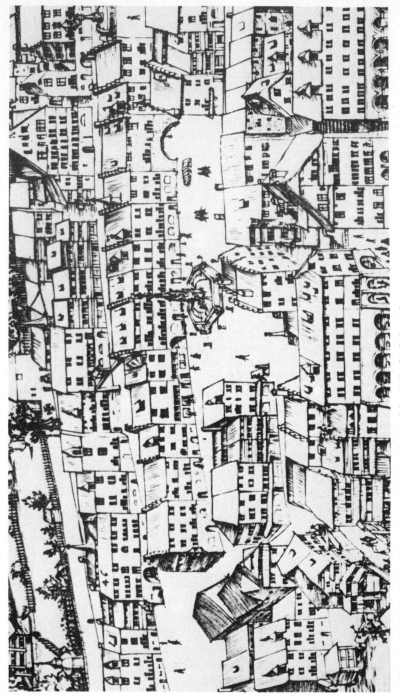

2 Sketch of the Weinmarkt at Lucerne from Martin Martini's *Stadtplan* of 1597

but not members of the minor clergy. Here again, therefore, very definite social limits applied as far as active participation in religious plays was concerned. The actor often had an interest in any profit the play might make, and he may have helped to finance it by contributing to the initial outlay. Most of the time, he had to pay for his own costume (and some plays demanded ornate and highly expensive costumes), as well as for the decoration of the stage-area allocated to the particular character he was playing.

Whether he was a member of the middle class, an alderman or a master-craftsman, such an actor was by definition an amateur. He may have played one or more roles in a Mystery play, but his social status was still naturally linked to his profession. And in this lies the paradox, to our eyes at least. For if these 'honourable middle-class men' from the cities prided themselves on their participation in plays, if their social status was in no way damaged by it, then quite the opposite was true of professional actors who were the object of public derision and harassment. The Church's vituperation against the acting profession had started with the very first *jongleurs*; as soon as the first professional or semi-professional companies appear (in the sixteenth century, according to local archives of the period), one finds similar prejudice towards actors. They were continually hounded and prevented from giving regular performances by municipalities and by individuals. However, in a good many cases their repertory was akin or even identical to that of the amateur bourgeois actors. This shows up clearly the extent to which the performance of religious plays was reserved as the privileged means of expression of a social group. Religious plays had become a manifestation of middle-class society.

That the performance of religious plays should be the privilege of a restricted social group in this way is not a phenomenon particular to the medieval western world. Such divisions have existed at other times and in other civilisations. But what is remarkable about the end of the Middle Ages in France is that religious theatre should have been used as the means of expression for a powerful group engaged also in other urban activities, in particular economic ones. It is just as if theatrical activity were intended to be a kind of 'metaphor' for the expression of power and for the social status which allowed access to power. The organisation and development of the play served to make this social dominance publicly manifest. In this respect, it must be noticed that the scope of expression open to this power went far beyond the confines of the simple religious play: most of the ceremonial demonstrations, processions, sporting events, traditional parades and visits by royalty were the handiwork of the same social group, and systematically excluded other members of the urban community.[16] The history of the ceremonies, festivals and plays of the Middle Ages is, in the last analysis, the history of the seizure by the middle class of all the city's major means of collective expression. No doubt this phenomenon was not to survive in this form during the post-medieval period, but it does show that the play, or the religious and civic ceremony, was originally conceived as something which qualified the social function of those taking part. Everything is resolved in the appearance, in the manifestation of the social being within a closed circuit, in a ceremony confined to the middle class where it acts out its social status on stage. Religious theatre had taken on a different ritualistic function: it was certainly no longer a religious ritual, but it had become a social ritual. Again, the Lucerne plays performed in the sixteenth century provide an especially clear example. At each successive performance, members of the same noble families claimed particular roles, asserting their legal *droit de succession* (right of inheritance), and many followed in their father's or grand-father's footsteps to play the same dramatic role.[17]

This 'privatisation' of all the functions of a religious play is also to be seen on the level of the theatre lay-out. Of all the areas in the cities which served for the staging of a play, the square was the most important. Now this square, as is the case for most of the other urban sites used, was by definition common land, an area open to the entire urban population, as opposed to the private dwelling areas. But this is qualified by the use made of common land during civic ceremonies and religious plays. For it is precisely this common, public ground which was 'privatised', enclosed, fenced off, and to which access was possible only on payment. This clearly shows the relationship between the 'privatisation' of land and social exclusion. For those having middle-class status and possessing assets and property in the city, the right to 'privatise' personal dwellings was extended to that of 'privatising' common land. By contrast, those who were totally or partially excluded from the integrated social groups were also denied entry to common land. The overall situation of religious theatre, as it appears at the end of the Middle Ages, is just as much the result of a gradual process of transformation in the social and economic structures of the city, as it is the end product of any particular theatrical development. However, it is no easy matter to understand this theatrical activity from an evolutionist's point of view. Any form of activity occurring within a given community is just as likely to proceed by fits and starts as it is with continuity. As far as religious theatre is concerned, the transformations involved were certainly very closely linked to the rise of middle-class power within the framework – a power which found a special form of expression in theatrical activity.

But the development of this activity took place both within the limits of a religious formulation, of which I have tried to indicate the ambiguity, and by a series of breaks with the ecclesiastical framework, initially in favour of the privatised urban framework, and subsequently of the urban community itself, which became an élitist group, excluding the majority of the people. By refashioning religious theatrical expression in accordance with middle-class status and middle-class opinions, the bourgeoisie was to provide the basis for much of the theatre's later development in the centuries which followed: 'privatisation' of theatrical space and activity, distribution of space according to the wealth and social status of the audience, shift from religious to social ritual. Can it not be said, then, that the 'collective message' conveyed by this theatre is the one passed on by the dominant section of urban society to their successors?

NOTES

1. Paris: Editions du Seuil 1972, p. 435.
2. E. Konigson, *L'espace théâtral médiéval* (Paris: Editions du CNRS, 1976).
3. M. Th. Caron, *La société en France à la fin du Moyen-Age* (Paris: Presses Universitaires de France, 1977).
4. 'The Manuscript of the "Miracles de Notre-Dame par personnages"', *Romance Philology*, XXII (1968–9), 15–22. 'The "Miracles de Notre Dame" Erasures in the MS. and the Dates of the Plays and the "Serventois"', *Philological Quarterly*, XLIX (1970), 19–29. 'Medieval Trade Guilds and the "Miracles of Notre Dame"', *Medium Aevum*, XXXIX (1970), 257–87.
5. Erich Köhler, *L'aventure chevaleresque, idéal et réalité dans le roman courtois* (Paris: Nouvelle Revue Français, 1974; original German edition, pp. 101 ff.
6. *Ibid.*, p. 117: 'La où il n'y a pas d'autorité ecclésiastique sévère et dogmatique exerçant un pouvoir déterminant, la constitution des mythes a été de tout temps la voie naturelle qui a permis d'éclairer l'impénétrable.'
7. Marcion, *Das Evangelium vom fremden Gott* (Leipzig, 1921), p. 264, cited in Köhler, *L'aventure chevaleresque*, p. 117.
8. Vladimir Propp, *Morphologie du conte* (Paris: Editions du Seuil, 1965). A. J. Greimas, *Sémantique structurale* (Paris: Larousse, 1966).
9. E. Konigson, 'Mythe des origines et romans familiaux dans les derniers mystères de la Passion française', *Revue d'histoire du théâtre*, 2 (1972).
10. Details and a list of these contracts can be found in Petit de Julleville 'Les Mystères', in Konigson *L'espace théâtral médiéval*. To begin with, the organisation of the play was mostly financed by the contractors (with occasional assistance from the City Treasury), and profits made were shared out on a pro-rata basis, according to amounts invested. The group was run in the same way as is a company, responsible to its shareholders.
11. *Histoire sociale de l'occident médiéval* (Paris: A. Colin, 1970).
12. Caron, *La société en France à la fin du Moyen-Age*, pp. 51 ff.
13. Many documents (see Konigson, *L'espace théâtral médiéval*) testify to the concern felt for the city's safety during the performance of Mystery plays, in the face of the threat posed by the unstable element of the population. While I am here referring only to the working class, the same kind of impoverishment existed among students, confronted by evermore lengthy courses of study and the scarcity of grants and bursaries.

14. Konigson, *L'espace théâtral médiéval*, p. 72–3, Les tableaux comparatifs des prix d'entrée et des salaires.

15. Most of the documents taken from archives relating to the Lucerne Mystery plays have been published – see particularly M. Blakemore Evans, 'The Passion Play of Lucerne', *PMLA* (1943).

16. J. Heers, *L'occident aux XIVe et XVe Siècles* (Paris: PUF, 1970), p. 243.

17. Blakemore Evans, 'The Passion Play of Lucerne'.

Kings and judges: Lope de Vega's
El mejor alcalde, el rey

J. E. VAREY

A significant number of Spanish plays of the Golden Age present a picture of rural life and, in particular, of the relationship of the social classes, which has in recent years been the subject of critical attention. In such plays, the king usually appears as the fount of earthly justice. The nobles are seen as owing allegiance to their king and, in their turn, as being under an obligation to deal justly with their vassals. The countryfolk owe duties of allegiance both to their lord and to the king. This secular hierarchy has its religious counterpart: the king is God's vice regent, and all classes of society should pay due respect to religion and fight, when the necessity arises, for both Cross and Crown.

The structure of this society is therefore basically of feudal origin, and it neglects, or deliberately ignores, many aspects of the actual society of the day. Spain in the seventeenth century continued to be a predominantly rural society, the peasant supporting with his labour the whole burden of government and society, owing tribute to his immediate lord, paying tithes to the Church and taxes to the Crown. More than half of the rural population were landless labourers; roughly a quarter were *labradores* (peasant farmers) who owned or leased the land they worked. It is true that a small proportion of the *labradores* were prosperous and that some regions of Spain were more favoured than others, but the general standard of living was low. The depression of the rural areas of Castile was accentuated by plague and famine towards the end of the sixteenth century and by a sharp increase in prices caused by monetary inflation. The last years of the reign of Philip III are characterised by an acute sense of the economic crisis through which Spain was passing, and which affected not only the labourer and the small farmer, but also the lower ranks of the nobility. The nobility of Spain was by no means a monolithic structure, as the plays might suggest. The great noble families of the sixteenth century, the *grandes* (grandees) and the *títulos* (titled families), looked down on the newer nobility, the *hidalgos* and the *caballeros*, many of whom had acquired their rank by procurement or by conferment. Whilst the *caballero* was usually an absentee landlord living in a town, the *hidalgo* might still live on his small estate, particularly in the north of Spain where penurious *hidalgos* were to be found, living in idleness – for many considered that their rank forbade them to undertake any work which could be considered menial – but excessively proud of the purity of their blood and jealous of their privileged position which ensured them immunity from taxation.

The role of the king is undoubtedly idealised in these country plays. Spain's imperial responsibilities had resulted in the growth of a large government bureaucracy, and the personal intervention of the king, of such importance under Charles V (1516–56) and the assiduous Philip II (1556–98), was considerably attenuated under Philip III (1598–1621) and Philip IV (1621–65). The important role assumed by the *privado* (royal favourite) in the early years of the seventeenth century gave rise to much concern. Lerma, under Philip III, and Olivares, in the reign of Philip IV, were the two most powerful figures of the age, and whilst it can be argued that the role of the *privado* was gradually evolving towards that of first minister of the Crown, there is no doubt that many thoughtful Spaniards considered that the king should take a more direct and personal part in the administration of his realm and in the exercise of justice.

Cutting across the social classes is the importance given in the seventeenth century to good lineage (*limpieza de sangre*). In many parts of Spain the racial mixture was high, but the expulsion of the Jews and, later, of the *moriscos*, put a premium on purity of blood. The geographical distribution of claims to nobility reflects the history of Spain. In the Cantabrian provinces – Guipúzcoa, Vizcaya, Asturias, and Galicia – a large proportion of the population considered themselves to be of noble origin, since their lands had never fallen to the Moors. They were thus, by definition, of good lineage, free from any taint of Moorish or Jewish ancestry. Furthermore, throughout the whole of Castile and northern Spain, the countryman felt himself in this respect to be the superior of the town-dweller, for the true old Christian (*cristiano viejo*) was to be found, or so he believed, more readily in the countryside than in an urban environment, where blood was more likely to be tainted by racial miscegenation.

The seventeenth century saw throughout most of Europe the expansion of towns and cities through an influx of country people, and in Spain the agricultural crises of the end of the sixteenth and beginning of the seventeenth centuries forced large numbers of country-dwellers to seek alternative employment in the growing urban centres. Whilst the duties of the noble, as depicted in the country plays, are very similar to those preserved in the sixteenth-century codes of the Orders of chivalry,[1] the role of the noble had in fact changed very considerably; the centralising policies initiated by the Catholic Monarchs, Ferdinand and Isabella, had produced a court society which kept many nobles from their local possessions for long periods of time, and the establishment of a capital in Madrid[2] localised their activities in this quickly growing, if somewhat artificial, centre of power. The older established cities, such as Toledo, Seville, and Barcelona, had, for historical reasons, somewhat different social structures; that of Madrid was changing and developing during the very period when the *comedia* was at the height of its success, and it must always be borne in mind that most secular plays were written for presentation in the commercial theatres of the big towns and cities.[3] The new urban population considered itself to be sophisticated, and its attitude to the country people appears in real life to have been one of condescending and conscious superiority: the ignorant countryman come to town is a staple figure of fun, and Noël Salomon has seen in such figures the reflection of a social phenomenon which he refers to as the 'animalisation' of the figure of the peasant for the enjoyment of an urban audience.

The relationship of social and economic realities to the dramatic world of the rural plays is therefore highly complex, and can only be comprehended if the plays are seen, as they must be, as primarily literary constructs. The moralistic view of country life as sane and virtuous, opposed to the vices of the town and the ambitions of the court, colours the entire presentation of the rural scene. The natural world, as seen from this standpoint, is God's handiwork, and the ordered procession of the seasons, the round of seed-time and harvest, the cycle of birth and death, are all evidence of the divine purpose. Man's envy, his ambition and his pride are boundless; nevertheless the lot of the countryman is not only dignified by his close association with the basic rhythms of life itself, but he is also less prone to those human failings which are at their most acute in the unnatural surroundings of the court and the town. Golden-Age plays are literary conceptualisations, and not socio-economic documents. And in their attitude to the failings of contemporary society, they tend to be conservative rather than revolutionary, reflecting the values of society and not its sordid realities.[4]

Lope de Vega's *El mejor alcalde, el rey* was published in 1635 in *Parte XXI* of the dramatist's plays. From a study of the versification pattern, Morley and Bruerton conclude that the play was probably written in the period 1620–3.[5] The immediate source of the plot is the fourth book of the *Crónica general de España* in the version of Florián de Ocampo (Valladolid, 1604), fols. 327v–328r. In this version, King Alfonso's love of justice is extolled, and as an example the case is cited of don Ferrando, a Galician lord, who deprived a *labrador* unjustly of his lands. The farmer went to see the King in Toledo, and Alfonso wrote to the lord ordering him to right the wrong he had committed. But the lord was powerful and, angered by the letter, swore that he would kill the farmer and refused to obey the King's commands, whereupon the farmer returned to Toledo with written evidence of what had happened. When the King was informed he set off for Galicia incognito, accompanied by two lords, and verified the truth of the reports he had received. He then confronted the lord, who was struck with fear and sought to flee. The King ordered his execution on the grounds that he had disobeyed his sovereign's commands. After the lord's death, the King went openly through Galicia, executing justice, and such was the fear that the report of this affair aroused that none dared commit any wrongful deed.

In Lope's version, don Tello is presented as a young man of spirit, living on his lands in Galicia, far from the court. Sancho falls in love with Elvira, asks and receives from her father, Nuño, his consent to the marriage and is counselled by the latter to approach don Tello, not only because his situation as vassal demands this duty but also because don Tello is rich and open-handed and may well provide Elvira with a dowry. Somewhat reluctantly, Sancho follows this advice, and is well received; don Tello gives him twenty cows and a hundred sheep and offers to patronise the wedding himself, together with his sister. As the marriage is about to take place, don Tello is struck by the beauty of Elvira and refuses to let the priest enter. That night his servants abduct Elvira. In act II we see how Elvira resists don Tello's advances, and how the latter's sister, Feliciana, advises patience. Sancho appears before don Tello, asking for justice against the abductor of his bride; the lord does not admit his own guilt, but swears to avenge the wrong done to his vassal. At this point Elvira emerges, his guilt is made plain, and Nuño and Sancho are driven from don Tello's castle with blows. Sancho, again following the advice of Nuño, determines to go and put his case before the King of Castile, at that point in time in León. Whilst Feliciana reproaches don Tello for his attempt to force his will upon a virtuous woman, the King receives Sancho, recognises his worth and gives him a letter to don Tello, ordering the latter to hand over Elvira immediately to Sancho and warning him that prompt punishment awaits those who transgress against the King's authority. When Sancho returns with this letter, he is again roughly treated; don Tello proclaims that he is lord and master in his own lands, and refuses the King's request. In act III Sancho returns to León, and Alfonso determines to ensure in person that justice is done. As in the chronicle, he travels to Galicia incognito, accompanied by two nobles. He presents himself as an *alcalde* (magistrate, or judge), and the two courtiers are taken to be the *alguacil* (officer of the peace) and *escribano* (attorney) who normally accompanied an *alcalde*. The proud lord refuses to acknowledge his authority in that capacity, but when the King reveals his true rank, he immediately submits and admits his guilt, made dramatically more effective by the appearance on stage of a dishevelled Elvira and her accusation of her lord. The King orders the rebellious vassal to be executed, but not before he has been first married to Elvira, thus righting the wrong he has done her and ensuring that she will inherit half of his estates. Don Tello's sister, who has, in act III, endeavoured to prevent her brother from using force and denounced his intentions, is made a lady-in-waiting to the Queen. And so the play ends.

A true story, says Lope, as told in the fourth part of the *Chronicle of Spain*, although, as can be seen, Lope has adapted the account given in his source to produce a dramatically more effective action centring on a case of honour.[6] From the chronicle Lope has derived the outline of the plot, and several details: the journey of the *labrador* to seek justice at the hands of the King, the letter written by the King, the angry reaction of the powerful and wilful lord, the King's journey incognito accompanied by only two noble companions, his verification of the truth of the affair before he passes final judgement, his confrontation with the noble, and the execution of the turbulent vassal. But, as Díez Borque has pointed out,[7] Lope has omitted in his play the theme of the violent acquisition of lands by the lord, and replaced it with the lord's violation of the bride of one of his vassals. In Lope's play Sancho pays two visits to the King, instead of the one visit to Toledo mentioned in the chronicle, with the result that the King's reactions are more gradual, and the audience is permitted to see him executing justice on three occasions in all. The rebelliousness of the vassal is thereby accentuated. The endings of the two stories also reveal important differences. Whereas the lord of the chronicle reacts with fear and endeavours to flee, don Tello immediately accepts the King's decision, underlining the futility of disobeying the King in person. Furthermore, whilst the King of the chronicle clearly uses the insolent behaviour of the lord as a salutary way of reminding all his subjects of his power, inspiring in them awe and fear, the King of the play is welcomed by all his subjects except the rebellious lord, and his clemency and kindness are stressed, as well as the impartiality of his justice.

The first 620 lines of act I of Lope's play establish a clear picture of the rural society of Galicia, in which province of Spain the action is set. The lord, don Tello, is presented as 'señor de aquesta tierra, / poderoso en paz y en guerra' (lord of those lands, powerful in peace and in war; I, 276–7); his servants and those who live at his expense number one hundred and thirty (I, 394–7). Nuño informs Sancho that it is only fitting that, when a marriage is arranged, don Tello should be informed of it:

> ... que el señor ha de saber
> cuanto se hace y cuanto pasa
> desde el vasallo más vil
> a la persona más alta
> que de su salario vive,
> y que los reyes se engañan
> si no reparan en esto,
> que pocas veces reparan.   (I, 429–36)

(The lord should be aware of all that is done and all that transpires, from the lowest vassal to the person of highest rank in his employment, and that kings deceive themselves if they do not pay attention to this, and it is very seldom that they so do.)

At this stage in the play, it is clear that don Tello's servants and vassals do not live in fear of him; he is beloved of the whole region, says Sancho, for so many reasons (1, .382), and his generosity is demonstrated by the open-handed way in which he provides Elvira with a dowry, causing Sancho and Pelayo to intone antiphonal praise of his generosity, virtue, valour, and piety (1, 446–50; cf. also 1, 476–7, 535). The gift is excessive, Sancho tells Nuño, but even more to be esteemed is the honour that don Tello has done them by offering to stand as sponsor at the wedding ('Y aunque es dádiva excesiva, / más estimo haberme honrado / con venir a ser padrino'; 1, 529–31). Ironically, as it is to turn out, Nuño praises don Tello's lack of pride in rank ('condición tan llana'; 1, 533), and Sancho agrees that he is the perfect model of a lord:

> Porque, en quitándole el dar,
> con que a Dios es parecido,
> no es señor; que haberlo sido
> se muestra en dar y en honrar.
> Y pues Dios su gran valor
> quiere que dando se entienda,
> sin dar ni honrar no pretenda
> ningún señor ser señor. (1, 547–54)

(For, if one takes away from a lord his generosity, which makes him similar to God, then he is no lord at all; nobility is demonstrated by open-handed generosity and in giving honour where honour is due. And since it is God's wish that his great worth be made known through his open-handedness, then no lord should pretend to be a lord if he does not show himself to be generous and willing to honour others.)

The social standing of don Tello and his way of life are established in the second *cuadro* of act 1,[8] where don Tello makes his appearance dressed for the hunt (SD, 1, 303), praises the beauty of the countryside (1, 306–8), and discusses the qualities of his hounds with his servants (1, 311–18). In an exchange with his sister, Feliciana, he recounts the delights of hunting wild boar and bears (1, 335–51) and, echoing a medieval and Renaissance *topos*, compares the chase to war: 'es digna de caballeros / y príncipes, porque encierra / los preceptos de la guerra, / y ejercita los aceros, / y la persona habilita' (it is worthy of gentlemen and princes, for it enshrines the precepts of war, exercises arms and maintains the body in physical perfection; 1, 355–9). There is, however, one moment during the dialogue with Feliciana which foreshadows the outcome of the play. His sister is concerned about the risks to his person that don Tello thus runs, and wishes that he would marry when, it is to be assumed, he would find other interests. Don Tello replies: 'El ser aquí poderoso / no me da tan cerca igual' (The fact that my power here is so absolute does not make it is easy for me to find a bride who would be my equal; I, 363–4). His pride, thus established, is to prove his undoing.

At this stage in the play, then, his vassals do not fear him, and praise his generosity and condescension. The highest honour that don Tello bestows on Sancho is, as we have seen, his consent to act as sponsor at the latter's wedding to Elvira. It is offered with true generosity but, ironically, leads to his prevention of the marriage, his eventual violation of Elvira and his just execution.[9] His persistence in his persecution of Elvira, despite her resistance, and despite the commands of the King, is due in large part to his pride, the feeling that he here displays that he is absolute lord and master of his own domains.

The social status of the other main Galician characters appears at first to be somewhat ambiguous. Nuño, according to Sancho's account, tills the soil: 'hombre que sus campos labra, / pero que aun tiene paveses / en las ya borradas armas / de su portal, y con ellas, / de aquel tiempo, algunas lanzas' (one who still preserves escutcheons in the time-worn coat of arms above the door of his house and, further, lances, I, 418–22). He is then, the representative of a family which is of noble origin but his wealth is limited. He appears to offer Sancho, as part of Elvira's dowry, a clumsily-built cottage ('esa casilla mal labrada', I, 202, the passage is defective, as can be seen from the versification). His daughter, Elvira, is virtuous, holds her reputation in high esteem, and is willing to obey her father in all he commands (I, 243–5). When Sancho teasingly tells her that her father has arranged her marriage to one of don Tello's squires, she laments the necessity to go and live in the palace (I, 253–8), a situation which reflects in miniature the Renaissance theme of the opposition between court and country life. Don Tello's servant, Celio, describes her to her master, and for the benefit of the audience, as

> ... la moza más gallarda
> que hay en toda Galicia,
> y que por su talle y cara,
> discreción y honestidad
> y otras infinitas gracias,
> pudiera honrar el hidalgo
> más noble de toda España.   (I, 504–10)

(the most mettlesome lass in all Galicia, whose beauty and grace, discretion and modesty and other infinite graces could bring honour to the most noble gentleman in all Spain.)

The social position of Sancho is clear in that he recognises don Tello as his master, serving him in the humble office of shepherd (I, 193, 384–6). But, he maintains, 'en Galicia, señores, / es la gente tan hidalga, / que sólo en servir, al rico / el que es pobre no le iguala' (the people of Galicia are of such noble birth, sirs, that the poor man is only beneath the rich man in the sense that he must serve him; I, 387–90). His parents, he recalls to Nuño, were 'pobres labradores, / de honrado estilo y de costumbres graves' (poor farmers, honourable and grave in their customs; I, 158–9). Celio recognises that Sancho is not stupid (I, 502), and the latter promises Nuño that he will display, as Elvira's husband, 'firmezas de labrador / y amores de cortesano' (the steadfastness of a countryman and the courtesy in love of a courtier; I, 569–70), again underlining the opposition between court and country.

The figure of Pelayo is, however, treated very differently. The role is written for the *gracioso*, the comic figure of the *comedia*, and he is presented as foolish and idiotic, displaying in the first *cuadro* a ridiculous love for Elvira (although he later shows no envy of Sancho when the latter's suit is successful). Pelayo is Nuño's servant, being in charge of his pigs (I, 125–30), a suitably low vocation which demonstrates the distance between them. The way in which he constantly intervenes during the scene in which Sancho is asking for Elvira's hand makes Nuño angry, and Pelayo is constantly referred to as an animal. He is thus one of those caricatures of the peasant to which Noël Salomon refers.

Don Tello's domains therefore represent a kingdom in miniature. Don Tello considers himself to be the absolute master, and he is repaid in duties and in respect by his underlings. Nuño is the equivalent of the nobility of the kingdom as a whole, a man of noble antecedents, although reduced in this microcosm of society to the status of a farmer. Sancho is an honourable workman, raised in society by his lord's gift of sheep and cows to a status similar to that of Nuño. Pelayo is the equivalent of the peasantry in the macrocosm. The name bestowed on the pigman is ironic, for it is that of the legendary hero who defeated the Moors at the battle of Covadonga and thus kept the north of Spain free from their suzerainty. The name further serves to point up the historical fact that, since they had never known Moorish domination, the people of the Basque provinces, of Asturias and of Galicia felt themselves to be of good stock (*de sangre limpia*), and therefore noble. But we should not seek to find in Lope a socio-economic thesis; the dramatist has chosen to set his play in Galicia, partly because his source indicated this choice and partly so that the society depicted in that distant region could be seen as a microcosm of Spanish society as a whole. We are to see what happens when a lord fails to look after the interests of his vassals and, indeed, actively works against their interests. Up to the actual moment when Elvira appears at the wedding ceremony, all seems to be well, although don Tello's arrogance, as well as his generosity, has already been demonstrated. With the appearance of the radiant Elvira, desire takes possession of don Tello's heart, and he is lost.

The wedding scene of the second *cuadro* takes place in the evening (I,

480–4). On the entry of Elvira, don Tello remarks to Feliciana that she is beautiful, and his sister replies that she is also graceful (I, 624). Don Tello sits next to the bride (I, 639–40)[10] and repeatedly exclaims at her beauty, although now in asides (I, 641–2, 646, 652–4, 656). He orders that the priest should not enter, thus deliberately frustrating a rite of the Church, giving as his excuse his desire to bestow yet further honours on the couple (I, 663–5). Sancho remonstrates, whilst Nuño obeys the lord's command that Elvira should retire, although he shows regret, in an aside as he leaves the stage, that don Tello should have attended the wedding ('ya me ha pesado / de que haya venido aquí'; I, 695–6). Don Tello and his sister take their leave, and Elvira arranges with Sancho that he should come to the house that night when she will let him enter, for she considers him already to be her husband, despite the fact that the religious ceremony has not taken place (I, 715–18). A marriage contracted by the pledging of the word without a religious ceremony had been customary in earlier centuries, but after Trent marriages, for obvious practical as well as religious reasons, took place in churches; nevertheless, the marriage by mutual consent continues to play an important part in literature. Elvira's decision is, however, undoubtedly one which could lead to loss of reputation and endanger her father's good name. The secret entry of the gallant into the house is one of the favourite plot devices of comedies of the period, but the result in this case is tragic.

In the third and final *cuadro* of act I night has fallen,[11] and don Tello, Celio and the others of his servants enter wearing masks. Don Tello tells Celio that he is motivated by jealousy that a countryman should enjoy the beauty that he himself desires:

> Yo tomé, Celio, el consejo
> primero que amor me dio:
> que era infamia de mis celos
> dejar gozar a un villano
> la hermosura que deseo.
> Después que della me canse,
> podrá ese rústico necio
> casarse; que yo daré
> ganado, hacienda y dinero
> con que viva; que es arbitrio
> de muchos, como lo vemos
> en el mundo. Finalmente,
> yo soy poderoso, y quiero,
> pues este hombre no es casado,
> valerme de lo que puedo.   (I, 736–50)

(I followed, Celio, love's first counsel, that it would be an affront to my jealousy to permit a countryman to enjoy the beauty that I covet. After I tire of her that rustic booby can marry her, for I shall give him a herd, land and money with which to live; that is what most desire, as we see often enough in the world. And, finally, I am powerful and it is my will, since this man is not married to the girl, to take what I want.)

Taking advantage of the fact that Elvira has opened the door of the house to, as she thinks, Sancho, they abduct her. Sancho arrives with Pelayo, but too late, and enter Nuño, lamenting what has taken place. Nuño believes that the attackers broke down the door by force (I, 791–2), and, although he was unable to recognise them because of their masks, Sancho is immediately aware that they must have been don Tello's men (even Sancho does not consider that don Tello would demean himself to such an extent as to take part in the act of abduction personally). How can there be any hope of earthly justice, laments Sancho, since don Tello is all powerful and the richest man of the realm? ('Pues, ¡es verdad que hallaré / justicia, fuera del cielo, / siendo un hombre poderoso, / y el más rico deste reino!'; I, 813–16). Nuño counsels patience. Not only does he trust Elvira to defend her honour but he suspects that don Tello will soon repent of what was clearly a youthful act of folly ('... que yo sospecho / que, como fue mocedad, / ya tendrá arrepentimiento'; I, 830–2). Don Tello, after all, is not a savage ('que no es bárbaro don Tello', I, 876). Sancho is, nevertheless, disconsolate, imagining what has probably befallen Elvira, whilst Pelayo, after first offering to stone don Tello's pigs in retaliation (I, 820–3), decides that the night's work has made him hungry, and goes off to the kitchen to fill his belly (I, 871–4).

The violent action of don Tello, then, in refusing to allow the wedding to proceed – thus preventing one of the rites of the Church from taking place – has led Elvira to offer to do what she would never have consented to under other circumstances: to permit Sancho to enter her home, and to give herself to him. This second action, which violates her respect for her father and his good name – even though she clearly considers the marriage to have taken place by free consent of the parties although without the blessing of the Church – facilitates in its turn the further violence of the abduction. An evening which begins with the gaiety of a wedding ends in a dark night of confusion, and in Sancho's desperate laments, tempered somewhat by Nuño's belief in the fundamental goodness of don Tello.

In act II we see that Nuño is not justified in his confidence, for he has not allowed for the consuming drive which passion engenders in don Tello. In the first *cuadro* we see Elvira stressing her honour (II, 881), and her wish to return to Sancho whom she considers to be her husband (II, 885–6). Don Tello sticks to the letter of the law: 'No es tu esposo; / ni un villano, aunque dichoso, / digno de tanta hermosura' (He is not your husband; nor is a countryman, although so fortunate, worthy of such beauty; II, 886–8). He pleads with Elvira to treat him less harshly, and asks her if she does not recognise that it is love which he feels for her. The audience is aware, from his speech to Celio before the abduction, that he is motivated by jealousy and that his passion is mere lust. Elvira, without this knowledge, nevertheless recognises his lust for what it is, and replies in neo-Platonic terms, that 'amor que pierde al honor / el respeto es vil deseo, / y siendo apetito feo, / no puede llamarse amor' (love which loses respect for honour is vile desire, and being no more than ugly appetite, cannot be dignified with the name of love; II, 895–8). Elvira thus rejects him by physical force and by intellectual reasoning (II, 919–21). If only she were his equal, laments don Tello, but the laws of the world forbid a match between people from such different ranks of society, and her lowliness would be an affront to his nobility (II, 949–58). Feliciana enters and counsels patience, offering to intercede on her brother's behalf. When Sancho and Nuño arrive, Elvira is told to hide. Feliciana advises her brother to treat them well, and not to forget what he owes to his station ('Trátalos bien, y no ignores / que importa a tu calidad'; II, 1005–6).

Sancho appeals to his lord's magnanimity. As a mere farmer, although a gentleman at heart ('Yo, sólo labrador en la campaña, / y en gusto del alma caballero'; II, 1031–2), he is not so much a rustic that he has never handled a sword. The moon can never be prevented from climbing to the heavens, he argues, not even by the sun, although she be masked by the clouds: an image which couples the idea of his ascent upwards to nobility of soul, occasioned by his love for Elvira, which even the sun (i.e. his lord, since the sun is first in the hierarchy of the heavenly bodies) cannot prevent, with the additional image of the clouds which mask the moon, referring to the masked men, satellites, as it were, of the heavenly bodies. He recounts how, in his despair, he had attacked with rusty sword a lofty tree, 'no porque el árbol me robase a Elvira, / mas porque fue tan alto y arrogante, / que a los demás como a pequeños mira' (not because the tree had robbed me of Elvira, but because it was so lofty and arrogant that it looked down on all others as petty; II, 1063–5). He tells don Tello that in the village rumour has it that the lord was the instigator of the abduction; but this cannot be true, he says, 'siendo quien eres tú' (since you are what you are; II, 1068).[12] In an allusive manner, Sancho has thus represented his suspicions that the abduction was the work of don Tello, and has threatened revenge. Don Tello at first hypocritically agrees to deal with the culprit harshly once he is caught; the offence is one not only against Sancho, but against his lord, who will know how to execute justice (II, 1083–6). He denies all knowledge of the whereabouts of Elvira; otherwise, he swears by his life, he would deliver her up ('Yo no sé dónde está, porque, a sabello, / os la diera, por vida de don Tello'; II, 1093–4), words which are at once proved false by the emergence of Elvira from her hiding-place. Don Tello orders his servants to kill Sancho and Nuño, and when Feliciana points out that the guilt does not lie with them don Tello replies that, even if Elvira and Sancho had been man and wife, the boldness of the two countrymen is excessive (II, 1105–10). Sancho and Nuño are driven from the stage with blows (SD, II, 1123), and don Tello turns angrily to Elvira, swearing that she shall be his by force, or he will not be able to look himself in the face ('que por fuerza has de ser mía, / o no he de ser yo quien fui'; II, 1129–30). Feliciana remonstrates that this cannot be said in her presence, and don Tello replies that he must have Elvira by force, or kill her ('he de forzalla, o matalla'; II, 1132). As Feliciana leaves the stage it is clear that she is turning against her brother: '¿Cómo es posible libralla / de un hombre fuera de sí?' (How can the girl be freed from a man who is beside himself with passion?; II, 1133–4), she wonders. As don Tello has moved further and further away from the norms of conduct expected from a noble, denying by his actions the nobility accorded to him by his birth and showing himself to be essentially ignoble, so Feliciana, who began by taking his side, moves gradually away from him; in some respects, she can be seen as the visible embodiment of his conscience.[13]

This attitude is made clearer in the third *cuadro* of act II, a short bridge passage in which it is revealed that Elvira is kept prisoner in a tower and is treated with cruelty. Don Tello's real motive force is no longer his passion, but the fact that Elvira has spurned her lord, despite his power and wealth (II, 1262–5). Feliciana promises to try to work on Elvira, and don Tello asks her to offer all kinds of gifts: indeed, were she his equal, he says, he would have married her ('y que si fuera mi igual, / que ya me hubiera casado'; II, 1289–90). Feliciana is somewhat surprised and tells her brother that all her efforts will be in vain, since an honourable woman cannot be conquered by any human interest ('porque una mujer / que es honrada, es caso llano / que no la podrá vencer / ningún interés humano'; II, 1298–1301). In the fifth and final *cuadro* of this act, we see don Tello again insisting that Sancho has no rights in the matter, since he was not married to Elvira (II, 1503; 1542–3). Sancho's view is that the priest knew well enough their intentions; however, his principal purpose in this *cuadro* is to deliver the King's letter, which don Tello receives trembling with rage (II, 1552). '¿Sabes quién soy?' (Do you know who I am?; II, 1559), he asks, and banishes Sancho from his territories.

> Villanos, si os he quitado
> esa mujer, soy quien soy,
> y aquí reino en lo que mando,
> como el Rey en su Castilla;
> que no deben mis pasados
> a los suyos esta tierra;
> que a los moros la ganaron. (II, 1580–6)

(If I have deprived you of this woman, I have the power to do so, for I am the king of my own domains, as Alfonso is the King of Castile; my forefathers do not owe their lands to him, for they wrested it from the Moors by their own efforts.)

Once again he cries 'Yo soy quien soy' (I am who I am; II, 1590), although it is of course clear from his actions that he is departing further and further from the norms of action which his birth and status require.

From Sancho's second interview with the King in act III, we discover that the priest had asked a much revered abbot to intercede with don Tello, but that he had been unable to move him to pity (III, 1685–92). In the second *cuadro* of act III, Elvira speaks from the tower which is her prison to her father, who praises her resistance. Don Tello comes upon the stage and says that he will never free her. Nuño and his supporters are the tyrants, he declares, in that they refuse to counsel Elvira to give way to his demands ('Vosotros sois los tiranos,/que no la queréis rogar/que dé a mi intento lugar'; III, 1871–3), a reversal of roles which neatly underlines the effect of the lord's unbridled lust which now subverts all human values in his eyes. At the end of the *cuadro* he tells Celio that he will overcome Elvira's disdain of him that very day (III, 1921–2). The rape then takes place as the King is making his preliminary inquiries, and the fourth *cuadro* opens dramatically with Elvira running onto the stage pursued by don Tello whilst Feliciana seeks to restrain her brother (SD, III, 2153). The audience is thus prepared for the dramatic entrance of the dishevelled Elvira in this final *cuadro* (SD, III, 2281), and for her long formal speech of complaint, from which it becomes clear that she was taken out into the country and raped (III, 2313–36). The final act of violence thus takes place in the presence of nature, as the speech underlines, and contrasts with the first *cuadro* of act I, in which Sancho and Elvira declared their love for each other, again in a country setting. It also ironically echoes don Tello's first appearance on the stage, dressed in hunting garb and conscious of the beauties of the countryside.

The play thus sees the disintegration of don Tello's personality: the young, well-loved lord degenerates into a savage monster who, infuriated by the way in which a countrygirl can spurn his advances, casts aside moral scruples, spurns religious advice, defies the code of his class and brings to dishonour the nobility of his birth. Desire for possession becomes lust, and lust in its turn gives way to anger; the main-spring of his actions, however, continues to be his belief that he is all-powerful in his own domains, and that there are no constraints which can affect him.

A *comedia* is a poetic play; Lope de Vega makes use of metaphor and simile, of allusions to classical mythology and to the medieval and Renaissance world picture, and of folkloric elements to reinforce the contrasts evident between his dramatic characters. These verbal devices are supplemented by the use of staging: costume, significant movement on the stage, grouping and levels of action, all are drawn upon to reinforce the theme of the play. Don Tello is, as we have seen, associated with the gentlemanly pursuit of hunting and is seen in the context of horses and hounds and the beasts of the chase. Nuño and Sancho are presented in relation to sheep and cattle; Pelayo is always associated with pigs. The hierarchy of the animal world thus reinforces the social hierarchy. The opening speech of act I is written in *décimas*, an elaborate stanza form, and begins with an apostrophe to the countryside of Galicia, placed on the lips of Sancho. Through the imagery, the love of Sancho for Elvira is related to the natural cycle, the spontaneous love of birds, beasts and flowers. The first meeting of Elvira and Sancho in that *cuadro* reflects both the Narcissus myth and the folk-poems in which a lover and his lass meet beside a clear-running stream. In act II Sancho compares his love to that of the ivy and vines clinging to a poplar, and finds now little solace in nature, although 'me pareció que alguna fuente / lloró también y murmuró turbada' (it seemed to me that some stream also wept and murmured in its perturbation; II, 1057–8). As we have seen, the rape of Elvira takes place also in the countryside, and thus don Tello besmirches the nature in which he himself had previously taken equal pleasure with his vassals. The ferocity of his later actions is foreshadowed in his descriptions of the wild boar and the fierce bear (I, 335–51) and Sancho compares him to a lion attacking a lamb (I, 841–4). Later in the play his ferocity is presented through comparisons with Tarquin and Amnon (III, 1911, 1924). Visually, the way in which he demeans himself by his actions is demonstrated in the scene in which Elvira appears on the stage balcony (representing in this instance the tower of her prison). Before her appearance above, even Celio confesses to Nuño that he is impressed by her valour (II, 1780–2, 1785–8). The words put into her mouth are lofty and noble in tone, and she shows herself grieved for the probable fate of Sancho. Although she does not directly confront don Tello in this scene, withdrawing immediately before his entrance, her appearance on the level which physically dominates the stage level at which he emerges is an indication to the spectators of her moral superiority, since this device is used in several other plays in which physical levels similarly indicate moral superiority and inferiority.[14] This stage picture is also related to the imagery of the speech of Sancho in act II, during his first confrontation with don Tello, in which he speaks of his love for Elvira as raising him upwards towards nobility of soul. In act III the gradual isolation of don Tello which results from his actions is underlined, not only by the words and actions of Feliciana and Celio, but by his physical isolation on stage in the final scene of judgement.[15] Stage pictures, then, as well as poetic images, serve to point up the theme of the play and to make its import simpler to follow by the audience.

King Alfonso is presented on stage on three separate occasions as the fount of justice. In act II, despite Sancho's fears that he will not be admitted to the King's presence (II, 1191–4), and that his suit will not be heard (II, 1203–10), the King is ever ready to receive a humble suppliant: 'Pues ¿quién a ningún pobre la resiste?' (Whoever refuses a poor man audience?; II, 1318). He urges Sancho to speak calmly (II, 1334) and not to weep (II, 1349), telling him that his role is not only to show mercy but to execute justice. Sancho should therefore explain who has done him wrong, 'que quien al pobre ofende, nunca es sabio' (for he who offends a poor man, is never a wise one'; II, 1354). Thus encouraged, Sancho tells his tale straightforwardly, in a way which impresses the King with his discretion and honesty. The King wastes no time in inditing a letter to don Tello, the time required to write it being taken up with a passage between Pelayo and Sancho in which they comment on the simplicity of the King's dress and manner, which contrasts with his valour. Describing don Tello's attitude to power, Sancho tells the King that 'él pone y él quita leyes: / que estas son las condiciones / de soberbios infanzones, / que están lejos de los reyes' (he makes and breaks laws, for such is the status of proud lordlings who are distant from their king; II, 1437–40), thus in effect giving the King knowledge that he did not have and making him aware that such proud and turbulent vassals indeed existed in his realms (II, 1430–1). The King is surprised at the great difference in attitudes between Sancho and Pelayo, and gives the latter money and the former his letter which, he tells him, will bring about the immediate release of Elvira.

The second scene of justice occupies the first *cuadro* of act III. Once again, Sancho is well received, 'porque el pobre para mí / tiene cartas de favor' (for me, a poor man always has letters of recommendation; III, 1665–6). He is indignant that don Tello should have refused to act as the King commanded, and asks if he tore up the letter. He did not physically do so, replies Sancho, but refusing to carry out the King's command was equivalent to his having done so (III, 1705–8). The King immediately decides that he must set out for Galicia and execute justice in person (III, 1726–8), overriding the contrary advice of his counsellors. He warns Sancho to tell Nuño that he is to get his house ready to receive him, but that none should be informed of the King's coming, on pain of death (III, 1749–53), and he further warns Pelayo that he must say no more than that the King is a noble from Castile, placing his two fingers over his mouth if he feels impelled to speak (III, 1755–62), a device with which Lope makes full play in the concluding *cuadros*, in which Pelayo is several times on the point of letting the cat out of the bag. Though Sancho pleads with the King that he is doing more than his simple estate demands and that it would be sufficient to send an *alcalde*, the King replies that the King is the best judge of all ('El mejor alcalde, el rey'; III, 1776).

In the third *cuadro* of act III, the King makes his appearance, supported by the two gentlemen, and with no other retinue. Nuño, warned by Sancho that a judge is at hand, tells the latter that the attempt to impose a judicial decision will be in vain:

> que un poderoso en su tierra,
> con armas, gente y dinero,
> o ha de torcer la justicia,

> o alguna noche, durmiendo,
> matarnos en nuestra casa.   (III, 1959–63)

(For a powerful lord on his own domains, supplied with arms, followers and
money, will either pervert justice or have us killed some night whilst we are
sleeping in our beds.)

The King and his two attendants are attired in travelling dress (SD, III,
2026). Nuño tells him of his fears, but the King replies that 'la vara del rey /
hace el oficío del trueno, / que avisa que viene el rayo' (the royal staff of
office is like thunder, for it gives warning of the impending flash of lightning;
III, 2043–5). He sets about drawing up the case by questioning witnesses,
asking them what they know of the affair of don Tello and Elvira.
Countrymen and women answer fearlessly and clearly, and the Count, one
of the King's two supporters, tells him that it is obvious that Sancho was
telling the truth (III, 2115–19). The King orders a priest and an executioner
to be at hand. In the final *cuadro*, after the sight of don Tello in pursuit of
Elvira, the King enters again and has himself announced by Celio. When
Celio asks what name he shall give, the King says simply, 'I' ('Yo'; III,
2201). Don Tello's fears, the King explains, will make it clear to him that
the King alone could call himself 'I' (III, 2210–12) and this surmise is
immediately proved correct when Celio returns:

> A don Tello, mi señor,
> dije cómo Yo os llamáis,
> y me dice que os volváis,
> que él solo es Yo por rigor.
> Que quien dijo Yo por ley
> justa del cielo y del suelo,
> es sólo Dios en el cielo,
> y en el suelo sólo el Rey.   (III, 2213–20)

(I informed my lord don Tello that you called yourself 'I', and he replied that
you should take your leave, for he alone, strictly speaking, can call himself 'I'.
The only being who could correctly and legally say 'I' in heaven above or on
the earth beneath, is God in his heaven, and the King on earth.)

Once again it is evident that don Tello regards himself as a King in
miniature. Celio is then told to announce the King as a magistrate or judge
of the King's household and capital ('un alcalde decid / de su casa y corte';
III, 2221–2). Don Tello then enters, surprised that a mere judge should have
sought him out in his own domains. '¿Qué diferencia tiene / del Rey, quien
en nombre viene / suyo?' (What difference is there between the King
himself, and one who comes in the King's name?; III, 2250–2), asks the
supposed judge. 'Si el Rey no viene a prenderme, / no hay en todo el mundo
quién' (Unless the King himself come in person to take me prisoner, there is
no one in the world who can do so; III, 2259–60), replies the lord. The King

thereupon discloses his identity, and at once don Tello submits to his authority and acknowledges his guilt. Elvira then appears on stage, making, as it were, the last speech for the prosecution. The King sentences the rebellious vassal to death, despite the Count's plea for mercy: 'Es traidor / todo hombre que no respeta / a su rey, y que habla mal / de su persona en ausencia' (Every man who does not respect his King, and who speaks ill of him in his absence, is a traitor; III, 2391–4), declares the King. Don Tello is first to marry Elvira, thus restoring her honour, and at the same time enabling her to receive half his estates, and then be executed. Feliciana, who, as we have seen, tried to mitigate the excesses of her brother, and later turned against him, is made lady-in-waiting to the Queen. Justice has been done, and has been seen to be done. The King has personally ensured that his writ runs throughout his domains.

An interesting point which has escaped previous commentators arises from the use which Lope has made in these final scenes of judgement of the actual person of the *alcalde de casa y corte* whose duty it was to maintain order in the theatres. At an early stage in the development of the Spanish *corrales*, the commercial theatres, it appears that, as in Elizabethan England, some favoured members of the audience were allowed to sit on the stage. According to the regulations for the theatres issued in 1608 by order of the Protector (himself appointed by the Royal Council), no one was to be permitted on the stage, other than the actors, nor was any bench or chair to be placed thereon for members of the audience.[16] The policing of the theatres at this early date was the responsibility of the Commisioners of the brotherhoods which owned the theatres and operated them for the benefit of the hospitals, and they were assisted by *alguaciles* (officers of justice). At a later date the Sala de Alcaldes de Casa y Corte, a body which derived its authority from the Royal Council, was given direct responsibility for the maintenance of order in the theatres. The lease of the theatres drawn up in 1625 refers to the maintenance of order by *alcaldes de corte*; they were to be permitted to use a box assigned to the Protector.[17] From detailed regulations for the conduct of the Sala, drawn up in or before 1630, it is clear that, by that date, the maintenance of order in the public theatres had passed under its jurisdiction. The regulations lay down that, among other duties, the *alcalde* charged with responsibility for the theatres must ensure that order is kept among the members of the public seeking admission and that all pay at the doors. As the time of performance draws near, he is to seat himself on the stage on a chair placed near the rear wall, and give the order for the play to begin. His bearing throughout should be such as to inspire respect for his authority.[18] These regulations do not refer to his subordinates taking their place on the stage, but a decree of the Royal Council of 1638 refers to his attendance with *alguaciles*. Commenting on this and

other instructions, Antonio Martínez Salazar wrote in 1764 that in this
period the *alcalde* sat on a chair on the stage, and that beside him stood an
alguacil and an *escribano* (attorney), but that in later years, with the introduction of more elaborate scenery, including wings, they were forced to
remove themselves to a box.[19] It is not clear when this move took place, but
the evidence at present available suggests that, when possible, the *alcalde*
continued to sit on the stage until a very late date. Whilst a document of
1654 speaks of the box set aside for the *alcalde*,[20] an account of the voyage
made by Cosme de Médicis to Spain and Portugal states that on 5
November 1668 the Prince visited the theatre in Madrid, and describes the
manner in which an *alcalde* sat on a chair on the stage, surrounded by his
ministers of justice.[21] Tomás de Guzmán, writing in 1683, speaks of the
alcalde sitting on the stage,[22] whilst a report of 1720, drawn up by Antonio
Montero de Pineda, states that the *alcalde* continued to take his seat on the
stage until shortly before that period ('de pocos tiempos a esta parte'),
dating the change to the period when the theatres were run by Juan Antonio
Peñón.[23] Writing in 1738, shortly before the two commercial theatres of
Madrid were rebuilt, Louis Riccoboni asserts that

> Below the *Cazuela*, and on two Sides of the Door by which they enter into the
> Pit, are two dark Boxes called *Aloxeros*, in one of which an *Alcade de Corto* [*sic*]
> (who is a Royal Judge) sits, having all his Retinue before him in a small
> Appartment which is in the Pit. This Magistrate, however, does not always sit
> here, 'tis only when the Scene is embarrassed by the Decorations; for at the
> simple Comedy, which they call *de Capa y Spada* [*sic*, for *de capa y espada*: 'cloak
> and sword plays'], he sits in a Chair, on one of the Sides of the Theatre, with
> two or three of his Officers behind him.[24]

This custom merits further investigation, but it is a reasonable supposition
that, at the time when Lope wrote *El mejor alcalde, el rey*, an *alcalde* was seated
on the stage during performances, attended by an *escribano* and an *alguacil*,
and that the custom persisted, when staging conditions permitted, until the
early years of the eighteenth century.

Lope de Vega has made subtle use of the practice. The King as executor of
justice (*justiciero*) is a *topos* of the *comedia*. In plays such as *Peribáñez* he
appears at the end and makes the final judgements; in other plays, such as
Lope's *El castigo sin venganza*, or Calderón's *El médico de su honra*, we also see
the ruler receiving suitors and despatching business. But in *El mejor alcalde,
el rey* the King as the executor of justice is, as the title suggests, the main
theme of the play. It is a play which confronts a microcosm with a macrocosm, Galicia with Castile. Don Tello rules his domain justly until he is
overcome with passion, lust and a frenetic desire to impose his will at all
costs, but he refuses to see himself and his territories as parts of a great
whole. The King rules Castile well and efficiently, but cannot be aware of

all that goes on in the more distant regions; once he is made aware of what is happening, he acts quickly, efficiently and impartially. Don Tello is made to realise his true place within the hierarchy of the state, and does so recognise his duties to his monarch and the way in which he has betrayed them. The King's commands should be obeyed by all, and all should obey the King's ministers of justice, for each is a direct representative of the King himself. It should not be necessary for the King to appear in person on every occasion, since his representative receives his authority directly from the King and should be obeyed as though he were the King himself.

The contrast between microcosm and macrocosm is also evident in the scenes of justice. The King of Castile admits the humblest petitioner, treats him kindly and gently, and is disposed to favour his requests should they turn out to be soundly based. Before coming to a decision he examines the evidence carefully, questions witnesses and checks his facts. Don Tello, on the other hand, who should similarly dispense justice to his dependants, is himself the author of the outrage of which they so rightly complain. He acts hypocritically, swearing to put right a wrong of which he himself is the author; when the truth comes out, he reacts violently, ordering at first the petitioners to be put to death and, when restrained by Feliciana, having them driven from his castle. The constant factor in these scenes is Sancho: he speaks as honestly to his lord as he does to the King, but whereas he can be straightforward and plain with Alfonso, with don Tello he has to employ hints and insinuations. Where a judge is biased and personally involved, the plain truth can be a dangerous weapon in the hands of the petitioner. Blinded by his lust and by his pride, don Tello considers Sancho to be a rustic clown; the King, on the other hand, appreciates his worth and listens with consideration to his plea.

The play, then, not only reinforces the power of the throne and makes an intriguing stage pattern which mirrors the actual trio of ministers of justice with another trio of actors who are playing similar parts, and are no doubt similarly dressed, but it also helps to reinforce the authority of the real *alcalde*. The play demonstrated to the audience that the *alcalde de casa y corte* whose business it was to enforce order in the theatre was himself the direct representative of the King's authority.

Earlier commentators saw in this and in similar plays a democratising Lope; more recent critics, such as Díez Borque, have pointed out that Lope's approach is conservative rather than revolutionary. Nevertheless, we must not consider Lope's attitude too much from a twentieth-century point of view. *El mejor alcalde, el rey* is one of a group of socially-conscious plays which reflect a feeling that all is not well in society. The tentative date of composition suggested by Morley and Bruerton, 1620–3, would allow for the play to have been written after the fall of Lerma (4 October 1618), when there was a hope for a time that perhaps the King would take a firmer hand, a more direct control, and that the rule of favourites would cease. Whether this is so or not, the play does plead for direct and honest application of the law, without the law's long delays and without the corruption which then seemed inevitable. In so doing, it looks back to the past, to an idealised and simplified society, in which the King played a more direct role as God's vice-regent on earth. Lope did not look forward, as his modern critics may, and as the eighteenth century certainly did, to a gradual and, it was to be hoped, inevitable progress towards a brighter future; he saw his ideal society in the past, a golden past to which, if all played their proper part in society, and if God's commandments were truly respected, society might once again return.[25]

NOTES

1. For the duties of the noble according to the code of the Order of Saint James, see J. E. Varey, *La inversión de valores en 'Fuenteovejuna'*, Lectiones, 5 (Santander: Universidad Internacional Menéndez Pelayo, 1976).
2. Madrid was declared the capital of Spain in 1561. In 1601 the capital was transferred to Valladolid, but returned to Madrid in 1606.
3. Performances in country towns and villages in the environs of Madrid have been studied by Noël Salomon, 'Sur les représentations théâtrales dans les *pueblos* des provinces de Madrid et Tolède (1589–1640)', *Bulletin Hispanique*, LXII (1960), 398–427.
4. For the historical background to this period, see John Lynch, *Spain under the Habsburgs*, vol. II (Oxford: Basil Blackwell, 1969); Antonio Domínguez Ortiz, *The Golden Age of Spain. 1516–1659*, trans. James Casey (London: Weidenfeld and Nicolson, 1971); and José Antonio Maravall, *Estado moderno y mentalidad social (Siglos XV a XVII)*, 2 vols (Madrid: Revista de Occidente, 1972). On *limpieza de sangre*, see Albert A. Sicroff, *Les controverses des statuts de 'pureté de sang' en Espagne du XVe au XVIIe siècle* (Paris: Didier, 1960); Américo Castro, *De la edad conflictiva* (Madrid: Taurus, 1961); and A. A. van Beysterveldt, *Repercussions du souci de la pureté de sang sur la conception de l'honneur dans la 'comedia nueva' espagnole* (Leyden: Brill, 1966). An essential work for the study of the rural plays is Noël Salomon, *Recherches sur le thème paysan dans la 'comedia' au temps de Lope de Vega* (Bordeaux: Institut d'Etudes Ibériques et Ibéro-Americaines de l'Université de Bordeaux, 1965), but see also, as correctives, R. O. Jones, 'Poets and Peasants', in *Homenaje a William L. Fichter. Estudios sobre el teatro antiguo hispánico y otros ensayos*, ed. A. David Kossoff and José Amor y Vázquez (Madrid: Castalia, 1971), pp. 341–55 and J. E. Varey, 'La Campagne dans le théâtre espagnol au XVII siècle', in *Dramaturgie et société*, ed. Jean Jacquot (Paris: Centre National de la Recherche Scientifique, 1968), I, 47–76.
5. S. Griswold Morley and Courtney Bruerton, *The Chronology of Lope de Vega's 'comedias'* (New York and London: MLA and OUP, 1940), p. 219.
6. Lope himself says in his *Arte nuevo* that the best plots are centred on honour, since they have the power to move the general public ('los casos de la honra son

mejores, / porque mueven con fuerza a toda gente'), lines 327–8 of his *Arte nuevo de hacer comedias en este tiempo*. See Juan Manuel Rozas's edition, in his *Significado y doctrina del 'Arte nuevo' de Lope de Vega* (Madrid: Sociedad General Española de Librería, 1976), p. 191.

7. Lope de Vega, *El mejor alcalde, el rey*, ed. José María Díez Borque, Clásicos Españoles (Madrid: Retorno Ediciones, 1973), pp. 87–8. All quotations in the present article are taken from this edition which, although not without errors, offers a reasonably sound text.

8. A Spanish play of the period is divided into three acts. Each act is divided into separate pieces of action which take place in a determined locale. Changes of location are indicated by brief moments in which the stage is left unoccupied; when the next actors make their appearance, it is taken that the location of action has changed, and the new locale is usually established by direct references in the speeches of the characters and, often, by dress. Nineteenth-century editors tended to divide each act into many scenes, determined by the entrances and exits of principal characters. It has more recently become the practice to speak of each whole piece of action taking place in one location as a *cuadro* (literally: 'picture').

9. Contrast the situation in Lope's *Peribáñez y el comendador de Ocaña*, where the highest honour granted to Peribáñez by his lord, that of bestowing on him *hidalguía* (a form of nobility), is at the same time part of a conscious plan to bring about his dishonour by seducing his wife. See J. E. Varey, 'The Essential Ambiguity in Lope de Vega's *Peribáñez*: Theme and Staging', *Theatre Research International*, n.s., 1 (1976), 157–78 (167–70).

10. Compare the similar scene in the final *cuadro* of act II of Tirso de Molina's *El burlador de Sevilla*; see J. E. Varey, 'Social Criticism in *El burlador de Sevilla*', *Theatre Research International*, n.s., II (1977), 197–221 (214).

11. Indicated to the audience by the actors' movements and failure to recognise each other (I, 753–4); costume, when Sancho and Pelayo enter dressed *de noche* (SD, I, 766); and speech, when Nuño, for instance, says later that he endeavoured to recognise the abductors by the light of the moon (I, 795–6). Or the significance of night scenes, see J. E. Varey, 'The Staging of Night Scenes in the *comedia*', *The American Hispanist*, II, 15 (1977), 14–16.

12. On the significance of this phrase, see Castro, *De la edad conflictiva*, pp. 79–99; and Leo Spitzer, '*Soy quien soy*', *Nueva Revista de Filologia Hispánica*, I (1947), 113–27.

13. On the character of Feliciana, see Sturgis E. Leavitt, 'A Maligned Character in Lope's *El mejor alcalde, el rey*', *Bulletin of the Comediantes*, VI, 2 (1954), 1–3; and particularly Albert E. Sloman, 'Lope's *El mejor alcalde, el rey*: addendum to a note by Sturgis E. Leavitt', *Bulletin of the Comediantes*, VII, 2 (1955), 17–19. Sloman sees Feliciana as a foil to the character of her brother.

14. See, for instance, Varey, 'The essential ambiguity in Lope de Vega's *Peribáñez*', 165–6; and, for the use of the same symbolism in Calderón, J. E. Varey, 'Imágenes, símbolos y escenografía en *La devoción de la Cruz*', in *Hacia Calderón. Segundo Coloquio anglogermano. Hamburgo 1970*, ed. Hans Flasche (Berlin and New York: Walter de Gruyter, 1973), pp. 155–70 (161–4).

15. This point was made by Margaret Wilson in a paper delivered at the Fifth

Congress of the International Association of Hispanists, Bordeaux, 1974: '*El mejor alcalde, el rey*: estructura, política y moral'. I am much indebted to Miss Wilson, who generously sent me a copy of her paper and allowed me to make use of it.

16. J. E. Varey and N. D. Shergold, *Fuentes para la historia del teatro en España, III. Teatros y comedias en Madrid: 1600–1650. Estudio y documentos* (London: Tamesis Books, 1971), p. 49.

17. Biblioteca Nacional, *Papeles de Barbieri*, Ms. 14004(1); quoted in J. E. Varey and N. D. Shergold, 'Datos históricos sobre los primeros teatros de Madrid: contratos de arriendo, 1615–1641', *Bulletin Hispanique*, LXII (1960), 186.

18. 'Noticias para el govierno de la Sala de Alcaldes de Casa y Corte', Archivo Histórico Nacional, Madrid, *libro* 1173, fols. 39v–41v. The document is undated, but precedes a decree of 4 July 1630. I owe this reference to the kindness of Professor N. D. Shergold, whose invaluable work, *A History of the Spanish Stage from Medieval Times until the end of the Seventeenth Century* (Oxford: Clarendon Press, 1967), pp. 390–8, should also be consulted.

19. Antonio Martínez Salazar, *Coleccion de memorias, y noticias del gobierno general del Consejo* (Madrid: Antonio Sanz, 1764), pp. 462–3.

20. Archivo Municipal de Madrid, 3–143–23, reproduced in N. D. Shergold, 'Nuevos documentos sobre los corrales de comedias de Madrid, 1652–1700', *Boletín de la Biblioteca de Menéndez Pelayo*, XXXV (1959), 224.

21. '... onde per evitare tafferugli che bene spesso li dentre seguno, per comodità dell'armi che chiascheduno porta allato e per vedere si la commedia merita d'esser rappresentata v'interviene un Alcalde con gran numero d'Alguazilli, il quale tenendo la sua vara in mano poco più grosse degli altri siede sopra una seggiola da una parte del palco e attorno a lui stanno in piedi i detti suoi ministri ...'. 'Memorie del Viaggio fatto in Ispagna dal Serenissimo Principi Cosimo di Toscana raccolte dal Marchese Filippo Corsini', quoted in Angel Sánchez Rivero and Angela Mariutti de Sánchez Rivero, *Viaje de Cosme de Médicis por España y Portugal (1668–1669)* (Madrid: Suc. de Rivadeneyra, 1933), p. 110, n. 1.

22. Tomás de Guzmán, *Respuesta a un papelón que publicó El Buen Zelo mahullador, alias, Marramaquiz, en que muerde, y araña con frialdades de ingenio, y ardores de invidia, contra las comedias, y sus aprobaciones* (Salamanca: Gregorio Ortiz, 1683), quoted in Emilio Cotarelo y Mori, *Bibliografía de las controversias sobre la licitud del teatro en España* (Madrid: Tipografía de la Revista de Archivos, Bibliotecas y Museos, 1904), p. 352.

23. Archivo Municipal de Madrid, 2–458–15. Peñón was involved in the lease of 1708–12; see J. E. Varey and N. D. Shergold, 'Datos históricos de los primeros teatros de Madrid: contratos de arriendo, 1641–1719', *Boletín de la Biblioteca de Menéndez Pelayo*, XXXIX (1963), 129–30.

24. I quote from the English translation: Louis Riccoboni, *An Historical and Critical Account of the Theatres in Europe* (London, 1741), pp. 89–90.

25. Part of the research on which this article is based was undertaken when I was in receipt of a Fellowship of the Leverhulme Trust, and I take this opportunity to express my gratitude to the Trust.

The social value of nineteenth-century English drama

MICHAEL R. BOOTH

Writing of a revival of Thomas Morton's *The Way to Get Married* (first performed in 1796) at the Olympic in 1867, the critic Dutton Cook declared that comedies of this school 'belong exclusively to the playhouse and the players. They reflect real life and manners in no way; as pictures of the period in which they were written they have no kind of value. They are mere theatrical contrivances for the display of the actor's peculiarities, for winning laughter at any price from the audience, and dismissing them amused with the slightest possible tax upon their reflective powers.'[1] Another writer a hundred years later states more generally and more bluntly that 'defending the relevance of nineteenth-century drama seems as hopeless as defending Benedict Arnold before the Daughters of the American Revolution'.[2] Presuming this means social relevance, then certainly the defence is never attempted, and, Benedict-Arnold-like, the nineteenth-century English drama stands convicted before the court of critical opinion of that worst of modern artistic and social crimes, Irrelevance.

These two points of view, a century apart, sum up much modern critical thinking about nineteenth-century drama. The other main charge, that this drama lacks literary merit and artistic stature, cannot be our concern here, although in passing we can note that the same Dutton Cook who castigated the early comedies for social irrelevance dismissed criticism on literary grounds as being itself irrelevant: 'They were never intended to be read. They would be almost as much out of place in a general library as the footlights themselves.'[3] The social case against nineteenth-century drama is essentially as Cook stated it: feeding upon its own past and its own theatrical conventions and techniques, the drama imitated itself rather than life, abandoning social truth and social relevance for the virtuoso display of star actors and the visual thrill of stage spectacle. Furthermore, the alleged meretriciousness of the dominant forms of light entertainment, such as pantomime and burlesque, combined with the fact that the most popular dramatic form of the century was the highly unrealistic and sensational melodrama, suggested that theatregoers preferred to pass their time in a world of glittering frivolity or of exciting dreams rather than the real world in which they lived. This is a reasonably accurate though necessarily abbreviated summary of a particular approach to nineteenth-century drama, and those who take it have not been endeared to their subject by the discovery of compensating literary skill or intellectual profundity: in fact just the opposite.

What 'social relevance' or 'social value' means is a relative matter about which it is necessary to be a little more precise before going any further. The argument that will be advanced here, that nineteenth-century drama has substantial social relevance and value, depends on the wide extent to which this drama, while not communicating social statistics, nor a naturalistic depiction of the way in which nineteenth-century man lived and worked, nor an exact account of social habits and cultural life, nevertheless conveys a great deal of interesting and absorbing information about popular social attitudes, social conflicts, social criticism, the ideals of a mass culture, and the way in which a century defined its character in terms of a dramatised social image. Whether that image corresponded to 'reality' is not so interesting a question as the question of the nature of that image. When it is realised that something between twenty-five and thirty thousand plays were performed in the course of the century, and that audiences ran into millions of people drawn from all social classes, then clearly we are concerned with a truly popular and gigantic entertainment industry employing at any one time many thousands of dramatists, actors, stage crew, and other theatre employees. The sheer mass of social information that industry produced cannot be dismissed as negligible.

All forms of nineteenth-century drama can be put forward as evidence for the ways in which playwrights spun their fabric out of the raw material of society and related their plays to the social concerns of the day. Because the Licensing Act of 1737 and the absolute power of the Examiner of Plays prevented the dramatist from writing seriously about religion, politics, and sex, his freedom to present social issues was circumscribed. However, until near the end of the century he was hardly in the vanguard of public taste and on the whole operated comfortably within the limits laid down for him. Such explicit political satire as *The Happy Land* (1873), a burlesque by W. S. Gilbert and Gilbert Arthur à Beckett, which caused great fuss and bother in the Lord Chamberlain's office, was uncharacteristic (except perhaps for pantomime) of a drama that was mostly cut off from participation in the artistic expression of political concerns in a highly political age.

One can, indeed, begin with some of these 'theatrical contrivances' fitted only 'for winning laughter at any price', as Cook puts it, in order to see to what extent the vast amount of light entertainment available on the nineteenth-century stage made any connections with social life. The turn-of-the-century comedy that he dismisses as irrelevant to its times, written by such authors as Morton, Frederic Reynolds, Thomas Holcroft, and

George Colman, had almost an entirely middle-class attraction; of the main dramatic forms only comedy and burlesque confined their appeal to the middle classes. This early comedy, while loosely structured and strongly episodic, was theatrically homogeneous in that the same half-dozen ideas are repeated from play to play: the patriotic exaltation of England and its soldiers, sailors, farmers, and men of commerce; the merit of the rustic and simple life; the condemnation of the aristocrat and town morals; the idealisation of virtue and charity. The most popular comedy of this school, which flourished from about 1795 to 1810, was Colman's *John Bull* (1803), significantly subtitled *The Englishman's Fireside*. It apotheosises the brazier Job Thornberry, a righteous and good-hearted tradesman, the John Bull of the title and the genuine representative of middle-class integrity and national worth. Although until the end of the play a ruined man, he makes the kind of speech entirely appropriate to his virtually allegorical character:

> Blunt or sharp, I've been honest. Let them look at my ledger – they'll find it right. I began upon a little; I made that little great, by industry. I never cringed to a customer to get him into my books, that I might hamper him with an over-charged bill for long credit; I earned my fair profits; I paid my fair way; I break by the treachery of a friend, and my first dividend will be seventeen shillings in the pound. I wish every tradesman in England may clap his hand on his heart and say as much, when he asks a creditor to sign his certificate.

Themes and speeches of this sort cannot exist apart from the life of their age. It is impossible to conceive of any work of art in isolation from the society and the period that gave it birth. In the particular case of early nineteenth-century comedy the restless bustle, the liberal sentiments, the rural ideals, the respect for agriculture and trade, the predilection for bourgeois characters and bourgeois social attitudes, the rejection of aristocracy and traditional standards of genteel behaviour, the patriotism and the francophobia are surely not unrelated to the political and social situation of Britain after the French Revolution and during the Napoleonic War. The presentation of ideal character and ideal virtue can be as socially revealing as the portrayal of everyday reality; not only the early comedy but also much of the century's drama thrives on ideals.

The principal ideal of Victorian society and therefore of the Victorian stage was the domestic, which meant the unapproachable virtue of woman, wife, and mother; the sacredness of ties between husband and wife and between parent and child; the sanctity of home and hearth; the inalienable right of the Englishman to enjoy domestic contentment and the ultimate impregnability of that contentment when threatened by outside forces. Such an ideal is at the heart of all kinds of Victorian drama and also strongly evident in the melodrama and comedy of the pre-Victorian period. In Victorian comedy and 'drama' the domestically ideal tendencies of comedies like *John Bull* and tragedies like Sheridan Knowles's *Virginius* (1820), which is unified around a father–daughter relationship, were enshrined in implacable dogma. The Victorian theatre as a whole became increasingly domestic, and comedy emphasised domestic themes as well as other concepts directly related to social developments.

One of its concerns was the proper relationship between husband and wife, both in the home and in that ever dangerous world outside. 'Marriage', says a male character in Edmund Falconer's *Extremes* (1858), 'is at once the most solemn and most beautiful mystery of this life ... the nobler the estimate individual man or woman forms of its obligations, the higher each must be lifted in the scale of humanity'. Sometimes the husband has to be reminded of the solemnity and beauty of this mystery, but much more often the wife must be brought up to the mark. The dashing young husband of J. S. Coyne's *My Wife's Daughter* (1850) has a hard struggle to adjust himself to a quiet domestic existence with his new wife, who exhibits suspicion and jealousy in nasty bursts of temper but eventually realises her faults and begs forgiveness. 'For this behold me humble and penitent', she cries, attempting to kneel before her husband; he raises her magnanimously and embraces her, to which she responds with 'Oh joy, joy! Dear Arthur, am I forgiven – my errors and your wrongs – forgiven?' Similarly, the wife of Palgrave Simpson's drama *Broken Ties* sees the folly of her pursuit of a career as opera singer apart from her family and is reconciled, with '*music tremolo*', to her husband. Her last words on the subject are:

> 'Tis mine again, the treasure flung aside,
> Domestic love, true woman's dearest pride.

The apparently ineffectual Mildmay of Tom Taylor's comedy–drama *Still Waters Run Deep* (1855), tyrannised over by the wife and aunt, proves his worth in the male world of business by exposing and humiliating a forger and swindler in the presence of the amazed females of his household, who immediately submit to his obvious masculine superiority. The aunt agrees with his dictum that 'there's only one master in this house', and the wife is told, 'I should prefer to win you by a lover's tenderness, but if I cannot do that I know how to make a husband's rights respected.' To this, Mrs Mildmay can only beg to be informed of her faults so that she can correct them, and say, 'I will honour and obey you, as a wife should.'

In comedy and drama where marital difficulties are prominent, it is clear that while much sympathy attaches to the lonely and neglected wife and obloquy to the indifferent husband – where this is the situation – the jealous, dominating, temperamental, and unfeminine wife receives short shrift, and that, whatever the agonies of the marital situation, adherence to the ideal necessitates a happy ending which too often is incredibly achieved by evasion of the real problem of incompatibility. Such endings mar two interesting comedies by H. J. Byron, *Cyril's Success* (1868) and *Married in Haste* (1876). In the former a popular dramatist and novelist, preoccupied with his writing and business affairs, pays little attention to his wife, and tensions rapidly develop between them. In the latter an artist is jealous of his wife's talent, for she is the better painter. Both plays deal with miserable couples rather than young lovers, and with the interesting question of reconciling creative talent with the domestic ideal. In another Byron comedy, *Partners for Life* (1871), this ideal in terms of its domestic comforts is strongly stated by the unhappy wife temporarily separated from her husband:

> I would rather lead a domestic life, if I had the opportunity – the pleasant late dinner with the curtains closed and the gas lighted – the music and the chat, and the cozy hour or two with coffee, and one or two of my husband's old friends smoking a cigar and talking of their old bachelor days – the calm pleasant close to the long day; how charming is the picture if it could but be realised.

The concern with marriage and the correct sort of marital relationship lasted both in comedy and more serious drama (although nineteenth-century comedy, as can be seen from the above examples, is often intensely serious) until the end of the century. The Mayfair comedies of Arthur Pinero and Henry Arthur Jones are most informative about the neurotic fear of a damaged reputation that forced upper-middle-class society to subscribe to a harsh moral code in public while deploring its destructive effect on the individual – such as Pinero's Mrs Tanqueray and Jones's Mrs Dane – in private. The society of these plays tries to preserve outward forms at all costs and frequently sacrifices the individual to them. In *Mrs Dane's Defence* (1900) the now blameless Mrs Dane is cast out from the love of a good young man because of past misdemeanours. Paula Tanqueray commits suicide because of the impossible strains of her joyless marriage and her socially inescapable guilty past. In Jones's *The Liars* (1897), Lady Jessica Nepean is forced to stay with her unpleasant and boorish husband while her adoring lover is driven to undertake an African expedition. Lady Susan in *The Case of Rebellious Susan* (1894), also by Jones, is pressured to return to a worthless husband and abandon her hard-won independence. Theo Frazer in Pinero's *The Benefit of the Doubt* (1895) must acquiesce in a humiliating and hollow form of agreement that will preserve reputation at the expense of her own feelings and her own personal freedom. In all these plays fear of social disgrace and the dreadful consequences of a socially irredeemable reputation determine the outcome, but it is always the woman who suffers the most, and it is usually the man who administers the inexorable laws of social justice which define social and personal morality. Any suggestion of women's rights is contemptuously dismissed, as it is in *The Case of Rebellious Susan* and quite a few previous plays that raise the issue.

Perhaps it is no wonder that women fall short and suffer as they do, considering the standard which they must ideally meet. The *raisonneur* of *The Case of Rebellious Susan*, who would make any modern male chauvinist look like a suffragette, tells an unfortunate feminist that there is an immense future for women at their own firesides, 'an immense future for women as wives and mothers, and a very limited future for them in any other capacity ... Nature's darling woman is a stay-at-home woman who wants to be a good wife and a good mother, and cares very little for anything else.'

The sophisticated drama of the 1890s was extremely sensitive to the social problems arising out of a phobic concern for public status and reputation, and these problems were seen as mainly relevant to marital and extra-marital relationships. However, such relationships and the ideal nature of woman must not be thought of as the only socially significant theme material for either late nineteenth-century dramatists or their predecessors. To stay with comedy for the moment, one can see even in an early play like *John Bull* and others of its type class antagonisms at work, especially those between the farmer and tradesman on the one hand and the townsman and propertied aristocrat on the other. The increasing domesticity of comedy and other forms of drama compelled playwrights to a greater awareness of the social milieu in which their characters lived and the material business of their daily lives. This awareness is not so detailed in comedy as it is in melodrama, but even so social themes of national importance are developed. In a comedy like *Money* (1840), by Edward Bulwer-Lytton, class bitterness is carried much further than in *John Bull*. The penniless sizar, Alfred Evelyn, sent down from university for horse-whipping a young lord who insulted him, and subsequently a dependant in the household of the ostentatious and unscrupulous Sir John Vesey, inherits a large fortune and is immediately fawned on by those who before had ignored or despised him. Several years before *Money*, in Douglas Jerrold's *The Golden Calf* (1832), a snobbish profligate sees the error of his ways and returns to the practice of his father's honourable trade. The mysterious friend who brings about this reform is the mouthpiece for a withering attack upon wealth and corruption:

> When 'tis not asked, 'What can a man do?' but 'What seems he to possess?' not 'What does he know?' but 'Where does he live?' and when this passion for appearance stays not with some hundred gilded nondescripts, but like one general social blight is at this moment found in every rank, in every walk – for a verity, we may not call the present age the age of gold or silver; but, of all ages else, the AGE OF OUTSIDES!

The principal character of Dion Boucicault's *The School for Scheming* (1847) pauses long enough in his frantic pursuit of wealth by dubious business means to observe, 'There's no reality anywhere – the very age is electro-plated – figures on the top – humbug underneath ... Facts exist no more –

they have dwindled into names – things have shrunk into words – words into air – cash into figures – reputation into nothing.'

The main themes of *Money* and several other comedies of the thirties and forties – class, wealth, social pride and ambition – form the backbone of later Victorian comedy, which enlarges the class theme with bitterness between the traditional landowner and well-born gentleman on one side, and the *nouveau riche* on the other, the dramatist's sympathy invariably lying with the former. Tom Robertson's comedies develop this aspect of class antagonism at some length. The social-climbing Chodd Jr of *Society* (1865), who believes that he can buy everything he wants in life, receives a deserved comeuppance in love and politics from a young man who inherits a baronetcy and a fortune to go with it. The low comedian of *Caste* (1867), a mechanic who purchases a plumbing and gasfitting business, is obviously on the way up in the commercial world. His hostility towards the elegant Captain Hawtrey is comically expressed but deeply felt: 'People should stick to their own class. Life's a railway journey, and Mankind's a passenger – first class, second class, third class. Any person found riding in a superior class to that for which he has taken his ticket will be removed at the first station stopped at, according to the bye-laws of the company.' Bodmin Todder of Todder's Original Patent Starch provides comic vulgarity in *Play* (1868). In *Progress* (1869) there is a sharp exchange of views on the eponymous subject between the son of a peer and a young engineer who has come to the old abbey (the ancient family home) to plan its demolition to make way for a railway; class hostility between them is also apparent. A clash between an earl and a factory owner is the basis of *Birth* (1870). The castle and the works are adjacent; the master buys out the aristocrat and occupies the castle. H. J. Byron's immensely popular and long-running *Our Boys* (1875) pits an arrogant baronet against a wealthy retired grocer. In Tom Taylor's *New Men and Old Acres* (1869), an old estate is saved from bankruptcy by the assistance of a Liverpool businessman who is devoted to his 'ledgers and dock warrants, noisy wharves, and dingy offices' and is 'proud of the name of a British merchant'. Of course he marries the daughter of Cleve Abbey, and there is a happy union between tradition and enterprise, property and the new meritocracy. The satire of the play is directed against the extremely vulgar and ostentatiously *nouveau riche* Bunter, who adores all things new and detests the old. Bunter's life-style combines, as he puts it, 'modern hopulence with modern elegance', and he speaks of his own estate in the following terms:

> Glass and iron are, I often say, the right and left 'ands of 'orticulture. Thanks to them and 'ot-water pipes, we can conquer climate and annilliate the helements! I've three acres under glass at Beaumanor Park, three-quarters of a mile of fernery; and our forcing 'ouses are considered equal to Chatsworth – at least, so my gardeners tell me. I don't pretend to know – still less boast.

What is a man, that he should set up his 'orn? A poor worm! You're 'ere to-day, and gone you are to-morrow!

Lady Matilda of Cleve Abbey describes the Bunters as 'odious parvenus – who seem to think society's a show, to be entered by paying at the door. If I hate anyone ... it's the Bunters, and the upstart class they belong to.'

The commercial undercurrents of plays like *The School for Scheming* and *New Men and Old Acres* become dominant motifs in a sizeable group of comedies, dramas, and melodramas about the business world and the impingement of that world upon the domestic ideal. Much of *Still Waters Run Deep* concerns the business acumen of the hero in exposing the nefarious financial dealings of the villain, and a major character of another Taylor drama, *Payable on Demand* (1859), a Jewish financier, is feverishly engaged in speculation on the eve of Napoleon's abdication. Indeed, Taylor has an abiding interest in tha domestic, moral, and social consequences of life in the City in contemporary rather than Napoleonic times. The second act of another of his plays, *Settling Day* (1865), is laid in a broker's office and is taken up by the efforts of the hero to cope with a financial crisis and save the firm; the financial strain of this crisis upon his married life is also a prominent theme. A much better known example of this interest is Taylor's *The Ticket-of-Leave Man*, one of the century's best and most famous melodramas, which traces the attempt of the ex-prisoner Brierly (wrongfully convicted) to rehabilitate himself by taking a job as a bank messenger in the City. The setting of the bank scene, and of all scenes of this kind in the mid-Victorian theatre, is carefully observed in a very detailed way: the reality and solidity of commercial life and its significance as an important social and dramatic theme is all the more convincing with an equivalent reality of sets and stage furnishing.

Brierly discharges the post honourably, but his past is revealed to his employer, who abruptly dismisses him on his wedding day. Brierly makes despairing efforts to find work but society refuses to have anything to do with him. Eventually he prevents a burglary at his ex-employer's premises, is given his job back, and is promised advancement in a City where 'there's no gap between the first round of the ladder and the top of the tree'. The ending is a happy one, yet along the way lies much suffering. East-End navvies are as hard-hearted as City bankers when it comes to a ticket-of-leave man, and Brierly condemns society as a whole in a bitter speech: 'I've tried every road to an honest livelihood and one after another they are barred in my face. Everywhere that dreadful word, jail-bird, seems to be breathed in the air about me ... sorry to part with me – no complaint to make – but can't keep a ticket-of-leave man. ... I've done no man a wrong – poor fellows like me should have no enemies.'

The social criticism both implicit and directly stated in *The Ticket-of-Leave Man* indicates an important aspect of the nineteenth-century melodrama, its use – necessarily limited by the powers of the Examiner of Plays – as a means of social comment and sometimes of social protest. In a century which saw the development of great metropolitan areas and large urban working-class populations, as well as enormous industrial expansion, it is not surprising that the drama responded with a considerable degree of social awareness. The growth of theatres in London's East End, on the south bank of the Thames, and on the fringes of central London meant that the working- and lower-middle-class patrons of these theatres, by far their dominant audience group, related closely to entertainment depicting melodramatic versions of their own lives set in their own habitats. Thus from the early Victorian period a large number of plays reconstruct the domestic environment of a class that had never before existed in such numbers and never before been taken seriously as a subject for drama. Daily life, the ordinary family under intense stress, the attempt to find and retain work (as in *The Ticket-of-Leave Man*) and the struggle against poverty, homelessness, crime, and drink constitute the subject of innumerable domestic melodramas. The content of these plays is that curious mixture of fantasy, myth, and verisimilitude of character and setting distinguishing domestic melodrama as a class, but the social concerns are real if luridly portrayed.

One of the major social problems of Victorian England was drink. A considerable body of literature, a great deal of legislation and, from about 1830, the rapid growth of temperance organisations attest to the seriousness with which the problem was taken. The temperance movement churned out poems, hymns, short stories, engravings, almanacs, primers, and novels to publicise the issues and persuade the wayward to the path of reform. The melodrama, with its built-in black-and-white morality and extreme emotionalism, was perfectly suited to the purposes of temperance appeal. From Douglas Jerrold's *Fifteen Years of a Drunkard's Life* in 1828 right to the end of the century the flow of temperance melodramas and plays concerned with the problems of drink was unchecked. The problem was usually seen in terms of the decline and degradation of a single family because of the husband's increasing propensity to drink, and its working out was usually horrific: poverty, starvation, *delirium tremens* (most realistically acted), crime, murder, madness, and death – unless, as often happened, the husband is reformed in time through the efforts of a loyal temperance-minded friend. Along the way the wife and children suffer terribly. The wife in Jerrold's play is murdered by her husband in a drunken frenzy, and Mrs Thornley in T. P. Taylor's *The Bottle* (1847) is killed in the same way, the instrument in the case being the dreadful bottle itself. *The Bottle* is an especially interesting example of the serious treatment of working-class characters in a working-class environment, set as it is in the streets, garrets, and public houses of poor areas of Finsbury and the City of London with a hero who is a mechanic (until dismissed from employment), a comic man who is a pieman, a comic woman who is a shoe-binder, and other characters of humble vocation. Both *The Bottle* and Taylor's sequel, *The Drunkard's Children*, are based upon the widely circulated temperance engravings of George Cruikshank; both were first performed at East-End theatres, and both were intended for local working- and lower-middle-class audiences.

Although temperance melodramas demonstrate a painful awareness of an important social question, the question itself is always examined in terms of the downfall or reformation of a single person with a completely free choice of drinking or abstaining. Despite the fairly realistic construction of a domestic setting and a family unit, social causes for drinking are largely absent, and there is no sense of environmental determinism. This is not surprising in melodrama, which is intensely romantic and sees the whole world in terms of individual goodness and evil, strength and weakness. However, another kind of melodrama has social connections, and, though individuality is again its most notable dramatic doctrine, what happens to the hero is seen as the effect of a larger social system. The melodrama of industrial discontent, of struggle between master and man, begins with John Walker's *The Factory Lad* (1832) and runs right through the century, culminating in Galsworthy's *Strife* of 1909. Such plays are doubly significant from the social point of view because not only do they dramatise the relationship between the factory worker and the industrial machine as represented by his employer or foreman, but this relationship is also paralleled by class antagonism much more bitterly expressed than in comedy. Domestic melodrama had since its inception in the early nineteenth century equated hero with peasant or cottager, and villain with propertied aristocrat, landlord, or squire, but industrial melodrama made the same moral equation between hero and factory hand, villain and master. This equation is not invariable: G. F. Taylor's *The Factory Strike, or Want, Crime and Retribution* (1838) condemns strikes and shows in a sympathetic light a generous millowner who must reduce pay because of business competition; later factory plays are hostile to strike leaders. More commonly, however, justice and morality are on the side of workmen and strikers.

A play with this approach is *The Factory Lad*, the earliest and most powerful of the industrial melodramas. Without the standard alleviating comic relief or even a happy ending it comes close to tragedy. A group of Lancashire workmen are dismissed by a millowner because he is mechanising his looms, which will save him £3,000 a year. ('Steam supersedes manual labour. A ton of coals will do as much work as fifty men, and for less wages than ten will come to.') The despairing men fail to persuade him to change his mind, and they break into the factory to smash the new machines, urged on to 'split into ten thousand pieces these engines of your disgrace, your poverty, and your ruin!' They fire the mill and flee, but are hunted down by soldiers and committed to trial by a corrupt justice named Bias. The dramatic narrative is centred on three characters, the contemptuous millowner, an honest workman with a wife and two young children, and an outcast poacher, half-crazed with poverty and suffering, who leads the attack on the factory and shoots the millowner dead at the committal proceedings. He has been a victim of local justice and the parish welfare system, both of which he denounces in a speech of direct social criticism:

> After begging and telling them what they know to be the truth – that you have a wife and five, six, or eight children, one perhaps just born, another mayhap just dying – they'll give you eighteen pence to support them all for the week; and if you dare to complain, not a farthing; but place you in the stocks or scourge you through the town as a vagabond! This is parish charity! I have known what it is. My back is still scored with the marks of their power. The slave abroad, the poor black whom they affect to pity, is not so trampled on, hunted, and ill-used as the peasant or hard-working fellows like yourselves, if once you have no home or bread to give your children.

It is the system that is at fault, not the individual victim, and it is the system that has turned the outcast into a revolutionary. He says, 'These times cannot last long. When man be so worried that he be denied food that heaven sends for all, then heaven itself calls for vengeance! No, the time has come when the sky shall be like blood, proclaiming this shall be the reward of the avaricious, the greedy, the flinty-hearted, who, deaf to the poor man's wants, make him what he now is, a ruffian – an incendiary!' These are strong words, but the villain of industrial melodrama is a particularly repulsive type who arouses savage hostility, a hostility based on class, wealth, and exploitation rather than personal character. The villain of *The Factory Lad* says scornfully of his hands, who not unnaturally object to their abrupt dismissal: 'Is England's proud aristocracy to tremble when brawling fools mouth and question? No; the hangman shall be their answer.' Seventy years later the factory manager of Arthur Moss's *The Workman's Foe* (ca. 1900) is even more vicious about his employees:

> I've climbed to power despite the envy and hatred of the workingman. And now I'll sweat as I please. I'll put the workman's head under my heel, and crush it with as little remorse as I would you. . . . Why should I care how little the workers earn as long as I'm successful? I made my position here by learning the art of riding roughshod over my fellows. I've climbed the ladder of fortune by hypocrisy and cunning, and, by sweating the workers, I and my employers may revel in luxury. Men of brains and cunning must rule the world.

The fact that speeches of this kind were put into the mouths of the capitalist and his henchmen for most of the century is socially revealing of the class bitterness long surviving in the popular theatre. Since these industrial melodramas also treat of such matters as automation, strikes, profits, and working conditions, they are exceptionally interesting for the social historian concerned with the folk myths of industry and labour in the nineteenth century.

Not only is nineteenth-century drama the first English drama to reflect the dreams, aspirations, and the sense of social injustice of the working class – indeed, to portray the working class seriously – but it is also the first to embody the realities of urban expansion. Its plays are oriented towards London, which is not surprising as the metropolis grew from a population of under a million in 1800 to three million in 1850 and six and a half million in 1900, and by the end of the century was dominating the theatrical life of the country to such an extent that a provincial theatre independent of the ubiquitous London touring company was virtually extinct. From T. W. Moncrieff's *The Heart of London* in 1830 to *The Great World of London* by George Lander and Walter Melville in 1898 the metropolis served as a moral and social symbol of evil and corruption; such plays often have a strong sense of urban topography and vividly suggest the life of the streets, the lodging houses, the tea gardens, the rich villas and elegant drawing-rooms. The juxtaposition of poverty and wealth, squalor and luxury, was a favourite device of the urban melodramatist. A further sharp moral contrast was obtained by bringing the country emigrant, frequently a young girl, a resident of the Eden-like village of rural melodrama, into the big city: the degradation of innocence, the bitter struggle against temptation, lost peace and lost virtue, the agonised present as contrasted with the tranquil past – these are several of the themes developed by the useful linking together of country and city. 'It be a dreadful and dreary place, this Lunnon, for them as are weak an wi' no hand to guide 'em', says the weary Lancashire miner-hero of Watts Phillips's *Lost in London* (1867) after searching for his wife all through the city, and his words could serve as an epitaph for many a fallen innocent in the wasteland of melodramatic London. Douglas Jerrold put the same point more fully and with specific social reference in the preface to his *Martha Willis, the Servant Maid* (1831):

> It is the object of the present drama to display, in the most forcible and striking point of view, the temptations which in this metropolis assail the young and inexperienced on their first outset in life. . . . This great metropolis teems with persons and events, which, considered with reference to their dramatic experience, beggar invention. . . . It is these scenes of everyday experience – it is these characters which are met with in our hourly paths that will be found in the present drama.

In an age which saw massive rural emigration into towns and cities in search of jobs, a possibly substantial proportion of the London audiences that saw the village melodramas of the pre-Victorian and early Victorian periods might themselves have come from the country; such drama must have closely related to their memories of home, the sense of contrast with their present condition and mode of life, and their dreams of simplicity and lost innocence.[4]

The argument so far advanced for the social value and significance of nineteenth-century drama has been based upon the evidence provided by comedy, melodrama, and the 'drama', that indefinable compromise between romantic melodrama and a materialistic, domestic, and prosaic age. Lest this seem too narrowly based an argument, something can be said in conclusion about the world of light entertainment earlier referred to, in this case especially pantomime, extravaganza, and burlesque, dramatic forms which might at first glance seem pure fun and quite removed from the sphere of social meaning.

Nineteenth-century pantomime is a curious mixture of fantasy – in the narrative part or 'opening' – with knockabout comedy and scenic trickery in the harlequinade, but both ingredients in this mixture were liberally infused with references to events of the day: politics, wars, fashion, trade, education, the price of goods, inventions and discoveries, building, transport, drink, and a host of other major and minor aspects of daily life. Leigh Hunt complained in 1831 of the decline of pantomime, which 'used formerly to be the representative of the Old Comedy, and gave us some good Aristophanic satire on the events of the day'.[5] In 1836 Charles Rice said that 'there is none of that poignant satire which used formerly to characterise this species of entertainment'.[6] However, matters must have improved. A French visitor to London, Francis Wey, saw the Surrey pantomime for 1855, *The Prince of Pearls*. In the harlequinade, as he described it, there 'comes a scene of political satire. The General Staff of the British Army drag themselves in on crutches; Cobden and his adherents are flogged like schoolboys; food adulterers are belaboured by the people.' Later, 'Admiral Napier had appeared in full-dress uniform, ordered a few Cossacks to be put in irons, shaken the editor of the *Times* by the hand, been chaired, then discarding his uniform danced a frantic jig with Harlequin.'[7] Topical allusions continued to be an important part of pantomime's framework of extensive social reference; for instance a note to the printed version of Drury Lane's *Jack and the Beanstalk* (1889) declared that 'the Libretto is subject to alterations from time to time for the introduction of topical allusions' – in other words such allusions would be constantly changing during the run to keep up with current affairs. [8]

This kind of topicality carries over to extravaganza and burlesque. From 1825 to 1855 J. R. Planché wrote revues for actor-managers like Madame Vestris, J. B. Buckstone, and Alfred Wigan. These pieces, with titles like *The Drama's Levée* (1838), *The New Planet* (1847), and *The New Haymarket Spring Meeting* (1855) were brisk, charming, light-hearted, satirical surveys of the drama and theatre of the day, as well as social and urban developments. In *The New Planet*, a revue prompted by the discovery of Neptune, the planets visit Earth with Mercury as a guide and see the sights of London, such as the Ethiopian Serenaders, the Polytechnical Institution, and the Egyptian Hall; there are many allusions to scientific discoveries. *The Drama at Home* (1844) contains a procession of current exhibitions, including Madame Tussaud, General Tom Thumb, and the Centrifugal Railway. The content of burlesque could be as closely related to contemporary life as that of Planché's revues. *The Enchanted Isle* (1848), a burlesque of *The Tempest* by Robert and William Brough, reflects the impact of the revolutions in Europe as well as other less significant occurrences. Caliban is turned into a revolutionary, and tells Prospero:

> Oh, blow your breezes!
> The love of liberty upon me seizes;
> My bosom's filled with freedom's pure emotions,
> And on the 'Rights of Labour' I've strong notions.

Later he enters marching to the music of the 'Marseillaise', *'with a Cap of Liberty on his head, a red flag in one hand'*. In the next scene Ferdinand, Ariel, and two fairies dance to rather different music, a fast waltz and then a polka, the polka being the dance craze of the 1840s. Another current musical fashion, the minstrel show, is alluded to when Prospero produces a pair of bones and accompanies Miranda *'à la Ethiopian Serenaders'* to the minstrel tune of 'Such a getting up stairs'. A contemporary reference of a different kind is made when Ferdinand is brought to Prospero's cell in the latest style: *'Railway music; a bell and steam whistle. A FAIRY SPECIAL rises through trap, C. with a flag, and holds it out as Railway policeman do. A noise of an approaching Train is heard. Shortly after enter a fairy Locomotive, R. with ARIEL and a SPECIAL as engineer and stoker, attached to a car, in which sits FERDINAND, attended by FAIRY SPECIALS.'* The theatrical light entertainment of the forties found the new railways an irresistible subject.

The songs of extravaganzas and burlesques frequently commented on the events of the day. Many burlesques of the sixties and seventies contained a topical song like the one in William Brough's *The Field of the Cloth of Gold* (1868), entitled in the printed text 'Song on the Topics of the Day', with a footnote explaining 'To be altered from time to time as occasion requires'. The song (to the tune of 'Oxford Joe') mentions the condition of Temple Bar, the Prince of Wales's visit to Ireland, Queen Victoria riding in Windsor Park, the result of the Boat Race, the British victory in Abyssinia, the question of closing public houses on Sundays, co-operative stores, and spiritualism. Songs of this kind are really musical newspapers; a satirical song cleverly aimed at a single topic is the anti-Darwinian patter song of Herman Merivale's *The Lady of Lyons Married and Settled* (1878), which begins:

Power to thine elbow, thou newest of sciences;
All the old landmarks are ripe for decay;
Wars are but shadows, and so are alliances.
Darwin the Great is the man of the day.

All other 'ologies want an apology;
Bread's a mistake – Science offers a stone;
Nothing is true but Anthrobiology –
Darwin the Great understands it alone.

and ends:

I'm the apostle of mighty Darwinity
Stands for Divinity – sounds much the same –
Apo-theistico-Pan-Asininity
Only can doubt whence the lot of us came.

Down on your knees, Superstition and Flunkeydom;
Won't you except such plain doctrines instead?
What is so simple as primitive Monkeydom,
Born in the sea with a cold in its head?

While the light entertainment of the nineteenth-century stage is socially valuable for the amount of information it contains about popular attitudes to current events, social habits, and the casual dress of contemporary life, comedy and melodrama deal more feelingly and intensively with larger issues and social themes of national importance. Sometimes such themes are treated on the level of fantasy and myth, but none the less seriously for that, and sometimes on the level of a domestic verisimilitude that comes close to social realism. Whatever the mode of performance, it is clear that this drama was closely engaged with contemporary society in a variety of ways over a variety of dramatic material. The extent of that engagement is one of the most interesting discoveries one can make about the nineteenth-century drama.

NOTES

1. *Nights at the Play* (London: Chatto and Windus, 1883), pp. 13–14.
2. Terry Otten, *The Deserted Stage* (Athens, Ohio: Ohio University Press, 1972), p. 1.
3. *Nights at the Play*, p. 13.
4. 'Home, Sweet Home' was written for a village melodrama, J. H. Payne's *Clari, or the Maid of Milan* (1823), and the theme of the village home was common in popular song as well as on the stage.
5. *The Tatler*, 28 December 1831.

6. *The London Theatre in the Eighteen-Thirties*, ed. A. C. Sprague and Bertram Shuttleworth (London: 1950), p. 11.

7. *A Frenchman Sees the English in the 'Fifties* (London: Sidgwick and Jackson, 1935), pp. 218–19.

8. A few years earlier W. Davenport Adams had begged for 'a minimum of topical allusions' in pantomime. ('A Plea for Pantomime', *The Theatre* (February, 1879), p. 27.)

Drama and society in Ibsen's *Pillars of the Community*

INGA-STINA EWBANK

Henrik Ibsen's thirteenth play, the two-part 'world-historical drama' of *Emperor and Galilean* (1873), opens on a confrontation of Christian faith and pagan philosophy during the Easter night of the year 351 in Constantinople; it closes, after ten acts of strident questioning of the human condition, with the death, twelve years later in Persia, of Julian the Apostate. More precisely, it closes with a scene in which spokesmen for both sides – the paganised Emperor's and the pale Galilean's – ponder the meaning of the life and death of Julian: is he 'a sacrificial victim of Necessity' or 'a glorious, broken tool of the Lord'? In the final lines, spoken by Macrina, the dialectic is not so much resolved as left leaning over the brink of the unspeakable: 'Let us not think to the bottom of this abyss.'[1] Ibsen's fourteenth play, *Pillars of the Community* (1877), opens on an edifying sewing circle in the house of Consul Karsten Bernick in a small Norwegian coastal town and closes, in the same room three days later, with the hero apparently purged of the falsehood on which he has lived for fifteen years and apparently having learnt that 'the spirit of freedom and the spirit of truth – those are the pillars of the community'. Put like this, it would seem that the turn to drama on contemporary social themes had meant to Ibsen not only a drastic narrowing of scope, in space and time, but also an equally drastic loss of depth in his exploration of the human mind. At the end of *Pillars* there appears to be no 'abyss' and so no suggestion that there is anything which cannot and should not be 'thought to the bottom'. Many would agree that the depth, and with it the characteristic Ibsen stance of questioning,[2] was to be recovered in the later prose plays, so that heroes like Rosmer, or Borkman, or Rubek (much like Brand before them) end up in an abyss, literal or metaphorical or both, leaving behind them questions as far-reaching and as ultimately open as any in *Emperor and Galilean*, rather than prescriptions for individual and social renewal. But few would grant *Pillars* any depth greater than that of the dry dock where the *Indian Girl*, safely returned by the twists of a 'well-made' plot, will undergo her 'thorough and honest repairs': a *Tendenzstück*[3] which, for all Ibsen's urge to join the main currents of European realism,[4] would seem to suggest nothing so much as that concern for social themes acts as a powerful narrower of dramatic art.

My aim in this paper is to question such views of the play: to suggest that the dramatic technique and (interrelatedly) the content of thought and feeling in *Pillars* are less superficial, less obvious, than has often been thought. My conviction that this is so has grown out of the experience of preparing a translation for the Royal Shakespeare Company's production of the play, directed by John Barton, which opened at the Aldwych Theatre, London, on 1 August 1977. Working through the play (and the drafts) word-by-word, and attending rehearsals where the words were turned into moments of imagined lives, have given me a new respect for both the structure and the texture of the play.

It is easy enough to use the later 'contemporary' plays as sticks to beat *Pillars* with, and in so doing miss the peculiar strengths of the earlier play.[5] To show what I mean, I will use the most obvious example. Put side by side with *John Gabriel Borkman* (1896), *Pillars* may well look like an immature version of the later play: of the story of the man who sells his love and his moral self for power and glory, abandoning Truth to embrace Mammon and the wrong sister (half- or twin-, as the case may be). Karsten Bernick reforms and is left at the end of the play 'on the brink of a new era' in which he will be cheerfully supported by both his women; John Gabriel Borkman ineluctably destroys himself and leaves the women behind as 'two shadows'. It may well look – as with Charlotte Brontë's two Brussels novels, *The Professor* and *Villette* – as if, in two forays into the same emotional fund ('det gjennemlevde', as Ibsen would call it[6]), the earlier one was hampered by considerations of objectivity, 'realism' and conventional audience or reader expectations (including the device of a happy ending), to the point where the creative imagination was strait-jacketed and its logic stultified. But appearances may be the result of looking through the wrong end of a telescope. A specific illustration is necessary at this point.

This is Bernick's vision of what he wants to do:

> Hvilken løftestang vil det ikke bli for vårt hele samfunn? Tenk blott på de store skogtrakter som vil gjøres tilgjengelige; tenk på alle de rikholdige malmleier som kan tas i drift; tenk på elven med det ene fossefall ovenfor det annet! Hvilken fabrikkvirksomhet kan ikke *der* komme i stand?
>
> (Ibsen, II, 337)

> (The boost it would give to our whole community! Just think of the vast forest regions which will be made accessible; think of all the rich deposits of iron ore which can be worked; think of the river, with one waterfall above the other! The industrial activity which can be started!)

And this is Borkman's vision of what he wanted to do:

> Alle maktens kilder i dette land ville jeg gjøre meg underdanige. Alt hva jord og fjell og skog og hav rommet av rikdomme – det ville jeg underlegge meg og

skape herredømme for meg selv og derigjennem velvaere for de mange, mange
tusen andre.

(Ibsen, III, 471)

(All the sources of power in this country, I had to command. All the wealth
that lay hidden in the earth and the mountains, in the forests and the seas. I
had to be master of it all ... To create an empire for myself and, by it, to
improve the lot of many many thousands of others.)

(Borkman, 62)[7]

From a 1970s point of view, of course, these two speeches are equally
damnable in their sentiments regarding pollution of the milieu. From a
more timeless point of view they are akin in that both attempt to justify, in
terms of social utility (not to say utilitarianism), an individual vision of
subjugating natural powers. In both, the vision is projected through a
rhetorical scheme of repetitions – both of words and of sentence patterns: in
the original, Bernick's row of imperative 'think's is flanked by two purely
rhetorical questions, and Borkman's 'all's are thrown into prominence by
inversion – to suggest *both* the absorption of the speaker in his vision *and* his
consciousness of an audience. Seen – or, rather, heard – in that context
alone, Borkman's could well be said to be the superior dramatic speech.
Ibsen achieves striking effects by simple means. The nouns and verbs
Borkman uses, with a self-evidence which suggests that to him they are not
metaphors, come from the vocabulary of a kind of heroic imperialism: he
sees himself as a Tamburlaine of Industry. In the original, the zeugmatic
use of the verb 'skape' – the verb of the first sentence in Genesis – to refer
both to his own 'empire' and to the improved 'lot of many many thousands
of others' holds, as in a nutshell, his megalomania *and* his urge to justify that
megalomania. Bernick's speech is more strained. Unlike Borkman, he has
to rely on routine adjectives of aggrandisement – 'vast', 'rich' – and his
verbs seem the outcome of a reaching for synonyms, as awkwardly as in an
official memorandum: 'be made accessible', 'be worked', 'be started'. His
climactic offering nearly sinks under a compound – 'fabrikkvirksomhet'
(industrial activity) – which has the same faint ring of business jargon.
Where Borkman's speech seems to enact an obsession, Bernick's talks,
however enthusiastically, *about* a subject.

But in the end such a comparison is odious, and Borkman's speech is not
just Bernick's twenty years on. First of all, Borkman's speech is different
because in another sense it *is* twenty years on: the years of imprisonment,
enforced and voluntary, have drained away the details of whatever concrete
projects he may have had in mind when he was arrested for embezzlement
and have left him with a dream-like vision of power. His industrial landscape is inside his head – as, of course, we experience much more extensively and poignantly in the play's last scene. Bernick's landscape is geographical and specific: it seemed right when, in the recent RSC production

of the play, Bernick (Ian McKellen) brought out a survey map and illustrated 'the vast forest regions ... the river, with one waterfall above the
other' from it. His language, like that of a general planning a campaign (and
on the RSC stage the analogy offers itself with special readiness), has the
power of fact under the fervour of vision. Even a hundred years on, Ibsen
can make an audience sense the imaginative appeal of nineteenth-century
Industrial Enterprise; and perhaps Bernick should more aptly be compared
with Thornton, in Mrs Gaskell's novel *North and South*, as he holds forth on
'the magnificent power ... of the steam hammer' and 'the war which
compels, and shall compel, all material power to yield to science'.[8] Mrs
Gaskell had the omniscient narrator's freedom to tell us about how a
listener is affected by

> the exultation in the sense of power these Milton men had ... they seemed to
> defy the old limits of possibility, in a kind of fine intoxication, caused by the
> recollection of what had been achieved, and what yet should be.[9]

Ibsen had to do it all through the dialogue. I hope I am not yielding to the
urge to defend Ibsen at all costs when I suggest that the very tension
between Bernick's 'kind of fine intoxication', on the one hand, and his
somewhat self-conscious officialese, on the other, is deliberate and functional: individual excitement having to clothe itself in the language of a
Pillar of the Community and persuade an audience. In this light, the
'fabrikkvirksomhet' is not a verbal anticlimax but a good, reliable mouthful
of a word, invoking the kind of planning and organisation which only
Bernick (in this community) can carry through.

For, finally, the dramatic context of Bernick's speech is utterly different
from Borkman's. Unlike Borkman, who is baring his soul to Ella Rentheim
alone, Bernick is in a thoroughly public situation, with thirteen other
characters on stage (or listening at the door to the verandah). He is 'selling'
the railway branch-line idea, in which his interests – as we are to learn in act
III – are more financially far-reaching and more suspect than most of his
present audience can imagine. In retrospect, the tension I have pointed to
in the speech can also be seen as a tension between sincerity and hypocrisy.
This is a feature which dominates much of Bernick's language, much of the
tone of the play as a whole, and, perhaps most importantly, the ending of
the play. I shall return to this point. For the moment I only wish to
underline what I hope my atomistic comparison of the two speeches has
suggested: that it is fruitless to discuss differences between *Pillars* and
Borkman as a mere matter of evolution, of Ibsen getting better and better at
doing the same thing. *Pillars* would seem to have some of its strengths
exactly where it does what *Borkman* does not attempt to do – that is, where it
dramatises man as a social being, in a particular society. In *Borkman*, the
compelling power of the play lies in the sense we are given that the hero, and

the few other characters, move in a medium entirely made up of their own obsessive visions of reality. Of *Pillars*, Ibsen might well have used George Eliot's words: 'It is the habit of my imagination to strive after as full a vision of the medium in which character moves as of the character itself.'[10] Only, as he was writing a play and not a novel, that medium had to be largely made up of other characters and what they say and do. *Pillars* has the longest cast list of any of Ibsen's 'contemporary' plays; it also conveys the strongest sense of 'community', as defined in the O.E.D. under II.7, 'A body of people organized into a political, municipal, or social unity', and II.7 (b), 'A body of men living in the same locality'.[11] *An Enemy of the People* (1882) may present a more acute picture of local politics and 'the damned, compact, liberal majority', but its dramatic conflict is the Romantic one of the rebel hero against society, and the focus is on the hero. The focus is on Bernick, too, but he is both pillar and product of his society – of a community of people who have been young together and have matured, or gone rotten, together; who share an ethos as they share a taste for coffee and for volumes of 'sermons, printed on vellum and in luxury binding'.

It is this density of social texture in the play which first makes it natural, to an English reader at least, to relate it to Victorian novels (some of which Ibsen had in fact read).[12] The community is Norwegian, beyond any superficial local colouring. It is well known that many strands in the social fabric – right down to names of characters and of ships like the *Palm Tree* – can be traced back to the small south-Norwegian coastal towns which Ibsen knew in his childhood and youth.[13] The nostalgia of the reference to how, in the old days, 'in the summer there were sailing trips, and walking trips as well', is both personal to the author and functional to the play, as a measure of the present joylessness of the community.[14] The contemporary social problems with which the play deals are either international, like coffinships and suppressed women, or they seem – to an English reader or audience – to roll several stages of social history into one. Because Norway was lagging a couple of generations behind the more industrially developed western world, Aune can be given both Luddite and Chartist grievances, and Bernick can hope to become a millionaire via the building of a first railway. History here helped Ibsen to an opportunity (to which English novelists, like Dickens, often helped themselves, in the face of historical accuracy) of making a community at a particular time representative of a large and varied number of social tensions. Not that it is the topical problems, as such, which make the social tissue of the play remarkable and representative: they are merely strands in a fabric woven to represent the oppressiveness of small-town life. For example, the position of women runs as a theme throughout the play, variously illustrated by the fates of Lona Hessel, Dina Dorf and Martha Bernick, commented on implicitly by many condescending remarks of Bernick's and explicitly in his and Johan's dialogue in act II, and brought to an apparently triumphant conclusion with Bernick's leaning over backwards to proclaim women the real pillars of the community. And yet the real importance of this theme is not that it turns the play into a Women's Rights document but that it is an integral part of the exploration of life in an oppressive community – one that also contains such examples of wifely adulation as Mrs Rummel, and such meek mutes as Nette and Hilda to whom it would never occur to refuse, as Dina does, 'to be a thing which is taken'. This absorption of the more topical issue into the general 'feel' of the play is adumbrated already in the earliest extant notes towards the play which Ibsen wrote in 1870. These begin with a paragraph on how the basic motif of the piece is to be the position of women in a men's world of self-important business; but, by the time he has sketched some characters and outlined some action (much of which did not survive into the finished play), he is clearly beginning to see the play as a kind of web of small-town life, and the notes end:

> There is a significance underneath; something symbolical, the liberation from all narrow conventions; a new free and beautiful life. This what the piece turns on. This matter and these interests to be illuminated from all sides.[15]

So, as the conventions of his fictive community – and the attempts to defy them – were illuminated from all sides, Ibsen's contemporary Norwegian town, much like the pre-Reform Bill England of *The Mill on the Floss* and *Middlemarch*, grew to be an image of a parochial, self-satisfied and stultifying society. In his later prose plays, society tends to be perceived, intensely but narrowly, as a congregation of ghosts – 'all kinds of dead old opinions and all manner of dead old faith', as Mrs Alving puts it – representative mainly on a symbolical level. The society of *Pillars*, like that of George Eliot's novels, is representative just because it has been so fully and intelligently – and therefore often comically – perceived. To take just one example, Rørlund's suspicion of things that go on abroad, in 'the big countries',[16] – part of a whole chain of passages in which the townspeople define themselves as 'us here in our community' – rings as uncomfortably true in present-day Norway, or England (or, for all I know, anywhere), as it must have done in 1877; and one can only regret that Ibsen did not preserve into the final version of his play that clinching piece of spiritual smugness which he gave to Rørlund in the first draft:

> The peace which we do not have within us, we can hardly expect to find without. And least of all abroad.[17]

Rørlund, the High Priest (or, as Lona insists on calling him, 'the Reverend') of the play's deeply unreligious and unmetaphysical community, is the clearest indicator that here, as in the great Victorian novels, social issues are also moral ones. Barbara Hardy has finely expressed how the Victorian art of fiction is essentially a moral art. It questions the nature and purpose of moral action, and at its best shows the difficulty and complexity of giving, loving and growing out from self in an unjust, commercialized, and denaturing society.[18]

The characters in *Pillars* have, with a few exceptions, the double problem of seeing their own self and of 'growing out' from it. Much of the play's rather cruel comedy comes from Ibsen's pressing home their inability to see that they have a problem. Dina Dorf might, on a purely social level (if such a thing exists), be a budding New Woman; but her voice, when she can find a language at all, comes out of the play as a cry for the free and beautiful life, away from 'an unjust, commercialized, and denaturing society'. What she wants the Americans to be, she tells Johan in act II, is 'natural', as against 'moral' in the town's sense of 'respectable'. The arrival of the circus near the end of act I is very unrespectable and the good citizens draw their curtains against it , but to her it is a rare token of a world elsewhere, an alternative society – which is presumably why it is in the play at all.[19] Whether or not there are reminiscences of *Hard Times* hovering here, Rørlund's catechising her on 'what is a beautiful thing?' is strangely like Gradgrind trying to get Sissy Jupe to define a horse. That a beautiful thing should be 'far away' is as impossible for him to conceive as is the real nature of her feelings for him: the desire, presumably, to escape the Bernick household at any cost. His engagement to her is a kind of spiritual rape, seen as such through the comic irony of his 'moral' references to Johan having practised 'all the arts of seduction' on 'this young woman, whom you covet'.

What Rørlund highlights – right down to his final comment that Dina was 'completely unworthy' of him – is that the social fabric of the play's world is based on a complete lack of sympathy. Sympathy is something given to causes, like the 'moral casualties', and then preferably in a material form, like the white underwear the ladies are sewing away at, or the 400 crowns which Bernick orders to be sent to 'the fund for feeding the poor'. But, just as the citizens collectively cannot imagine anything good outside their own community, so each of them, on the whole, suffers from an inability to see anything from anyone else's point of view. One could almost chart the whole play as a series of confrontations with the refrain, outspoken or implicit, of 'you don't understand'. It also means that many of the play's comic moments stem from the audience's awareness of the unbridgeable gap between a question and an answer, between two visions which will never meet. Any voice which does not speak with the received standard language of the community is immediately silenced. It can be by absurd logic, as in the passage from the second draft of the play, discussing the book which Rørlund has been reading to the ladies, about a landslide which saves a small community from corruption by making it necessary to move its railway line to another valley:

Dina. But what happens to the people in that other valley?
Rørlund. Dear girl, we have to assume that the other valley was uninhabited.[20]

Or it can be by translation into clichéd metaphor, as when Martha heretically declares that 'down there in the schoolroom, I often wish I were far away, out on the wild sea', only to be told by Rørlund:

... of course you don't mean that literally; you mean the great stormy community of men, where so many are wrecked.

Or it can be by simple refusal to accept the premiss, as when Dina questions the blanket condemnation of 'the big countries':

Dina. But don't a lot of great things get done too?
Rørtlund. Great things ...? I don't understand ...

It may seem that I have been evading the central confrontations of the play: those between Bernick and Lona; and also the central moral and social issue of Bernick's lie, fifteen years back, on which he has built himself up into a pillar of the community. But I have been trying to describe 'the medium in which character moves'; and perhaps by now it is clear how much Bernick is part of that medium. As a cell in the social tissue, he repeats the pattern of the whole: unable to see himself as he is, unable to recognise in anyone else an 'equivalent centre of self',[21] but supremely able to hide both inabilities behind the justification that he is acting for the good of the community. Having seen this, and having recognised that Bernick is one of those of us who, in George Eliot's words, take 'the world as an udder to feed our supreme selves', we must now part company with Victorian fiction and remember that we are discussing a play. For the most remarkable aspect of Ibsen's art in *Pillars* is ultimately the way he uses his *dramatic* structure and language to control our responses to Bernick and the medium in which he moves. Seen from a bird's-eye viewpoint, the play has the clear thematic outline of a satire with a soft ending, emphasised by repeated symbols in language and action (the ships, the pillars, etc.) and articulated by Lona Hessel. This is the *Tendenzstück* which criticism finds so 'obvious'. But on stage (whether literally or in the mind) the play is a *process*: of communication between author and audience, in which we find ourselves in an ever-shifting relationship with the material he presents – now laughing, now pitying; now condemning from a comfortable distance, now feeling that 'there but for the grace of God ...'. Henry James wrote in his essay 'On the Occasion of *Hedda Gabler*' that, with *Hedda Gabler* and all the rest of Ibsen's plays,

we have stood in an exceptionally agitated way in the presence of the work of art, and have gained thereby a peculiarly acute consciousness of how we tend to consider it;

and the exceptional agitation he puts down to the fact that

under its influence we sweep the whole keyboard of emotion, from frantic enjoyment to ineffable disgust.[22]

I cannot think of a better way of describing how the Aldwych audiences in the summer of 1977 reacted to *Pillars*.

In his famous speech to the Kristiania students in September 1874, Ibsen declared his faith that 'to write is essentially to see',

> but, remember, to see in such a way that what has been seen is experienced by the recipient as the writer saw it.[23]

We tend perhaps too easily to stress the romantic–symbolic aspect of Ibsen's notion of the writer as a seer, forgetting the equally important second half of the sentence, about his control over our responses. The long period between the first conception and the final completion of *Pillars*, and the many notes and drafts extant (with possibly still more lost) to show how he struggled with what to say and how to say it, provide external evidence that special attention should be paid to the art of the play. The internal evidence of dramatic structure and language confirms that such attention is worth-while, and that Ibsen is very carefully making us 'see' and 'experience' the world of the play as he saw it.

It is more difficult than one might imagine to find a formula to describe the plot structure of *Pillars*. The age-old one of 'a crisis triggered off by a homecoming' works only if we allow that Lona's and Johan's homecoming is into a family and a community already set on the edge of crises of their own: the restlessness of Dina; the reluctant amorousness of Rørlund; the unwillingness of young Olaf to be brought up (like a sturdier Paul Dombey) as part of Bernick and Son; the railway business, which is at a particularly critical point; labour relations in the shipyard, where the workers are resentful of the move from manual to mechanised labour and aggrieved at the sackings which have taken place; the hostility of the Press, about to make anti-Bernick capital out of the prolonged presence in the town of the dissolute crew of the *Indian Girl*; and so on. This list – which could have been prolonged – in itself shows that we are not dealing with a straightforward, linear plot, but with a web of interrelated actions. Nor do these actions add up to a consorted drive towards exposure: although in the last and climactic scene Bernick reveals his life-lie to the shocked community, we have known who did it ever since Bernick talked with Johan in act II. Nor do we have the same snow-balling sense as in later Ibsen plays – *Rosmersholm*, for example, or *Ghosts*, or *Borkman* – of the past slowly gathering meaning and force until, in the end, it crushes the protagonist. The past in this play is something of a *donnée*, and Bernick is remarkably uncrushable. If, after all these negatives, we have to reduce the plot structure of *Pillars* to a formula, it seems to me that the closest we can get to our experience of it is to describe it as a progressive – and progressively disturbing – exploration of the gap between avowed and actual states of affairs, between sincere and hypocritical sentiments.

There is considerable structural parallelism between the first and the last act of the play. Both are 'public', in the sense that they bring almost the entire cast together on stage (and act IV also uses as many extras as a theatre management can afford). Both are built out of social ceremonies: the sewing and coffee party in act I, the celebratory procession in act IV, with music and banners and illuminations (but without the torches which glorified the occasion when Ibsen himself was similarly honoured by the Kristiania students in 1874). Act I serves as exposition and act IV as resolution; but both are at the same time lively images of the ethos of the community. We do not yet know in act I that Bernick is not the pillar he appears; but there are ample signs that things are not what they seem: in the inflated, pharisaical rhetoric of Rørlund and of Bernick himself when he appears; in the gossip of Mrs Rummel & Co; and above all in the many moments where speech and action clash in blatant satirical deflation. Rørlund expatiates on 'the good and pure home, where family life is seen in its most beautiful form ... where peace and harmony dwell', and Betty Bernick is distracted by the loud noises from the Pillars discussing business in the next room. Bernick, too, describes the family as 'the core of the community ... a small, close circle, where no disruptive elements cast their shadow ...', and the arrival of the foreign mail sends the Pillars scuttling off. These are the 'obvious' Ibsen moments, carried into the later plays where, if anyone refers to the prospect of 'youth knocking at the door', one can be sure that there will instantly be a real live specimen of youth knocking. But in this play their blatant irony is essentially part of Ibsen's technique for making us 'see' the community. Act IV is equally blatant, with Rørlund's elaborate speech and Rummel's statement that 'A citizen's home should be like a show case' beating against Bernick's and the audience's full knowledge of the state of affairs. The celebration put on for Bernick is in some interesting ways used like the masque at the end of many Jacobean plays, with the same clear irony of the reversal of an expected outcome as we find in Revenge masques, from *Antonio's Revenge* to *Women Beware Women*. The Presenter's speech by Rørlund, the giving of emblematic gifts to the Pillars, even the tonal mixture of solemnity and amateurism (as when Rørlund, surpassing even himself in oily rhetoric, makes great show of using 'the prosaic and blunt word ... a railway') set the scene apart, like a play-within-a-play, and so give to Bernick, as he starts to reply to the speech of homage, something of the electrifying power of the masquers 'taking out' the audience. As he not only reveals himself (partly, at least) for what he is but also brings his moral points to bear on his stage audience, the analogy is more with the purgative masque of a play like *Cynthia's Revels* than with the Revenge tradition. I do not for a moment believe that Ibsen was consciously or unconsciously

3 *Pillars of the Community*, Aldwych Theatre, 1977. A Royal Shakespeare Company production, directed by John Barton. Group scene from act IV

drawing on features of Elizabethan–Jacobean drama; the point is that his structural devices produce some of the effects, both theatrical and moral, which that drama often relied on for its dénouements. Like most play masques, and also like the sewing party in act I, the celebration aborts. Ian McKellen spoke Bernick's lines of dismissal –

> Good night! And please take all this show away. These things are out of place here now –

in a tone of quiet intimacy with the audience in the theatre, doubly striking after the conscious rhetoric of his appeals to his stage audience –

> Fifteen years ago I rose to the top on those rumours; whether I am now to fall by them, is something each one will have to decide for himself –

and the effect was strangely like the breaking-through of illusion in Prospero's 'Our revels now are ended.' There was no longer a transparent fourth wall between us and the actor; and the play was no longer something calling for a detached and satirical response. For a moment it reached right into our own 'here and now'.

If acts I and IV are 'public', II and III are in a sense 'private', in that they are constructed as series of smaller group confrontations, often just of two characters. In act II the dialogues of, respectively, Bernick and Johan, and Bernick and Lona are focuses where past and present motivations are illuminated. We are made steadily more aware of Bernick's duplicity and the hollowness of the community's respectability, and we are likely to respond to Bernick much as Lona does: 'What right have you to stand where you're standing?' His unremitting refusal to tell the truth is presented with a grimly comic effect: when the act reaches its climax, with Rørlund's 'revelation' that Johan was Dina's mother's undoer and ran away with Old Mrs Bernick's money, and when we think Bernick has his back to the wall at Johan's appeal to him to tell Dina the truth, then he wriggles out of the situation with the absurd adroitness of a Richard III and Richard Nixon rolled into one –

> Not another word! This is a moment for silence –

and slips off to the Chamber of Commerce.[24] In act III Bernick is on stage throughout (except for the last couple of minutes, when he is in his own room but still audible), visited, in singles or groups, by most of the rest of the cast. This is a darker and more complex act. Bernick's position becomes more desperate and his resolution to hide the truth at any cost hardens correspondingly. When 'any cost' includes the life of Johan, with all the crew of the wretched *Indian Girl* thrown in, his attitude cannot be accommodated within even the grimmest comedy. But we are not allowed, either, to respond simply with James's 'ineffable disgust', for Ibsen lets us listen to Bernick's soul-searching, albeit (typically) conducted in very roundabout

4 *Pillars of the Community*, Aldwych Theatre, 1977. Ian McKellen as Karsten Bernick and Judi Dench as Lona Hessel

terms and with Rørlund as an unwitting catalyst. And in the three-cornered dialogue with Johan and Lona he presents such a persuasive argument why only he himself is capable of providing 'a possible future of greatness and blessedness' for the community, and why therefore Johan's 'life's happiness' must be sacrificed for 'the prosperity of your birthplace', that we well understand how Lona comes to accept the argument. Action, at this stage of the play, lies entirely in speech; and, though, from the outside of the situation, we recognise that Bernick is substituting a perverse kind of utilitarianism[25] for ethics, he dominates the dramatic action and so compels a kind of allegiance from us.

So far I have spoken of the two middle acts as if they were 'private'; but they are really not any more so than the first and the last act. For, in the quick-slow-quick rhythm by which scenes follow upon one another, business is forever encroaching upon domestic affairs, public matters upon private ones. As the personal crisis mounts at the end of act II, Bernick is called away because 'the railway is hanging in the balance'; and Johan and Bernick's heart-to-heart talk is interrupted by Krap sticking a pile of more or less illicit purchase contracts under Bernick's nose. It seems to be a principle of construction in the play constantly to let one sphere of action erupt into another – making us, of course, see that there is little point in speaking about 'private' versus 'public' spheres, rather than moral and immoral ones. In the theatre, this principle produces a kind of montage effect which makes nonsense of the complaint that 'Ibsen's observance of the unity of place – a feature he took over from French drama – ... leads to some awkward situations', especially in the opening scene.[26] It is not just that Mrs Bernick, paraphrasing Lady Eden, might well say that the railway runs through her garden room, but that the whole play would be less expressive if the different acts had different locations – the shipyard, the Chamber of Commerce, etc. As it is, the setting which Ibsen describes with customary care in his stage directions, and which he then uses to the full in the action, becomes a perfect image of the world as it looks from the Bernick point-of-view. The garden room is its hub, and outside it, as it were in concentric circles,[27] are the areas of increasing otherness: the verandah, the street, the sea, and 'the big countries'. In itself, the garden room is a microcosm of the community, thanks to the four doors which serve to let in – and out – its representative members. The Pillars argue loudly about the railway, just off-stage in Bernick's study, while the women sew and their conversation, dominated by Mrs Rummel, emphasises the gulf between the men's sphere and the women's: Mr Rummel, says his wife proudly, 'is so used to speaking at public meetings, you know'. The Pillars invade the stage and insist on the women staying on the verandah, as the railway question is 'too complicated for the ladies'. When he needs an admiring audience, Bernick invites them in – the groupings and movements thus helping us to see here what Lona is to point out to Bernick in the closing moments of the play: 'You don't see the women.'

It seems to me part of the deliberate structural art of the play that it opens *both* with the Aune–Krap dialogue *and* with Rørlund reading to the ladies from *Woman as the Servant of the Community*.[28] The superimposition, in the theatre, of the one image on the other – remembering, too, that the Pillars are meeting next-door – makes a wealth of social comment. Aune and Krap, in a nicely stylised dialogue, engage in a stichomythic interchange. Why, asks Krap, does Aune agitate the workers?

> *Aune.* I do it to strengthen the community.
> *Krap.* That's odd! Mr Bernick says it undermines the community.
> *Aune.* My community is not Mr Bernick's community, Mr Krap. As chairman of the Working Men's Association I must ...
> *Krap.* You are first of all foreman of Mr Bernick's shipyard. You have first of all your obligation to the community called Bernick & Co. For it is on *that* we all depend for our livelihoods.

The background presence of Rørlund and the ladies – the silk of their dresses no doubt brought by the ships Aune helps to build; their sense of community soon to be summed up in Rørlund's thanking God 'that things are as they are with us' – crystallises into a visual image the paradox which the dialogue turns on: the divisiveness and yet interdependence within the community. Ibsen has found simple theatrical means of making a comment which a novel would leave to the omniscient narrator (like Dickens on Tom-All-Alone's, in *Bleak House*). What, finally, he also makes us see and experience through (literally) the traffic of the stage, as it converges upon the garden room, is the multiplicity of simultaneous pressures upon human beings. If, as I have suggested, we find it more difficult to condemn Bernick in act III, this is partly because we see him beset by pressures from every direction. We see not only what is wrong, but why it is wrong.

Like the structure of the play, its language demands of us more flexible responses than it has usually been given credit for. A post-Watergate audience is, as was apparent at the Aldwych, peculiarly alert to the subtlety with which Bernick's moral evasiveness is realised: to his preference for the word 'untruth' ('usannhet') over 'lies'; his tendency to substitute *interpretations* of facts for facts themselves;[29] to turn confessions into self-dramatisations. Bernick is, of course, by far the subtlest speaker in the community: the other Pillars, including Rørlund, demonstrate their inanity, moral shortsightedness, or even perversion, as blatantly as 'Holy-Michael' Vigeland when he trusts to Providence as long as the freight-rates in England are high enough to make it worthwhile. They – and particularly Rørlund – revel in 'poetic' metaphors, which are obviously empty clichés. Their rhetoric cries out to be seen as false.

But this is by no means the only mode of speech in the play. It is one of the

play's chief satirical devices; but the verbal texture as a whole is full of
surprises and contrasts. There are a number of plain-speaking voices,
notably those of the 'Americans', Lona and Johan. Lona, on her truth-
mission, is deliberately provoking in her own vocabulary and in the way she
deflates the rhetoric of the 'moral' people. On the other hand, she has an
emotional rhetoric of her own when she wants to make a point – to ask for
'fresh air', or to tell Bernick that his whole life is built on 'quicksands'.
Dina's language (as in the scene with Rørlund which forms such a contrast
to the sewing party) is simple and direct. At times – such as the revelatory
group scenes which conclude acts II and III – she is almost inarticulate, and
we sense that for her there is really no meaningful language in this community. For others there are two languages: Mrs Rummel, for example,
who can sum up the fate of Dina Dorf's mother with a literalness which
suggests callousness –

> She didn't last long, either. She was a fine lady, you know, and not used to
> working. So it went to her chest, and then she died –

and then immediately turn to Pillar-type imagery to describe how this 'ugly
business' affected the Bernicks:

> It's the dark spot in the sunlight of their happiness, as Rummel put it once.

Martha is the only character in the play with a lyrical language to express
deep emotion. The scene where she tells Lona of her long and fruitless love
for Johan stands out from the rest of the play, in its sad loveliness. The
nostalgia is rendered in a kind of prose poetry, through images like the
endless spinning, but also through utterly literal statements:

> I've loved him and waited for him. Every summer I waited for him to come.
> And then he came ... and he didn't even see me.

Martha, at other times, shows us that rhetoric, too, can be sincere. Out of
context, her appeal to Johan's conscience –

> Have you forgotten that a woman died in distress and shame for your sake?
> Have you forgotten that for your sake a young child's life was poisoned? –

might sound like the usual moral jargon of the community. In its context it
is a cry wrung from the heart.

The case of Martha is a reminder that, with Ibsen as with Shakespeare,
whether he writes prose or verse, we cannot make the assumption that
rhetoric is necessarily false, 'insincere'. So much of it *is*, in *Pillars*, that we
tend to be particularly on our guard against elaborate expressions of feeling,
patterned speeches, emotive metaphors. So much of what characters say
has a palpable design on their interlocutors that we tend to look for ulterior
motives under each statement. All this applies, of course, in a special way to
Bernick himself. A few times he gives his egotism away without realising it:

it tends to be particularly in relation to the women, as when he tells Lona
that his and Betty's marriage is a success because 'over the years she has
learnt to bend her own nature to fit in with mine'; or when he 'explains'
Martha to Johan:

> ... of course she has enough to take an interest in; she has me and Betty and
> Olaf and me [*sic*]. People shouldn't think of themselves in the first place, least
> of all women. We all have a community, large or small, to support and work
> for. That's what *I* am doing, at any rate.

So much for Number One. But for a good deal of the time he is much more
aware of the effect of his words on the person he is speaking to; and our
response to him has to be correspondingly more complex. Indeed, the
dramatic power of Bernick's character seems to be founded in the versatility
of his rhetoric: we have to stand before it, in James's phrase, 'in an
exceptionally agitated way' and with 'a peculiarly acute consciousness of
how we tend to consider it'. His scenes with Lona, and his scene with her
and Johan in act III, are full of twists in logic, tone and style. They move, in
leaps, from the rankest hypocrisy to disturbing sincerity:

> *Bernick.* ... With my spotless reputation so far, I can take this matter on my
>   shoulders, carry it into the open, and say to my fellow-citizens: 'Look, this I
>   have raised for the good of the community.'
> *Lona.* Of the community?
> *Bernick.* Yes, and not *one* will doubt my intentions ... [...] And isn't it the
>   community itself that forces us to take crooked paths?

But always – as in the sentence which follows almost immediately, 'So my
conscience acquits me in this respect' – the intention is self-justification,
and the aim (achieved, too, in this scene) is to manipulate the other
person(s) in the right direction. The one time his defences are down is in the
scene with Lona in act IV. The procession to honour him is approaching; the
Indian Girl is sailing towards certain disaster; Johan and Dina are on board
the *Palm Tree*. All he can say – 'dully', in Ibsen's stage direction – is 'Too late
... and to no purpose ...'. As Lona tears up the two incriminating letters,
his sense of a wasted life finds direct expression:

> *Bernick.* ... It's too late now; my whole life's been thrown away now; I can't
>   go on living after today.
> *Lona.* What's happened?
> *Bernick.* Don't ask me ... But I *must* go on living all the same. I *want* to live ...
>   for Olaf's sake. He'll make everything right and atone for everything ...

There are at least three leaps of thought in this last short speech: the first,
before 'But I *must* go on living ...', revealing his sheer urge to survive; the
second, before 'for Olaf's sake', showing that he is, as always, justifying his
own will through a motive outside himself; the third, before 'He'll make
everything right' proving the insincerity (unrecognised by himself) of the

second by its marvellous illogic. It is really, then, Olaf who should live for *his* sake. The future which is implied for Olaf here – 'to atone for everything' – is like the 'mission' which Mrs Borkman plans for Erhart; and it makes the next twist in the plot all the more effective: a few moments later it looks as though Olaf is sailing towards death on the *Indian Girl*. In the fifth and last extant draft of the play, this speech is very different:

> *Bernick.* Don't ask me! Not live! Yes, I want to . . . live, live . . . work . . . it will be recompense enough.[30]

The late modification of the speech is a fine stroke, both in terms of plot and of psychological insight. Without the gesture towards Olaf, the draft speech is merely a token of Bernick's grit and resilience; with it, the final version speaks of man's capacity for self-deception.

I find it difficult not to believe that Ibsen was shifting the character and the play in the same direction when, between the fifth draft and the final version, he extensively modified the section of the last act which deals with Bernick's speech of 'confession' and his 'reform'. It is true that in the printed text Bernick is more honest about his business transactions. In the draft he evades telling his fellow-citizens that turning the properties over to a public company was an afterthought; in the printed text he is outspoken. But, however sincere he may think himself, the habit of making capital out of his honesty persists and he soon turns it to his own advantage:

> *Bernick.* I have no right to approval; for what I have decided now, was not what I had in mind from the beginning. My intention was to keep everything for myself, and I still believe that these properties can best be put to use if they remain in the hands of *one* man. But you may choose. If you so wish, I am prepared to manage them, on your behalf, to the best of my ability.
> *Voices.* Yes! Yes! Yes!

From this he moves, in both versions, on to an examination of his own conscience and his community's; but only in the final text is this clearly turned into a community ritual where the Age (i.e. what is outside Bernick) receives much more attention than his own inner guilt. Ironically, he begins,

> But first my fellow citizens must know me as I am,[31]

only to continue:

> Then let each one scrutinise himself; and then let it be clear that from this evening we begin a new era;

and then to lavish on the 'museum' to be made of the old era all the elaborate imagery of hollowness, white-washing, etc., which we know so well from Rørlund's speeches in the first act.

He approaches the moment of confession very self-consciously – 'And now I come to the main item I have to settle with my community' – and with such a stagey account of Johan and Dina's escape (including a pause for audience reaction and an aside to Betty) that it is difficult not to feel he protests too much in the sentence with which he takes off:

> You shall know everything. *I* was the guilty one, fifteen years ago.

He moves away from the moment of truth by – in the final text only – a beautifully balanced elaboration of his statement – one, too, which sends the ball, as it were, into his fellow-citizen's court:

> ... Fifteen years ago I rose to the top on those rumours; whether I am now to fall by them is something each one will have to decide for himself.

The nature of that decision is surely foreshadowed –

> When peace has returned to your minds, it will appear whether I have lost or gained by speaking out –

for there is a shade of moral blackmail here: if I have 'lost', he implies, then you are as good as saying that you prefer hypocrisy to truth. From this we move, again in the final version only, to the extraordinary anticlimax of his confession:

> I still have more ... much more ... to repent of, but that is a matter for my own conscience alone. Good night!

This is hardly to let them know him 'as I am'; nor to let them 'know everything'.

It seems undeniable that Ibsen, as he was finalising the text, made Bernick more self-conscious, not to say calculating, in his handling of his stage audience. I do not think that he was turning Bernick into a charlatan and the ending of the play into complete irony. But I do think that he was warning us about taking the conversion *and* the 'new era' at face value, and that he was making us ask questions about Bernick's sincerity. Certainly no actor of the part can escape those questions. In the RSC production, Ian McKellen began this scene by making Bernick speak from the depth of his consciousness of guilt; then, via the ladder of rhetoric which Ibsen has provided, and with an ever-growing enjoyment of his own powers of rhetoric, his Bernick moved towards the surface, feeling what he said rather than saying what he felt. Thus he left the theatre audience in what the more impatient critics called a 'muddle' and the more thoughtful ones saw as challenging. I think Ibsen would have liked this, for the muddle, if we 'think it to the bottom', turns out to be something of an 'abyss'.

English nineteenth-century writers liked to explore the 'streamy' nature of human consciousness, perhaps most concisely imaged in a fragment of a poem by Matthew Arnold:

> Below the surface-stream, shallow and light,
> Of what we *say* we feel – below the stream,
> As light, of what we *think* we feel – there flows
> With noiseless current strong, obscure and deep,
> The central stream of what we feel indeed.[32]

These lines could well be a paradigm for an Ibsen play like *Rosmersholm*, where the whole action of the play consists in Rebekka and Rosmer working, gradually, from the surface of what they *say* they feel, *via* what they *think* they feel, to the 'strong, obscure and deep' area of what they feel indeed – where they cannot live, only (in a terrifyingly apt image) leap into the mill-stream. But in *Pillars* the paradigm hovers as a tantalising possibility only. It hovers, because it may be that we are in touch with what Bernick feels indeed; it tantalises, because – as we have just seen – it may be that he just *thinks* he feels it, or even just *says* that he feels it. If that is so, what about 'the spirit of truth and the spirit of freedom'? Where is the true self? Perhaps the real horror of life lived – as all human life must be – in the society of men is that there is no such thing as truth? 'I do but ask; my call is not to answer', Ibsen wrote in his verse letter to Brandes while he was working on *Pillars*. There are, it seems to me, enough questions left at the end of *Pillars* for the eleven remaining plays.

There is also another intimation of the abyss: in the unspeakable horror of what Bernick intended to happen to the *Indian Girl* and all who sailed in her. He leaves it out of his public confession, but, as we saw, Ibsen adds a reminder of it in his final version of the play ('I have still more ... much more ... to repent of ...'). He adds yet another reminder, at a stage where in the draft there is only calm of mind, when close to the end he makes Bernick exclaim:

> Where have I been? You will be horrified when you know.

The 'when'[33] leaves the matter disturbingly open: is there a catastrophe yet to come, tomorrow, when Bernick tells them of the depths of evil to which he has been brought? Or is the 'when' a kind of rain-cheque, never to be cashed? The questions are essential to the after-effects of the play; and – as so often in Ibsen – those effects are an essential part of our experience of the play. That he added these lines seems to me to indicate Ibsen's awareness of all that had apparently been evaded in the resolution, and his insistence that we, the audience, should be aware. We *could* rest with the optimism of Lona and Betty at the end, and with their sense of a new beginning – echoed in Aune's jaunty turn to the new machinery[34] and Martha's vision of a clearing sky. But none of them know what we know, or have tried to look into Bernick's mind as we have. If we respond not only to the single voices but to the play as a whole, we are left, I think, with Henry James's insight:

Whether or no we may say that ... we know Dr Ibsen better, we may at least
say that we know more about ourselves.[35]

And that is no mean achievement for a hundred-year-old social drama.

NOTES

1. This is my literal translation of the original, 'La oss ikke tenke denne avgrunn til
bunns' (*Henrik Ibsen: Samlede Verker*, ed. Didrik Arup Seip, Oslo, 1960; II,
319),rendered more idiomatically, but with the loss of Ibsen's image of
thought-movement, by James Walter McFarlane in his translation of the play;
'Let us not seek to the bottom of this abyss' (*The Oxford Ibsen*, 8 vols, London:
Oxford University Press, 1960–77; IV, 459). In this paper translated quotations
from Ibsen are, unless otherwise indicated, my own. Quotations from *John
Gabriel Borkman* are from the 'English Version' of the play, by Inga-Stina
Ewbank and Peter Hall (London: Athlone, 1975), hereafter referred to as
Borkman. Quotations in Norwegian from Ibsen's plays are from the three-
volume edition referred to above and hereafter referred to as *Ibsen*, while his
drafts, speeches and letters are quoted from the centenary edition, *Henrik Ibsen:
Samlede Verker*, 21 vols, ed. Francis Bull, Halvdan Koht, Didrik Arup Seip (Oslo:
Gyldendal, 1928 – 57), hereafter referred to as *S. V.*
2. 'I do but ask; my call is not to answer': cf. p. 94, below.
3. See Roman Woerner, *Henrik Ibsen* (Munich: Beck, 1910), II, 57–61. My attention
was drawn to Woerner's view by James Walter McFarlane, whose essay on
'Meaning and Evidence in Ibsen's Drama' in *Contemporary Approaches to Ibsen*, I,
ed. Daniel Haakonsen (Oslo: Universitets Forlaget, 1966), pp. 35–50, contains
the most persuasive argument for an ironic ending to *Pillars of the Community*.
4. The impact on Ibsen of Georg Brandes's lectures on 'Main Currents in
Nineteenth-Century Literature', the first volume of which was published in
1872, is well known.
5. I have done so myself, in 'Ibsen and "The Far More Difficult Art of Prose"', in
Contemporary Approaches to Ibsen, II, ed. Daniel Haakonsen (Oslo: Universitets
Forlaget, 1971), pp. 60–83.
6. *S. V.*, XV, 393; cf. Ewbank, 'Ibsen and "The Far More Difficult Art of Prose"',
pp. 61–2.
7. I have returned to a somewhat more literal translation than that in the printed
version, in order to show the rhetorical pattern of the original.
8. Elizabeth Cleghorn Gaskell, *North and South*, Everyman ed (London: Dent,
1961), p. 75.
9. Gaskell, *North and South*, p. 157.
10. J. W. Cross, *George Eliot's Life, as Related in her Letters and Journals* (3 vols, London,
1885–6), II, 361.
11. This is why I have preferred *Community* to the traditional *Society* in the translation of Ibsen's play-title. The Norwegian word, *samfunn*, covers a range of
meanings, from society at large to an organisation like 'arbeidersamfunnet' (the
Working Men's Association). Rørlund refers to 'disse store samfunn' (the big
countries), and Krap calls the firm of Bernick & Co a 'samfunn'. The necessity
of translating it by several English words, according to context, obscures the

obsessive frequency with which 'samfunn' occurs in the text. The other noun in the title, *'støtter'*, raises a problem too, in that it really means 'supporting pillars', and that the verb 'støtte' (support) is used in the text with ironic reference to the title. Thus at the end of act II Lona tells Bernick: 'Du skal opp og støtte samfunnet ...' (You are supposed to go and support the community.)

12. Cf. Michael Meyer, *Ibsen: A Biography* (Harmondsworth: Penguin 1974), pp. 46, 246.

13. See for example Halvdan Koht's Introduction to *Pillars* in *S.V.*, VIII, 9–28.

14. The line, which is not in the final version of the play, occurs in the first draft *(S.V.*, VIII, 169) and was incorporated into the RSC acting text.

15. See *S.V.*, VIII, 156.

16. Cf. note 11, above.

17. See *S.V.*, VIII, 170.

18. Barbara Hardy, *The Moral Art of Dickens* (London: Athlone, 1970), p. 4.

19. A number of colleagues, after seeing the Aldwych production, have asked why so much is made of the circus when it arrives, and why nothing is made of it later in the play. Not, apparently, a 'well-made' device.

20. See *S.V.*, VIII 195. This passage in the draft was incorporated into the RSC acting text.

21. George Eliot, *Middlemarch* (Harmondsworth: Penguin, 1970), p. 243.

22. Henry James, 'On the Occasion of *Hedda Gabler*', *New Review* (June 1891); reprinted in Michael Egan ed., *Ibsen: The Critical Heritage* (London: Routledge, 1972), p. 235.

23. See *S.V.*, XV, 393.

24. 'This is a moment for silence': the Norwegian phrase cannot be literally translated. It uses the passive form of the verb *tie* (to be silent, not to speak), which gives the impression that Bernick is thrusting the responsibility away from himself. At the Aldwych Theatre, it proved, audiences laughed at this line in an uncomfortable fashion which dispersed the tension of the scene, and it was replaced by the less literal 'This is not the time to speak'.

25. Ibsen intensely disliked Mill's *Utilitarianism*, which he read in Georg Brandes's translation and, in a letter to the translator dated 30 April 1873, berated as 'philistine sophistry'. See Meyer, *Ibsen*, p. 385.

26. Herman J. Weigand, *The Modern Ibsen: A Reconsideration* (New York: Dutton, 1960), pp. 23–4.

27. The semi-circular set on the curtainless stage of the Aldwych Theatre aided this impression of a Bernick-centred universe.

28. The better translation of this title would be *Woman as the Servant of Society*, but I wish to stress at this point the juxtaposition of various *samfunn*. Cf. note 11, above. – Ibsen's first draft of act I opened with Rørlund and the ladies only, leaving Aune till act II.

29. Aldwych audiences were unfailingly amused by Bernick's line to Lona and Johan in act III: 'Now we come to the fact which can be interpreted in different ways ...'.

30. See *S.V.*, VIII, 232.

31. '... know me as I am': the original, '... kjenne meg til bunns' cannot be translated literally; but the image – 'to the bottom' is the same as used by

Macrina in the speech from *Emperor and Galilean* quoted on p. 75, above.

32. See *The Poems of Matthew Arnold,* ed. Kenneth Allott (London: Longman, 1965), p. 543. These lines were published in *Cornhill Magazine,* xx (November 1869), 608, as part of Arnold's essay on 'St Paul and Protestantism'. I first encountered them in Lionel Trilling's brilliant study of *Sincerity and Authenticity* (London: Oxford University Press, 1972), p. 5.

33. It is more disturbing than the 'if' incorrectly given in some translations. Archer has 'when'; McFarlane implies an 'if' in his freer version: 'It would horrify you to know'; and Ellis-Fermor, who has 'when', incorrectly plays down the horror by translating 'I vil forferdes' as 'You will be shocked'.

34. This phrase appears only in the final version, as does Bernick's repetition (three times) of 'thorough' and (twice) 'honest'.

35. James, 'On the Occasion of *Hedda Gabler'*, p. 235.

Little tragedies: Russia's other drama

DONALD RAYFIELD

There can be few countries where the history of the theatre and the history of drama follow such different lines as in Russia. From the middle of the eighteenth century, a few decades after its introduction, to this day, a very European theatrical tradition has flowered in Russia: the lunacies of Tsar Paul or the menaces of Stalin have barely checked the theatre's growth. But it is a theatre in which spectacle, histrionics and, more recently, theories of acting, production and direction have often been far more prominent and original than repertoire. It is easy to give an account of the rise of Russia's great theatres, actors and directors, from Volkov to Vakhtangov; it is hard to put together a coherent history of the dramatic repertoire, for Russia's drama has no real continuous history.

We can enjoy Ibsen without necessarily feeling our ignorance of the Norwegian repertoire to be a major drawback. But to accept the genius of Gogol and Chekhov somehow forces us to acknowledge that Gogol is separate from Chekhov, and that Chekhov is separated from the present day. However close the examination or far-reaching the analogies, we cannot establish anything like the continuity that runs from Molière to Anouilh, or from the Jacobeans to Edward Bond. The threads are short: Gogol's *Government Inspector (Revizor)* is clearly in the same tradition of distorted classical comedy as Kapnist (1790s) or Griboyedov (1820s); Chekhov's plays appear to re-use the formula proposed by Turgenev's *Month in the Country (Mesyats v derevne)* half a century before. But the major Russian dramas, the very few that have a European stature and renown, seem to be islands without any sign of an archipelago.

There are many reasons that can be proposed. The most obvious is that of the milieu: of all the literary arts, drama is the most sensitive to control or repression. Poetry can be written for posterity or oneself; novels can be written 'for the drawer' or for publication abroad, but there is little that impels a man to write a play without hope of performance. The Russian theatre, fostered as it was by the state, was even more hesitant to allow improvisation, scandal or public criticism than western European theatres; and it was much easier to bring pressure – whether by making the play unfashionable, arresting the producer or switching off the electricity – on a play than on a novel or a poem, between whose producer and consumer there are so few intermediaries. Those very intermediaries – the actors, the theatrical 'committees', the censors, producers and the consumers too – have had very much closer links with the state establishment than the literary magazines, editors and publishers who played such a part in the nineteenth-century Russian novel or in Russian poetry.

Just as striking a factor is the strangely unprofessional nature of the Russian dramatist. With one major exception, Ostrovsky, none of the major Russian playwrights owed his full allegiance to drama. The most original of the eighteenth-century playwrights, Fonvizin, was at his best and most creative as a satirist–journalist, a civil servant and a moralist. In any overall view of Pushkin, we must see his plays as a phase through which he passes in a movement from lyrical poetry to prose, fictional and at the last factual, in a continuous search for greater detachment and objectivity. Gogol's conception and exploitation of the theatre, despite his innate genius as a mimic, make one think of his plays as those of a story-teller at prayer. Turgenev writes plays after discarding narrative poetry and before settling for the novel. Chekhov makes incursions into the theatre without ever abandoning the devices and complexities of the story-writer. Tolstoy turns to the theatre only once he is convinced of the immorality of imaginative prose. Even Griboyedov, whose *Woe from Wit (Gore ot uma)* is arguably the finest verse comedy of the classical tradition, and who never produced any work of art remotely comparable with this one completed masterpiece, must be classed as as amateur in his handling of drama as a genre, for the classical mould of the play is grotesquely cracked by the Romantic striving for which he could not – or would not – find new channels.

The Russian dramatist is, then, rarely in his true element. Often he flounders; only occasionally does he cavort. This 'amateurism' accounts for the sporadic triumphs and the frequent failures of Russian drama. Pushkin's *Boris Godunov,* where classical and Romantic modes clash, where exposition, lyricism, comedy, tragedy and rhetoric are formlessly compounded, is more typical than such rare sucesses as Turgenev's *Month in the Country* or Chekhov's *Seagull,* where the constraints of the genre are broken only to reform magically into a new dramatic structure.

Yet there exists in Russia another, less haphazard dramatic tradition – an incursion from lyrical poetry into drama – whose masterpieces are just as original, and not so chimerical, as Griboyedov's, Gogol's or Chekhov's. Pushkin's 'little tragedies', symbolist drama and Blok's *Rose and Cross (Roza i krest)* in particular, are virtually unknown outside Russia and rarely performed anywhere in the world. But in the span of a century, they link into a coherent tradition of lyrical drama, extraordinary in its exploitation of deliberately limited resources. A cursory reading and a little advocacy can give the European theatre an entire new facet.

The writing of lyrical drama, as Pushkin's work shows, is a spontaneous, organic and at first unconscious process. Russian poetry inherited from its French and its classical sources a view of the poet as a demiurge, in whom the ordinary human being and the inspired priest of Apollo, the member of society and the recluse, are often at odds. Pushkin's persona often divides into two conflicting aspects, one the naive, impulsive and eternally young prodigal, the other the wise, cold blooded, eternally old cynic. In much of his work the two aspects are irreconcilable. Lensky is killed by Onegin (*Yevgeni Onegin*), Mozart by Salieri (in the little tragedy of that name). But the dialogue begins in the lyrics that mark his maturity: the return from exile in 1824. More and more freqently, a lyric takes the form of a dramatic dialogue, and the lyrical wholeness of elergy divides into contrasting moods which characterise contrasting characters. Thus, *The Conversation of the Bookseller and the Poet* (*Razgovor knigoprodavtsa s poètom*, II, 191)[1] begins as the poet's monologue, built out of typically Pushkinian parallelisms, contrasts of rhythm, ordered imagery of earth and sky, symmetry of vowel sounds, crescendi of assonance, which is periodically interrupted by the bluff and inharmonious bookseller's questions and reproaches. But the two lines eventually collide: two or three words – 'glory', 'freedom' – echo, and, as in all really dramatic writing, the gap between the characters is bridged. The poet's disillusionment and the bookseller's cynicism are common ground: the poet's last words slide into prose: 'We'll come to terms. Here's my manuscript.' From the fission of lyrical poetry, true dramatic development has been born.

In *Boris Godunov*, there is just as strong a contrast between the language of the characters; but neither Boris, who stems from Racinian tragedy and the classical hero's paralysis, nor the false Dimitri, who embodies the patricidal vigour of *Sturm und Drang*, come from within the poet. They are not a fission of a lyrical persona, but characters born from two different dramatic traditions, whose incompatibility drains the whole play of life and form. In establishing lyrical drama – the drama of the miniature – Pushkin had to abandon the heterogeneous cast of traditional comedy and tragedy and to propagate characters by a vegetative process, so that their common origin in a divided self is never lost.

There have been few writers as cautious and circumspect as Pushkin in their approach to genre. Pushkin's prototype dramas are disguised as extended lyrics, just as that prototype of the Russian novel, *Yevgeni Onegin*, is presented to us as – in all but sub-title – a Byronic poem, just as his most original works are claimed to be translations. There are several dramatic scenes which precede the overt return to drama marked by the little tragedies of 1828–30. One of the most striking is the alleged *Scene from Faust* (*Stsena iz Fausta*; II, 283). On the one hand it is a pastiche so convincing that even a sophisticate might be sent back to Goethe to seek for the original

German On the other hand, it expresses the same symbiotic antipathy between Mephistopheles and Faust that we find between the bookseller and the poet and which we shall find between Mozart and Salieri. Their impatience with each other, their ability to grasp at once (even if perversely) what the other only hints at, give the impression of two characters linked in a bondage as unbreakable as the ties between two halves of a schizophrenic. The compelling dramatic power of Pushkin's lyrical drama stems precisely from this sense of thraldom, of cognation, of *ego*, and *alter ego*. The dramatic dialogue is shortened to great intensity, since there is little need for exposition or extraneous subject-matter in a conversation between such complementary characters as bookseller and poet, Faust and Mephistopheles, Mozart and Salieri. We divine instantly their common interests and their conflict.

The little tragedies, though not written to a common formula, are very closely linked. The 'canon' of four – *The Covetous Knight* (*Skupoy rytsar'*), *Mozart and Salieri*, *The Stone Guest* (*Kamenny gost'*), *A Feast During the Plague* (*Pir vo vremya chumy*) – were already conceived in 1826, during the painful months Pushkin spent on his father's estate, in the despairing aftermath of the Decembrist revolt. They were all completed in the miraculous autumn of 1830, while cholera quarantined Pushkin on the estate at Boldino. To this canon we must add *Water-nymph* (*Rusalka*), conceived likewise in 1826, but, like so much of Pushkin's best work of the 1830s, unfinished, and a play usually known as *Scenes from the Times of Chivalry* (*Stseny iz rytsarkikh vremyon*), written in 1835 and uncompleted, though complete in itself.

The four 'little tragedies' at first strike one as studies, rather than fully realised works of art. They are all based – or appear to be – on an existing work or, in the case of *Mozart and Salieri*, a well-known anecdote. Thus *The Covetous Knight* is claimed by Pushkin to be a translation from Chenstone (as Shenstone was known in Russia), *Mozart and Salieri* in one manuscript fair copy is described as being 'from the German', *The Stone Guest* uses the alternative title of Molière's *Don Juan* and the characters from the Da Ponte–Mozart opera, while *A Feast During the Plague* is in fact what Pushkin claims it to be, a translation and adaptation of a scene from John Wilson's *City of the Plague*. The literary dependence is thus only partly mystification. We have seen how Pushkin implies that his *Scene from Faust* is a translation, a disclaimer which is part modesty and partly a pledge of allegiance; but it is equally true of Pushkin's maturity that every new genre is approached through a self-imposed apprenticeship. The deliberately restrained invention of the 'little tragedies' not only counterpoises the anarchic spawning of the scenes of *Boris Godunov*, but channels Pushkin's energies into developing techniques that can eventually reduce a historical panorama into a play. The *Scenes from the Times of Chivalry* are proof that the restraint and the new techniques were working towards a new type of historical play. In his prose work, too, Pushkin worked along a similar path, writing pastiches of picaresque, sentimental and romantic narration before producing a masterpiece of historical writing, *The Captain's Daughter*, in which all three genres are synthesised in a new and personal mode.

But it would be foolish to discard either Pushkin's prose or the 'little tragedies' as mere exercises of style. Just because they are the antithesis to *Boris Godunov* in their length and range, or because *Scenes from the Times of Chivalry* amounts to a synthesis of *Boris Godunov* and the little tragedies, does not diminish their extraordinary qualities. For underneath the familiarity of their subject matter lies a lyrical theme quite unique in European drama: the internal conflict between inspiration and intellect, the fundamentally amoral nature of artistic genius. These are aspects of a theme already raised in Pushkin's lyrics, not only in *The Conversation of the Bookseller and the Poet*, but in lyrics such as *Poèt* where the 'most contemptible of the children of this world' is transformed by the arbitrary touch of the divine word into a 'wild savage ... full of sounds and confusion' (III, 2). Now the two personas can lock in combat on the stage and resolve the dualism of the creative mind.

The Covetous Knight is on the surface a study of avarice, as single-minded in its preoccupation as Molière's *L'avare*. But its second scene, where the baron fingers his treasure in a candle-lit cellar, is a monologue so full of intense emotion, that we begin to identify with a magic rite. The miser's coins are rich with associations:

> Of how much human care
> deceit, tears, prayers and curses
> it is the weighty representative.

rich with unrealised possibilities:

> like a demon
> I can control the world from here; if I should wish, halls
> will be erected,
> a playful troupe of nymphs will run
> into my magnificent gardens. (v, 342)

By the end of the monologue, which occupies almost half the play's length, we are so saturated with erotic and predatory imagery, that we sense that these coins are not sterile detritus of vice, but the fertile symbols of all the sensual and mental impressions that the poet's mind has accumulated and refuses to relinquish. The imagery of the baron's speech takes up that of the poet's monologue in the *Conversation*. The poet, too, in his first inspiration is accompanied by a demonic spirit which gives him the illusion of power over nature; Pushkin's poet hoards his experience with the jealousy of a lover 'over the gifts of his young mistress' (II, 342), just as the covetous knight gloats secretly over his treasures 'like a young rake waiting for a rendezvous with some sly debauched girl' (v, 342). The poet prefers a sheet of white paper to a poem that squanders his inspiration to the mob; the baron prefers to conceal his cellar from 'unworthy eyes' rather than 'squander what I have obtained by blood'.

In the *Conversation* the poet is opposed by the bookseller, that 'charlatan double who sells us' as André Gide defined the worldly side of the artist. In *The Covetous Knight* the opposition is more than verbal; the baron's son is determined to get an allowance from his father and in the tempestuous quarrel of the third and final scene drives the miser into a fatal rage. In a mere seven or eight minutes' dialogue, the monologue's forebodings are swiftly turned into tragic action: the lyric is realised as drama, lyrical tension as movement. The son however is more than the avenging normality of the real world, which we expect in classical comedy and tragedy. He is the same force of dissemination, prodigality, debasement which the bookseller represents. Father and son differ in their estimation of money, just as poet and bookseller differ in their estimation of the manuscript. As the Jew who tempts the son to murder in the first scene of the play puts it,

> the youth sees in a money swift servants
> and recklessly sends them here and there.
> But the old man sees them as trusty friends
> and guards them like the apple of his eye.   (v, 338)

We may regard *The Covetous Knight*, as do Russian critics, as a study of a monomaniac; we may take it as an exercise in dramatic compression, as a terse portrait of patricidal times (patricide being an ill-concealed *Leitmotiv* of Pushkin's life and Russian history) in which the present is thinly disguised by the Middle Ages. But, to link the play firmly with Pushkin's oeuvre and the lyrical drama that is to come, we must see it ultimately as a study of the poet's inner purgatory.

Mozart and Salieri, which follows the then new tradition in holding Salieri to be guilty of poisoning Mozart out of jealousy, takes the pattern of *The Covetous Knight*, only to reverse it. Here it is only Mozart, the victim, who squanders his inspiration, improvising without a thought for his music's permanence, laughing when a blind violinist murders his *voi che sapete*. Mozart differs from the covetous knight not only in his carefree prodigality, but in his self-assurance. Not even the ominous spectral figure that commissions his requiem mass can disturb his conviction in his own genius and in the moral order that genius and goodness are inseparable. Mozart is the artist if not without fear, at least without reproach – the Romantic whom Pushkin so much envied, even when he appears to disdain his naivety, and whom we also find in Lensky (*Yevgeni Onegin*), and in the Italian improviser of the unfinished prose and verse work, *Egyptian Nights (Yegipetskiye nochi)*. Just as Yevgeni Onegin is drawn to Lensky only to kill him, and the Maecenas Charsky is drawn to the Italian improviser only to recoil in disgust, so Salieri feels for Mozart an affection so great that he cries for the first time in his life and feels at the same time such an envy and indignation that genius should light on an idler, rather than on his hard-working self, that he poisons the first man he has come to love.

Salieri's monologues open and close the first scene and close the second and last scene: they are the core of the play, just as the baron's monologue is the core of *The Covetous Knight*: the nucleus from which murder springs. Like the baron, Salieri broods over a world in which nothing is real except what he has laboured to accumulate and what he now stands to lose to Mozart: recognition as a genius. In this world there are no realities outside his mind: the play opens:

> All say: there is no truth on earth.
> But truth does not exist on high ...   (v, 357)

and concludes with the same cynicism, tempered only by a question mark:

> And Buonarotti? or is it a tale
> of the stupid senseless mob – and
> the Vatican's creator was no murderer?   (v, 368)

At this point we stumble on the strangest characteristic of lyrical drama: its moral relativity. There is no force for good, not even for common sense or received wisdom, without which we are unaccustomed to measuring the tragic process. Mozart's naive faith, we might argue, is just as much hubris or hamartia as Salieri's ruthless disloyalty. Tragedy does not lie in the fatality that separates Mozart or Salieri from the herd, but in the peculiar structure of the artist's mind in which the two must coexist until one silences the other and, at the same time, the mind they share.

The other two little tragedies seem less capable of expressing anything purely Pushkinian. *The Stone Guest* ties Pushkin firmly to the dénouement by which Don Juan, at his moment of apparent triumph in his last conquest, the faithful widow of his victim, dares to invite the victim's statue to dinner and nobly takes the hellish consequence. *A Feast During the Plague*, being mostly translation, limits Pushkin even more narrowly. Yet we are right to draw analogies, for within the framework Pushkin has imposed on himself, the common thematic material is only more rigidly expressed. In these two plays, the conflict is not so much between two elements of the creative intellect as between the amoral compulsions of the artist and the outside world that threatens him with extermination. Don Juan and the chairman of the feast both exude vital energy and creative imagination in opposition to a deadly and unchanging outside. They are conventional tragic figures in their inner drive to take on the world with maximum defiance, by compounding their crimes and indecencies. They are unconventional, in that the sole energy and poetry of the plays repose in them so that our final reaction is the sympathy which all great lyrical poetry must engender, not the pitying and terrified withdrawal which the last stages of tragic nemesis force upon us.

Don Juan and the chairman are singers. In act II of *The Stone Guest*, Laura, Juan's mistress turned friend, sings to the guitar a song (which Pushkin has left for the producer to improvise) and shocks her guests by telling them the words are by Don Juan. In *The Feast*, the chairman's song, which replaces, rather than translates the song in Wilson's original, is the pivot of the whole play. Don Juan's poetic nature is made more explicit in the monologue that opens scene ii, when disguised as a monk he is to embark on his most unlikely seduction. He wonders what he is going to say to her:

> ... Bah! what comes into my head,
> I'll say, without preparation,
> like the improviser of a love song ...　　　　　(v, 390)

the *improvizator* (improviser) being in Pushkin's *Egyptian Nights* the personification of spontaneous poetry. Even Leporello, in the *commedia dell' arte* tradition as disillusioned a servant as can be, impatiently tells Juan:

> ... Your imagination
> will finish the picture in a minute:
> I think it's quicker than a painter's ...　　　　　(v, 378)

Neither Molière nor Da Ponte portray a Don Juan with such instinctively subtle timing and psychological insight as Pushkin's. His approach to Donna Anna, the fatal thrill he communicates when he reveals himself as her husband's killer all reinforce the image of Juan as an inspired demon. The drive to satisfy his desire, at the cost of his life if need be, links him not only with the other monomaniac heroes of the 'little tragedies' as an incarnation of a deadly sin (avarice, envy, lechery) but with the Pushkinian conception of the poet.

In considering *A Feast During the Plague*, we must concentrate on the songs, as on the monologues of *The Covetous Knight* and *Mozart and Salieri*. They are the lyrical source of the action. They are also the sole original part of the play, if we discount the act of selection and cutting. Wilson's *City of the Plague* is an extensive drama, relying to a degree on Defoe's *Journal of the Plague Year* and strongly coloured by a Protestant ethos in its contrast between the frivolity of the aristocrat and the earnestness of the bourgeois in times of crisis. From Pushkin's extract almost all the Protestant positive thought has evaporated. The priest enters at the end to cast a pall on the proceedings, but goes before he can be established as anything but an importunate omen from a grim outside. Pushkin's feast occupies the entire play and rises from a regrettable episode to a noble counter-attack in a world of suffering and grief.

The first of Wilson's songs, a Scottish ballad, is brilliantly transformed by Pushkin into a morbid Romance. The second begins as Wilson intended, only to veer off from a desperate glorification of perversity in the face of disease into a Romantic poem which expresses one of the most fundamental Pushkinian paradoxes:

> There is ecstasy in battle,
> and on the abyss's dark edge
> and in the enraged ocean
> amid dreadful waves and stormy darkness
> and in the Arabian hurricane
> and in the breathing of the Plague.
>
> In everything that threatens perdition
> are hidden inexplicable pleasures
> for the hearts of mortals –
> perhaps a pledge of immortality,
> and happy is he who in the turbulence
> is able to win and know them. (v, 419)

This is the same pleasure that the covetous knight feels in the blood and tears associated with his money or Don Juan in his dangerous seductions: the same demonic urge which Pushkin sensed in all poetic inspiration.

The song at the hub of the lyrical play is perhaps the most important element that Pushkin took from Wilson. It replaces the exposition, the extended informative dialogue, the chorus and all the more time-consuming devices of conventional drama as a means of 'knotting' the action, the *zavyazka* to which we oppose the *razvyazka*, or dénouement. In the two unfinished miniature plays that follow the 'little tragedies', the song plays the same explicit part as in *A Feast During the Plague. The Water-nymph (Rusalka)*, though unfinished, leaves us in no doubt about the fatal outcome. A prince deserts his mistress, the miller's daughter, in order to marry. She drowns herself, is transformed into a *rusalka* and through the daughter she had conceived by the prince, lures him back to the river. It is at the prince's wedding feast that the note of impending doom is sounded. The first song is a real folk song, recorded by Pushkin; the second, sung by a mysterious voice in the choir, introduces the discordant images of the river and the drowned girl. In other respects, *The Water-nymph* belongs more to Pushkin's exercise in folk modes, rather than in lyrical drama, but the song plays the same constructional role as in *Scenes from the Times of Chivalry*.

The *Scenes*, it can be argued, stand out with Blok's *Rose and Cross* as the major achievement of historical drama in Russia. The play takes the vital step of freeing itself from recorded history, from the shackles that make *Boris Godunov* so halting. The times can be pinpointed only by the imminent invention of gunpowder, the place only by the Frankish names. No real historical characters overshadow the imagination. And yet, or therefore, a very convincing portrayal of the Middle Ages emerges. Pushkin's plan (written in French), of which the first half of the first part was realised, shows the lyrical scope of the play:

> A rich draper. His son (poet) in love with noble demoiselle. He runs away to be a groom in her father (an old knight)'s castle. The demoiselle scorns him. Her brother brings someone who wants her hand. Young man humiliated. He is thrown out by her brother at the demoiselle's request.
>
> He goes back to the draper. Old bourgeois' anger and sermon. Brother Berthold comes. Draper lectures him too. Berthold seized and imprisoned.
>
> Berthold busies himself in prison with alchemy – discovers gunpowder. Peasants revolt, stirred up by young poet. Castle besieged. Berthold blows it up. The knight (mediocrity personified) killed by a bullet.
>
> Play ends with reflections and by the arrival of Faust on devil's tail (discovery of printing, a different artillery).   (v, 618)

As the *Scenes* stand, they end with the poet (Franz) captured by the knights, his death sentence commuted to life imprisonment as a reward for his brave songs which now give such pleasure to the demoiselle. The songs are significant not only for what they express, but for their very existence: they give the poet–rebel a function even to those that hate him. Pushkin, kept at the court of Nicholas I after the failure of his friends, the Decembrists, must have put much of his own predicament into the ironic fate of Franz. The songs may be an expression of the poet's innermost feelings; they are merely an entertainment to those that commission and hear them. The dichotomy of poet and bookseller has become that of prisoner and warder.

The *Scenes* are written not in the blank verse of the 'little tragedies' which evolved from the sometimes pallid iambics of *Boris Godunov* into a highly flexible medium, but in the most laconic prose. The songs thus irrupt like flashes of light in the greyness: like Don Juan or the chairman of the feast, Franz sings as an act of fearlessness, in the shadow of the gallows. The first of his songs is a revised version of a lyric, *Legenda*, written six years earlier, a lyric later to inspire much of Dostoyevsky's *Idiot:*

> A poor knight once lived in the world,
> taciturn and simple
> . . . .
> He had one vision,
> that no mind could grasp,
> and the impression
> cut deep in his heart . . .   (v, 481)

It celebrates the same single-minded possession by first inspiration as the words of the poet in the *Conversation*. But here it plays an ironic double role. Franz, in the beginning of the play, is as obsessed with chivalry and tournaments as Albert, the baron's son in *The Covetous Knight*. His ill-treatment at the hands of the demoiselle and her brother lead him to join the forces of revolution, and yet to the last Franz is helplessly in love with the demoiselle, the châtelaine whose prisoner he is now physically as well as spiritually. While the 'poor knight' of his song has sacrificed himself for the *lumen coelum, sancta rosa,* he has thrown his life and talent away for a haughty and cruel woman of the world. The song sets out his ideal and at the same time the horrible disparity between that ideal and the cause for which he has lived.

Pushkin's life is a story so rich in events and passions, that one hesitates to draw biographical analogies, lest the distinction between life and art be blurred. Nevertheless, one of the necessary characteristics of lyrical drama is its biographical origin. The more Pushkin strove for extended and objective forms, the more striking the accidental parallels between the recurrent themes of his personality and those of his *dramatis personae.* The relations of Franz and the castle unwittingly echo those of Pushkin and the court, just as Mozart and Salieri, Don Juan or Walsingham (the chairman of the feast) embody much of the private poet. Later lyrical drama in Russia differs only in that it is *explicitly* autobiographical.

Of all Pushkin's dramas, only *Mozart and Salieri* was ever performed in his lifetime, and that on two occasions only. Not only the ever-watchful censorship of Nicholas and the Third Department, but the innate conservatism of Russian theatres, which welcomed only patriotic pageantry or slick vaudeville from contemporary playwrights, must be blamed. When the Russian theatre became almost free, from 1856 to about 1863, its repertoire wavered between two poles: the historical play that was to develop into the classics of Russian opera by the last decades of the century, and the 'realist' play which dealt with problems of class and morality with only a more melodramatic touch than the novel. From the 1850s to the 1890s, poetry was felt to be a subordinate form of literature, whose task was more and more civic, moral and even scientific. When lyrical poetry was itself reduced to the isolated work of unfashionable recluses, lyrical drama hibernated.

The signal for an awakening came from the very genre that had weakened drama throughout Europe in the middle of the nineteenth century: opera. The signal came, however not from Russian opera, which explored an idealised Russian history and a heavily harmonised Russian folk music, but from Wagner. Wagner's operas, though performed in Russia, had few imitators among Russian composers, but his texts and his sources had an influence just as strong on Russian as on French poets.

Excepting the *Ring* cycle and *Die Meistersinger,* Wagner stands out (oddly enough) as a Celtic composer: the themes of *Parsifal* and of *Tristan und Isolde* and of *Der fliegende Holländer* are Celtic, not Germanic. In the poetry of Mallarmé and of Maeterlinck, in the stories and in *Axël* by Villiers de l'Isle-Adam, we see the Celt in his Wagnerian twilight, the last of the poetic and magical races of Europe, besieged by the prosaic and practical Germanic and Roman civilisations, driven into the sea and mists of antiquity.

This vision of Mallarmé's *Elbehnon* coincided with the Russian symbolists' and decadents' view of the poet, hounded by forces of expediency, by the 'iron age' of Pushkin's bookseller. In the juvenilia of Aleksandr Blok, at the turn of the century, Celtic mists envelop a personification of the poet who has in him the same dramatic possibilities as Pushkin's.

Russian symbolism, however, was only partly prompted by the *poètes maudits* of France. Like symbolists everywhere, they were poet–schoolmasters, well-read in the classics. Just as Mallarmé's *Hérodiade* updates Racine's Phèdre into an androgyne, self-sufficient poet, so schoolteachers such as Annensky and Sologub turn their expertise in Greek drama to good account. Annensky, the director of Russia's greatest school and an acknowledged Euripidean scholar, produced in his *Thamyris the Zither Player (Famir-kifared)* not only a surrogate for the lost play by Euripides, but a powerful myth of the singer who challenges the muses and is blinded by them for his pains: the myth, like symbolist myth, emphasises the absolute perfection which symbolist poetry strives for and the price paid for failure.

But neither Annensky's pseudo-classical plays, nor Sologub's *The Wise Bees' Gift (Dar mudrykh pchyol)* came within a mile of being staged. The lyrical poetry of the symbolists was, by 1904, more widely accepted in Russia than in any other European country, but, for all its experimental movements, the Russian theatre kept its doors shut. Perhaps the reason was that the parody had reached Russia before the original. Chekhov's *Seagull* has a play within a play, which is perhaps meant as a real essay in the new theatre, rather than a parody; but the effect on the other characters of Treplev's invocation of the spirit of the world, like the effect on most audiences, is comic. The extratemporal yearning, the Satanic symbolism, the sense of cosmic spirit which Chekhov had detected in Maeterlinck, were seen through the prism of a failed playwright. It is arguable that Chekhov, in his last play, *The Cherry Orchard*, wrote a work whose ultimate meaning is expressed in symbols and whose characters no longer function along the lines of conventional dramatic psychology – so the symbolists themselves argued – but audiences and directors had difficulty enough accepting Chekhov as a 'realist', without trying to cope with any symbolic plane.

Yet the nature of symbolist poetry in Russia drove it again and again towards dramatic form. When the symbolist movement began to splinter in 1906, the isolated poets took refuge in classical Russian poetry, as though to learn from Pushkin, Baratynsky and Tyutchev how to cope with the shattering of a pléiade and a culture. (Was not the catastrophe of December 1825 very like the bloody events of 1905, in that it shook the very assumptions on which poets went on writing?) That Pushkinian stoicism, which can be stylised as 'a feast during the plague', colours the work of those symbolists who surmounted the crisis, and in particular the poetry and lyrical drama of Aleksandr Blok.

In approaching Blok we must admit that we are not dealing with a poet of the same order as Pushkin. Blok's lack of a self-critical faculty, and his somewhat mediocre, alternately fey and dour intellect make him a poet of great unevenness. His work, though certainly symbolist in more than allegiance, forms a biographical chain, in which there is only one high plateau and one peak: some of the lyrics of 1906 to 1914, with the drama *Rose and Cross* of 1913, and the long poem *The Twelve (Dvenadsat')* of 1918. Everything he wrote functioned as a diary; only at these points does his work also function as universal art.

Blok was attracted to the theatre by his circle of aquaintances, by the theatricality that coexisted with his native reticence and by the increasing complexity of his lyrical persona. Unlike Pushkin, he had a theatre prepared to meet him: the Kommissarzhevskaya theatre, by 1906 under Meyerkhold. Meyerkhold had broken away from Stanislavsky, with the revolutionary conviction that a 'conditional' *(uslovny)* theatre, which abandoned all attempts to produce a facsimile of real life, was the only means of producing drama attuned to modern symbolism. It was Meyerkhold who argued to Chekhov that methods other than Stanislavsky's were needed to stage the subtleties and overtones of *The Cherry Orchard*. It was Meyerkhold who agreed to stage Blok's *The Puppet-theatre Man (Balaganchik)* with Maeterlinck's *Miracle of St Anthony*.

Like all his lyrical dramas, *The Puppet-theatre Man* stemmed from a lyrical poem; a boy and girl watch a puppet-theatre in which one of the puppets suddenly jumps over the footlights to scream for help.

> I'm bleeding cranberry juice
> I'm bandaged with rags!
> There's a cardboard helmet on my head
> and a wooden sword in my hand.[2]

Typical of Blok's grotesque second book, this jump from play to reality is transferred to the drama. Here Pierrot and Harlequin compete for Colombina in the familiar Petrushka puppet-play of Russian provincial market performances, which Stravinsky and Diaghilev were later to exploit. But the play has new dimensions. The author periodically bursts onto the stage to try and stop an apparently unscripted development; the mystics of St Petersburg who conjure up Colombina are just caricatured as the author; the cranberry blood and cardboard of the poem turn the pathos into a cruel grimace. Blok seemed to be caricaturing his relationship with his wife and his friend and foe Andrei Bely, with his fellow-symbolists and to all his earlier work. Yet, for him the play had worked: he wrote to Meyerkhold (22 December 1906):

> *The Puppet-theatre Man* had to be put on by you; for me there is a purifying element in it, a way out of lyrical solitude.[3]

The public may have been driven to 'whistles and roars of hatred inter-rupted by resounding yells'; his father-in-law, the chemist Mendeleyev may, as gossip had it, have died of the shock of what the play revealed of his family's private life; but Blok held on to lyrical drama as a purgative and an escape from lyrical poetry.

The other plays of 1906 were less eagerly awaited by Meyerkhold. In any case, *The King on the Square (Korol' na ploshchadi)* was too overtly a political allegory and *The Stranger (Neznakomka)* too similar to the Virgin Mary to pass the censorship. *The Stranger* had to wait until 1913 for a performance. It suffers from the same weaknesses as *The Puppet-theatre Man*: satire of savage indignation but without wit, save perhaps for an extraordinary surreal conversation on cheese and the Gogolian touch by which two drinkers in a bar are Verlaine and Hauptmann, just as Gogol's *Nevsky Prospekt* introduces two German shopkeepers called Schiller and Hoffman. Now, however, the poetic persona has split not into two but into three. Instead of the melan-choly Pierrot and sanguine Harlequin, Blok sees the poet as a being only momentarily whole, who divides into a trinity of Stargazer, Man in Blue (the Pierrot) and Middle-Aged Gentleman – spirit, heart and flesh. The *neznakomka* is the 'eternal feminine' which gives them all their reason to be: but, in Blok's degraded world, she can respond fully only at the lowest and simplest level to the flesh, leaving Stargazer and Poet mourning for their lost astral rhythm and ideal. The formula for *Rose and Cross* is born.

Between the grotesque mixture of caricature, guignol and lyricism of *The Stranger* and *Rose and Cross*, there is a distance so enormous that the seven years that separate them are not enough to account for the anomalous wholeness of Blok's last play. Only *Song of Fate (Pesnya Sud'by)*, a more psychological autobiographical work of 1908, rejected by Stanislavsky and never performed, stands between the two plays. *Rose and Cross* invents a whole new technique of collage, that Blok was to use once more in *The Twelve*. The mixture of quotation, translation, reminiscence, pastiche and invention in fact reminds us of Pushkin's *Feast* or *Scenes*.

Despite its title, the *Rose and Cross* have nothing to do with Rosicru-cianism, and the literal symbolism is the least important aspect of the play. What is most important is the distance that Blok has put between his subject-matter and his biography, so that a whole imaginary world can be composed. It began, not as a play, but as a ballet scenario for music by Glazunov, in which Blok could embody memories of Brittany where he had spent the summer of 1911 and could give rein to his fascination with medieval history. All that was Blokian in the scenario was to be the contrast of the troubadour from the Celtic north with the castle and châtelaine of Languedoc.

But the scenario became too explicitly poetic; within weeks Blok was writing an opera. By January 1913 it was a play. But the operatic structure –

in fact, Wagnerian structure around a group of *Leitmotive* – remained. Incidental music, at one point to have been composed by Rachmaninov, was in fact written, but the revolutions of 1917 interrupted rehearsals and the play was performed for the first and almost the last time in the northern town of Kostroma in 1920.

There can be few plays in any repertoire which can be interpreted on so many levels: as a historical play of Celtic versus Latin, of the tensions of the thirteenth century; as a political allegory, in which Russia is the châtelaine, the castle the state, and the knight Bertran the helpless intelligentsia forced to side with the castle against the peasantry; as yet another self-dramatisation like *The Puppet-theatre Man* or *The Stranger;* as the penultimate drama in the death of the 'eternal feminine'; as a Masonic play on Necessity and the oneness of Joy and Suffering. Blok felt compelled to offer an exegesis for Stanislavsky's theatre (MKhAT):

> *Rose and Cross* is not an historical drama . . . landowner's morals of any age and any people do not differ . . . It is first of all the drama of the *human being* Bertran; he is not the hero, but the reason and heart of the drama; the poor reason sought to reconcile the Rose of untried Joy with the Cross of accustomed Suffering . . .[4]

But the best approach to the play is through the song whose phrases torment the heroine until, finally, Gaetan the Breton poet sings it at the May festival:

The hurricane roars
the ocean sings,
snow whirls,

Momentary time flashes past,
we dream of the blessed shore!

In the dark clefts of night
the spinning wheel buzzes and sings.
An invisible spinner looks
into your eyes and spins fates.

The sunset looks into the eyes
of the knight like a streak of fire,
and starry nights burn
over fateful destiny.

A world of unlimited delight
is given to the singing heart,
the roaring ocean calls
to a fateful and aimless journey.

Give yourself to an impossible dream,
what has been doomed will come,
an unalterable law to the heart
is that Joy–Suffering are one!

Your future path is wandering,
the roaring ocean calls.
Joy, o Joy–Suffering –
pain of wounds still unknown!

Everywhere – trouble and losses,
what awaits you ahead?
Set up your shaggy sail,
mark your strong armour
with the sign of the cross on the breast!

The hurricane roars,
the ocean sings,
snow whirls.

Momentary time flashes past,
We dream of the blessed shore![5]

Gaetan's song is one of the strangest knots of Russian poetry. If we unravel it, we find threads that lead back to Pushkin's *Feast* – the hurricane and the ocean of the chairman's song; threads that lead back to the political–philosophical poem, *Two Voices (Dva Golosa)* of Tyutchev; and further back to Goethe's stoically Masonic *Symbolum,* where the necessity of suffering is propounded as the nobility which distinguishes humanity from the starry world of the gods. Threads lead back to Blok's poem *Neznakomka* (which precedes the play of the name), in which an 'enchanted shore' is glimpsed through the veil of the fateful stranger, and forwards to the imagery of wind, snow and the cross of *The Twelve.* The song resumes the themes of the play, makes sense of the scattered phrases and prepares us for the crucifixion of Bertran, the human persona of the poet, as he dies guarding the châtelaine's bedroom

Yet, like the chairman's song in Pushkin's play, it is not entirely original. From Barzaz-Breiz, *Chants populaires de la Bretagne* and similar sources, Blok had culled druidical wisdom on the dominance of Necessity and Pain, and Breton refrains, 'Snow fell, wind blew', which are attuned to the mood and landscape of his lyrics. The list of sources that Blok provided in his *Notes* – Provencal, French, Breton, Cornish – forces us to look at *Rose and Cross* as a collage, as many-layered as *The Twelve* in its references. The alien material somehow brings to life the satire and the stylised plot that lie so heavily on Blok's earlier plays.

The poetic persona is, as usual, a trinity: Gaetian, pure poetry, Celtic mists, insanity, grey-haired age; Bertran, neither wholly a poet nor wholly a human being; Aliskan, the page-boy, entirely animal. All of them are exploited by Izora, the châtelaine, who responds to the song of Gaetan, the carnality of Aliskan and – the essential tragedy of the play – can find nothing to love in the self-abnegating and adoring Bertran. Like all Blok's incarnations of the eternal feminine, whether the Beautiful Lady of the troubadours or Russia, she is too far fallen to answer any but the lowest calls. Only in dreams and in song does her spiritual nature still flicker and this drives her to send Bertran north to search for the singer of the song that torments her. With the prophetic note which is Blok's most disturbing poetic quality, the play ends in war erupting around the castle, a war in which Bertran is fatally wounded, fighting the peasantry with whom he sympathises, while Izora, taking refuge in fornication, ignores the tragedy that awaits her.

In the last three years of his life, Blok's genius was paralysed. There exist a number of sketches for historical dramas, some of which explore the synthesis of the lyric and dramatic still further, but none of which came near realisation. The lyrical drama, however, even in years of war, revolution and civil war, did not wholly die. But it needed a poet with the same self-dramatising urge as Blok to create drama comparable with *Rose and Cross*.

That poet was Mayakovsky. To him belongs the re-invention of the narrative poem in Russia, an exhibitionist, pyrotechnic expression of despair, mockery, ambition and sheer energy and invention, which owes not a little to Apollinaire's *Chanson du mal-aimé*. The fundamental conceit of Mayakovsky is as old as his technique is new: the unrequited love of the troubadour for the châtelaine. A poem such as *Flute and spine (Fleyta-pozvonochnik)* is a drama reduced to a monologue, as an orchestra might be turned into a one-man band. The poet is the attacker who supplies his silent audience with their own lines of protest, his beloved with her evasions, whose subject is himself, as demonstrative and button-holing as Walt Whitman (whose influence in Russia in the 1910s was enormous). A man who could declaim to an audience of Russian bourgeois in 1915, 'Darling Germans' ... is a man who creates drama out of the moment.

The transition from narrative poem to drama, such as *Vladimir Mayakovsky* by Vladimir Mayakovsky, is gradual. It is towards the end of his life, however, when Mayakovsky begins to feel the same unrequited love for the party and the state that he once felt for women alone, that Mayakovsky extends into fully-fledged drama. Just as Pushkin branches out from a conversation between a bookseller and a poet, Mayakovsky takes a *Conversation with a tax inspector (Razgovor s fininspektorom)* as a means of establishing the misunderstood role of the poet in a suspicious society. A play such as *The Bed-bug (Klop)*, particularly in its second half where the hooligan-poet suddenly attracts our commiseration, stranded as he is in the antiseptic utopia of the future, contrasts lyrical yelps of despair from the poet caged in the zoo with the prosaic sense of the woman he once spurned and the brand new world that wonders at him. It is a contrast essentially identical with that of Pushkin's little tragedies and Blok's dramas.

Lyrical drama was hardly attuned to the demands of socialist realism of the 1930s. Only Bulgakov, who, thanks to Stalin's whim, enjoyed a precarious immunity, could experiment with the form in his plays on Molière and Pushkin, in which the naive poet and diabolical society are opposed. The only director able, or reckless enough, to stage such plays was Meyerkhold and by 1940 he had been judicially murdered. But as long as poetry is written in Russia, lyrical drama will not be extinct.

NOTES

1. All references to Pushkin's works are to volume and page of the ten-volume edition *Polnoe sobranie sochinenii*, ed. B. V. Tomashevsky (Moscow, 1962–6).
2. Aleksandr Blok, *Sobranie sochinenii*, 8 vols. (Moscow–Leningrad, 1960–3), II, 67–8.
3. Blok, *Sobranie sochinenii*, VIII, 170.
4. Blok, *Sobranie sochinenii*, IV, 530.
5. *Ibid.*, pp. 507–8.

Synge's communities and dissenters

W. A. ARMSTRONG

. . . if it's a poor thing to be lonesome, it's worse maybe go mixing with the fools of earth

Much criticism of John Millington Synge has a retrospective colouring. Some important critics persistently look back to the Romantics of the early nineteenth century for explanations of his work. This tendency is very apparent in Ronald Peacock's essay on Synge in *The Poet in the Theatre*, where he is described as 'a very romantic writer', 'of the latest progeny of Rousseau and Herder', 'with a nostalgia for the primitive', and 'a lyrical response to nature'; 'a romantic', adds Peacock, 'the more exquisite for being tardy'.[1] A similar retrospective method prompts the Keatsian thesis of Alan Price's book, *Synge and Anglo-Irish Drama* (1961) – that Synge's drama springs from a contrasting of dream and reality. A Wordsworthian comparison is encouraged by Una Ellis-Fermor's contention that Synge exemplifies 'an extreme form of nature mysticism'.[2]

That Synge was a mystic in the full sense of the word, I very much doubt. That he was a neo-Romantic who pursued dream at the expense of reality, I cannot accept. Nor can I accept the final verdict of Peacock's essay, which describes Synge as 'a fortuitous visitor in our sky, shedding a brilliant and decorative lustre but no fertilising warmth'.[3] What I would stress, on the contrary, is that Synge was not an Irish Georgian, a latter-day Romantic, but a poet who had assimilated Darwin's as well as Wordsworth's conception of nature, a thinker who had important ideas in common with Bernard Shaw, a dramatist who had anticipated the symbolic situation of isolation and danger characteristic of the work of Ernest Hemingway, Samuel Beckett, and Harold Pinter.

Isolation was a recurrent situation in Synge's life as well as his plays. In his letters to Molly Allgood, his fiancée, he used to sign himself 'Your old tramp'. Like the tramps and tinkers in his plays, Synge chose to isolate himself from all social and political communities except the peasant ones of the Aran Islands and the west of Ireland, and even in those he was something of an outsider – for, but not of, them. He came from Evangelical

Protestant stock, but a rift with his family and their religion began in his teens and became permanent. In an autobiographical fragment, Synge records that he read a book by Darwin when he was fourteen, and that the theory of evolution raised such strong doubts in his mind that by the time he was seventeen he had renounced Christianity. Darwin sharpened his awareness of the fact that the struggle for existence is continuous and life is lived dangerously. When Synge entered Trinity College, Dublin, at the age of seventeen in 1888, he found no friendship or community to compensate for his alienation from his family and its Protestant faith. He ignored student activities; his main enthusiasms were music, the Irish language, and Irish antiquities. After he graduated, he entered into another kind of alienation when he left Ireland and lived in Germany and France. While in Paris he met Maud Gonne and became interested in the highly nationalistic principles of the Irish League, but he resigned from this organisation because he believed that the regeneration of Ireland would come by evolution not revolution, and that regeneration involved aesthetic as well as political values. Even when Synge was participating in the work of the Irish National Theatre, he was isolated to a degree. His outlook and plays were quite different from those of Yeats, Lady Gregory, and the other dramatists of the movement. When *The Shadow of the Glen* was accepted for production at the Abbey Theatre, two of the best players, Dudley Digges and Maire Quinn, refused to act in it and withdrew from the theatre. There was hissing and booing at the end of the first performance, and in the nationalist press the heroine who goes off with a tramp was stigmatised as an insult to Irish womanhood. *The Well of the Saints* also ran into trouble; Willie Fay, one of the leading actors, objected to a sarcastic reference to a priest in Synge's dialogue, and when the play was performed it was widely attacked as a caricature of the Irish character. But these discouragements were trivial by comparison with the abuse which greeted the production of *The Playboy of the Western World*. There were riots in the Abbey Theatre every night for four nights; a nationalist journal vilified the play as a 'vile and inhuman story told in the foulest language we have ever listened to from a public platform',[4] and even responsible writers like Stephen Gwynn and W. J. Lawrence severely censured its moral tone. Among the Abbey actors there was a strong animus against the play. Willie Fay later recorded how his brother and he begged Synge to turn Pegeen into 'a decent likeable country girl' and to cut out the torturing of Christy with hot turf, but, he adds, 'we might as well have tried to move the Hill of Howth as move Synge'.[5]

Synge's isolation from family, religious, political, and theatrical communities corresponds to a basic and recurrent situation in his plays. In each play there is a central character whose intuitions lead him to move away from a community less perceptive than he is; this archetypal outward movement sometimes sets the character at odds with the ideals of the community and sometimes leads him to the brink of disaster, but Synge convinces us that the adversity, the alienation, and the danger are justified because of the intensification, the inner development, and the enriched vision achieved by the dissenting protagonist. His protagonists could be described as culture heroes in the higher sense of the word 'culture' because they are persistently concerned with the quality of life; security and communal life matter less to them than their vision of the truth or of the good life and the living of it.

A psychic experience which Synge had in the summer of 1899, when he was twenty-eight, shows how his senses and sub-conscious mind co-operated with nature to prefigure several of the characteristic themes and sensations of this basic situation in his plays. It is enlightening to compare Synge's description of the experience with the factual account given by Edward Stephens, his nephew. Synge was staying at Castle Kevin, a country house south of Dublin, with his mother and two friends of the family, Madeline Kerr and Edie Harmar. One evening, Stephens records, Synge 'was sitting in the porch with a fixed expression on his face and had not noticed that Miss Kerr had left him. Edie Harmar, when she saw his ghastly appearance, gave an exclamation which recalled him to consciousness. He explained that he had been looking down into the valley at two fields which had taken on the appearance of great eyes because in the distance they formed oval spaces of equal size and, in each, similar clumps of dark trees surrounded by white mist formed eyeballs. He said that by gazing at these he had become entranced, and it was some time before he regained his normal composure.'[6]

Synge's account of this experience differs from his nephew's in some important particulars. His alteration of the facts to create a distinctive imaginative pattern has much in common with his alterations of the source-materials of his plays. He lifts the experience out of the country house and the circle of family and friends. He says that it happened while he was wandering alone, collecting moths in the Wicklow Hills. He describes it as a 'psychical adventure' which gave him 'a singular acquaintance with the essences of the world'. These 'essences' are embodied in the following narrative:

One evening when I was collecting on the brow of a long valley in County Wicklow wreaths of white mist began to rise from the narrow bogs beside the river. Before it was quite dark I looked round the edge of the field and saw two immense luminous eyes looking at me from the base of the valley. I dropped my net and caught hold of a gate in front of me. Behind the eyes there rose a black sinister forehead. I was fascinated. For a moment the eyes seemed to consume my personality, then the whole valley became filled with a pageant of movement and colour, and the opposite hillside covered itself with ancient doorways and spires and high turrets. I did not know where or when I was existing. At last someone spoke in the lane behind me – it was a man going home – and I came back to myself. The night had become quite dark and the eyes were no longer visible, yet I recognised in a minute what had caused the apparition – two clearings in a wood lined with white mist divided again by a few trees which formed the eye-balls. For many days afterwards I could not look on these fields even in daylight without terror.[7]

The 'essences' described here involve wandering, isolation, nature, danger, reverie, and art. Solitary wandering leads to a confrontation with natural powers, which induce first a sense of peril then a feeling of absorption in nature, which is followed by the metamorphosis of the hillside into structured works of art.

Before Synge attempted to incorporate these 'essences' into plays, he encountered them in the Aran Islands. An intense feeling of isolation emerged from the wordless keening of the islanders, expressing 'the mood of beings who feel their isolation in the face of a universe that wars on them with winds and waves'. Danger was a continuous condition of existence for the man of Aran, but it brought with it a sharpening of his senses: 'the danger of his life on the sea gives him the alertness of a primitive hunter'. This alertness attuned him to his environment; for Synge, 'the supreme interest of the island lies in the strange concord that exists between the people and the impersonal limited but profound impulses of the nature that is round them', and the men of Inishmaan 'seemed to be moved by strange archaic sympathies with the world'. He also found affinities with art and artists in the moods of the islander; 'the long nights he spends fishing in his curagh bring him some of the emotions that are thought peculiar to men who have lived with the arts', and he traces 'an affinity between the moods of these people and the moods of varying rapture and dismay that are frequent in artists'. This was the community that Synge admired most, but he acknowledges that its heightened responsiveness to man, nature, and the universe was intermittent, and that most of its thought was bounded by the daily commonplaces of survival. 'Yet it is only in the intonation of a few sentences or some old fragments of melody that I catch the real spirit of the island,' he wrote, 'for in general the men sit together and talk with endless iteration of the tides and fish, and of the price of kelp in Connemara.'[8]

A dichotomy between an islander with sharpened intuitions and islanders trammelled by the routines of survival is one of the main themes of *Riders to the Sea*, written in the summer of 1902. In this play the hard lot of the Aran Islands community is symbolised by the sea and the wind, which impose a dangerous struggle for existence upon it. At the outset, Maurya, the aged mother, and the other characters are presented in contrasting relationships to this fate. We hear how Maurya has been 'crying and keening' for nine days because of her fear that her son Michael has been drowned and that she will lose her remaining son Bartley in the same way if he tries to go to the mainland to sell horses. Maurya is isolated from the other characters because they accept their hard lot with a rigid and inarticulate stoicism.

The contrast in attitudes is finely conveyed in theatrical terms by stage business. Intent on the routines of survival, Cathleen kneads dough for a cake, puts it in the oven, then works at a spinning-wheel. When Maurya rakes the fire, Cathleen reproaches her for shifting the hot turf away from the oven. Even more significant is the business concerning the rope and the boards, which are expensive commodities for the islanders. Maurya wants to preserve the rope for a ceremonial purpose – to lower Michael's coffin into the grave after his body has been found – but this hope is denied her when Nora hands the rope to Bartley so that he can make a halter for his horse with it. Bartley refuses to make a coffin out of the boards, and this puts him further at variance with his mother, who will not give him her blessing when he leaves. Even when she hurries after him, she is unable to speak the blessing because she is appalled by the apparition of Michael riding on the grey pony behind Bartley.

Maurya's account of her vision of Michael on the grey pony is a turning-point in the play; her daughters already know that Michael is dead and Maurya's intuition of this fact makes them begin to respond at last to her other intuitions of doom. Soon afterwards news arrives that the grey pony has knocked Bartley into the sea and that he has died on the rocks. Ironically, the pony intended to bring subsistence to the house has helped to destroy the last of its breadwinners. Maurya and the community react in different ways to the disaster. The men kneel by the door and the women sway and keen. The women have come nearer to the emotional state that Maurya was in at the start of the play. But Maurya has progressed beyond that state; she is now more composed and forward-looking than she was; she will no longer care, she says, 'what way the sea is when the other women will be keening'. In the final moments of the play, she develops still more when her imagination raises her to pity for all mankind – 'for every one is left living in the world' – then to the tragic vision of the essential human situation so finely expressed in her last words: 'No man at all can be living for ever, and we must be satisfied.'[9]

Maurya is never at one with her community. At the beginning of the play, she is at odds with it. In the final phase, she is above it, thinking and feeling on a higher and more articulate plane of sympathy, understanding, and imagination than any of those around her. The contrast between dynamic character and static community is a persistent theme in Synge's drama. *The Tinker's Wedding*, which dates from 1902, is his simplest treatment of it. The play has its origins in a story he heard in Wicklow about a priest who refused to marry a tinker and his mistress when they failed to bring the tin can they had promised him as part of his fee. Synge intensifies the conflict by adding the episode in which the tinker, his mistress, and his mother retaliate by bundling the priest into a sack and throwing him into a ditch. Another important addition is the stage business in which Sarah Casey, the mistress, rams the wedding-ring on the priest's finger. It was Sarah's desire for the sort of respectability represented by the priest and his flock which had led to the request for a wedding ceremony. When she pushes the ring on to the priest's finger, she is symbolically passing the buck of respectability back to him. By the end of the play she has completely renounced the torpid, property-owning community of the priest, having discovered that she prefers the nomadic, easygoing life of the tinkers, which is free from the avarice and guilt-complexes that the priest has exhibited.

There is a richer treatment of a similar theme in *The Shadow of the Glen*, another play that Synge began in 1902. He develops his theme in terms of the psychic state of a particular locality, and drastically modifies his source-materials to show his heroine abandoning a way of life accepted by many peasant communities. In the Aran Islands, he heard a story of how a man pretended to be dead in order to catch his wife with her lover, how the plan succeeded, and how the husband killed them both. In the play, old Burke pretends to be dead and Nora, his wife, is visited by Michael Dara, her lover, but Synge's ending shows Nora leaving the house with a tramp and Burke and Dara complacently drinking together. Old Burke and Dara represent the way of life which Nora renounces for that of the Tramp. The action of the play is closely integrated with its setting. Synge places it in the Wicklow Mountains, a region of desolate glens and shepherds' huts, with heavy rainfall throughout the year; a region which vividly illustrates a key-idea in the play, the Darwinian idea that life is a struggle for existence for man and beast alike. Nora tells the Tramp that she married old Burke because she had to live and he had the means of subsistence: a farm, a few cows, and some sheep. Synge emphasises that this struggle inevitably ends in decay and death. Nora cannot help thinking of the time when Michael and she will grow old and die. Because of the pressure of these laws of struggle and decay, Michael is more interested in acquiring old Burke's property than in Nora. When old Burke suddenly comes to life and orders Nora out of the hut, he invites Michael to stay with him and he is quite content to do so. The play ends with Michael drinking a toast to old Burke and wishing him long life. There is a penetrating irony in this ending. Like one of his own sheep, Burke is anxious for company. We know enough about the bleak life of the glen to be certain that he has not long to live, despite Michael's good wishes. Burke and Michael thus come to symbolise a blinkered life of appetites, self-preservation, and herding-together. The Tramp, on the other hand, symbolises an outflowing life of movement, altruism, and imagination. We hear that his imagination enables him to see 'great wonders' when he travels. When Burke orders Nora out of the hut, the Tramp invites her to join him in this active and perceptive existence. Burke's life is equated with the coughing of a sick sheep whereas the Tramp's is associated with the sun and the songs of birds. Burke and

Michael are coarsened by one law of nature, whereas the Tramp asserts a higher law of movement and responsiveness to beauty. When Nora goes out into the rain with the Tramp, she transcends the one and endorses the other.

The Shadow of the Glen is more successful in communicating what is renounced than what is endorsed. These two aspects of Synge's basic situation are more fully conveyed in *The Well of the Saints*. He again places his setting in a mountainous district in the east of Ireland. His plot derives from a French play of the fifteenth century about a blind man who carried a lame man on his back. When they were miraculously cured by the remains of St Martin, the lame man cursed the saint for bringing his easy life to an end. Synge alters this by making his leading characters a blind man and a blind woman. He invents the all-important episodes showing how happy they are when they become blind again and how they abandon the village community in which they have been living.

Each of the three acts of *The Well of the Saints* is associated with a certain season. In the first act it is early autumn when a saintly friar restores the sight of Martin Doul and his wife Mary. Both are at once disillusioned. Prompted by a perverted sense of humour, the villagers had persuaded Martin that Mary was beautiful, and he is appalled to find that she has sparse grey hair and eyes like a pig's. They quarrel bitterly. The second act shows them at odds with the village community as well as each other. The season is now wintry and cold, and Martin finds it the colder because he can see the grey clouds and the red nose of the smith for whom he has to work. He is attracted by the fair hair and fine skin of a young woman of the village, Molly Byrne, but she scorns his offer of a life spent wandering together in the warm south. The second act ends with Martin cursing the smith and Molly. In the third act, the season is early spring; Martin and Mary have become blind again and are drawn to each other once more. Both find new illusions to live by; Mary looks forward to having hair of unrivalled whiteness, Martin to having a long silky beard which will make the quality stop and give him money. When the saint tries to restore their sight again, Martin knocks the can of holy water out of his hand. The villagers throw stones at them and they set off for the south.

It is part of the irony of this play that all the characters have illusions and that the deepest response to life is that of the two blind characters. The saint talks of blindness as the result of sin, but Martin and Mary are happier and more perceptive of truth when they are blind. Molly Byrne and the smith think they make a far finer pair than Martin and Mary, but another villager carries conviction when he tells Molly 'it's more joy dark Martin got from the lies we told of that hag . . . than your old man will get from you, day or night, and he living by your side'. For all their vanity and illusions, the blind pair have far finer perceptions and greater courage than the village community. Their senses of hearing, touch, and smell are acute and give them a delight in nature which none of the others enjoys. This is well conveyed in the final act when Mary remarks, 'There's the sound of one of them twittering yellow birds do be coming in the springtime from beyond the sea, and there'll be a fine warmth now in the sun, the way it'll be a grand thing to be sitting here, quiet and easy, smelling the things growing, and budding from the earth.'[10] As before, Synge is emphasising how physical deprivation can sharpen the senses and stimulate the imagination. Even more than before, he associates movement and danger with this enlightenment; when Martin and Mary set off for the southern regions, the smith warns them of deep rivers and the danger of drowning.

Synge explores his basic theme more deeply in *The Playboy of the Western World* because he shows more fully the workings of the inner resources which enable his protagonist to transcend the community he renounces. The play has its origins in an anecdote that he heard in the Aran Islands about a Connemara man who killed his father with a turfing spade and fled to the Aran Islands where the inhabitants hid him from the police. When he recorded this story, Synge ascribed the behaviour of the islanders to their hatred for English jurisdiction. As usual, he made fundamental changes when he turned his source-material to dramatic use. He added the train of events showing the resurrection of the father and the bitter departure of father and son from the community which had given asylum to the young man. He set his play in County Mayo, not the Aran Islands. He obviously thought the psychic state of this locality better suited to his theme. When Synge visited Mayo in 1904, he found a great contrast between the beauty of the landscape and the desolate, monotonous life of the inhabitants. Correspondingly, at the outset of the play Pegeen Mike finds life so barren that she wistfully recalls the exciting days when a villager got six months in jail for maiming a sheep, and remembers how he was so good a story-teller that he could make old women shed tears. Her yearning for violence and poetry are typical of every member of the community except the timid Shawn Keogh. Consequently, when Christy Mahon appears with his story of having killed his father with a loy for trying to force him into a loveless marriage, he is welcomed and lionised by the villagers, and especially by Pegeen. They welcome him, not out of hatred for the law, but because he brings them a vivid tale and incarnates a myth. The picturesqueness of his tale delights them and his violent deed appears to them sub-consciously as an archetypal act of rebellion. They do not ponder the fact that it represents rebellion not only against patriarchal tyranny but also against one of the traditional institutions of the Irish peasant community – the arranged marriage. Pegeen herself is under pressure from her father and the parish priest to marry Shawn Keogh, a spineless man of property. In act III, however, there is a series of ironic reversals. Christy's father appears and the villagers are angry at the loss of their myth. But when Christy fells his father with a loy they are horrified at the reality of the myth. They tie Christy up and burn him with hot turf. The final irony comes when Christy departs with his father and Pegeen ruefully realises that there was something genuinely heroic about him, that she has lost the 'only playboy of the western world'.

This play is Synge's most sustained exercise in tragicomic irony and his most detailed study of how imagination can transform and develop character. In the latter respect it illustrates one of Bernard Shaw's strongest convictions about the workings of the evolutionary process. Stimulated by the admiration of the Mayo villagers, Christy's imagination eventually makes him worthy of the myth he has precipitated. His early stumbling phrases give way to accomplished story-telling about his violent deed; in act I, his first timid confession is simply, 'I killed my poor father': his second minimises his violence, 'I just riz the loy and let fall the edge of it on the ridge of his skull', but his lionising by the villagers prompts more and more vivid exaggerations; in act II he first claims to have split his father's head 'to the knob of his gullet', then to have cleft it 'to the breeches belt' with one blow.[11] Pegeen makes him conscious of his touch of the poet when she declares, 'it's the poets are your like, fine fiery fellows with great rages when their temper's roused' (*ibid.*, p. 81). Once it is brought to life, Christy's imagination enables him to see the desolation of his previous existence; 'There wasn't anyone heeding me in that place saving only the dumb beasts of the field' (*ibid.*, p. 83). It also makes his growing passion for Pegeen articulate, ardent, and rhythmical. 'If I wasn't a good Christian,' he tells her, 'it's on my naked knees I'd be saying my prayers and paters to every jackstraw you have roofing your head, and every stony pebble is paving the laneway to your door' (*ibid.*, p. 149).

Christy's furious cursing of his resurrected father at the end of act II is another climax in his development. He is now becoming the bold young man instead of pretending to be one. His growing courage and initiative are illustrated when he rides to victory in the horse-race on the beach at the start of act III. The prizes he receives imply a tribute to a poet–warrior rather than an amateur jockey: bagpipes, a fiddle 'was played by a poet in the years gone by', and 'a flat and three-thorned blackthorn would lick the scholars out of Dublin town' (*ibid.*, p. 145). The blackthorn prefigures the next stage in his development when he fells his father for the second time. Another stage comes when Pegeen leads the community in its attack on him and he recognises that he no longer has any roots in it: 'I'll quit the lot of you and live from this out like the madmen of Keel, eating muck and green weed on the faces of the cliffs' (*ibid.*, p. 169). His development is complete when he leaves the village with his father. Christy knows that his relationship with his father has permanently changed, that he is now the dominant personality. 'I'm master of all fights from now', he tells him (*ibid*., p. 173). The irony and eloquence of his thanks to the villagers – 'you've turned me into a likely gaffer in the end of all' (*ibid*., p. 173) – gives an aura of triumph to his final exit, though, unlike Nora Burke and Martin Doul, he has no sympathetic companion with him when he breaks away from the community. But he has an awakened imagination, an awareness of his life's ironies, courage, and self-sufficiency.

Of all Irish myths, the story of Deirdre was the one closest to Synge's concern with protagonists who break away from a community. The departure of Deirdre and Naisi for Alba at the end of act I of *Deirdre of the Sorrows* parallels a climactic gesture to be found in most of his previous plays. Deirdre knows that it has been foretold that she will be the ruin of the three sons of Usna and have a little grave to herself and a story about her that will be told forever. Once this has been affirmed in act I, the ending of the play is predestined, but Synge's treatment of the myth is made distinctive by his motivation of Deirdre and Naisi. The argument with which Deirdre persuades Naisi to defy King Conchubar and flee with her from Ulster is characteristic of Synge: 'Isn't it a small thing is told about the ruin of ourselves,' she tells him, 'when all men have age coming and great ruin in the end?' (*ibid*., p. 211). In reaching for joy on the brink of danger, she has a characteristic in common with Nora Burke, Martin and Mary Doul. Like them, too, she moves away from a community to a life close to nature when Naisi and she settle in Alba for seven years.

The most important of Synge's alterations of the myth is his motivation of the decision of the lovers to return to Ulster. In the myth, Deirdre returns unwillingly. In the play, when Fergus is sent by Conchubar to persuade them to return, he warns Naisi that their love will fade if they linger alone in Alba, and Deirdre overhears Naisi concede that 'I've had a dread upon me a day'd come I'd weary of her voice . . . and Deirdre'd see I'd wearied' (*ibid*., p. 227). Sooner than see their love decay, she urges him to accept Conchubar's invitation: 'isn't it a better thing to be following on to a near death, than to be bending the head down, and dragging with the feet, and seeing one day, a blight showing upon love where it is sweet and tender?' (*ibid*., pp. 231–3). This concern with the intensity as opposed to the length of life is another motive very characteristic of Synge. He deems his dissenters right to search for fulfilment, but Deirdre expresses his basic pessimism about their situation when she suppresses her lover's hopes of escape with the words, 'There's no safe place, Naisi, on the ridge of the world' (*ibid*., p. 231).

At the close, with Naisi murdered and Deirdre a suicide, Conchubar is left facing the prospect he had long dreaded – old age, decay, and loneliness. These are fears that he has in common with Old Burke, but unlike him Conchubar eventually recognises that his self-concern has been a vice when he confesses, 'I know well pity's cruel, when it was my pity for my own self destroyed Naisi' (*ibid.*, p. 257). By the end of the play, the community headed by Conchubar is disintegrating. Revolted by Conchubar's broken pledge of safety for the lovers, Fergus sets Emain Macha on fire and declares his lasting enmity to 'a thief and a traitor' (*ibid.*, p. 267). *Deirdre* is unique among Synge's plays in that it shows dissenters returning to the community they had rejected and in that a community is shown divided against itself.

Some readers of Synge's plays have wondered why only one of them is set in the Aran Islands despite his great affection for their inhabitants. The approach adopted in this essay suggests a reason. Synge turns to less enlightened communities – cruel, callous, hypocritical, and complacent – to sharpen the conflict between his dissenters and their social environment. His continuous interest in this conflict is shown by the persistence with which he drastically alters his source-materials to create it. The communities represented in *The Shadow of the Glen, The Well of the Saints*, and *The Playboy of the Western World* demonstrate the fact that 'human kind cannot bear very much reality', and the protagonists break away from them because they have intimations of things not dreamt of in their philosophy. Synge concentrates on the happenings leading to tension and fracture; only in *Deidre* does he treat later events. The break sometimes involves danger which makes the dissenters seem feckless, but what the communities regard as hubris, Synge vindicates as an act of liberation. Struggle and decay are inevitable; it is the quality not the quantity of life that matters. Enlightenment is often associated with a passionate act of violence; Sarah Casey rams the wedding-ring on the priest's finger: Marin Doul dashes the can of holy water from the hand of the saint: Christy Mahon fells his father with the loy. The dissenters are never reconciled with the communities; they accept their lonesomeness and find fulfilment in their imaginations and nature. Some of them are Darwinian enough to realise that decay is certain and there is no safety on the bleak ridge of the world. Like some of his best twentieth-century successors, Synge offers no apocalyptic hopes. We must learn to live on the ridge.

NOTES

1. London: Routledge, 1946, p. 89.
2. *The Irish Dramatic Movement* (London: Methuen, 1954), p. 163.
3. *The Poet in the Theatre*, p. 97.
4. Review by Arthur Griffith in *Sinn Féin*, 31 January 1907.
5. W. G. Fay and C. Carswell, *The Fays of the Abbey Theatre: an Autobiographical Record* (London: Rich & Cowan, 1935), pp. 212–13.
6. *My Uncle John*, ed. Andrew Carpenter (London: Oxford University Press, 1974), p.129. The illustrations between pp. 94 and 95 in this book include two photographs of Castle Kevin, both showing the porch.

7. Quotations from Synge throughout this article are from *J. M. Synge: Collected Works*, gen. ed. Robin Skelton, 4 vols. (London: Oxford University Press, 1962–8). This quotation is from *Autobiography* in vol. II, *Prose*, ed. Alan Price (1966), p. 10.

8. *The Aran Islands*, in *Prose*, pp. 75, 132, 75 fn. 1, 142, 132–3, 74 (two quotations). These page references follow the order of the passages quoted in this paragraph.

9. *Collected Works*, vol. III, *Plays* (Book I), ed. Ann Saddlemyer (1968), pp. 25–7.

10. *Plays* (Book I), pp. 92, 131.

11. *Plays* (Book II) (1968), pp. 73, 103, 119.

The Italian futurist theatre

JULIE R. DASHWOOD

From the time when Marinetti[1] founded futurism by publishing the first futurist manifesto in 1909, the movement was characterised by its desire for total renewal. For the futurists, literature, painting, sculpture, theatre, music, dance, morals and politics should all be inspired by the discoveries which had changed man's physical environment, and which should also correspondingly change his perceptions. Their theories were centred on the industrial age, which had produced the machine and electric light, brought about the growth of cities and revolutionised means of transport and communication. They welcomed the products of industrial society with an all-embracing optimism, seeing them as the means by which man would dominate his environment and be able to extend his knowledge infinitely. Their faith in the present and the future led them to adopt an aggressive stance, advocating boldness, love of danger, courage and rebellion and making these essential elements of their poetry. In 1909, Marinetti wrote 'Oggi, più che mai, non fa dell'arte se non chi fa della guerra'[2] (Today more than ever only those who make war can create art). The industrial age was one of speed and change, and these were also basic to the futurists' love of the modern, and their rejection of the past, whose art and society were described by them as static, lethargic and inward-looking. In the first manifesto, Marinetti wrote: 'Noi affermiamo che la magnificenza del mondo si è arricchita di una bellezza nuova: la bellezza della velocità'[3] (We declare that the magnificence of the world has been enriched by a new beauty: the beauty of speed). In 1913, he described closely the effects of the speed of transport and communications on modern sensibility, saying that man was now aware not just of his immediate surroundings, but of the whole world. He was able to overcome the limits of time and space, and to live through events both far and near, in fact, to be everywhere at the same time.[4] *Simultaneità* (simultaneity) is the word used by the futurists to describe these extensions of perception. Different times, places and sounds, both real and imagined, are juxtaposed in their works in an attempt to convey this new concept to their public. The desire for simultaneity was accompanied by one for synthesis. The futurists held that the speed of modern life exacted a corresponding speed of communication in art, which was therefore to convey the essence of emotion or situation without the need for long explanation or description.

Man's relationship to the new dimensions revealed by science and technology therefore provided much of the material for the futurists. But if on the one hand the powers of man were extended indefinitely by his discoveries, on the other, they claimed, his very nature should change as a result of these discoveries. He should, in fact, become like a machine, abandoning the weaknesses and sentimentalities of the past. Influenced as they were by the superman of Nietzsche and D'Annunzio, the futurists wrote of their own god-like being, who was aggressive, tireless, inhuman and mechanical. Early heroes were those in direct contact with machines: car-drivers, pilots, journalists, telegraph-operators and the like. Later, the hero became a fusion of man and machine, assured of immortality as his parts were interchangeable. This semi-mystical being, a prefiguration of the robot, also provided subject-matter for futurist works of art, and machines themselves came to provide techniques for the realisation of the works, especially in the visual arts and the theatre.

Marinetti was determined from the outset to bring his movement to the attention of the greatest possible number of people. In common with many other innovators in the arts of the time, he believed that art and literature could have a determining influence on society, and he described futurism as 'la nuova formula dell' Arte-azione'[5] (the new formula of Art-action). The artist therefore became the leader and promoter of the new ideas, and the forger of links between art and action, art and society. Marinetti had edited the periodical *Poesia* (1905–9) in Milan, but by 1909 he had come to regard the activities of this period as too limited. Action was required, and he wrote that: 'Bisognava assolutamente cambiar metodo, scendere nelle vie, dar l'assalto ai teatri e introdurre il pugno nella lotta artistica'[6] (It was absolutely necessary to change methods, to go out into the streets, to make assaults on theatres and to bring blows into the artistic struggle). The desire for ceaseless activity, the advocacy of courage and heroism and the insistence on aggression, then, led the futurists to go beyond mere theorising. They involved themselves in a great deal of direct action, including their *serate*, or evenings, which usually consisted of readings from futurist works of literature, and which often ended in a brawl. Theatres were often used for the *serate*, and typical of most of these is the one held at the Teatro Lirico, Milan, in February 1910. The programme was a powerful mixture of poetry, politics and polemics. One of Paolo Buzzi's anti-Austrian poems was read, and Marinetti brought the evening to a premature close when he shouted 'Long live war, sole hygiene of the world! Down with Austria'. A riot broke out, and Marinetti was arrested on stage. Formal protests the next day from the Austrian and German consuls assured the total success of the evening.

The *serate* gave the futurists some experience of the theatre. Marinetti himself already had this to some extent from his early plays, *Roi Bombance* (1905) and *La donna è mobile* (1909),[7] and he recognised the importance of the theatre, and that of the *spettacolo* (performance) in general,[8] for his movement. Art exhibitions were held, as were meetings, speeches, 'staged' quarrels in public, and later cinema and radio were used. These public performances became an ideal means of direct communication with the public, in the expectation that the audience would react directly and physically to what they saw and heard. Marinetti and his group delighted in hostility, and in the cat-calls, fruit and vegetables which usually accompanied this. In his *Manifesto dei drammaturghi futuristi*[9] (manifesto of the futurist dramatists) of 1911, which also has the title 'The delight of being hissed at', he advised playwrights to despise their audience. Deliberate provocation of the audience, partly for the sake of being aggressive and partly in order to break down the barriers between the audience and the actors, became one of the important techniques of the futurist theatre, and influenced the staging of their plays. The futurists, then, realised the importance of using theatres and theatrical techniques very early on, but the evolution of the idea of a specifically futurist theatre is a relatively slow one. The rest of this article will consider the various stages in the development of the futurist theatre, and will aim to show how the theatre became the ideal medium for one of the most vital and creative phases of futurism.

It was with the *Manifesto dei drammaturghi futuristi* that Marinetti began to formulate his theories on the theatre as such, although in retrospect this manifesto seems very cautious and tentative. In it he demanded that the authority of the author over the actors should be absolute. In this way the actor would be prevented from relying on easy effects to please the public, and would have to give a deeper and more serious interpretation of his role. This concern does not reappear in the later manifestos, although Marinetti obviously felt the need here to face the problem of the actor. The solution he suggested was not practicable for himself, as he was not particularly well qualified to direct plays, nor was he greatly interested in the technicalities of production. It has been argued, with some plausibility, that precisely because the futurists lacked experience of stagecraft it was some years before adequate productions of their works were possible.[10] He went on in the manifesto to denounce the themes of the theatre of realism of the time, represented in Italy by Marco Praga and his emulators, saying that love and the eternal triangle had been portrayed too much in literature. Greater virulence, however, is reserved for plays based on history and mythology, which were the stuff of much of D'Annunzio's theatre. These historical reconstructions, Marinetti wrote, taking as their main characters Nero, Julius Caesar, Napoleon or Francesca da Rimini, ran directly counter to the need to adopt themes from modern life. He insisted that 'Bisogna introdurre nel teatro la sensazione del dominio della Macchina, i grandi brividi che agitano le folle, le nuove correnti d'idee e le grandi scoperte della scienza, che hanno completamente trasformato la nostra sensibilità e la nostra mentalità d'uomini del ventesimo secolo' (We must bring into the theatre the sensation of the domination of the Machine, the great tremors which run through crowds, the new currents of ideas and the great discoveries of science, which have completely transformed our sensibility and our mentality as men of the twentieth century). His statements here are generic, but there is also in the manifesto a slight indication of the need for synthesis, which became one of the fundamental principles of the futurist synthetic theatre: 'L'arte drammatica non deve fare della fotografia psicologica, ma tendere invece ad una *sintesi della vita nelle sue linee più tipiche* e più significative' (Dramatic art must not be psychological photography, but must rather tend towards a *synthesis of life in its most typical* and significant lines). The ideas advanced in this manifesto were not used in plays until later, although when Marinetti adapted act II of his play *La donna è mobile*, renaming it *Elettricità*, in 1913, he referred to it as a *sintesi futurista*.

He was not, however, content to leave his excursions into the theatre at this point, and he turned his attention to a kind of theatre which seemed to him to be the perfect model for all his ideas. This was the Variety Theatre, which had developed from the music hall and the *café chantant*. The Variety Theatre, with its programme of unrelated numbers, and its dependence on the virtuosity of the individual artist, was anti-realistic and it had a popular appeal unknown to the official theatre of the time. By contrast with the reverent silences of the official theatre, it allowed and even depended on the spontaneous reactions of the audience, and even, in the case for example of conjurers, relied on the participation of the public. Italy in the early twentieth century had at least two outstanding performers in this kind of theatre, Leopoldo Fregoli and Ettore Petrolini but, in spite of their popular success, they were largely ignored by theatre critics, as was the genre as a whole.

Marinetti published his *Manifesto del teatro di varietà*[11] in 1913, and said that he found in Variety all the elements necessary for a new approach to the theatre. He said that it was free from tradition, dogma and masters, and so able to invent 'nuovi elementi di stupore' (new elements of astonishment). He found, that is, a weapon with which to attack the technical, aesthetic and social limitations of the theatre of his time. Wanting a total renewal of the theatre, he held up the improvisation, eclecticism, flexibility and audience-participation of the Variety against the official theatre, the better to emphasise the negative aspects of this 'teatro minuzioso, lento, analitico e diluito, degno tutt'al più dell'età della lampada a petrolio' (meticulous, slow, analytic and diluted theatre worthy, at the most, of the age of the oil lamp). He found all the means for the preparation of the new sensibility here: heroism, cynicism, action, laughter and synthesis. The protagonists, clowns, acrobats, dancers, jugglers and conjurers, were naturally dynamic and anti-academic. All this provided a natural basis for renewal. Marinetti wanted to take up the Variety Theatre and transform it into a 'teatro dello stupore, del record e della fisicofollia' (theatre of amazement, record-setting and body-madness). To psychology, Marinetti opposed body-madness, defined here as action, heroism, life in the open air, dexterity and the authority of instinct and intuition.

The futurist *serate* anticipated some of the points made in this manifesto, but in itself it also acts as a forerunner for many of the later futurist theories on the theatre. The references to synthesis, action, movement and daring, the interest in a new kind of character, the need to induce the spectators to take part in the action on the stage all foreshadow the many theoretical writings of Prampolini,[12] Depero[13] and Balla.[14] Marinetti himself took up in particular the idea of breaking down barriers between audience and actors, and this became one of the main points in his other two theatre manifestos, *Il teatro futurista sintetico*[15] (The futurist synthetic theatre) of 1915 and *Il teatro della sorpresa*[16] (The theatre of surprise) of 1921. He did not allow this concept to remain at a purely theoretical level. He knew already what the direct intervention of the author with his audience could achieve from the reaction of the press to incidents like his own appearance at the performance of his play *La donna è mobile* at the Teatro Alfieri, Turin, on 15 January 1909. The play seemed destined to be a flop until he appeared on stage himself to thank the organisers of the whistling for the honour done to him. This intervention was hailed by the press as 'un gesto nuovo nelle cronache delle prime rappresentazioni' (a new gesture in the annals of first nights).[17] As a result of the publicity campaigns of the futurists, and the interest aroused by descriptions like this, many audiences came to have certain expectations of what an evening with the futurists, and especially with Marinetti, ought to be. A detailed account of the events at the Teatro Dal Verme, Milan, on 16 January 1914, was given in the newspaper *Corriere della sera* on the following day.[18] The anonymous writer noted, interestingly, that: 'E chi agì non furono i futuristi, ma il pubblico, specialmente quello delle gallerie' (And it was not the futurists who acted, but the members of the audience, especially those in the circles). He went on to describe what happened during Marinetti's reading of his poem *Assedio di Adrianopoli* (Siege of Adrianople): 'Quando egli rievoca il *bum bum* dei cannoni, tutta la folla fa *bum bum*' (When he recalls the boom boom of the cannons, the whole crowd goes boom boom). Here, and in the performances at the Galleria Sprovieri in Rome, some of the theories of the *teatro di varietà* were put into practice.

Until 1915, however, material for the appearance of the futurists was provided by their manifestos and poems, by the music of Luigi Russolo[19] and the early plays of Marinetti. They also began to include scenery and costumes designed by the futurist artists, principally Balla and Depero. But the performances remained on the level of interesting experiments, and had little effect, in Italy, on the theatrical tradition. Their influence was felt more strongly outside Italy, for example by the dadaists with their Cabaret Voltaire, and in Russia. It was not however the intention of the futurists to remain on the sidelines, but to change the whole concept of the theatre. With their manifesto of 1915, *Il teatro futurista sintetico*, Marinetti, Settimelli[20] and Corra[21] set out all their ideas for renewal in the theatre, and their hopes for resulting changes in society. They mounted a violent attack on the values of the traditional theatre, and made euphoric statements about the new futurist theatre. All the important concepts developed by the futurists were, for the first time, applied directly to the theatre, which from now on was to be synthetic, atechnical, dynamic, simultaneous, alogical, autonomous and unreal. The old theatrical genres of farce, vaudeville, sketch, comedy, drama and tragedy were to be replaced by 'le battute in libertà, la simultaneità, la compenetrazione, il poemetto animato, la sensazione sceneggiata, l'ilarità dialogata, l'atto negativo, la battuta riecheggiata, la discussione extralogica, la deformazione sintetica, lo spiraglio scientifico ...' (free exchanges, simultaneity, interpenetration, the short acted poem, the dramatised sensation, laughter in dialogue form, the negative act, the re-echoing exchange, discussion beyond logic, synthetic deformation, scientific glimmerings ...). For the first time, some *sintesi teatrali* (theatrical syntheses) were written, both before and after the publication of the manifesto, which had in the manifesto their theoretical justification. The *sintesi* were works of extreme brevity and concentration, in which the conventional three-act play was replaced by *attimi* (moments) intended to capture the essence and atmosphere of the event or the emotion as it happened. Movement, gesture, sound and light became as important as the written word, and in some cases came to replace words altogether. This reduction to what the futurists regarded as the essential part of the action was intended to create an immediate and dynamic contact with the public, so that the audience responded intuitively to the play.

In 1915 and 1916 the companies of Berti, Tumiati, Zoncada and Petrolini all performed the *sintesi* on tours of Italy. Public reaction was initially hostile. After Italy's intervention in the First World War, however, in May 1915, patriotic approval was given to some of the aims of the manifesto and to those *sintesi* intended to appeal directly to hatred of Austria–Hungary and Germany and to glorify war. The futurists had been the first, in 1914, to demonstrate publicly against Austria and for intervention in the war. The manifesto stated the need to accompany these demonstrations with an 'azione artistica sulla sensibilità italiana, che vogliamo preparare alla grande ora del massimo Pericolo' (use of art on Italian sensibility, which we want to prepare for the great hour of maximum danger). Books and periodicals were no longer adequate vehicles for this work: only the theatre could carry it out. 'NOI CREDIAMO DUNQUE CHE NON SI POSSA OGGI INFLUEN-ZARE GUERRESCAMENTE L'ANIMA ITALIANA, SE NON MEDIANTE IL TEATRO' (We believe therefore that the only way to arouse the Italian spirit to war is through the theatre). The desire to use art to arouse and maintain a certain state of mind amongst the public is here very apparent. Images of war and aggression had abounded in the works of the futurists from 1909 onwards. They had declared war to be 'la sola igiene del mondo' (the sole hygiene of the world). As has been seen, they joined battle with enthusiasm, both aesthetic and physical. They had found a partial focus for their adulation of war in the war in Libya (1911–12), but now it became one of the major considerations of the group. Examples of *sintesi* written to appeal to Italian patriotism are Marinetti's *L'arresto* and Umberto Boccioni's *Kultur*, both performed during the tours of 1915 and 1916. In *L'arresto* (The arrest) a number of critics and observers are gathered in a comfortable room, and express their disapproval of the war. Suddenly from the trenches a young soldier cries: 'O venite un po' voi signori pessimisti, a far quel che facciamo noi! (Come on, you pessimists, and do what we're doing!). One of the critics, described as spiteful and gouty, is forced to pick up a rifle and fight, with a gun instead of with his tongue. The soldiers, from being participants in the war, become spectators, and watch the critic fighting the Austrians until he is killed by a bullet. The police arrive, and one of them says: 'È gia cadavere!' (He's already dead!), to which a soldier replies: 'Arrestate almeno il suo fetore passatista' (At least arrest his passatist stink). *Kultur* represents the struggle between Latin genius and unbearable Germanic pedantry, which destroys all creativity by making it the subject of arid study.

Syntheses such as these were applauded, especially in 1916, and helped to create an atmosphere more favourable to the experimentation of the futurists. It is worth saying that many of the *sintesi* remain schematic, like the ones described above, and that their value for the most part lies in their experimental nature. It is however worth analysing the approach of the futurists to the theatre in these works as they are the first practical real-isation of their manifestos. Extended plot and action give way to brief and essential moments; logic and realism are abandoned in favour of a mingling of reality and imagination, the banal and the incredible, or even the supernatural; simultaneity of time and space is seen as the only means of presenting the complexity of life to the audience; characters are no longer such, but rather become allusions or syntheses, and the cast comes to include animals, flowers, noises, objects and so on; the element of surprise is dominant; at all times, the theatre and society of the past are attacked. Time in the theatre is no longer chronological, but is, to use Marinetti's terms, 'created' or 'invented', and is used for dramatic rather than naturalistic effects. *Dissonanza*[22] (Dissonance) by Corra and Settimelli has a fourteenth-century setting in which a lady and a page exchange impassioned hendecasyllables. They are interrupted by a man asking for a match, and then continue as before. Similarly, space is no longer unitary, but can be used by the dramatist to show different situations at the same time, with no regard for verisimilitude. In Marinetti's *Simultaneità* the life of a modest bourgeois family installed around a table reading, preparing accounts and sewing is juxtaposed with that of a prostitute preparing her toilette. A dim greenish light surrounds the family, while a very bright electric light is focused on the cocotte. The two groups seem unaware of each other until the end, when the family falls asleep and the cocotte moves towards them. She throws all their work on to the floor, and then continues to polish her nails. She is, Marinetti wrote, not a symbol but a synthesis of luxury, disorder, adventure and waste, all things both desired and regretted by the family. He said that time and space were fused here, and a new dynamism and simultaneity were created. Evident here is Marinetti's wish to contain reality in a moment rather than an act, using light and gesture to convey his meaning rather than words.

The cocotte is not a naturalistic or psychological whole, and in this is typical of many of the protagonists of the futurist theatre. 'Il signore grasso e panciuto' (the fat, paunchy man) in Marinetti's *Un chiaro di luna* (Moonlight) is described by the author as an alogical synthesis of many emotions: fear of the future, of the cold and solitude of the night, of his vision of life in twenty years' time and so on. Even, at times, only part of the actor is seen by the audience. In Marinetti's *Le basi* (The bases) the curtain is raised so that only the legs and feet of the actors are visible. The actors are instructed to give the maximum expression to the scenes by using the movements of these limbs. The same approach is used in *Le mani* (Hands) by Marinetti and Corra. In this case, only gestures of the hands are used to convey emotion and situation. Among the protagonists in his *Caccia all'usignolo* (Hunting the nightingale) Govoni[23] lists the sound of bells, voices of drunkards, the rustling of wind, the interplay of light, moonlight, the voice of the nightingale, the movement of lizards, voices from the town, breathing, sighing, the sound of the clock, a cat, a hoopoe and a dog. Animals, inanimate objects, sounds, light and movement come, therefore, to be as important as human actors, and even, at times, to replace them. Marinetti's play *Vengono* (They're coming) is subtitled *dramma d'oggetti* (drama of objects). Servants continually move eight chairs and an armchair around the stage as the majordomo receives different orders from his masters. Marinetti intended to give the impression that the chairs gradually acquired a life of their own through these movements. Finally, they are placed diagonally across the stage, and an invisible spotlight is used to project their shadows on to the floor. As the spotlight is moved, so the shadows move making it appear as though the chairs themselves are going out of the French window. Marinetti wanted the three most important 'characters' in his *Teatrino dell'amore* (Little theatre of love) to be the little theatre itself (in this case, a puppet-theatre), the buffet and the sideboard. Depero's *Colori* (Colours) is entirely abstract, consisting only of sound and light.

Accompanying the reduction of human actors to a secondary role, or their total disappearance, is the reduction of words to very brief exchanges, or to nonsense. The characters in Mario Carli's[24] *Stati d'animo* (States of mind) have lines written in *parole in libertà* (words in freedom) or which are meaningless, and use gesture and tone of voice to convey their different emotions. Three *sintesi* by Cangiullo[25] are an attack on the whole theatrical tradition, as well as on the use of words in the theatre. In *Non c'è un cane* (There isn't a soul about), called a synthesis of night, the protagonist is the Man who isn't there. On a cold, deserted street at night, a dog (*cane*) crosses the road. Cangiullo's *Detonazione* (Detonation) is called a synthesis of the whole modern theatre. The setting is the same as in the previous synthesis, but this time, after a minute of silence, there is a revolver-shot. We are told that his *Decisione* is a tragedy in fifty-eight acts, and perhaps more, but that it is useless to perform fifty-seven of them. The final, brief act concludes with the words: 'Questa è una cosa che deve assolutamente FINIRE!' (This is something which absolutely must finish).

Parody is also used to attack not just the traditional theatre but contemporary society as well. *Passatismo* (Passatism), by Corra and Settimelli, consists of three brief, identical and static scenes, set in 1860, 1880 and 1910. An old man and an old woman hold the same conversation in each. At the end of the third scene, both die, identically, of a heart attack. Further assaults on surrounding realism are provided by Boccioni[26] in *Il corpo che sale* (The body which rises). Here, the tenants of a block of flats see a body rising up past their windows. They call the portress, who explains calmly that this is the body of the lover of the fifth-floor tenant, sucked up every day by his mistress's eyes. The portress will not allow him to use the stairs, as she is concerned about the good reputation of the building. In Paolo Buzzi's[27] *Il pesce d'aprile* (The April Fool), a dead wife announces the death of her husband to the priest. The unexpected, the weird and the supernatural are all elements used by the futurists, as is the grotesque, or the resolving of tragic situations into comedy and the reverse. The conclusion of Balla's *Per comprendere il pianto* (To understand grief) is 'Bisogna ridere' (You must laugh). Iacopo, protagonist of *Verso la conquista* (Towards the conquest), by Corra and Settimelli, renounces his debilitating love for Anna in order to fulfil his self-appointed mission as a hero. On leaving her, however, he slips on the skin of a fig, and dies after falling downstairs.

Some of the *sintesi* obviously made great demands on the ability of the audience to understand the new idiom. Of the audience, however, more was expected than mere comprehension and reaction to the futurist theatre. In *Dalla finestra* (From the window), by Corradini and Settimelli, the spectators themselves are listed among the characters. At the beginning of the play, we are told that:

> Tutti gli spettatori che sono qui, personaggi–protagonisti, per comprendere il dramma devono porsi per suggestione nei panni di un paralizzato che non può né muoversi né parlare, a cui solo viva e chiara è rimasta l'íntelligenza imprigionata nella carne morta e che si trova in letto presso a una finestra, con le persiane aperte dal vento nelle tre notti lunari di cui fan parte gli *attimi* della azione.

> (All the spectators who here are characters and protagonists, in order to understand the play must try to imagine that they are paralysed and cannot move or speak, with only their intelligence, imprisoned in the flesh, left alive and unclouded; that they are in bed next to a window, with the blinds opened by the wind in the three moonlit nights which make up the *moments* of the action.)

The audience is asked, then, not just to react, but to participate directly in the mood of the play.

These were the themes and techniques used by the futurists to convey their ideas to their audiences. The manifesto of the synthetic theatre had claimed that: 'Il *teatro futurista* saprà esaltare i suoi spettatori, cioè far loro dimenticare la monotonia della vita quotidiana, scaraventandoli attraverso un *labirinto di sensazioni improntate alla più esasperata originalità e combinate in modi imprevedibili*' (The *futurist theatre* will be able to excite its audience, that is make it forget the monotony of everyday life, by hurling it through a *labyrinth of sensations expressed with the most exacerbated originality and combined in unpredictable ways*). While the success of the dramatists in achieving this ambition was varied, serious attempts were made to create a new theatrical idiom, and to work upon the sensibilities of the audience in a new way.

The futurists were not, however, always in control of their medium, and as one critic wrote of the productions of the *teatro sintetico* at Bergamo: 'Durata complessiva dello svolgimento dei dieci numeri del programma una trentina di minuti; durata complessiva degli intervalli due ore'[28] (Total length of the performance of the ten numbers of the programme about thirty minutes; total length of the intervals two hours). One possible reason for this inadequacy of performance is that the *sintesi* were generally performed at this time by companies used to the traditional theatre, and who were unused to the demands made by the futurist theatre on actors and producers. Another is that Marinetti and the others did not give serious attention to the kind of actors, stages and scenery best able to interpret their works. He was content to maintain the dynamic of the futurist theatre by provoking the public and preparing for battle with each performance. The lines just quoted indicate one result of this inattention to technique. Another newspaper critic, Enrico Novelli, writing in *La Nazione*, Florence, on 10 March 1916 described the *sintesi*, identified the difficulties posed by them and proposed solutions to the problems raised. He wrote:

> Rapidi schizzi, appunti, vedute di scorcio, compenetrazioni, nostalgie, ricordi, attimi filosofici, lampi di ultra-umanità: questi, più o meno potrebbero essere tanti *motivi* di espressione del teatro sintetico. Ma perché il pubblico potesse riceverne una sensazione immediata e potesse, perció, giudicarne convenientemente, abbisognerebbero due cose: un teatro adatto: una compagnia apposita. Un teatro fornito di tutte le più assurde complicazioni scenografiche e meccaniche: una compagnia costituita da elementi agili, vibranti, assuefatti a dare in una sola intonazione il *riassunto* di una *parte* intera: comici futuristi insomma.[29]

> (Rapid sketches, notes, foreshortened views, interpenetrations, nostalgia, memories, moments of philosophy, flashes of extreme humanity: these more or less are among the *motifs* expressed by the futurist theatre. But for the audience to gain an immediate sensation of them so that it could assess them suitably two things would be required: a suitable theatre: a special company. A theatre containing all the most absurd scenographical and mechanical complications: a company made up of agile, vibrant elements, trained to give in a single intonation the summary of an entire role: futurist comedians in fact.)

This very clear exposition of the requirements of the futurist theatre evoked no response amongst the futurist dramatists. Not until 1921 did Marinetti and Cangiullo form a specifically futurist company, although two established comedians, Luciano Molinari and Ettore Petrolini, both belonging to the Variety Theatre, showed interest in the *sintesi* and included some of them in their programmes, with some success. Marinetti tried to claim that Petrolini was a futurist. He was, however, an independent artist whose personal style coincided to some extent with that proposed by the futurists, and not one who was fundamentally influenced by them.

It was the visual artists who first gave serious thought to the kind of stage-design most suitable for the futurist theatre. Prampolini, Balla and Depero were the artists most closely involved in this work. In March 1915, Balla and Depero signed *Ricostruzione futurista dell'universo*[30] (Futurist reconstruction of the universe), a manifesto which indicates many of the directions followed later in their designs for the stage. They wrote of the limitations of the flat plane, and the need to create a synthesis in the visual arts of atmosphere, interpenetration of planes and states of mind. To achieve this, they proposed the creation of the plastic–dynamic complex, which was to be abstract, moving, odorous and noise-creating. Influenced by the work of Boccioni and Severini, and also by the cinema and machine, the artificial landscapes of Balla and Depero prefigure closely the abstract, spatial, architectural and constructivist approach which was the basis of their work for the theatre. The myths of the industrial age, speed, aggression, the modern and the machine, became their means of expression.

Prampolini was influenced by their theories, and in 1915 published a *Manifesto della scenografia e coreografia futurista*[31] (Manifesto of futurist scenography and choreography). He wrote that it was false to think of the stage as an independent artistic entity, as the set should live out the action on the stage in a dynamic synthesis. This synthesis between set and action should result from the collaboration of author and designer. Instead of interpreting the intentions of the author, the set should acquire its own *ordine emotivo* (emotional capacity), thus arousing feelings which aid the action of the play. More than this, it should arouse emotions which the script or the action cannot convey, and to this end, it was necessary to use the stage not to create a photographic representation of reality, generally realised through a painted set. Space should instead be filled by an 'Architettura meccanica incolore, potentemente vivificata dalle emanazioni cromatiche di una sorgente luminosa' (Mechanical architecture, colourless and powerfully brought to life by the chromatic emanations of a source of light). The designer should create dynamic combinations of colour, light and shade, and therefore enable the actor to achieve dynamic effects impossible in a realistic setting. Abstractions, described by Prampolini as the interpretative equivalents of reality, were needed, to arouse emotion directly in the audience. He even went a step further, and looked forward to the abolition of the actor, and his replacement by pure light and chromatics. A synthesis of light, colour, movement and plot, therefore, was the major proposal of Prampolini's manifesto. His new, dynamic techniques were to some extent inspired by the moving images of the cinema, and it is not a coincidence that he designed his first sets for the cinema. His designs for the theatre foreshadowed Bragaglia's *luce psicologica* (psychological light) of 1919, and Ricciardi's *teatro del colore* (theatre of colour), also of 1919. His theories developed to the point where, in his manifesto *Atmosfera scenica futurista*[32] (Futurist scenic atmosphere) of 1924 he proposed an 'architettura elettro-dinamica polidimensionale di elementi plastici luminosi in movimento nel centro del cavo teatrale' (electro-dynamic, polydimensional architecture composed of plastic luminous elements moving in the centre of the well of the theatre). Prampolini's work for the *teatro della pantomima futurista* (futurist pantomime theatre) in Paris in 1927 represents his last contribution to the futurist theatre as such, but by then he was working as an independent artist, and was not in direct contact with Marinetti and the others.

Prampolini was the most coherent theorist of futurist design for the stage, but Balla and Depero also made important contributions. Balla put some of Prampolini's ideas into practice in his combinations of light and music for the *Ballets Russes* of Diaghilev in a production of Stravinsky's *Feu d'artifice* at

5 'Selvagetti. Teatro plastico', by Fortunato Depero, 1918. Private collection, Milan

the Teatro Costanzi in Rome in April 1917. Depero began to create his plastic characters in 1915, and in 1917 he created his *Scena plastica floreale* (Plastic floral scene) for Stravinsky's *Le chant du rossignol*, although in the event his sets and costumes were not used. His work with the Swiss Gilbert Clavel led him to the idea of a puppet-theatre, the *teatro plastico* (plastic theatre), in which he substituted puppets for actors, finding in them a greater freedom and more play for his imagination. The characters in his plastic dances were *selvaggi* (primitive beings), harlequins, men with golden whiskers and stylised animals, coming from an imaginary world of machines and automata (see plate 5). His examination of the links between space, volume, light, colour and line took him into the realm of fantasy and magic, and so into an art which was totally non-realistic. The artists and stage designers, then, worked with Diaghilev and Stravinsky, and also with the composer Malipiero. Often they used futurist means of expression to interpret non-futurist works. It remained for the authors to form a theatrical company consisting of actors able to interpret their plays.

Marinetti, Settimelli and Dessy[33] tried to do this about a year after the end of the First World War. Very little information is available about this venture, and the productions met with little success. At this point, Marinetti and Cangiullo realised that the *teatro sintetico* had lost its momentum, and proposed the examination of some of the aspects of the *teatro di varietà* which had not yet been taken up. Surprise, one of the key elements of their *teatro di varietà*, became the major element in the new theatre which they described in their *Manifesto del teatro della sorpresa* (Manifesto of the theatre of surprise) of October, 1921. While underlining the merits of the *teatro sintetico*, they wrote that the aim of the new theatre was to involve the spectator completely in the performance. The author should therefore be able to 'provocare nel pubblico parole e atti assolutamente impreveduti, perché ogni *sorpresa* partorisca nuove sorprese in platea, nei palchi e nella città la sera stessa, il giorno dopo, all'infinito' (provoke in the audience words and actions which are totally unexpected, so that every *surprise* gives rise to new surprises in the pit, the circles and in the town on the same evening, the following day, and infinitely). They returned to the protagonists and programme of the *teatro di varietà*, and so to *fisicofollie* with the participation of gymnasts, athletes, illusionists, eccentrics and conjurers. The programme was to consist of a *teatro–giornale* (theatre–newspaper) of futurism, a *teatro–galleria* (theatre–art gallery), readings of free-word poems, dances, dramatised poems and musical improvisations for piano, piano and voice, orchestra and so on. Improvisation was therefore the means of creating surprise, and was intended to create further improvisation on stage and generate it among the audience and beyond the confines of the theatre itself. This represented a final break with the traditional concepts of time and space in the theatre, as the action and improvisation should have infinite repercussions.

The new company which was to perform the works of the *teatro della sorpresa* was gathered around Marinetti, Cangiullo and Rodolfo De Angelis, a man who had begun his career in the *caffè-concerto* and who was also writer, painter, editor and later song-writer. They had to face the difficulty of putting together a company made up of participants from many different branches of entertainment, and capable of great flexibility. De Angelis later described some of the problems encountered in forming the company:

> Un vecchio attore napoletano, Cecchi, che aveva recitato per oltre un quarto di secolo con Federico Stella, mi chiese lo scioglimento del contratto dopo due prove. Finalmente raccogliendo un po' dappertutto elementi disparati: attori da prosa, ballerini, comici di caffè-concerto, giovani intelligenti e animosi,

amanti del teatro, e belle dame desiderose di pubblicità, riuscii a mettere insieme il complesso occorrente.[34]

(An old Neapolitan actor, Cecchi, who had acted for more than a quarter of a century with Federico Stella, asked me to end his contract after two rehearsals. Finally gathering disparate elements from everywhere: prose-actors, dancers, comedians from the *caffè-concerto*, courageous and intelligent young people, theatre-lovers, and beautiful women seeking publicity, I managed to put the necessary group together.)

De Angelis also indicated the difficulties faced by the instrumentalists, who were seated among the audience, and yet had to play together. Then a choir of forty or fifty members capable of following and singing a futurist score was not always readily available.

Continuity in the company was provided by the contributions of Marinetti, Cangiullo and De Angelis, as the participation of most of its members was brief and occasional. This fluctuating, disparate and at times amateur company made its début at the Teatro Mercadante in Naples on 30 September 1921, and flopped miserably. The greatest success of the company's tour of Palermo, Rome, Florence, Genoa, Turin and Milan in October 1921 was at the Salone Margherita in Rome on 12 October.[35] The evening began when Cangiullo and some instrumentalists took their places among the audience. From a box, Cangiullo conducted an orchestra composed of a trumpeter and two violinists to the accompaniment of less polite noises from the audience. Then Cangiullo's *Cielo e Ciglia* was greeted by showers of fruit and vegetables. As the evening continued, the audience invaded the stage, Bragaglia was attacked as he applauded the performers and finally the actors responded by physically attacking the audience. Little apparently was heard of the *strabilianti sorprese* (astounding surprises) promised by the posters, although surprises of a different kind were provided by the actors and public. The action did not, however, end in the theatre. As the audience left, some of its members tried to carry away their chairs, but were prevented from doing so by the attendants. Marinetti was followed from the theatre by about three hundred people, and after an exchange of insults became involved in a fight. Finally, the police intervened and escorted him to his hotel. Although the work of Pirandello and, to a lesser extent, that of the writers for the theatre of the grotesque, Chiarelli, Rosso di San Secondo, Antonelli and Cavacchioli, had begun to transform the Italian theatre since the time of the *teatro sintetico*, the futurist theatre was still obviously vital enough to arouse extremes of hostility and approval. But its most interesting and innovatory phase came to an end with the last tour of the *teatro della sorpresa* in 1924. After this, Marinetti's colleagues in the enterprise followed independent careers, and some ceased to take part in artistic activities altogether.

The remainder of the story of the futurist theatre can be equated largely with the activities of the founder and leader of futurism. Marinetti had continued to write plays on his own account, independently of the *teatro della sorpresa*, even when his company was at its most flourishing. But from *Il tamburo di fuoco*, written in 1921, onwards, the plays generally show a return to more traditional structures. This play has more in common with those written before he became interested in a specifically futurist theatre than with the *sintesi* and the *sorpresa*, a tendency which he acknowledged himself when he called it a 'dramma impressionista' (impressionist play). His gradual return to order after the battles and experimentalism of the futurist theatre can in part be explained by the social and political climate in Italy in the 1920s. While making due allowance for the necessarily ephemeral nature of much of the futurist theatre, depending as it did on improvisation, performance and production rather than on written texts, and for the impossibility of prolonging a series of theatrical experiments which to a large extent had run their course, his gradual return to tradition does run parallel to the strengthening of the fascist hold on the state. Especially after 1924, the year of the Matteotti murder and the Aventine secession, the fascist party was able to gain control of all the organs of the state. The official desire for stability and control, and the repressive climate of censorship and ultimately dictatorship did not permit the anarchy and heated polemics, artistic and political, which had been the key-note of so many futurist activities. It would no longer have been possible to use the stage to carry these debates into the public arena and to provide an alternative to the fisticuffs of the fascists.

Some of the futurist rhetoric of nationalism, heroism, youth, élitism and athleticism was absorbed by the fascists, and Marinetti and some of the other futurists had supported the fascist movement enthusiastically from the outset. He and others did resign from the movement when it began to show more authoritarian and right-wing tendencies in 1920, but he returned to acceptance of the party and the regime in 1922, and he never again protested openly at any of the measures taken by the fascists. On 18 March 1929, he accepted membership of the *Accademia d'Italia*, which was the reward offered by Mussolini to the artists who had supported him. So the man who, twenty years previously, had proposed the destruction of museums, libraries and academies of all kinds ultimately fell into line with those who had the blessing of the regime.

As has been said, some of the themes and tendencies of futurism prefigure closely those of fascism, and for this reason it is not possible to equate futurism with the modern experimental theatre of the absurd or of 'happenings'. Some of the techniques of the early avant-garde of the twentieth century have certainly been acclaimed as total innovations in the post-war theatre, and this view needs to be corrected. Ideologically, however, there is no connection between these different phases in the theatre.

NOTES

1. F. T. Marinetti (1876–1944). The foundation manifesto was published in French in *Le Figaro*, Paris, 20 February 1909. The Italian version was published in *Poesia*, v, nos. 1–2, (February–March 1909). The futurists used the words 'passatismo' and 'passatista' (passatism and passatist) to define a state of mind which was static, traditional, professorial, pessimistic, pacifist, nostalgic, decorative and dilettante, in fact, to describe everything which, in their view, was the antithesis of futurism.

Unless otherwise indicated, quotations from the futurist manifestos and writings are taken from the critical edition of Marinetti's works: F. T. Marinetti, *Teoria e invenzione futurista*, edited with introduction and notes by L. De Maria (Milan: Mondadori, 1968). There is a good selection of the manifestos in translation in *Futurist Manifestos*, edited and introduced by U. Apollonio (London: Thames & Hudson, 1973). All the translations in this article, however, are by the author.

2. Marinetti, *Prefazione* to G. P. Lucini, *Revolverate* (Milan: Edizioni di 'Poesia', 1909), p. 9.

3. Marinetti, *Teoria e invenzione*, p. 10.

4. *Ibid.*, p. 60.

5. *Ibid.*, p. 201.

6. *Ibid.*, p. 201.

7. Marinetti's plays can be found in F. T. Marinetti, *Teatro*, ed. G. Calendoli (Rome: Vito Bianco, 1960).

8. V. M. Kirby, *Futurist performance* (New York, Toronto, Vancouver: Dutton, 1971).

9. Marinetti, *Teoria e invenzione*, pp. 266–9 (here called 'La voluttà d'esser fischiati').

10. G. Antonucci, *Lo spettacolo futurista in Italia* (Rome: Studium, 1974), p. 27.

11. Marinetti, *Teoria e invenzione*, pp. 70–9.

12. Enrico Prampolini (1894–1960) painter, theorist and designer for stage and cinema.

13. Fortunato Depero (1892–1960) painter and designer.

14. Giacomo Balla (1871–1958) painter and designer.

15. Marinetti, *Teoria e invenzione*, pp. 97–104.

16. *Ibid.*, pp. 142–4.

17. Now in G. Antonucci, *Cronache del teatro futurista* (Rome: Abete, 1975), p. 39.

18. *Ibid.*, p. 56.

19. Luigi Russolo (1885–1947) painter, theorist and composer.

20. Emilio Settimelli (1891–1954) author, theorist and playwright.

21. Bruno Corra (pseudonym of Bruno Ginanni Corradini, b. 1892) playwright and theorist.

22. These *sintesi* can be found in *Il teatro futurista sintetico* (Milan: Istituto editoriale italiano, 1915).

23. Corrado Govoni (1884–1965) poet.

24. Mario Carli (1889–1935) author and journalist.

25. Francesco Cangiullo (b. 1884) poet, playwright, theorist and journalist.

26. Umberto Boccioni (1882–1916) painter, sculptor, theorist and playwright.
27. Paolo Buzzi (1874–1956) poet, novelist and playwright.
28. Antonucci, *Cronache*, p. 93.
29. *Ibid.*, p. 103.
30. Now in *Archivi del Futurismo*, ed. M. Drudi Gambillo, T. Fiori (Rome: De Luca, Vol. I, 1958), pp. 48–51.
31. Now in *Sipario*, no. 260 (December 1967), pp. 55–8.
32. *Sipario*, pp. 50–1.
33. Mario Dessy (b. 1902) journalist and writer.
34. R. De Angelis, *Caffè-concerto* (Milan: S.A.C.S.E., 1940), pp. 283–4.
35. Antonucci, *Cronache*, pp. 148–55.

Communist *kabuki*:
a contradiction in terms?

BRIAN POWELL

On 7 March 1949 the members of a *kabuki* company called Zenshinza with their families – over seventy people in all – joined the Japan Communist Party. It is this company to which the words 'communist *kabuki*' in the title refer and about which the question is asked. The three ideographs used for the name Zenshinza mean Forward Advance Company, a rather cumbrous name in English. While the Japanese is certainly incongruous, especially in traditional *kabuki* circles, it is not cumbrous, and the Japanese name will be used in this article. The names of the Zenshinza actors will appear in the normal Japanese order, that is, family name before given name. *Kabuki* actors are conventionally referred to by their given names and this convention has been followed here after the first full reference.

It is a truism in Japan that *kabuki* is 'feudal'. To answer the question in the title one only needs to list the 'feudal' characteristics of *kabuki* and one will conclude that of course communist *kabuki* is impossible in any meaningful sense. Zenshinza must therefore be either a freak or a fraud. In practice it is not as simple as this. Zenshinza's contribution to the development of modern Japanese theatre in the widest sense has been great and its achievements considerable. Others may say that Zenshinza represents neither *kabuki* nor communism, but this depends on a definition of those terms. Formally at least Zenshinza remains a company of mainly *kabuki*-trained actors all of whom are full members of the Japan Communist Party.

The word *kabuki* is relatively easy to define. As a living theatre form it is known in the West through actual performance by *kabuki* companies on tour. Its history is available to the general reader in a number of books written in English and other western languages.[1] From these one can see that an entertainment form known as *kabuki* became recognisable as commercial theatre during the second half of the seventeenth century. By this time plays with plots were being performed by groups of actors before audiences who had paid money to be allowed to watch. From its inception, usually placed in the early years of the seventeenth century, *kabuki* had been an actors' theatre. Its earliest repertory had consisted of crude sketches designed to show off the dancing talents and other charms of the performers, male and female. The open association of prostitution with these performances had led to government bans on the appearance firstly of women (in 1629) and then boys under the age of fifteen (1652). A further stipulation was that the events portrayed on the stage should be rather closer to those of ordinary, everyday life than they had hitherto been. There was thus both a negative and a positive side to government interference in the new art and at the hands of the adult male actors who remained there evolved a distinctive drama form.

At the beginning of the eighteenth century the three major cities of Edo (modern Tokyo), Kyōto and Ōsaka each had areas that might be compared to London's West End. A number of theatres would be clustered together offering a variety of forms of entertainment in competition with each other. It is in this period that *kabuki* tradition begins, as many of the changes that have been brought about since then have been refinements of the basic conventions established at this time. The tradition itself had two main dimensions, the one artistic and the other institutional, and no account of *kabuki* can be considered complete without reference to both of them.

The art was the art of the actor, not the composite art of playwright, director and actors, which we now regard as the norm. The playwright, or teams of playwrights, wrote plays in order to please the actors, who altered them at will. There were no directors; the actors directed themselves. The individual creativity of the actors was often subject to some restraint, either financial or officially imposed, but throughout *kabuki* history it has been possible for the exceptionally talented and self-confident actor to introduce changes into his art that have later been recognised as artistically significant. *Kabuki* was fortunate in producing at the end of the seventeenth century three actors of great brilliance and very different styles who established new standards of artistic accomplishment.[2] There were other such individuals later in the eighteenth and nineteenth centuries and innovations in the artistic interpretation of various classic roles were not infrequent.

It is important to realise, however, that the effect of these artistic changes on the institutions of the *kabuki* theatre was minimal. At any time during the eighteenth and early nineteenth centuries a theatregoer might have been delighted at the brilliance of one of the actors appearing before him, but the institutional framework within which the production actually reached the stage hardly changed during that period.

The institutions of the *kabuki* theatre may be broadly divided into two categories, firstly those connected with the actors who appeared in any given performance and secondly those involving the externals of the performance, especially the theatre management.

The acting world of eighteenth- and nineteenth-century Japan was organised in families. It became almost impossible to embark on an acting career if one happened not to have been born into one of the established acting families; and, conversely, it was almost impossible not to become an actor if one had been born the son and heir of an acting family.

Not all acting families were equal by any means. Although in most cases the members of an acting family could usually be assured of working for much of the time, the type of role that would be given was rigidly controlled by a conventional hierarchy among the families. A few families, such as the Ichikawa, achieved fame and position because of the brilliance of their heads at an early stage of *kabuki* development. The leading roles were always played by the members of these few families. Actors in other families always played the subordinate roles and members of the lowest class of acting families were condemned permanently to walk-on parts. In the circumstances of Japanese society during this period a hierarchical system of this kind, even in an artistic sphere, was generally accepted by those who were part of it; we should not automatically imagine that the bit-part actors were deeply discontented at what would seem to us to be injustice. There was a modicum of flexibility, in that an obvious nincompoop born to a famous actor could be persuaded to turn his hand to other things and might be replaced by means of adoption by a bright scion of a low-class acting family. In general, however, the system ensured that the mediocre actor would be the star provided he had been born appropriately, and the genius might spend a lifetime carrying spears if he had not. The system had the positive effect of imparting a sense of security to members of a notoriously insecure profession and to members of a class in Japanese society which was constantly subject to interference from above. It had a negative effect in that power and influence inside the theatre inevitably accumulated in the hands of the famous acting families, who therefore had a strong vested interest in preserving the *status quo*.[3]

There was also a strict hierarchy within single acting families. The eldest son was expected to succeed his father. One should also include in the families of famous actors the sons of other, often lower-class acting families, who had been accepted as disciples of the master. The personal relationships between these various family members were, as one might expect, vertically organised and strictly controlled. The master's word was law and could not be challenged. Blood relatives spent many hours in practical training. The disciples, when they were not fulfilling some menial duty for the master, often had to be content with learning by silently watching the master in rehearsal or performance. Meaningful dialogue between the master and his pupils about the interpretation of a given role or scene was almost unknown.

Japanese society from 1615 to 1868 was officially divided into four classes. These were, in descending order of precedence, the *samurai*, the peasants, the artisans and, at the bottom, the merchants. *Kabuki* actors were regarded as belonging to a class so low that it was not included in the official classification. Of the four official classes the merchants enjoyed a prosperity and financial influence out of all proportion to the low social position accorded them by the *samurai* rulers. There were thriving business communities in all the main towns and in the course of time a distinctive merchant culture came into being. It was in this cultural milieu that *kabuki* (and the woodblock print) developed and it is therefore not surprising to find a strong element of commercialism in this form of theatre.

The financing of a theatre was in the hands of the owner of the theatre or his agent, and the actors depended on these functionaries for their livelihood. Once funds had been raised for a season of productions, contracts were signed by the actors, usually of a year's duration. Money to back a season of plays was as hard to find in Japan as it has been anywhere. Unless a sympathetic backer with an interest in the theatre could be found, the terms on which money had to be borrowed were very hard. Everything had to be done to maximise the commercial success of a theatre. Much pressure was put on the actors to perform what the public wanted to see. It must be said that in general the actors responded readily to these pressures. Apart from the obvious fact that commercial success was in their interests, too, in the case of failure the theatre owner or manager might simply disappear, leaving the debts to be shouldered by the actors.

The commercialism of *kabuki* had two important consequences. Firstly, it became the custom only to perform selected scenes from plays, usually the scenes which showed off the leading actors' talents to best advantage. It also had the effect of confirming the subordinate position of the playwright, who worked as one of a team creating plays at the specific behests of the actors. Secondly, it reinforced the traditional idea of the theatre as a place for social gathering. Theatregoing was not only, or perhaps even mainly, to watch and appreciate the play. One almost always went in quite a large group and, as a full programme took most of the daylight hours, one needed various other services such as food and drink, toilets, and, if it was an all-male party, perhaps some feminine company. These were provided, not by the theatre itself, but by nearby tea-houses which, when the authorities allowed it, were linked to the theatre by covered passages. The tea-houses would delegate one of their employees to look after a certain group of patrons and throughout the performance these stewards would be bringing food and especially drink to their customers in the theatre or would be conducting them out of the theatre for a period of relaxation at the tea-house.

In the course of time clearly understood relationships developed between those who ran these ancillary services on the one hand and the theatre management and the actors on the other. Once these relationships had been established, they were difficult to break, even if the financial advantage shifted sharply either one way or the other. A whole nexus of such relationships developed which fully integrated the theatre into merchant society during the Edo period.

Thus although *kabuki* has rightly been described as a lively theatre form, the institutional framework within which it pursued its sometimes inspired artistic aims was essentially conservative and naturally tended to perpetuate itself as such.

This then was the situation in 1868 when, after two and a half centuries of seclusion, during which the country was officially closed to the outside world, a transfer of power (the Meiji Restoration) took place and the new government opened Japan to western culture. The years 1868 to 1912 are referred to as the Meiji period (the reign name chosen by the Emperor) and during these forty-four years Japan modernised herself economically and culturally at an astonishing rate.

By a happy historical coincidence the first thirty years of the new era witnessed the exceptional talents of three *kabuki* actors who revitalised the art of *kabuki* acting, generally acknowledged to have degenerated during the middle part of the nineteenth century. Each in his own way added depth to the portrayal of the character types in which he specialised and it was due mainly to these three actors that *kabuki* was able to establish itself as part of the new Meiji culture, perhaps more successfully than any other traditional art form.

It may be appropriate here to add a note on the two other forms of traditional Japanese theatre. Both the *bunraku* puppet theatre and *nō* are well known in the West and active in Japan today. For a century and a half before the Meiji Restoration, however, both were overshadowed by *kabuki*. Puppet theatre, after a burst of popularity under Japan's greatest playwright during the first quarter of the eighteenth century, soon gave way before the greater spectacle of *kabuki*. *Nō* was closely identified with the regime which was overthrown in 1868 and most performances were private affairs organised by the *samurai* rulers for their own enjoyment. *Nō* was much in disfavour in the early years of the Meiji period. Japanese theatre effectively meant *kabuki* at this time.

In Japanese writings comparing Meiji Japan with the West one often comes across a number of words for 'logic' or 'reason'. Many Japanese at the time perceived the difference between the Japanese and the western traditions in terms of structures based on or ignoring logic. If certain premises were given, certain consequences followed logically from them. The western theatre was seen as eminently logical compared with *kabuki*. Given that a play had a certain theme, the development of the plot and the characters and the emphasis of the acting would be a logical expression of it. Given that drama was an art form, those who went to watch it would do so because, logically, they wished to see a performance of a play. This type of argument has many ramifications which cannot be examined here, but even at this level of superficial generalisation one can see that it could have considerable force when applied to the situation in the theatre in immediate post-Restoration Japan. Travellers were soon visiting the West and observing its 'logical' theatre. Would they be satisfied with Japanese 'illogical' theatre – *kabuki* – when they returned home?

They were not, and *kabuki* was subject to reforms of three kinds during the Meiji period. Firstly, an actor of historical dramas attempted to inject a little logic into his performances. In 1878 Ichikawa Danjūrō 9th, the head of a famous acting family dating back to the seventeenth century, pioneered a form of play which became known as *katsurekigeki*, plays of living history. He carried out research into the historical background of the period plays which he was to perform and tried to ensure as much historical accuracy as possible in the costuming and the scenery. He also made his delivery more like that of everyday speech, particularly when performing new plays.

During the earlier 1870s Danjūrō had worked with an energetic theatre manager, Morita Kan'ya 12th, who had attempted to adapt some of the institutions of *kabuki* to the modern age. In his new theatre, opened in 1878, the activities of the various theatre stall-holders and the tea-houses were strictly controlled and a fixed price system imposed. A box office (previously the theatres had not always been able to exercise strict control over the sale of 'tickets') and toilets were installed. The powerful and influential were invited (with some financial inducement) to attend the theatre and many did so. Both Danjūrō and Kan'ya later joined some of the statesmen and scholars who had been introduced to *kabuki* through this theatre in establishing a Drama Reform Society (in 1886). Tsubouchi Shōyō, the great translator of Shakespeare, and Itō Hirobumi, the national father figure of Meiji Japan, were both members. The Drama Reform Movement was important in that it involved 'outsiders', hitherto kept strictly apart from the theatre. Some of these outsiders had had direct experience of western theatre, which they knew to be part of middle- and upper-class culture. No doubt they had been impressed by the elegant audiences in the theatres of London and Paris. The first Drama Reform Society criticised *kabuki* as being full of obscurity and nonsense, of obscenity and vulgarity. Japanese theatre should be reformed into a thing of delicate beauty, which could be watched by ladies and gentlemen without misgivings.

The third type of pressure towards change exerted on *kabuki* came from the new big business of Meiji Japan. It was realised, in particular by two energetic brothers, that entertainment organised along the lines of the new joint-stock companies could be very profitable indeed. In 1892 these two brothers formed a company which was later known by the name of

Shōchiku. Their company quickly took over the main theatres in the Kyōto–Ōsaka region and in the decade from 1905 to 1915 also gained almost complete control of all Tokyo theatres.[4] Under Shōchiku *kabuki* was certainly organised along eminently 'logical' western lines.

What effect did these changes have on traditional *kabuki* of the pre-Meiji period? The audiences did not like Danjūrō's 'living history plays' and during the last years of his life he reverted to classical *kabuki* performed in the time-honoured way. Only historians of the theatre remember *katsurekigeki* today. The Drama Reform Movement certainly succeeded in confirming the social acceptability of *kabuki*. Later historians have, however, credited it with little else. Its discussions were mainly confined to peripheral matters, such as seating arrangements or lengths of performances, and *kabuki* theatres came to adopt many aspects of western theatre architecture. In itself, however, the Drama Reform Movement only scratched the surface of *kabuki* tradition.

As the Shōchiku company established its near monopoly position, much of whether *kabuki* would fundamentally change or not would inevitably depend on the management policy of its new commercial masters. Shōchiku's policy, still followed today, can be summed up briefly as having three main elements: (1) to mount programmes which consisted of excerpts rather than complete plays, (2) to have the lead parts played by star actors, and (3) to encourage group theatregoing by offering special terms to organisations wishing to give their employees a treat.

The new commercialism had reaffirmed the old commercialism of the pre-Meiji period. The acting families remained pre-eminent and conservative. The audiences had shown they did not approve of change. To be sure they now sat in numbered seats, but they still ate from their lunch boxes and wandered in and out at will during the performance. The institutions of *kabuki* remained essentially what they had been before the Meiji Restoration. Progress still depended on the occasional actor of brilliance and initiative, but Danjūrō's experience had shown what limited scope even such an actor had.

It was in circumstances such as these that a group called Taishūza, Theatre of the Masses, was formed in 1929 by a number of *kabuki* actors. The group was closely linked to the Marxist arts movement and one of its leaders has subsequently suggested that it was not unconnected with the illegal Japan Communist Party.[5]

Until the formation of Taishūza the term communist drama could only be used in relation to the development of *shingeki*, new drama. During the Meiji period, while *kabuki* was responding at best only partially to the new age, various attempts were made to foster the growth of an independent modern drama – anti-traditional and anti-commercial. In 1924 these efforts came to fruition with the formation of the Tsukiji Shōgekijō, Tsukiji Little

Theatre. This company of young actors and actresses had their own very modern, western-style theatre, and performed a varied repertory of western drama in translation and, from 1926, plays by contemporary Japanese playwrights.[6]

Tsukiji Shōgekijō was mainly supported by progressive young intellectuals who were ecstatic in their welcome of its performances of German Expressionist plays. Most of those who patronised Tsukiji Shōgekijō were caught up in the craze for Marxism which had swept a large section of the Japanese intelligentsia off its feet. It was not only social scientists and historians who were affected. Novelists and poets and other creative artists saw in Marxism the solution to the problems which they faced in building a twentieth-century Japanese culture. Although one does not immediately think of poets and playwrights as good organisational material, it was felt necessary to set up elaborate organisations – societies, leagues, federations – to co-ordinate the activities of Marxist and Marxist-inclined writers and artists.[7]

The first national league of such writers was established in November 1925, and one of its sections was concerned with drama. The years 1926 and 1927 were years of great debate about Marxism and they also saw the formation of legal left-wing political parties and the resurrection of the still illegal Japan Communist Party. Many splits and realignments took place among the various political groupings, and the arts, including drama, were also subject to this tendency. By the end of 1926 all artists who wished to be acknowledged by the left-wing arts federation had to show their 'consciousness of a [Marxist] objective' in their works. Playwrights emerged who tried to accomplish this. After the mass arrests of suspected communists and sympathisers in March 1928 some unification was achieved in the left-wing drama movement and in 1929 a federation for drama alone, called PROT in the conventional abbreviation of its Esperanto name Proletarea Teatoro (Proletarian Theatre), was formed. By this time the political requirements made of 'proletarian' writers (as they may now be called following Japanese usage) had been narrowed, and 'proletarian realism', which enjoined seeing the world from a strictly communist viewpoint, was the creative method to be followed. In 1929 and early 1930 proletarian drama achieved some notable successes and its influence rapidly spread. Proletarian drama was now being performed by a large number of *shingeki* groups throughout Japan, including the larger of the two groups into which Tsukiji Shōgekijō had split in 1929. It would not be an exaggeration to say that proletarian drama almost monopolised the Japanese modern drama movement at this time. Late in 1930 the Japan Communist Party was successful in establishing total control over PROT and a new form of 'agit-prop' drama was initiated, whose object was strictly political. In 1932 a bold, but misguided, declaration of the movement's international links (with Moscow) brought on the intensified police drives that finally smashed the PROT organisation completely in 1934.

The positive results of the proletarian drama movement are usually only recognised in Japan by those who share its ideology. It cannot be denied that Marxism has deeply influenced all *shingeki* since the 1920s, for better or for worse. In 1934 the organisation for left-wing drama was smashed, but the idea lived on. The sometimes heroic, sometimes circumspect attitude of the artistic Left in the militarist later 1930s ensured that all subsequent playwrights would have to define their ideological position against the yardstick of Marxism.

During its heyday proletarian drama achieved some important successes, if its activities are seen in the context of the development of a modern drama. It brought people into the modern (as opposed to the commercial) theatre who had never been there before. In addition a brief but substantial unity was achieved between all the human elements of a stage production: the playwright, actors, audiences and critics, something unknown in *shingeki* previously. The immediate negative effect of communist domination of *shingeki* is clear. Progressively from late 1930 onwards the artistic character of drama was subordinated to political aims to such an extent that much dramatic writing became unrecognisable as plays in any previously accepted definition of the term.

The *kabuki* actors who founded Taishūza in 1929 were all young and most came from lower-class acting families. There had been a general slump in the entertainment business in 1929 and these actors had been the first to suffer. They had been forced by Shōchiku to accept salary cuts and even redundancies. They formed a society to protect themselves and then broke away from commercial *kabuki* altogether by founding Taishūza. Soon afterwards the new company was strengthened by the addition of actors from another group which had just disbanded. This was the Kokoroza (Soul Theatre, after Evreinov) which had been a partly *shingeki*, partly *kabuki* group since its inception in September 1925. It had been linked closely with the proletarian drama movement. Its leading member had been a *kabuki* actor named Kawarasaki Chōjūrō, who had travelled to the Soviet Union in 1928 and had returned an admirer of it. Chōjūrō had close connections with several of the leaders of the *shingeki* movement. Taishūza thus became a mixed *kabuki* and *shingeki* group, with professional *kabuki* and semi-professional *shingeki* actors. It continued Kokoroza's links with the proletarian literary movement and performed both modern and period plays. At about the same time the famous acting family headed by Ichikawa Ennosuke also broke away from Shōchiku and formed a company of its own. This was Shunjūza (Spring and Autumn Company), but its first production, of a Soviet play by Tretyakov, was a failure, and the venture collapsed soon afterwards. Ennosuke himself and a number of the other leading actors returned to the Shōchiku fold. The remainder joined with Taishūza to form Zenshinza in May 1931. It had thirty members at its foundation.[8]

The three acknowledged leaders of Zenshinza were Kawarasaki Chōjūrō, Nakamura Kan'emon and Kawarasaki Kunitarō. Chōjūrō was the only one from a major *kabuki* family. He had been trained both by Ichikawa Danjūrō 9th (perhaps the most famous *kabuki* actor of all time) and Ichikawa Sadanji 2nd. Chōjūrō might in his own right have been expected to become a famous actor. Kan'emon and Kunitarō were different. Kan'emon was the scion of a minor acting family and, though genius was seen in him at an early age, within the traditional *kabuki* system he would only ever have played small parts. Kunitarō was the son of an artist, and as an outsider trying to make his way in *kabuki* would similarly have had to be content with insignificant roles.

At the founding meeting of the new company the following resolutions were passed:

(1) The company's finances should be open and the actors' salaries, conventionally secret, should be decided in general meetings.

(2) The status system of [traditional] *kabuki* should be abolished.

(3) The equal rights of all members as human beings should be recognised. That is to say, the organisation of the company should be rationalised and members should help each other whatever the task in hand.

Zenshinza mounted its first production in June 1931. Three plays were performed, all newly written. The first was entitled *Kabuki Ōkoku* (The Kingdom of Kabuki) and was a satirical description of the contemporary world of *kabuki*. The audiences for this first production were very poor, sometimes numbering fewer than the actors. Every single member of the group was mobilised to distribute advertising material around Tokyo, but audiences for the second production in July were not much better. A subsequent tour to Okayama did not produce improved results. Financial difficulties and the problems associated with them caused many internal tensions during the first months. True to its declaration Zenshinza held frequent and sometimes very protracted meetings of the whole company to discuss the various issues.

Towards the end of 1931 Zenshinza began to realise that to survive it would have to compromise its principles to some extent. A backer was found for a December production, but he wanted Zenshinza members to appear in a play on a war theme. This was to be a joint production with a company which specialised in such plays. The leader of this second company, an actor famous for his performances of military heroes, was to head the cast. Needless to say, such an arrangement was anathema to many members of Zenshinza. A general meeting was held, and the issues were very clear. Either Zenshinza would not appear at all and risk going out of existence or it would have to swallow its principles. In the end a compromise was reached. Both the war play and a famous proletarian play were performed in the same programme. According to one of Zenshinza's main actors, the war play ended with a rendering of *Kimi ga yo*, the Japanese national anthem, and the proletarian play with the Internationale.[9]

Once Zenshinza had accepted the need for survival if they were to achieve anything at all, the way was open for the next compromise, this time of a more fundamental nature. There was a possibility of a longterm arrangement with the Ichimuraza, one of the three 'Edo theatres' with a history dating back to 1651. But the Ichimuraza management made various demands. The first was that traditional *kabuki* star billing should be restored. Up to this time on posters and advertising material the Zenshinza actors had been listed in strict alphabetical order as this was in accordance with the principles laid down at the founding meeting. The second demand was that Zenshinza should perform a play entitled *Chūshingura* (The Treasury of Loyal Retainers).[10] *Chūshingura* was written in the mid-eighteenth century and since that time has enjoyed unbroken popularity. In the modern period there have been numerous adaptations for film and television. The theme, which was based on a historical event, is the vengeance taken by forty-six *samurai* on the man who had caused the disgrace and death of their lord. Because of the precautions taken by their future victim nearly two years passed before the revenge was finally achieved, but during this time the forty-six never lost sight of their goal. Sustained by their feelings of loyalty towards their dead lord they sacrificed all that was dear to them in order to accomplish their object. The play ends with the burning of incense before the spirit of the lord who is now avenged. Historically, however, there is a sequel to the episode which adds significance to the legend of the Forty-seven (originally there had been forty-seven, but one had died). By exacting vengeance these *samurai* had placed themselves outside the law and they should have been punished. The military ruler of the time, however, impressed by their selfless and steadfast loyalty to their dead lord, was at first inclined to pardon them and then after discussion with his advisers granted them the honour of self-inflicted death by disembowelment (*seppuku* or *harakiri*). Glorification of the *samurai* virtues and the concept that a criminal act may be condoned if it is carried out in a spirit of loyalty and absolute sincerity have unpleasant associations with militarism in modern Japan and there was uproar in Zenshinza when the Ichimuraza's demand was made known.

But *Chūshingura* was performed, with great success, and star billing was reintroduced. Zenshinza soon became famous for its performances of *Chūshingura* and at least one classical *kabuki* play was included in all future programmes. By the end of 1932 plays with left-wing content had become

6A A scene from Zenshinza's first production of *Chūshingura* in 1932. Left: Nakamura Kan'emon; right: Kawarasaki Chōjūrō

6B Left to right: Nakamura Kan'emon, Kawarasaki Kunitarō and Kawarasaki Chōjūrō on stage together in 1956. The actor to the far right is Arashi Yoshisaburō

rare, but Zenshinza seemed to be firmly established. In October 1932 it managed to pay its actors a salary for the first time and everyone's salary was decided at a General Meeting. An acting school was organised and a monthly magazine published.

Zenshinza started in 1933 with a policy statement. It had four headings: (1) Rationalisation of *kabuki* plays; (2) Providing a stimulus for *kabuki*; (3) Training of progressive theatre people; (4) Productions of progressive plays. Four slogans were adopted for 1933: (1) Zenshinza to the masses with all speed; (2) From individualism to collectivism; (3) Face problems square on; (4) Once we decide on something, let's do it at once.

Productions continued. Zenshinza now had a national reputation and requests from provincial theatre managements started coming in. Classical *kabuki* and new plays were performed. One of the latter was a piece written especially to incorporate the latest popular hit song. In July Zenshinza signed a contract with Shōchiku, the very company whom the members had been execrating for the previous five years at least. In September the first Zenshinza film was made and contracts with two big film companies followed in 1935. Zenshinza was making a lot of money.

Towards the end of 1933 it drew more attention to itself by disregarding a hallowed *kabuki* tradition. It decided to perform *Kanjinchō* (The Subscription List) in spite of the fact that the leading role, Benkei, was regarded by the main Ichikawa family as their monopoly. Chōjūrō performed it without obtaining permission or paying royalties. The production was a triumphant success and ironically confirmed Chōjūrō's position as a member himself of a leading acting family. Zenshinza was now generally recognised in the *kabuki* world. To round the year off Zenshinza performed an adaptation of Schiller's *The Robbers*.

By now Zenshinza's repertory fell regularly into three categories: *kabuki*, *shingeki* and *taishūgeki* (popular drama), and this was to remain the pattern throughout the 1930s and early 1940s.

Notwithstanding the low position in the traditional hierarchy which its actors had originally occupied, Zenshinza built up a high reputation for superlative productions of classical *kabuki*. The company became known for a certain style of acting, referred to as *aragoto* (literally 'rough-stuff'), which had been the hallmark of Edo (Tokyo) *kabuki*, as opposed to the more realistic, even effeminate style of western Japan, during the pre-modern period. The leading actors of male roles in the main Ichikawa family were the principal exponents of this style and in 1840 Ichikawa Danjūrō 7th had established a corpus of plays whose leading roles required a high level of *aragoto* technique. These were known as the Eighteen Favourite Plays of Kabuki and became the exclusive preserve of the main Ichikawa family. *Kanjinchō* (one of the Eighteen) had been performed without permission, but in 1936 the Ichikawa accepted the realities of the situation and gave their approval for a Zenshinza production of a second play from the corpus. During the following years some of Zenshinza's most successful productions were of other plays from the Eighteen Favourites.

Most of the *shingeki* plays which Zenshinza performed were written by playwrights who in the 1920s had been associated with the proletarian drama movement. In the circumstances of late 1930s Japan, as expansionism abroad continued and the military tightened their hold on the government, plays with overtly left-wing themes could no longer be written and many left-wing playwrights turned to historical subjects. Fujimori Seikichi, famous in Japan for his earlier proletarian plays, was one such playwright, and from this period he wrote plays regularly for Zenshinza. In the early 1940s the company had a close association with a playwright named Mayama Seika. Mayama, who had been writing plays and working in the commercial theatre for over thirty years, had never himself been connected with the proletarian drama movement, but as a writer he was interested in historical personages whose lives had been governed by strong beliefs and convictions. Mayama and Zenshinza seemed ideally suited to each other and Zenshinza benefited greatly from its association with him.

The 'popular drama' section of Zenshinza's repertory was represented by both plays and films. It was the theatrical counterpart of *taishū-bungaku* (mass literature), a term coined in the 1920s to describe the literature produced to meet the demands created by the new mass-communications media. Popular drama in Japan was like popular drama anywhere in the West, highly commercialised, mostly superficial and usually melodramatic, but occasionally redeemed by a playwright of distinction. One such was Hasegawa Shin, whose swashbuckling but sympathetic gangland heroes found appropriate expression in the very successful productions of Zenshinza.

Zenshinza also made films during this period. Ten were shot between 1935 and 1940 under contract to Japan's two largest film companies, Nikkatsu (four) and Tōhō (six). Twice Zenshinza films were judged to be in the Best Ten films made during a certain year.

Not surprisingly Zenshinza was now financially secure. From the foundation of the group there had been hopes of one day creating an artistic community which would not only act together but also live together. In 1937 this was achieved by the construction of a large-scale study centre, including rehearsal rooms, offices and living accommodation. This was enlarged in 1940 and 1942. A community life was established in which everything was decided by general debate. It is said that at the beginning even the leaders of the group had to accept the standard of accommodation laid down as appropriate to the size of their families. All facilities for normal life were available at the study centre and everyone, including the wives and children, partook collectively in the activities of the company.

Internally, however, the years 1938 and 1939 were a time of great stress for Zenshinza, partly caused by the general circumstances of the theatrical world. After the China Incident of July 1937 (the start of Japan's war in China) *kabuki* for some reason went into such serious decline that the newspapers began to speculate on its complete collapse. *Shingeki*, on the other hand, began a remarkable run of success which lasted well into 1938. This situation posed some problems for Zenshinza. From the beginning it had performed *shingeki* plays and it included among its membership a number of actors and actresses who were only trained in *shingeki* techniques. But Zenshinza was still essentially a company of *kabuki* actors, and the great majority of the *shingeki* plays which it performed were set in the pre-modern period. The problem was complicated by the fact that, despite the vigilance of the censors, the successes which the *shingeki* companies were currently enjoying were mainly productions of plays which could be considered left-wing in inspiration. Apart from the content of the plays themselves, attendance at performances given by *shingeki* companies formerly linked with the proletarian drama movement was regarded by intellectuals as the only form of protest against militarism open to them. Encouraged by this indirectly expressed but genuine revival of the Left, the *shingeki* group within Zenshinza increased their resistance to classical *kabuki* and all reactionary themes and were successful in forcing the abandonment of a planned production of a Mayama Seika play concerning a famous modern Japanese general. Flushed with this success the group subsequently opposed the production of an eighteenth-century *kabuki* domestic drama, but this time Chōjūrō asserted his leadership and the play was performed very successfully. Several members of the *shingeki* group then resigned. Zenshinza had acknowledged itself as primarily a *kabuki* company. Chōjuro remarked, perhaps a little complacently, on the celebrations in Moscow to mark the thirtieth anniversary of Stanislavsky's death. Meyerhold, Stanislavsky's more revolutionary disciple and the idol of Japanese progressive theatre people in the 1920s, was already forgotten.

One may describe Zenshinza's record during Japan's wars in China and in the Pacific as either patriotic or time serving. Given the company's left-wing history and associations, perhaps the latter description is more appropriate. In 1939, with government support and encouragement, it performed a dramatisation of a novel advocating Japanese immigration into occupied Manchuria. This production was subsequently made into a film. Much of the film version was shot on location in Manchuria and a smiling Chōjūrō was photographed by the press shaking hands with a local Japanese official. Later the same year (1940), just after the two largest *shingeki* companies had been forced to disband by the authorities, who disapproved of their political coloration, Zenshinza identified itself even more strongly with the militarist government by performing a play as part of the celebrations to mark the 2,600th anniversary of the founding of the Imperial Japanese State. The performance won a prize.

During the last few months of the war, several Zenshinza members were called up and the rest were evacuated to the country, where they played to local communities. This experience was useful to Zenshinza when it found that within two years after the end of the war no Tokyo theatre was interested in full-length Japanese plays. There was more money to be made showing American films to the Allied Occupation forces. Zenshinza took to touring and specialised in playing Shakespeare to audiences of young people in school auditoria. The aim of this Youth Theatre Movement, as it was called, was to enable as many young people as possible to appreciate great works of world literature. In this Zenshinza was highly successful. It is estimated that the total audience for its production of *The Merchant of Venice* eventually reached a million.

And so to 7 March 1949 when after three days and three nights of almost continuous discussion at a General Meeting the members of Zenshinza decided that they would all join the Japan Communist Party (now, under the Occupation, legal for the first time in its existence). It was, Chōjūrō said at the time, a harder decision to take than the one which had resulted in the group being formed eighteen years previously. The event caused a sensation and much speculation about the motivation behind the decision. There were those who said that it was based on hard commercial calculation. The stronger of the two labour union federations was communist-backed and it could mobilise large numbers of members to watch Zenshinza performances. This would probably be more profitable than continuing the schools performances. It is true that the Left was riding high at the time and such considerations may well have played a part. However, audience numbers could hardly have been the sole topic of a three-day and night discussion. The slogans adopted by the company for 1949 had already included a reference to worker audiences and it is likely that in the new atmosphere of freedom of speech Zenshinza was moving to resurrect its early left-wing idealism. Perhaps also the linking of the company with the Communist Party in such a spectacular way was intended to compensate for what many saw as its collaboration during the war.

As predicted, joining the Japan Communist Party opened some doors for Zenshinza but closed many others. On the one hand touring performances (often linked with appearances in political demonstrations) attracted wide support from workers and their families in areas where the Communist Party was strong. On the other most headmasters would have nothing more to do with Zenshinza and police harassment began to increase. After the first heady few years of Occupation encouragement of democracy the 'Reverse Course' had started and American policy made the rebuilding of Japan as a strong economic power the first priority. Communism, although still legal, came under pressure again, and as in the 1920s the authorities regarded with especial concern the power of professional actors to influence audiences. Kan'emon was particularly pursued by the police in Hokkaidō and a number of (in retrospect) amusing incidents occurred. Make-up is a useful disguise for a hunted actor. The police were chagrined to discover on two occasions that they had arrested a musician in mistake for Kan'emon; even more humiliating was to be told that Kan'emon was actually appearing on stage, but to fail to capture him and then to arrest an actor playing the same part who was not Kan'emon at all. Kan'emon created a sensation by fleeing secretly to Peking and the early 1950s, while he was there, was a difficult period for Zenshinza.

By this time, however, the company had a wealth of experience in many different types of theatre: in large-scale performances of classical *kabuki* and modern plays, in films and latterly in touring. In the later 1950s and the 1960s this experience was used to good effect. Touring remained, and remains, central to Zenshinza's activities and five groups would be performing in different parts of Japan at any one time. Performances by the whole company in major urban theatres have not been neglected, and a new mass audience has been created through appearances on television. The repertory remains much the same as before, with some slight shift of emphasis towards domestic dramas in the *kabuki* productions. In 1974 Zenshinza, apart from its usual touring activity, performed in five major Tokyo theatres, it appeared on three different television channels, and it started three new projects in children's and study theatre. In 1976 it celebrated its forty-fifth anniversary and it is moving towards its fiftieth with confidence and vigour.

To return to the title of this article: is the communist *kabuki* created by Zenshinza a contradiction in terms?

Kabuki has been defined here as an art form which is fundamentally conservative. The institutional conservatism of the pre-modern period has been carried over into the modern age. Artistically *kabuki* was, and is, also conservative, but in the past century, as in the pre-modern period, artistic innovation and creativity have been possible when an actor of genius has appeared.

The use of the word 'communist' in the title is inexact in one sense. Although the joining of the Japan Communist Party by Zenshinza *en masse* was a sensational event, the group's ideological stand did not change significantly at that time. Historically Zenshinza grew out of the proletarian arts movement of the 1920s. Whatever one may say about the ideological shifts of this movement, its members were always united in the belief that art should be closely connected with a Marxist *Weltanschauung*. The ideological differences between those Marxists who actually joined the Japan Communist Party in the 1920s and those who did not do not seem very great to a non-Marxist. Ideologically the Left in Japan has been almost totally Marxist. Practically it has been both very difficult and very easy to become a member of the Japan Communist Party over the past fifty years. In the late 1920s such a step meant an underground life or certain imprisonment and possibly torture. In 1949 it was a limited act of faith which many people in all walks of life took. The circumstances of pre-war and post-war Japan are so different that it would be almost meaningless here to limit the definition of communism to membership of a communist party. Here it should be taken to refer to an ideological commitment to Marxism on the part of creative artists.

Marxism in 1920s Japan, however, had a further significance for Japanese intellectuals and writers. It was a stage, perhaps the final triumphant stage, in a modernisation process. Japanese proletarian literature developed at such an amazing speed that most of the West – excluding of course the U.S.S.R. – was left trailing behind. In this respect Japan had become more modern than the western countries which she had been emulating. Now logic was on Japan's side. Japanese Marxist writers of the 1920s considered the literature which they were writing to be more logical than anything comparable in western capitalist societies. Left-wing literature and arts were ahead of contemporary society, which was developing much more slowly. There was an element of idealism in the attitude of the writers towards their work and what they hoped to achieve by it.

The question of the title must now be rephrased: can a highly developed and deeply conservative pre-modern art form be subjected to changes based on a modern ideology and still flourish in a society which has itself been rather slow to change? And is the resulting art product recognisable as being both progressive and traditional, or is this impossible?

The answer to the first of the two new questions is not difficult. If one accepts that Zenshinza art fits the description given, then one cannot deny that this art has flourished and still flourishes in modern Japanese society. Zenshinza has not only performed *kabuki* successfully in large urban theatres; it has proved over nearly fifty years that high quality performances of *kabuki* plays can attract audiences from a great variety of different social groups. Through Zenshinza *kabuki* has flourished in Japanese society more widely than ever before.

The answer to the second question – whether Zenshinza's art is a successful fusion of communism and *kabuki* – is more complex, and requires that *kabuki* again be considered in its two main aspects, artistic and institutional. As has already been mentioned, *kabuki* art was essentially the art of the actor. Kan'emon has become Zenshinza's main spokesman on acting technique and he has written a number of books on the subject. In a recent work the following sentence occurs near the beginning: 'It is required of the actor that he pays particularly careful attention to polishing his technique of movement (what the audience sees) and delivery (what the audience hears), so that he can be seen and heard in every corner of the theatre.'[11] Elsewhere in this book he lays emphasis on ensuring that the audience obtains what it has paid for. These seem rather obvious points to make, but Kan'emon's practical approach is very different from much of the writing on modern drama *(shingeki)*, which has been highly theoretical. His ideas are in the long *kabuki* tradition of serving the audience – as opposed to involving, leading or educating it – and in this respect Zenshinza has been credited with standards as high as one would expect from commercial *kabuki* companies.

Kan'emon has also tried to go beyond this, and Stanislavsky's theory of acting has exerted a considerable influence on his thinking. He sees a danger that traditional *kabuki* technique alone can lead on the one hand to mannerisms and on the other to forced delivery and movement which may interrupt the smooth flow of the action. He hopes that the internalised psychological training of the Stanislavsky system will help prevent these shortcomings.

Perhaps more significant than this is the way in which Zenshinza has attempted to change some of the institutions of *kabuki* and in doing so has enabled them to be re-evaluated as part of the artistic aspect of the form. For example the strict system of the acting families was abolished and to a large extent casting is done according to individual talent (it is also a matter for corporate discussion and decision). A corollary of this has been that dominance of the production by the performances of one or two actors has been restricted. It would be difficult to claim that it has been completely eliminated, as Chōjūrō, Kan'emon and Kunitarō have usually played the lead parts, but Zenshinza is renowned for its ensemble playing, something almost unknown in commercial *kabuki*. This has been a natural by-product of breaking down the traditional relationships that have always existed between acting families and of establishing corporate life in their place.

Kawatake Shigetoshi, Japan's most eminent theatre historian, singles out the establishment of communal life as the most significant reform of Zenshinza.[12] It was a goal set by the company within a short time of its foundation and fought for hard. On the many occasions during the 1930s and 1940s when principles were heavily compromised, the justification was often given that by this means alone the financial basis of communal life could be made secure. By the simple fact of a group mainly of *kabuki* actors living together and attempting to establish a community based on equality and co-operation, the conservative aspects of *kabuki* art were bound to undergo some change.

A change has certainly taken place. It is very tempting to suggest that it is a change for the better – that a performance by a company of actors co-operating in conveying the meaning of the play is somehow superior to a performance where the lesser actors are only foils to the self-important and domineering lead actor. This would be a western view, but it is one which Japanese theatre critics have increasingly come to adopt. Not only has there been this qualitative change in *kabuki* performances as a result of Zenshinza's beliefs, but more Japanese than ever before are watching *kabuki* plays as plays rather than spectacles.

Zenshinza's left-wing stance has affected its general approach to *kabuki* in several ways. The logical left-wing position must be that *kabuki* is feudal, has no place in modern Japan, and cannot therefore be allowed to stay as it is. *Kabuki* actors traditionally have altered plays to suit themselves. Why not rewrite the plays in one's repertory in order to give them a left-wing interpretation? This is an extreme position, which was, briefly and unsuccessfully, adopted by Zenshinza in the 1950s. A more moderate variation of this is to give emphasis in the production to scenes where there is a more realistic representation of ordinary life in the pre-modern period. These are the scenes which commercial *kabuki* would usually omit, as there would be little scope for the lead actors to display their special talents. Zenshinza has often adopted this middle course and in doing so has earned the praise of critics who have admitted to gaining a new insight into the play as a whole. A third approach – the one now generally taken by Zenshinza – is to see *kabuki* historically as an art form produced in a feudal age by the creative energy of the social class most oppressed during that age (in Japan's case, officially at least, the merchants were at the bottom of the scale). *Kabuki* should thus be regarded as an expression of the resistance of that class to the oppressive feudal authority. As a socialist one can justify oneself in performing this drama if one can recreate it as it was. So one studies the circumstances in which a play, perhaps two hundred years old, was originally created and performed, and one tries to mount a new production which is historically accurate. Thus in a curious way the need to reconcile an artistic belief with a political ideology has brought about a re-examination of classical *kabuki* and an attempt to rediscover the original significance of its plays as works of art.

The preceding paragraph may sound like chop logic, but such theoretical problems have always been taken seriously in Japan. There has been a degree of youthful idealism in the Japanese Left which can appear to have a cynical aspect when an encounter with reality forces compromise. Zenshinza has had this idealism in good measure. Compromises were certainly made, but it was because Zenshinza was left-wing that communal life was established, equality practised and new productions of theatrical classics brought to millions of people. Zenshinza's 'communism' has shown itself able to reform *kabuki* without destroying it.

NOTES

1. For example: Earle Ernst, *The Kabuki Theatre* (New York: Grove Press, 1956); James R. Brandon, *Kabuki: Five Classic Plays* (Cambridge, Mass: Harvard University Press, 1975); A. C. Scott, *The Kabuki Theatre of Japan* (London: Allen & Unwin, 1955); Zoë Kincaid, *Kabuki – the Popular Stage of Japan* (London: Macmillan, 1925); Charles J. Dunn and Bunzō Torigoe, *The Actors' Analects* (Tokyo and New York: Columbia University Press, 1969).
2. Ichikawa Danjūrō 1st (1660–1704), Sakata Tōjūrō 1st (1647–1709) and Yoshizawa Ayame (1673–1729).
3. There are exceptions to all generalisations. In the mid-nineteenth century the son of a theatre tobacco-stall-holder succeeded through dogged determination in becoming a star actor (Ichikawa Kodanji), but such men were very rare.
4. Ishizawa Shūji, *Shingeki no Tanjō* (The Birth of New Drama) (Tokyo: Kinokuniya Shinsho, 1964), 8off.
5. Toita Kōji ed., *Taidan Nihon Shingekishi* (Dialogues on the History of Japanese New Drama) (Tokyo: Seiabō, 1961), 185.
6. There is only one book in English concerning *shingeki:* J. Thomas Rimer, *Kishida Kunio, Toward a Modern Japanese Theatre* (Princeton University Press, 1974). See also: A. Horie-Webber, Modernisation of the Japanese Theatre; the *Shingeki* Movement', in W. G. Beasley ed., *Modern Japan* (London: Allen & Unwin, 1975), 147–65. For Tsukiji Shōgekijō see: B. Powell, 'Japan's First Modern Theatre, Tsukiji Shōgekijō and its Company, 1924–26', *Monumenta Nipponica*, xxx, 1(1975), 69–85.
7. See: George Tyson Shea, *Leftwing Literature in Japan* (Tokyo: Hōsei University Press, 1964).
8. Information concerning Zenshinza is taken mainly from Sakamoto Tokumatsu, *Zenshinza* (Tokyo: Ōdosha, 1953).
9. Kawarasaki Kunitarō, *Engeki to wa Nani ka* (What is Drama?) (Tokyo, Popurasha, 1974), 86–7. This incident is not mentioned by Sakamoto.
10. The full title is *Kanadehon Chūshingura*. There is an English translation: Donald Keene, *Chūshingura* (New York and London: Keen, 1971).
11. Nakamura Kan'emon, *Kabuki no Engi* (Kabuki Technique) (Tokyo: Miraisha, 1974), p. 16. My translation.
12. Kawatake Shigetoshi, *Nihon Engeki Zenshi* (A Complete History of Japanese Drama) (Tokyo: Iwanami Shoten, 1959), p. 950.

The political in Britain's two national theatres

BERNARD CRICK

The Royal Shakespeare Company, in its theatres in London and Stratford, meets the obligations of a national theatre as comprehensively as does the company at work in the new complex of theatres on the south bank of the Thames. These obligations were formulated in the National Theatre Committee Handbook of 1909:

   (i) to keep the plays of Shakespeare in repertoire
   (ii) to revive whatever else is vital in English classical drama
   (iii) to prevent recent plays of great merit from falling into oblivion
   (iv) to produce new plays and to further the development of modern drama
   (v) to produce translations of representative works of foreign drama, ancient and modern
   (vi) to stimulate the art of acting through the varied opportunities which it will offer to members of the company.

In considering the intricate relationships between drama and society in Britain in the 1970s, we will naturally regard with special interest the ways in which these heavily subsidised national institutions treat political issues.

I write as a political philosopher who happens to be an addicted theatregoer. I have reviewed some of the plays discussed here, but in conditions of relative leisure.[1] Unlike newspaper reviewers, therefore, I have always been able to read the text or acting script (after the performance, on principle and also to preserve the basic dramatic joy of surprise). And unlike most literary critics, I shall limit myself here to a discussion of specific recent productions. The choice of plays may therefore seem rather random, but the procedure has some advantages. It should reveal how our national companies perceive politics in plays in general, rather than in the specifically 'political' theatre, or in drama of 'commitment'. One of my main points is that politics is important in plays which do not invite those labels.

Literary critics sometimes worry that drama is debased or simplified by intense political commitments. While this is not necessarily so, I share their worry, since political sincerity is no excuse for bad drama. Indeed I add to it a concern of my own craft: that dramatising politics in some contemporary ways can debase politics. A strident, wholly partisan view of politics expressed in one-sided dialectic is essentially undramatic. The perennial is reduced to the topical, the transitory and the arbitrary. I invoke what I conceive to be the tradition of Aristotle, Machiavelli (of *The Discourses*), Montesquieu, J. S. Mill, Tocqueville, and Hannah Arendt – a tradition that sees politics as a way of mediating between conflicts of values and interests: ideally, the mediation elevates (Hegel), but if that is not to be, at least a practical, humane compromise can be struck (Burke). Elsewhere I have defined politics as the creative conciliation of naturally differing interests and ideals.[2] I would add that I expect there to be politics even in the classless society. We will never be rid of it: it is a perennial human activity that reflects our freedom (whether as gift or curse) to choose different preferences and values. We can choose better or worse, but the manner of our choosing should be *political*: that is, through public discussion, recognition of alternatives and other people's perspectives, and acceptance of reasonable procedures, not through command based on a single view of authority enforced by power.

The inference is clear. Politics, in this sense, has many similarities with drama. Both involve contrast, clash or conflict of differing viewpoints, values or characters, often in changing or different circumstances. Both of them may find or seek some resolution, but the manner of reaching that resolution is what makes a decision political rather than autocratic or arbitrary, or play a political drama rather than propaganda, or 'triumph', or *tableaux vivants*. Most dramas, indeed, have some politics in them, in this sense, however small or incidental.

The image conjured up by 'political theatre' is all too often the converse both of what I mean by 'political' and of what I mean by 'drama'. 'Committed theatre' is, indeed, a better phrase; for politicians or *le tempérament humain et politique* are often the prime target of the committed playwright. For him, all important questions have already been decided: it remains only to dramatise the answers so that people (the theatregoing public? the streets?) can understand them better, be proselytised by them or, if the audience are the converted already, kept on heat. I am far from saying that 'committed theatre' cannot on occasion make good drama. The ends may be pre-judged, but the means may be open to debate, permissible objects for play. For example, the RSC recently put on David Edgar's *Destiny*. Having heard that it dealt with the rise of fascism in the West Midlands, I felt sure it would be awful; but it turned out to be what I had often imagined but never expected to see: a strongly committed left-wing play able to understand and empathise with different types of fascism in conflict with one another, each well embedded in rich and diverse characters. Or consider Shaw. His deliberate propaganda can lead to good drama because he allows his devils so many good lines, and gives them memorable characters, indeed considerable intellectual dignity. They may sometimes be caricatures, but they are caricatures of plausible ideas, not simply of class interest and class malice, as are the cardboard figures of 'them' in agit-prop theatre. On the one hand, there is Brecht's profound and dramatic *Galileo*, on the other the shallow claptrap of *The Days of the Commune*. On the one hand, there are the genuine political dilemmas, necessity of state against character and loyalty, of John Arden's *Armstrong's Last Goodnight*; but on the other, the strident, stereotyped rant of *The Ballygombeen Bequest*.

So to look at our two national companies is to allow a chance, for once, to see how well political themes are handled in the best plays, classical or modern, whether politics is a main theme or only incidental. So much good drama already contains good politics. I mean, of course, a good understanding of politics. For politics is concerned with dilemmas and alternatives, with the clash of values and interests, and with uncertainties as to which is which. Nothing is more dramatic than politics. But whereas the *theatricality* of politics is understood all too well, very many 'political' playwrights and producers mistake commitment for politics, or the end of an argument for the beginning. Drama thrives on moral dilemmas. If we think that there should be no moral dilemmas, or no 'problematic' after the revolution, then indeed we *ought* to chase out the poets and the playwrights or turn them simply into official foghorns.

One further justification for only considering the RSC and the National Theatre Company: here we can observe the effect of political material on a very general audience, not a politically selected gathering (as in the fringe, or Unity Theatre of yore). We should never forget a simple difference between drama and other art forms – which accounts for so much of the peculiar and perennial tension between the State and the Stage – that a play must be performed in public, usually to an unrestricted audience. We sit and we see how our fellow-citizens react, and reactions are hard to control, not simply when political satire is overt, but also, say, when the RSC Feste is played as a professional comic, desperate to keep his job – a little jab of reality which visibly disturbed and stirred many of the audience. We should never forget that a performance involves not just the audience watching the actors and the actors reacting to the audience but also the audience – as in any *polis* – anxiously watching each other.

FEUDAL POWER

Whether politics is seen as of perennial or only of topical problems, is well revealed in productions of Shakespeare's histories. Directors in our national companies have, on the whole, shown considerable political sense. The politics is there in the text – is it not? What a bore it used to be thought. But Hall, Barton, Hands and Nunn have, with their respect for the text and for language, not for partisan reasons, brought it back to life. In rescuing so many of the minor parts and the minor lines from the neglect of the bad old star system, they have necessarily repoliticised plays that used to be seen as simply dramas of noble characters, flawed, floored or overawed. The RSC's Roman plays of 1973–4 are a fine example, particularly *Julius Caesar* and *Antony and Cleopatra*. Trevor Nunn gave them a political unity: political firstly in the sense that he saw them as plays primarily about politics, even in their original intention (so much Elizabethan political thought used or was possessed by the many-sided image of Rome) and, secondly, as ways for the contemporary theatre to discuss the perennial issues of politics.

Nunn did not try to twist Shakespeare into being topical, as did Jonathan Miller, or actually abuse him for not being topical, as does Charles Marowitz: he simply brought out perennial issues of justice versus reason of state. Having heard that they were 'political', I began to attend with my usual prejudices. I feared at the worst that it would be all 'production', and that the politics of the Romans would simply be those of the director's personal affirmation: the telling us what to think, or the feedback mirror of trendy sentiments, such as the great rubbish of the RSC's *US* Vietnam pantomime of 1966, which was all burning Buddhist monks, butterflies and wicked Yankees. At the best, I feared the more subtle mistake of John Barton in the *Wars of the Roses* or 'the matter of England' plays, that politics is simply a struggle for power, one noble beast tearing another down, in a purely Hobbesian world of 'life is a restless search of power after power that ceaseth only in death'. Somehow Barton missed the level of political ideas: the feudal preconception of loyalty expected and loyalty betrayed, of honour upheld and honour sacrificed for interest.

In the Romans, however, I saw, and kept on going back to see, Shakespearian theatre and thought about Shakespeare of a very high order indeed: productions poised between bringing out all that he meant and pointing up certain things that should peculiarly worry us.

Only in *Julius Caesar* did the politics go wrong. Today we are very unsubtle in our perceptions of different types of autocracy. We are such good democrats, that we hump together crudely all types of autocracy. A feudal nobility is one thing, the Roman senatorial class another; but both had in common a political situation in which no one man, not even a feudal king, not even a Roman consul, could become dictator (a constitutional office) and assume absolute authority without gaining the support of powerful fellows. There was no army to be commanded as one: feudal levies and Roman legions followed their local commanders who had to woo them and give them constant success and rewards.

What we feared partly happened. Caesar was a fascist. He was surrounded by guards dressed in black leather who drilled with Prussian precision, not with feudal or Roman practicality. The programme notes got it half right by stressing the enormity of 'dictator for life', but then they betrayed their misunderstandings of autocratic senatorial or oligarchic politics by including photographs of Mussolini and (to show no fear or favour) of Mobutu – quite the wrong images. This instantly weakens the play, for tyrannicide is now prejustified and the retribution only follows because of the impure motives of Cassius (envy) and Brutus (pride). But surely the act itself must at least be questionable for the play to work well? The political reflection upon a Roman or a feudal notable who has become protector and who may seek to become king (so close to the Bolingbroke theme) is coarsened if the director suggests that there is no doubt at all that Caesar got what was justly coming to him. The text shows Caesar dedicated to the good of Rome, proud and wilful certainly, perhaps in danger of being a tyrant, very likely to be so if he listened to Antony too much, but far from certainly so. Also, as his perceptive remarks on Cassius show, he is no fool. That he is a lesser man than the role he plays only makes him like Richard II or Henry IV, conscious of the politician's need to act: it does not, in a modern radical sense, 'unmask' or expose him as unequivocally a tyrant.

The temptation of contemporaneity was, however, too great. Caesar becomes a fascist, so the moral dilemma of to kill or not to kill almost vanishes, and Cassius and Brutus merely coincide: the issue between them and Antony–Octavius is simply settled by force of arms, the strongest winning. As in *Henry VI*, politics is then simply portrayed as a struggle for coercive power. And psychological interest in the play has then to be sustained by a wholly eccentric reading of the stoic Brutus as an over-educated neurotic and youth-of-our-times who loses his cool in a most un-Roman way.

In spite of these flaws in the actual content of political thought, no one could mistake from the production that Shakespeare expected his audience to discuss seriously the ethics of tyrannicide and to see analogies with their own politics in the republican versus oligarchical debate. It argues considerable political sophistication that *Julius Caesar* could be written and played in Elizabethan London (just as it does for President Nyerere personally to have translated the play into Swahili).

A proper sense of topicality was conveyed by the very speed of the production. It marched at a remorseless and frightening pace, as of events beyond control and men struggling vainly to contain them or catch up. And Antony is established in his turn, for if Caesar is a fascist then Antony is a pure opportunist; whereas surely Antony is, for all his faults, a loyal man and, perhaps because of his self-indulgence, a more human man than the ice-cold operator Octavius – there is even a suggestion, perhaps, that he is more human than Brutus. His repeated 'honourable men' is not just an unworthy sneer at Brutus's alleged hypocrisy, but is a genuine lament for the dying feudal world of honour, loyalty and friendship, here violated by the killing of one's master; that world which Falstaff blows away in his speech on honour.

Despite this, *Julius Caesar* could be made to follow from *Coriolanus* because everywhere the republican symbols were stressed – SPQR indeed. Proud trumpets accompany the assassination of Caesar which became a Delacroix-like tableau of tyrannicide, *sic semper tyrannis*, as even Lincoln's assassin cried. They repeated the assassination scene in slow motion, once in triumph, and then yet again as a nightmare to haunt with its moral ambiguity for both actors and audience. Here Trevor Nunn was morally so right: realising the necessity of violence, but never revelling in it. In both plays, the power, the sheer physical power, of the people, is never far from the stage, whether for good or ill, spontaneous or arranged.

Antony and Cleopatra is also political all through, even though now the people are absent as a force. Common soldiers speak clear political common sense right at the beginning, and these lines were emphasised massively:

> *Philo.* Nay, but this dotage of our general's
> O'erflows the measure ...
>   His captain's heart
>   ... reneges all temper,
> And is become the bellows and the fan
> To cool a gipsy's lust. Look where they come!
> Take but good note, and you shall see in him
> The triple pillar of the world transform'd
> Into a strumpet's fool. Behold and see.
>
>   (I, i, lff.)³

And see we did, the most marvellously political Cleopatra with an 'infinite variety' indeed of charms and lusts. 'The old ruffian' Antony could not keep up with her and she hardly seemed to know in her own mind whether she was coming out of policy or going out of passion. 'Know you not me?' she cries when he thinks she is betraying him to Octavius. But she cannot answer that herself, neither Janet Suzman as Cleopatra nor, I suspect, the closest student of the play. For the gipsy is a very mixed up young middle-aged woman indeed, and was rightly played as such. The only trouble is that then one got carried away by all the imperial symbols (not republican now) of the production, as well as by the fast pace of the finely pointed political dialogue in all the minor characters, so that one sat there nearly shouting: 'Go home, you fool, mend your fences. Rome needs you! pay attention to politics!' One sides with his unfortunate loyal soldiers, but it can hardly be a tragedy simply of personal sloth and political ineptitude.

Since it cannot really be shown, as there was some hint at doing, that Cleopatra is as clear-headed as Octavius in wanting the whole world for herself and is simply using Antony, then the gipsy must also have majesty, must be played as something of a female Henry VIII, so that her fall and death are even more terrible than Antony's. An invented pageant of their crowning in gold as gods is inserted before the first words of the play, presumably to build up the 'majesty and mystery' of kingship or charismatic authority lacking in the actual acting of the part. And they must have between them – Shakespeare did know about it – a real love, indeed a mysticism of love.

How odd now to remember that Olivier and Vivien Leigh in 1951 could simply do the play as a love duet, if in Roman rather than Illyrian dress, and that most of the bit parts were then either cut or gabbled through. But now, as often, in restoring it as a play with so many great small parts and complex cross-currents, the director has allowed the balance to swing too far. Surely much of the play is about the rival claim of politics and love, of the public and the private; it is not *just* about the neglect of politics for sexual passion. Is this not also a message for our time?

But again, despite some uncertainties, possibly weaknesses in the principals, the play was made magnificent by that quite admirable team-playing which is the hallmark of the RSC. Every small part was given its full value and the play emancipated from the stars in all sorts of good ways which reveal Shakespearian thoughts too often lost, particularly political thoughts. One example is the first scene of act III. Antony's captains have won a battle in Syria, and Silius urges Ventidius to press on to Mesopotamia.

> Oh, Silius, Silius!
>   I have done enough. A lower place, note well,
> May make too great an act, for learn this, Silius:
>   Better to leave undone than by our deed
> Acquire too high a fame when him we serve's away.

And there is the common soldier who speaks out of turn but who is so right about not fighting at sea. Again, on the eve of Agincourt, the common soldier sees the odds more clearly: the king has got them into such a mess that only heroism will save them. No blame is attached to Ventidius and the others for deserting Antony when his cause is lost – as if Shakespeare anticipates Thomas Hobbes in suggesting that 'honour' and 'loyalty' have been the great killers of men, so that obedience should rationally go to him who can effectively enforce the peace – even the cold and nasty Octavius. But there are feudal distinctions there too: the close personal follower, the member of a noble household, is in a different position, as even Hobbes recognises. Enobarbus is not just a 'captain', he is a companion. Rationally, like a good bourgeois utilitarian, he deserts when all is lost. But unlike all the others he suffers, he is torn; the old ethic of feudal loyalty has him in its deadly grip: so that when Antony forgives him 'nobly', he kills himself miserably, not even quickly and cleanly.

Images and customs of autocracy are, thus, as peculiar and varied as those of democracy. They cannot be lumped together, as they were in *Julius*

Caesar. Caesar as *princeps* was top dog, but top dog among champions. Obviously those absurd fascist *squadristi* of the Stratford stage could not accompany him into the Senate House. He could not be well-guarded, for he was a politician in enforced and sweaty intimacy with fellows. But he was thinking of going too far. If I had wanted a topical image for the programme, I would not have been so seeming-daring as to have a photo of poor old Musso, the dictator, but I would have been really daring and more accurate by showing Nixon, Wilson, Heath, or even De Gaulle – bad and arrogant politicians, but politicians nonetheless.

TUDOR POWER

The question of whether to adopt a political approach or an a-political approach to many classical plays is a false question. The real task is to discover what kind of political assumptions motivate the play, always having in mind the difficulty of a modern audience who will probably assume that feudal kingship was autocracy and not immediately grasp (without the director's help) the sharpness of conflict between the different political ethics of honour, loyalty and reason of state when the three coexist in the same dramatic situation. Or we will comfortably and liberally think of all 'reason of state' as wicked, rather than – as Shakespeare and his audience critically assumed – often a path towards peace, justice and order against the feudal anarchy of honour and dynastic or personal loyalties. (They were connoisseurs of the doctrine of 'the lesser evil', while we are so often hypocrites, enjoying its benefits and denouncing or denying its claims.) These issues can be brought to life by a relatively straightforward playing of the *Henry IV* plays and a particular reading of *Henry V*. Indeed, the plays, as produced by Terry Hands at the RSC in 1975–6, stressed a general modern dilemma: whether to follow an ethic of honour and loyalty or one of utility.

I would like to have offered him for the programme notes (which can be so helpful, or not) a passage from Hobbes to follow that speech of Falstaff's:

> *Falstaff.* ... honour pricks me on. Yea, but how if honour pricks me off when I come on? How then? ... Who hath it? He that died o'Wednesday ... Therefore I'll none of it. Honour is a mere scutcheon. And so ends my catechism.
>
> (*I Henry IV*, v, i, 139 ff.)

> Honour consisteth onely in the opinion of Power. Therefore the ancient Heathen did not thinke that Dishonoured but greatly Honoured the Gods, when they introduced them to their Poems, committing Rapes, Thefts and other great but unjust or unclean acts ... Scutcheons, and Coats of Arms hæreditary, where they have any eminent Priviledges, are Honourable; otherwise not: for their power consisteth either in such Priviledges, or in Riches, or some such thing as is equally honoured in other men. This kind of

Honour commonly called Gentry, has been derived from the Antient Germans.

(Thomas Hobbes, *Leviathan*)[4]

One suspects that old Thomas Hobbes may have had Falstaff's speech in mind when he turned his mockery against honour, the conceptual lynch-pin of the feudal ethic. 'Brutus *was* an honourable man', while 'Yours in the ranks of death' was what traditional apologists for political obligation had worked towards; reasons and beliefs that would lead men to follow their lord and master, or at least the oath-bound cause, to death or glory and not to count the cost to themselves. But Falstaff, and Hobbes in his philosophical treatise, were among the first to popularise and to justify a purely prudential utilitarian obligation.

To Hobbes the only aim of civil society is to preserve peace and individual life. 'When armies fight', he disarmingly observed, 'there is on one side or both, a running away; yet when they do it not out of treachery but fear, they are not esteemed to do it unjustly but dishonourably.' Jack Falstaff was never traitor, only coward. I have a fancy that the turncoat Stanley must have been very close to the hearts of Hobbes, Shakespeare and of Shakespeare's audience; that Stanley who sat on his horse waiting at Bosworth Field until he could bring peace at last by changing sides; by deserting his declining King, he made what had been a probable victory for Henry Tudor certain, total, and lastingly decisive. Having been obsessed for some time with Sir John Falstaff's anticipation of the philosophy of Hobbes, I was happy to hear Terry Hands remark that they kept the character of Henry VII in mind throughout rehearsals and they tried to imagine what kind of relationships an Elizabethan audience would have seen between Bolingbroke and Hal, the progress from *Henry IV* to *Henry V*.

The plays got the now familiar RSC treatment in producing historical sequences in Shakespeare: (1) unity of design; (2) an overall conception linking the plays and treating them as a larger unity; (3) a sense of politics and a stress on contemporary relevance; (4) a great quickness of pace; (5) clear speaking and faith in the text; and, above all else, (6) much care and thought for each minor part and scene in ensemble playing of the highest possible order.

The key lay in the treatment of the character of Henry IV himself. He was played by a character actor, Emrys James, which in itself was a useful shock. Traditionally the part has usually been played as epitomised by Sir John Gielgud in Orson Welles's film, *The Chimes at Midnight*: the noble, tortured, sleepless, high-minded king, worried for the peace of England when he dies leaving such a son, and remorseful for some act of usurpation, far in the past, by which Bolingbroke had gained the crown. The audience is so sympathetic to this good king that, while they think it very noble of him to worry about some slight skulduggery in the past (killing a king), they so readily see that the noble Henry IV is more of a king in character and ability than was Richard that they think all the better of him for crying over the spilt milk (royal blood). If it were not for the poetry, this reading of the part would invite a director to cut some of those sleepless scenes, since the audience might even become rather impatient at his going on so about those far-off days (a decade before).

Emrys James, however, portrayed him as politician Bolingbroke, boasting to his son of how well he played the king and courted the citizens compared to dead Richard; and still playing the king to keep his head and to ensure his clan's succession, which happened to be the best security for peace in the realm. We see him almost livid with jealousy at news of Hotspur's victories, but when Hotspur speaks his famous speech, 'When I was dry with rage and extreme toil / Breathless and faint, leaning upon my sword,' Bolingbroke first eyes him with malign cynical admiration (as if 'what fine acting, what a figure for a prince's part!'), but then openly scoffs, laughs in his face when he gives the heroic account of his brother-in-law Mortimer's fight with Glendower. 'This vile politician Bolingbroke' (Hotspur's words) can admire good resolute propaganda, but his old tummy turns with disgust to see that this roaring lad actually believes what he says. The King, after all, flatly says, 'He never did encounter with Glendower.' And provocatively adds, 'I tell thee, he durst as well have met the devil alone.' John Gielgud spoke all this remotely, as if the noble King had been given false reports traducing such men of honour and was repeating them in good faith. Emrys James said it as if it were true, and as if everyone there knew it to be, including Northumberland. The 'honour' of Hotspur is made to look sincere, indeed, but destructive, anachronistic and foolish. The audience is torn two ways, neither of them utterly nice – and that is politics. This is in the text. And this is the kind of political rather than heroic eye that the modern RSC directors have always had.

Now, of course, Emrys James did rather overdo it. To see him walking round the Northumberlands in circles cackling, was, at first, to think that he was still playing his mad King John. It took me a few minutes to see that he was over-registering the cynical politician, not the mad tyrant. But the dramatic limitation of the traditional reading of the part is that if the King has already reached (apart from insomnia) a substantial serenity and inner release from the sins of his youth, because of his hard work in the prime business of kingship, namely care for the peace of the realm, this contradicts the dramatic point that such release can only be achieved by his son, not by his Bolingbroke self at all. The kingship Hal knows he will have to assume is a very practical kingship, which needs the myths of honour and divine stewardship, but is political, prudential and bourgeois in spirit. Hal relaxes amid backstage company while waiting for his call to take the centre of the stage. He indulges Falstaff and is indulged by him.

Falstaff here personifies irresponsibility, perpetual childish naughtiness and adolescent indulgence (so comic in an old man). It was plainly necessary for England for Hal to cast the fat knight away; but the Prince was not corrupted by an evil Falstaff – that is only what his father said in family quarrels held in public. He was simply indulging himself in irresponsible company, acting irresponsibly between bouts of duty, before the institution closed in totally around the man, making it necessary for him to act the king twenty-four hours a day, even act an heroic king in the pattern of Hotspur if policy dictated transmuting civil into foreign strife.

If we assess the Stratford *Henrys* by the six features of production I have identified above, it will emerge how sensible (with one bad lapse) is their reading of the political relationships.

Firstly the unity of design. I put design before the intellectual conceptions because this is a director's theatre. One has the feeling that everything follows from the director having thought of certain key symbols or patterns. In the *Wars of the Roses*, it was steel: great hanging, square screens of grey and bronze metal and the frightening clash and echo of medieval two-handed swords with five- or six-foot steel blades. In the Romans, it was symbols of power, republican then imperial, the fasces, the banners with SPQR, but used economically, as ever, with a very few realistic objects on a long, bare stage. Now in the *Henrys*, the selective realism of dress stressed the propaganda and mythology of kingship, the putting on and taking off of rich, ceremonial, sometimes sacred garments, but work-a-day leisure gear, as it were, underneath (and sometimes battlegear): a great stress on actors acting actors. Something like all those shows or pageants of power put on by or for the great Queen, to mask a more precarious reality. In *Henry V* this was carried to an extreme. The first scene at the English court was played in modern rehearsal dress – track suits and sweaters. Only the Ambassador is in medieval magnificence. But as war is decided upon, the nobility of England don their costumes. And parts of the King's 'costume' are his speeches reverting back to feudal 'honour', donned for necessity of national war. The common soldiers are, however, seen as the Old Contemptibles, dressed half-way between battledress of the 1940s and the padded jackets of Brecht's own definitive production of *Mother Courage*; and they talk all too realistically about the odds and the motives. This worked well. Chorus's appeal to our imagination works when we are aware of the props. The Chorus himself remained in modern dress throughout. And it is Emrys James – the actor who played Henry – again. So Henry IV introduces his son's triumph, his seeming eradication of the curse on Bolingbroke and his issue, just as in the first part of *Henry IV*, the King, after his opening scene, actually stays on stage, still and shadowy, to watch sadly his son wake Falstaff in the tavern and plan the Gad's Hill Massacre.

Secondly, an overall conception seemed to be there, because of the overall design, but was in fact harder to sustain. The play of *King Henry V* does, after all, have almost as little relationship to the *Henry IV*s as any of the comedies do to each other. And the two parts of *Henry IV* really are two different and self-contained plays. The prince's reconciliation to the tasks of kingship is fully resolved in Part One and even the rejection of Falstaff is clearly implicit. Part Two does have some marvellous scenes, but it is episodic and repetitive. The temptation to treat the scenes as separate set pieces is greater. As a result, there was too much comic business between Shallow and Silence, so that the humour and sadness of Sir John's affable Hal-like condescension to these clowns, under the shadow of his own impending overthrow get lost or muted. But a play is a play and takes place on a stage, not in the mind of a scholar. The two plays of *Henry IV* can be played as if one, and in the theatre they can gain by such treatment.

Thirdly, a sense of politics, even down into the lesser parts, and a stress on contemporary relevance were there unmistakably. Northumberland and Worcester, for once, were three-dimensional, power-hungry men: Worcester resolute, Northumberland fearful, no mere attendant lords. The full text of the conspiracy scene at Southampton was given which, though hardly Shakespeare's finest hour, shows both the *politique* needed to export domestic quarrels to France and the risks involved. And having seen war-like Douglas in *Henry IV Part One*, one was inclined to listen seriously to the arguments in council against not going abroad at all with Scotland still unsubdued.

Fourthly, the great quickness of pace, sustained by the bare stage, and the familiar RSC convention of one group of actors coming on stage before the others are off; and now, beyond that, sometimes lingering and listening throughout the next scene. They not merely had a Brecht-like alienation effect, but were also, when seen in character, threatening. The thrust and rake of the stage (a gradient of 1 in 12) sustained both the pace and the sense of proximity without any of those overworked gimmicks of galloping through the audience. This was marvellous theatre: the sense of events hustling men.

Fifth, clear speech and faith in the text were never sacrificed to business, action, 'production': there was none of those signs that actors and directors are convinced the audience does not want to listen, and should therefore be given something to watch. I still look back with anger to all the naked bottoms and bongo drums with which the National Theatre in 1973 successfully destroyed the words and meanings of the *Bacchae*. In the *Henrys* we were given an almost complete text of the plays; and when there were difficult words or concepts, they were not smothered in stage business. On the contrary, for a moment the swift pace slowed and the lines were pointed. Indeed, even all those long political speeches of Henry IV, that long exposition of the Law Salic of the Bishop of Ely, were not cut but were delivered clearly and intensely. We were made to feel what follows from such logic. Actions will follow, but later. It was unforgivable of Olivier (as Robert Speaight has said), all those years ago but still on celluloid, to guy the Bishop of Ely. For this just turns Henry V into a patriotic predator, rather than someone with as good a dynastic claim as any to the old French lands of the Plantagenet, Angevin, Anglo-French dynasty.

Sixth and lastly, there was great care for every minor part and scene. As in the Romans, much of the most telling political commentary is found in minor scenes and parts which used to be so much in the shadows when the great stars shone too brightly. The Northumberland scenes were all excellent: he appeared so much more calm and powerful than Bolingbroke himself, but was in fact crippled in his pursuit of power for his family by his fear for his own life. Hobbes's individualism does not work well for dynastic, feudal loyalties.

Only in the scene of Henry's renunciation of Falstaff did their political sense falter, in a lapse back to the unsubtle view of autocracy. For the King appears not just in the splendour of coronation robes, but transfigured in a huge and impersonal golden suit of armour. The director has said that it was meant to show the machine taking over the man; but I saw the gold as others did, as a symbol of divine transfiguration. They made just such a mistake in a recent production of *Richard II*; as if Shakespeare had the mid-seventeenth-century theory of the divine right of kings in mind. This anachronism is a bad misreading of Shakespeare's politics. The divinity that hedges a king is not to his person, as Stuarts and Bourbons claimed, but to the dynastic principle of descent. To break that is to strike at the heart of the feudal system of obligation and honour to superiors and to family loyalties; but in the name – and hence the dilemma – of better governance.

Granted, the Tudors tried to have it both ways. But the rejection of Falstaff by a man (the son of Bolingbroke) acting the part of king is made inevitable, hence not free and tragic, if the coronation is seen as divinisation. We are meant to feel the heavy need for 'reason of state', for 'the matter of England', of Hal becoming Henry and casting off Jack Falstaff, not because of any sacerdotal necessity. The doctrine of the divine right of kings is one of those precise concepts that often get misapplied, through secular ignorance, to almost anything in the past involving kings and religions.

POLITICISATION TOO FAR

I shall stay with Shakespeare a little longer, for production of the classics in some fresh manner is the great test of modern directors. And they have been lucky, for a 'fresh manner' can be achieved simply by going back to the text, a fuller text, and to the minor parts (the famous 1946 season of the Old Vic was the beginning of an attempt at ensemble playing, but only the beginning: all my memories are of Richardson and Olivier themselves).

The National Theatre directors have avoided extravagances like Jonathan Miller's *Merchant of Venice*, with Shylock as a frockcoated nineteenth-century banker. But applying a sense of politics of our times to the histories is one thing, elsewhere it is more problematic. Consider recent productions of *Twelfth Night, Hamlet* and *King Lear*.

The RSC's *Twelfth Night* of 1974–5 could not, at first glance, have been less political. It was marvellously lyrical: a celebration of one night of misrule in an artificial kingdom of self-love. The director had, for once, absolute faith in the script-writer. Peter Gill gave us a straightforward production, with no great tricks or reinterpretations, no sign that he was obsessional in any way, only many marks of thought, bringing out things not often noticed and playing down things over-noticed. (I have seen swings, saws, custard pies, coloured bladders, weak bladders, pails of water, and God knows what else besides, swing into action as heavy comics and directors have shown their lack of trust in the lines as written – as the kitchen upstages the court.) The simple strength of this production was that it had confidence in the comedy of Viola, Olivia and Orsino: it got the social relationships right. High life is high comedy (social ambiguities), and low life is low comedy (drunkenness and lust). Is this a banality? But I have seen so many productions in which Sir Toby and his crew are the comedy and Viola and Olivia are simply romantic. *A Midsummer Night's Dream*, too, is often damaged in this way, by Bottom upstaging the comedy of Puck and the courtly lovers.

Here from the start it was clear that Orsino was fooling himself, acting extravagantly, not to be taken seriously in his passion for Olivia. He is not guyed as a person: on the contrary, the cult of hopeless love is guyed. And Olivia, in an important new reading, was no longer the stately, majestic, beauty. Mary Rutherford was very much like the merry tom-boy Hermia she played in Peter Brook's great production of the *Dream* (1970), and also fooling herself, like the Duke, by plunging into the game of an equally fashionable cult – that of extravagant mourning.

So Illyria is, at first glance, totally removed from the real world. Seen as a tract, it could only be an anti-Puritan tract against the folly of earnestness. There is nothing to do but amuse oneself. But the production suddenly shows us that amusing others is harder graft. Traditionally the most artificial of the characters, Feste is in this production pulled down to earth: he is not the sweet fool we have come to expect, the gentle, witty zany, someone to fit easily in a great lady's entourage, more like a naughty domestic animal, a Christopher Smart's cat or John Skelton's parrot, than a wilful human servant. No, Ron Pember was a hard-bitten, professional comic, working all the time, watching the audience's reaction, fearing that the fashion for him will pass and that he will prove boring, but equally fearing that he will one day go too far. One mistake, one gag mistimed, one insolence too close to the bone, and his next job might be as porter with Macbeth in cold Scotland. (And so it was.)

He speaks with the accent of a Petticoat Lane salesman, or the last stand of the dregs of the music hall. Far from powdered and pretty, he is perpetually in need of a shave. His voice has a rough, sardonic, cutting edge. He is most un-Illyrian, a reminder of the outside world, of servitude and even death. He sings 'Then come kiss me, sweet and twenty,/Youth's a stuff will not endure' harshly, almost mockingky, a profane version of the Duke's idyll of true love thwarted; not an erotic encouragement, but a reminder of old mortality. He is closer to Rahere than to Touchstone.

The reality of Feste jarred at first, but then actually accentuated the deliberate artifice of the high-life comedy, which otherwise seems 'just a play'. Certainly it makes Viola's lines on Feste become not just a condescending compliment to a servant, but a rather more profound and melancholy reflection on the human condition:

> This fellow is wise enough to play the fool;
> And to do that well craves a kind of wit.
> He must observe their mood on whom he jests,
> The quality of persons, and the time;
> And, like the haggard, check at every feather
> That comes before his eye. This is practice
> As full of labour as a wise man's art;
> For folly that he wisely shows is fit;
> But wise men, folly-fall'n, quite taint their wit.   (III, i, 57–65)

For there is this dying fall within the play, as in Feste's own last song. And at the end another pardonable liberty, the director gave us Antonio standing with his back to the audience, like Feste also left alone, for he had loved Sebastian (why not?). Yet the high life on its own is too artificial for us to feel sadness amid laughter, so the little political touch, Feste's whiff of cold reality, was more than pardonable, it was profound.

Such a directorial liberty shows a sense of political and social reality, but does not seek to politicise the whole play. One could fearfully imagine lame beggars and hungry poor being intrude on the stage to watch the fruits of exploitation, as was done recently to politicise (yes) *King Lear*. But that enormity in a moment. First, *Hamlet*.

Peter Hall's 1976 National Theatre production of *Hamlet* got a bad press. Few critics seemed bold enough simply to say that Albert Finney ranted, that Fortinbras had played the Prince prematurely. Most blamed the production as being astonishingly and deliberately static and old-fashioned. I blame both. But the reason why the production was so immobile, stagey and undramatic seems to have been missed: it was a failure in political thought.

Hall put the production firmly in a political context. The stage was made deliberately shallow by a wall right across it with a single central door, so that all characters and extras, more extraneous than I had seen for twenty-five years (ten players, twelve rioters, eight councillors with grey beards) all lined up in a shallow semi-circle around the throne and watched the great ones, reacting but little. Hierarchy was stressed. The court was made the context. The issue was the succession to the throne of Denmark. The uncut text, with all the politics about Old Norway and young Fortinbras in it, so seldom heard, and a very powerful reading of Claudius by Denis Quilley, strengthened this interpretation. Claudius was every inch the 'new prince', almost deadpan, even if the lower lip would tremble for the nonce; but who asks too nicely how a man came to power, if he can keep the realm at peace? And who better: Claudius or Hamlet? Well, in the end the guilt of Claudius is too great a primordial curse; but so are the instability and incompetence of Hamlet. Fortinbras from a neighbouring kingdom it has to be; and Horatio speaks for Denmark in its hour of need. Good government must come first.

Now all this is in the text, and is often suppressed or not noticed. I remember the Hamlets of Olivier and Guinness and do not suspect that Gielgud's was very political. But the political issue, if a powerful peripheral theme, is not the storm centre of the play. Hamlet himself is, of course, more important. The tragedy, certainly, is not just that Hamlet does not get his rights, but that he is not *fit* to be king; and yet the play does centre on the man, not on the realm of Denmark. It is not one of the English histories, where the context matters, nor is it like the Roman plays, with their deep analogies with English history and specifically with Elizabethan politics. If the minor parts *should* be politicised, Polonius, for example, given back his dignity, the Prince must still o'er tower them. The RSC did much better with the late Buzz Goodbody's small-theatre, modern-dress production of *Hamlet* for a cast of fourteen. There were deft political touches. The lines, for instance, where Polonius instructs Reynaldo to spy upon Laertes are usually got through quickly.

> *Polonius.* You shall do marvellous wisely, good Reynaldo,
> Before you visit him, to make inquire
> Of his behaviour.
> *Reynaldo.*   My Lord, I did intend it.
>
> (II, i, 3–5)

But in the RSC production, the actor gave it with a deprecatory, cocky little half-sneer, as if to say, 'Don't tell me how to suck eggs. I've learned all I can from you about the business. Why don't you retire and let me take over?'.

He was thrusting, junior executive, an arrogant company creep. Of course it is there: what other meaning can the scene have? The big fish eat the little fish, but every dog must have his day. Polonius, like Caesar, was no fool: rather he had been the embodiment of 'politique' wisdom, Cecil or Burleigh-like, but now on his way out. Ambition sours and destroys every human relationship at court.

The modern dress neither distracted nor seemed a gimmick. The King, George Baker, wore a marvellously over-well-cut chairman of the board suit, perhaps a little bit like Prince Rainier; just as Gertrude was, bless my soul, got up like Mrs Simpson. He is so rational and commanding that if the state of Denmark is to avoid inflation and industrial anarchy, it must be him at the helm, however he got there. Whereas Hamlet is the non-political humanist and intellectual, so intelligent, so much more civilised and profound; but could a man of such volatility and indecisiveness, a bit manic-depressive even, be king, be trusted with the care of the state?

Ben Kingsley played the Prince as feigning mad, which is too dangerous a game for Hamlet, for playing at it drives him into madness, able to recover but each time with diminishing coherence; and if his energy grows throughout the play, it loses any rational sense of direction. Ben Kingsley was hardly the Prince, more a humanist–courtier, unsure (like Horatio) about what he is doing there at all; but Hamlet the man lets us hear every word of his soliloquies, every word being thought over, as if thought really is decisive. 'To be or not to be.' We really wonder what conclusion he (and we) finally will reach. But when he warns Ophelia off him, 'I'm very proud, revengeful and *ambitious*', that is his sane side, as when he complains that Claudius stood 'between the election and my hopes'. Part of him would rather be back with Horatio in the seminars of Wittenberg, but part is indeed ambitious, caught up in the court, quite apart from motives of filial vengeance and dynastic justice. This was a great reading in a great production, precisely because it saw the complementary relationships between the dramatic and the political, the heroic and the social; unlike Peter Hall's production which could have had as subtitle, 'The Business of Good Government'.

With the 1977 Stratford production of *King Lear*, it was, however, the RSC's turn to go too far. The curtain rises to reveal Kent and Gloucester in frockcoats, and as the court assembles we find the three sisters in turn-of-the-century court dress, glistening, sharp bare shoulders; and then the King appears in cream imperial Franz Joseph costume, medals and sashes and all, in high top boots which jut up ludicrously when he sits on his throne, almost reaching his chin, making him appear both puppet and petulant autocrat. The use of such a precise historical or imaginative locale shows us instantly what the production is supposed to be about: tyranny, or more precisely the whimsicality and arbitrariness of absolute power. Lear is not a feudal monarch. He does not have to conciliate his fellow-nobles. Unlike in the histories, there appear to be no rival military powers before his abdication. So he can banish Kent as quickly and with as little dispute as he can divide his kingdom. Lear is a new monarch, *rex absolutus*. Regan and Goneril are on the edge of their nerves; with this old man anything could happen, whatever has been said beforehand. They push their advantage and luck ruthlessly and speedily; they are frightened and tense, but they are true daughters of their father's will and wilfulness.

The directors, Nunn and Barton, plainly thought they had found a contemporary political inwardness to render the strange old story plausible to us, some real motivation for launching old Lear out on the blasted heath to howl against humanity. Great pains were taken to show that Lear, even more than Antony or Hamlet, is not fit to govern. The production had Lear embodying the folly of arbitrary will, the bloody consequences for inhabitants that follow from giving kingdoms away as if they were personal gifts. And the interpretation worked very well at the beginning. Donald Sinden, who played Lear, had played Henry VIII five years before, so the face and presence of the wilful, childish, petulant, but also majestic and powerful autocrat were right. It is almost as if Henry VIII when he was old had three daughters and he decided to divide the kingdom between Mary, Anne and Elizabeth, none of whom lived happily for a moment afterwards. 'Better had thou not been born than not to have pleased me better', says Lear to Cordelia. 'Quod principi placuit legis habet vigorem', Thomas Cromwell had reminded King Henry that the late Roman law so spake (what pleases the king has the force of law). He sits on the dragon throne and stamps his boot impatiently for the flattery of the daughters to begin. Regan actually stammers with fear, though her vicious intent is clear-cut within.

Even into Goneril's house the reinterpretation wears well. The ugly sisters do, quite frankly, have quite a lot to put up with. Lear and his knights burst into the house like a Romanov hunting party (or perhaps the Hapsburgs in the Carpathians), dressed like peasants, stinking like peasants, drunk as lords and firing off their guns with rowdy extravagance. The two sisters are needlessly cruel to the half-senile old man, but god! he is a handful, all whim and will and neither reason nor policy. Even the court of Denmark was far bettered ordered.

The costuming in this production does present some difficulties. Lear on the heath stripped down to his woollen combinations is downright silly, and a French army in capes and kepis distracts our attention, as does Cordelia reappearing in long khaki skirt and tunic, a military tailoring half fit for the Countess of Athlone inspecting her regiment leaving for Flanders, and half for Fanny's First Fight with the Fascists. Alas, it distorts as well as distracts. For to cry on their reunion:

> Oh my dear father! Restoration hang
> Thy medicine upon my lips, and let this kiss
> Repair those violent harms that my two sisters
> Have in thy reverence made. (IV, vii, 26–9)

while all kitted out with Sam Browne and bullet pouches is to create a quite meaningless paradox. She does what she has to do against the grain of her gentle nature, she does not find a new, true nature in political crisis and battle. She is not the devil's disciple. And a group of wretched poor are twice interpolated between scenes at the beginning, singing a non-textual ballad about what a rotten lot it is to be poor – an apparently arbitrary and crude piece of Brechtian routine.

Doubts about the design are, however, only preliminary to a graver doubt. The design in itself could have been amended. The directors need not have been so consistent with time and place. In *Henry V's* last campaign they began in actors' rehearsal gear, moved into medieval finery but ended aptly in drab trench clothes. Similarly with *King Lear*, what the directors needed at the outset to establish the politics of autocracy or absolute monarchy, need not by itself have dictated the costuming of later scenes. But integral to the production was a resolute determination to give the play a time and place, to stop Lear himself rising out of the play to comment too freely and terribly on the eternal human condition.

They seem to have treated *King Lear* as if it were one of the histories, a part of the 'matter of England'. It is about a quarrel in a noble house, the tearing of a country to shreds by fratricide and patricide, so strong and terrible is the *libido dominandi*, the lust for power, generating other lusts, not rising from them. It was a kind of trial run for the 1977–8 *Henry VI* cycle and an echo of Barton's *Wars of the Roses*. The playing of Goneril and Regan made this initially very plausible. Their behaviour is almost to be respected, considering what life at Lear's court must have been like. Royal folly and cruel caprice lead to downfall, but humanity, in the shape of Cordelia returned and Lear briefly reborn is asserted, however temporarily and precariously, at the end. The death of Lear and his favourite daughter is disaster but not utter defeat for the human spirit: they were reconciled, they became themselves again without the royal robes. Indeed in his long smock and flowing beard he seems transfigured from Czar into Tolstoy.

But Lear also faced the storm. And so far I have said nothing of the scenes on the heath, the mad scenes. Making the play a history almost forces a playing down of these scenes, if not to nothing at least to very little, only to a rather odd happening which holds up the action. We are to feel that the King says such dreadful things because he is mad (and serve the old tyrant right), not because in madness he gains a terrible insight (however speculatively the playwright may have meant it) into the human condition. It is one thing – and always to the RSC's credit – to have escaped from the old-fashioned star system, but it is another deliberately to mute Lear and to play down or simply to mismanage the dark and strident middle scenes. There is a political element, certainly; but it is only a small one. Schiller firmly labelled his *Don Carlos* 'a domestic drama in a Royal House'; and this *Lear* almost came down to that, as if dynastic rivalry produced the savage condition of England, not the extremities of natural man. How much more moved one was at the traditional but almost unbearably intense Lear of Tony Church in Buzz Goodbody's 1972 Other Place production when a few characters stood in a Beckett-like metaphysical abstraction, exposing tortured human nature, not products of some Brechtian time and social condition.

The tight sense of time and place imposed on *Lear* is at odds with the language. And the driving sense of event piling upon event, beyond the control of the royal actors, the directors' style and the message in the history plays, seems oddly eccentric in this most episodic and loosely structured of the tragedies – a drama more expressionistic and metaphysical than narrative and political.

So determined are they to politicise it and to tie it down in time and space (and a time, moreover, very close to us) that when the Fool in the storm on that 'brave night to cool a courtesan' utters his ironic prophecy:

> When every case in law is right;
> No squire in debt, nor no poor knight;
> When slanders do not live in tongues;
> Nor cutpurses come not to throngs;
> When usurers tell their gold i' th' field,
> And bawds and whores do churches build –
> Then shall the realm of Albion
> Come to great confusion.
> Then comes the time, who lives to see't
> That going shall be us'd with feet   (III, ii, 85–94)

and adds: 'This prophecy shall Merlin make for I live before his time', they deal with this foolish anachronism on the Bard's part by the simple and economic means of cutting it. Yet this absurd anachronism is important. Shakespeare himself prevents any attempt to anchor the play in history. And it is so often remarked what pains he took (compared, say, to *Macbeth*) to take all references to Christianity out of the play and even, as far as possible, most Christian presuppositions: part of the matter, at least, is speculation about what happens to man's mind and reason when isolated in extreme situations of both cruelty and of compassion, or in nature without society. The world is a prison, he seems to say, and we are Fools indeed to think that dreams of better kings and of social justice will take away the doom of tragedy and grief from man's mortal and perhaps salvationless lot.

Why should the directors have done it this way? Perhaps extraneous extras furnish a clue, as does also a haunting double page photograph in the programme of Victorian poor children in filthy overalls, three rows of them, but here endlessly repeated, forming a human pyramid of repetitive poverty-stricken faces – under which is quoted:

> Poor naked wretches, wheresoe'er you are,
> That bide the pelting of this pitiless storm,
> How shall your houseless heads and unfed sides,
> Your loop'd and window'd raggedness, defend you
> From seasons such as these? O, I have ta'en
> Too little care of this! Take physic, pomp;
> Expose thyself to feel what wretches feel,
> That thou mayst shake the superflux to them,
> And show the heavens more just.   (III, iv, 28–36)

So we are to read this as a kind of prophecy of the welfare state (more incredible than Merlin's), rather than sympathy for what any Jacobean, Shakespeare almost certainly, could only see as part of the inevitable suffering of humanity.

As this theme of social injustice has no warrant at all in the text of the play and does not follow from the well-perceived but overdone political dimension of Lear as autocrat rather than feudal monarch, where did they get it from? In Bertolt Brecht's key essay *Über experimentelles Theater* of 1939, he asks:

What is alienation? To alienate an action or a character first of all simply means to deprive that action or character of anything matter of course, well known or obvious and to arouse amazement and curiosity about it. Let us once again take the example of Lear's rage at his daughters' ingratitude. By means of empathetic technique the actor can present this rage in such a way that the spectator would regard it as the most natural thing in the world, so that he'd be incapable of imagining that Lear could not be angry, so that he has full solidarity with Lear, identifies with him, entirely, and grows angry himself.

By means of the alienation technique, on the other hand, the actor represents Lear's anger in such a way that the spectator can be amazed at it, that he can imagine different possible reactions of Lear's than simply one of anger. Lear's attitude is alienated, that is it is represented as peculiar, striking, remarkable, as a social phenomenon that need not be taken for granted. This rage is human but not general for all humans, there are people who do not feel it. The experiences that Lear has do not rouse rage in all people at all times. Rage may be an eternally possible reaction of human beings, but this rage, the rage that expresses itself in this way and has this cause, is conditioned by its time. Thus to alienate means to historicise. It means to represent actions and persons as historical and hence as transient....

What is gained by this? The gain is that the spectator no longer sees the people on the stage as utterly unchangeable, beyond influence and helplessly delivered up to their fate. He sees that this man is as he is because the

conditions are as they are. And the conditions are what they are, because the
man is what he is. . . . and man is received in the theatre as the great changer
who is able to take a hand in natural processes and social processes, and no
longer simply accepts the world, but masters it.[5]

Might one of the directors have read this and seen it as the final challenge to
their school of modern, politically conscious production, to historicise even
Lear? All very well for some types of play, but surely not for *Lear*? Brecht
himself never, in fact, produced *Lear*. An historical *Lear* can be, as this is, a
perfectly coherent and enjoyable production. But at such a low level. So
much is lost. I was not harrowed, only interested. And this, presumably,
was the narrowing, Brechtian rationalising effect intended. But on the
lower level, as a student of politics, I must hint at certain well-known
dangers to that very freedom that Brecht thought he was talking about if
one tries to politicise everything. Everything can be made politically relevant, but a world in which everything must be politically relevant would be a
world of unfreedom, not the realisation of true politics. How much I have
enjoyed and praised the Hall–Barton–Nunn style of producing the histories
and their rediscovery of the political elements in the complex compounds of
Hamlet and *Antony*. But everything tragic is not history and politics. Will
thoughts such as Lear expresses simply not occur *ex hypothesi* in the classless
society? We might be happier, but we would certainly be poorer if so.

MODERN POLITICS

There are plays whose main concerns are the dilemmas of politics, or the
differing values of the public and the private life. The National has done
very well for some of them, not over-politicising them. Büchner's *Danton's
Death*, of course, almost defies ideological simplification: it is both the
tragedy of Danton the man and of the inflexibility, and ultimate cruelty, of
Robespierre's principles. There is a sympathy with *La Revolution* which the
conservatives must dislike, but a sense of tragedy that is hardly 'the noble
example' or the clear-cut enemy sought for in revolutionary theatre. Their
production of Beaumarchais' *Marriage of Figaro*, while a simpler play, was
exactly what a national theatre should do, a surprise for most of us,
something we all heard of, but few seen – or we may have *thought* we had seen
it, for Da Ponte had taken the political guts out of Beaumarchais for
Mozart. What we now saw had something to do with the bourgeois, French
revolution (as the literary histories have told us), not just the chastening of
aristocratic arrogance and excess by the humane and sentimental values of
the opera.

Satire can pose difficulties. *The Captain of Köpenick* mocks the idiocies of a
very specific society, so if the audience cannot be trusted to have some sense
of what the old Kaiserreich was like (*nothing* like Nazism) and if the (much

wasted) programme notes cannot be used sensibly, refuge has to be taken,
alas, in over-playing the broad comedy. Indeed, Paul Schofield had similarly over-done the main role in the RSC's *Government Inspector* of a few years
before. Shades of autocracy cause difficulties for modern directors habitu-
ated to stark images of twentieth-century totalitarianism. Some satire,
while grotesque, should evoke the wry smile of recognising a fitness, not the
guffaws of harmless catastrophe. After seeing Ton Stoppard's highly political *Travesties* done by the RSC (political in the sense that it was a double
swipe at Dadaist irresponsibility and at the Leninist social theory of art), I
suspect that his earlier *Jumpers* was meant to be more political. Perhaps we
were meant to be generally worried about the future under the rule of the
rational-seeming 'Radical Democratic Party', not merely to sympathise
with a solitary moral philosopher holding out. But that one part – either as
written or as played – was too farcical and rich.

Best of all modern political plays has been, I think, John Arden's *Armstrong's Last Goodnight*. Here is the explicit theme of the good man and,
indeed, the poet, Sir David Lindsay, the king's herald, trying privately by
'politic guile', 'Machiavel's art' and 'through craft and through humanity'
to overcome without bloodshed the disturber of the peace of the border,
Johnny Armstrong. He fails. His misplayed strategies lead to the death of
his friend. In the end, he has to don his herald's clothes again, to betray his
office 'for necessities of state' by luring Armstrong to ambush and a sudden
hanging. A dishonourable act will, none the less, maintain peace between
the kingdoms and save many a life. Our sympathies are divided. This was
Arden the realist. His later plays, in collaboration with Margaretta D'Arcy,
are all *engagé* and either shallow or, as in *The Island of the Mighty*, a vast
cauldron of strange, incompatible and unmeasured ingredients. He has
moved from having a profound sense of politics into being a propagandist.
And, as a person, why not? My only point is still, however, that drama
thrives on dilemma and on conflict, not even on the best resolutions.

A movement in the other direction is shown by Trevor Griffith, a committed dramatist taken up by both the national companies. They have
responsibilities to new playwrights, certainly; but they can also be dangerous to new playwrights, particularly when these great institutions ape the
fringe. Griffith had his *Occupations* very well presented by the RSC at The
Place, a small and intimate theatre, good for small audiences, minority
plays, tryouts and informality. *Occupations* was about Gramsci and Lenin –
well, a Lenin-like figure, anyway, and certainly the historical Gramsci. The
play never moves outside the assumptions of Marxism. But there develops a
deep and genuine clash both of personality and of doctrine between
Gramsci and Kabak, the Soviet agent, sent either to stiffen socialist mili-
tancy in the Fiat strike of 1920 or, if the strike failed, to conclude a trade deal
with Fiat, which he does. The harsh Leninist–Marxism confronts the

humanistic Marxism of Gramsci, to which a dash of anarcho-syndicalism is added by the author. The drama works psychologically, the protagonists are full characters as well as ideological types, and they work upon each other.

Then, however, he wrote *The Party* for the full stage of the Old Vic. It was a good idea, a trendy left-wing television producer holding a party to bring together (irreconcilable) elements of the advanced Left, while they watch on television the Paris students' uprising. But the characters relevant to the action were cardboard figures: a lot of fashionable over-production crept in, bedroom scenes with mirrors, nothing to do with the main theme. There had to be a lot of lecturing at the audience, since 'the National crowd' would need much more explanation than the students at The Place. The programme read like discussion notes for a seminar at the Workers' Educational Association, and a drunken wise-fool of a playwright, whose main role is to expose the shallowness of the trendy television producer, has to be wrenched out of character at the end to prophesy revolution by popular spontaneity rather than by the tactics of any party. It was bad. I did not see a version that subsequently toured student unions, but many say that it was better: the over-production was out and the audiences more fitting and responsive.

Griffith, however, came back to the National with a Nottingham Playhouse production of *Comedians*, a truly rich and complex image of the war between consumerism, art and political commitment. An evening class for comics sees its decent old teacher defending the traditional craft, fit for the family, against both the calculating, smutty debaser ('give 'em what they really want') and the zany revolutionary ('shock the bastards into thinking'). They both let him down and go their own way at the audition. Parliamentary politics is doomed: fascism and anarchism will be left to fight it out. I do not share the author's catastrophic view. But the play is the richer for being open-ended and for having, in the traditional masks of comedy and the art of teaching about art, found rich metaphors for debasement, doomed tradition and the hope of transformation.

Two superficially similar young left-wing playwrights, David Edgar and Howard Barker, have been taken up by the RSC, and divide rather like the two souls of Mr Griffith: the tortured enthusiast (who can dramatise) and the conceited demagogue (who can only preach in theatrical images). As I have said already, David Edgar's announced theme of the fortunes of fascism in the West Midlands (in *Destiny*) did not warm my blood like wine, at least the everyday blood I use for understanding and delight, rather than that saved to be spilt in the last fight. But, despite a conventional ending, of capitalists hiring fascists to fight trade unionists (as dramatically simple-minded as it is historically silly), the main body of the play was about types of fascism and nationalism in conflict with each other, together with subplots of different kinds of compromise made by 'decent' or ordinary politicians. And each idea was well embedded in plausible characters who are rarely seen on the stage. Howard Barker, on the other hand, in *That Good Between Us* has a number of unrelieved and largely undifferentiated bastards *all* grinding down the workers and their friends, when a social democratic government, in a slightly future *Clockwork Orange* Britain, takes off the kid gloves and reveals itself for the oppressive, violent class force it really is. The author achieves remarkable dramatic images: the first naked gang rape on the stage (to my knowledge), beatings, bicycles, punts, burials, striptease, and groaning beds. A series of scenes succeeded each other at great pace, as only the RSC directors can achieve, as if the stage were screaming to be cinema; and, in the end, to make a really partisan point, the result was as full of technically and psychologically shocking images as much modern cinema, and as pointless, mindless and undramatic. We didn't know what was going to happen next, but we knew exactly what was happening all the boring time. Even in adolescent religious days I was bored by sermons, however bizarre their quotations from the Old Testament, and rationally puzzled about why all this incitement to a change of life should be aimed at those already converted.

Political theatre is at its worst when it sees politics simply in terms of violence by undifferentiated oppressors against equally undifferentiated oppressed. Politics is, indeed, about conflict: but conflict by all means available, violence, fear, propaganda, and (perhaps most of all) by argument, persuasion and example. Every tyrant, even, has to persuade someone, or he would not be able to sleep at night. Political theatre is at its best when it makes us aware of the price to be paid, always, for progress, or at best the plausibility and equal authenticity of differing ideas. Such is drama. All good drama has some political element in it, some choice between real alternatives. If choice is lacking, as in Maoist text, or if it is made clear that Caesar *must* die, Falstaff *must* be forsaken, Hamlet *clearly* is or is not fit to be king, or if the play is a mere history lesson with a known result and fixed course (as equally Robert Bolt's recent *The State of Revolution* or Brecht's *The Days of the Commune*), then both drama and politics are diminished.

NOTES

1. I have used materials from reviews contributed to *The Times Higher Education Supplement* and *The New Review*. I thank the editors for permission.
2. Bernard Crick, *In Defence of Politics* (Harmondsworth: Pelican, 1964).
3. Quotations from Shakespeare are from *The Complete Works*, ed. Peter Alexander (London: Collins, 1951).
4. Thomas Hobbes, *Leviathan*, introd. A. D. Lindsay, Everyman's Library (London: Dent, 1914), part I, chapter 10, p. 47.

5. *Über experimentelles Theater*, a lecture first delivered in Stockholm in May 1939, and in revised form in Helsinki in October 1940. It is reprinted in *Schriften zum Theater 3* (Frankfurt: Suhrkamp Verlag, 1963). The quoted passage is on pp. 101–2. I am grateful to Joyce Crick for showing me this passage, for convincing me of its significance, and for translating it.

German social drama in the 1960s

HANNE CASTEIN

On looking back over the last thirty years of German theatre, one is struck by the fact that the subject-matter of the majority of the important plays is political. Post-war drama in West Germany, Switzerland and Austria is of more direct social relevance than most other contemporary theatre in the West. There have, to take one indicative example, been several plays set in mental hospitals – Friedrich Dürrenmatt's *Die Physiker* (The Physicists, 1961), Peter Weiss's *Marat/Sade* (1962–4), and Martin Walser's *Der schwarze Schwan* (The Black Swan, 1964) – but in each case the playwright's concern was not with his characters' 'insanity' but with the psychopathology of the society for which the asylum setting was used as a metaphor.

There have been some alternatives to social and political drama; for example, the influence of the theatre of the absurd dominated the German stage in the 1950s, through productions of plays by Anouilh, Ionesco, and Beckett. But the more original plays in German have come from playwrights with an interest in public and social rather than in personal and metaphysical questions. The reason for this predominance of political plays is that in Germany there was a unique necessity to come to terms with the recent past, above all to analyse cause and effect of the most extensive attempt at genocide in human history. The first resulting plays in the late forties were about the Second World War – we think of Wolfgang Borchert's *Draussen vor der Tür* (The Man Outside, 1946) and Carl Zuckmayer's *Des Teufels General* (The Devil's General, 1946), which were popular with audiences but did not attempt to analyse the sources of fascism. In the late fifties Max Frisch's *Biedermann und die Brandstifter* (The Fire-Raisers, 1957–8) and his *Andorra* (1958–61) went further and looked into the root causes of fascism, and of anti-semitism in particular.

This paper is concerned largely with plays written in the 1960s. At the beginning of that decade a whole crop of plays set out to examine society from a new point of view. Retrospectively this view was defined by Peter Weiss in his *Notizen zum dokumentarischen Theater* (Notes on Documentary Theatre, 1968): 'Nicht individuelle Konflikte werden dargestellt, sondern sozial-ökonomisch bedingte Verhaltensweisen.' (It is not individual conflicts that are portrayed, but human behaviour conditioned by socio-economic factors.)[1] There was in addition a revolutionary departure from the political parable plays of the fifties in favour of a new form of drama based on fact and documentation. This drama was optimistically charged with the task 'zur Wahrheit ... vorzustossen' (of penetrating to the truth)[2] and testified to a new generation's belief 'dass die Wirklichkeit, so undurch-schaubar sie sich auch macht, in jeder Einzelheit erklärt werden kann' (that reality, however impenetrable it may seem, can be explained in every detail).[3]

The playwrights this paper will concentrate on – Rolf Hochhuth, Heinar Kipphardt and Peter Weiss – rejected the main contemporary dramatic movements when they formulated the concept of their alternative *realistisches Zeittheater* (realistic theatre of the time).[4] Apart from Schiller's important influence, Hochhuth shares with Weiss a frequently acknowledged indebtedness to Erwin Piscator's concept of a political, documentary theatre. The nature of the relationship between Piscator's spectacular productions of the 1920s and the 'documentary' theatre of the sixties still needs to be precisely defined. But we know of Piscator's great interest in the young playwrights in the last few years of his life: he was the first to produce the most important plays written in the new genre. He opened the new building of the Freie Volksbühne (West Berlin) with Hochhuth's *Der Stellvertreter* (The Representative) in 1963 and in the same theatre he directed productions of Kipphardt's *In der Sache J. Robert Oppenheimer* (In the Matter of J. Robert Oppenheimer) in 1964, and Weiss's *Die Ermittlung* (The Investigation) in 1965. Hochhuth acknowledged the great debt he owed to Piscator's work by dedicating his second play *Soldaten* (Soldiers) to him in 1967, and Piscator in turn paid tribute to the new generation following in his footsteps. He remarked in the epilogue to an edition of his *Das politische Theater* (Political Theatre): 'Mir scheint, ich setze die Schriftsteller, die in den zwanziger Jahren mit mir arbeiteten, in ihrem Wert nicht herab, wenn ich sage, dass Stücke, wie sie mir seinerzeit als Ideal vorschwebten, erst heute etwa von Hochhuth, Kipphardt oder Weiss geschrieben werden, Stücke, die sich der Faktizität des Dokumentes, der Strenge exakter historischer Analyse unterwerfen, ohne dabei auf die Freiheit der Gestaltung verzichten zu müssen.' (It seems to me that I am not undervaluing the writers working with me in the twenties when I say that the sort of plays I was aiming at then as my ideal are written only now by, for example, Hochhuth, Kipphardt or Weiss – plays submitting to the factual nature of documents and the discipline of exact historical analysis without having to renounce creative freedom.)[5]

When Piscator comments on the relationship between historical fact and creative freedom in documentary drama, he touches upon the key issue in the debate surrounding the plays of Hochhuth, Kipphardt and Weiss.

Before attempting to consider this complex matter, I should like to raise some simpler questions. What encouraged this sudden re-emergence of political plays with a heavy stress on documentary evidence after almost thirty years? The most remarkable initial impulse appears to have been the spate of Nazi trials beginning in the early sixties which attempted to get at the objective facts behind the Third Reich, and which involved the extensive publication of evidence and trial records in the national press. And it was the televised trial of Adolf Eichmann in 1961 that sparked off the first of these documentary plays, Hochhuth's *Der Stellvertreter* (1963), and two years later Kipphardt's *Joel Brand*. The Frankfurt Auschwitz trials (1962–4) prompted Weiss's *Die Ermittlung*. These plays established the genre of documentary drama as a new form in German theatre. The process coincided more or less exactly with a general move to the left in German politics, and it was to peter out in the early seventies with the unmistakable swing to the right.

One might have spoken simply of the *political* theatre of the sixties in Germany, if the plays of that period had not shared a striking preoccupation with the use of documentation. The playwrights went about using this documentary evidence in various ways. There were what one might call 'pure documentary plays' where trial records were scenically arranged. (The important examples are Kipphardt's *In der Sache J. Robert Oppenheimer*, Weiss's *Die Ermittlung*, and Hans Magnus Enzensberger's *Das Verhör von Habana*.) Another category might be called 'historical–biographical', and the main plays would be Tankred Dorst's *Toller* (1969), Weiss's *Trotzki im Exil* (Trotsky in Exile, 1970) and Dieter Forte's *Martin Luther und Thomas Münzer oder die Einführung der Buchhaltung* (Martin Luther and Thomas Münzer or The Introduction of Book-keeping, 1970). Thirdly, a large number of plays make use of documentary material in the text itself and also append chunks of it in the printed version.

Hochhuth's plays belong to this third category. His first play *Der Stellvertreter*, which inaugurated the movement, was not only an overwhelming box-office success but it also, because of its highly controversial subject-matter, received a good deal of international attention. Hochhuth condemned the attitude of the Catholic Church and especially that of God's representative, Pope Pius XII, to the extermination of the Jews under Hitler. The play alleges that the Pope declined to intervene on behalf of the Roman Jews, although their arrest, deportation and extermination were made known to him. While Hochhuth's play is of course largely fictitious, he takes great pains in the often very detailed stage directions to point to the authenticity of his reconstruction of the historical events. This function is particularly served by his appendix to the play, *Historische Streiflichter* (Historical Spotlights), which prints some of the play's documentary source material. Hochhuth describes his own method of using this material in the

introduction to the appendix: the events of the play were 'nicht wie eine
Reportage dem geschichtlichen Ablauf nachgeschrieben, sondern zu einem
Spiel verdichtet' (not recorded as in an historical report, but creatively
shaped into a play).[6] Hochhuth prefaced his later play *Guerillas* (1970) with
a discussion of his theatre's use of factual information. He sharply rejects a
news-reel approach to historical, realistic drama: 'Wochenschauen
unterhalten mit dem eingängigen Irrtum, der fotografierte Ausschnitt der
Realität sei realistisch.' (News-reels entertain, committing the common
error, that a photographed slice of reality is realistic.)[7] Hochhuth turns to
Schiller for a formulation of the historical playwright's dilemma: 'Der
Neuere schlägt sich mühselig und ängstlich mit Zufälligkeiten und
Nebendingen herum, und über dem Bestreben, der Wirklichkeit recht nahe zu
kommen, beladet er sich mit dem Leeren und Unbedeutenden, und
darüber läuft er Gefahr, die tiefliegende Wahrheit zu verlieren, worin
eigentlich alles Poetische liegt. Er möchte gern einen wirklichen Fall voll-
kommen nachahmen und bedenkt nicht, dass eine poetische Darstellung
mit der Wirklichkeit eben darum, weil sie absolut wahr ist, niemals koin-
zidieren kann ...' (The modern writer frets and worries about accidents
and matters of little importance and in the attempt to come very close to
reality he burdens himself with meaningless and insignificant material.
During all this he runs the risk of missing the underlying truth which is the
essence of creative literature. He would like to offer a perfect reproduction of
a real event, forgetting that a literary presentation of it, because it is true in
an absolute sense can never coincide with reality ...)[8] Unlike the authors of
historical plays of the past, Hochhuth claims strict historical accuracy as
well as literary merit. To uncover the historical truth behind political events
has become one of the important functions of the modern playwright, and
Hochhuth sees himself here at the beginning of a new tradition: '... viell-
eicht bin ich der erste Stückschreiber, der stets darauf beharrt hat, dass
uns *keine* willkürliche Behandlung der Historie mehr zusteht. Wenn Lessing
schrieb, der Dichter sei der Herr der Geschichte – ich habe mich stets als ihr
Knecht gefühlt.' (... perhaps I am the first playwright who has always
insisted that we are no longer entitled to *any* arbitrary treatment of history.
Lessing wrote that a writer is the master of history – well, I have always
considered myself her servant.)[9] Hochhuth insists that factual accuracy and
literary truth can be reconciled: 'Die bereits greifbaren Fakten intuitiv zu
einem Ganzen zu verbinden, zu einem Ganzen der Kunst und der Wahrheit
bleibt das hohe und selten erreiche Ziel der Dichtung, die sich *gerade*
angesichts eines so erdrückenden Rohmaterials und aller kompilatorischen
Mühen nicht ihre spezifische Freiheit nehmen lassen darf, die allein dem
Stoff erst die Form gibt.' (It is the great and rarely achieved aim of literature to combine factual matter in a union of art and truth. Especially in
the face of an overwhelming mass of raw material, art must not allow

itself to be deprived of its particular freedom which alone gives form to this material.)[10]

The critical discussion of documentary drama has tended to ignore what Hochhuth, Weiss, and Kipphardt have had to say about their plays. In a representative study, these playwrights are accused of being responsible for a 'Regeneration des Stoffes' (a reinstatement of the dominance of plot over form).[11] But the playwrights' concern with questions of dramatic language and form expressed itself in many theoretical statements, as for example in the prefaces and appendixes to their plays. More importantly, there is the elaborate structure of the plays themselves, and in the cases of Weiss and Hochhuth their highly stylised language, a free rhythmic, or irregular verse.

In an interview in America Hochhuth put the case for this surprising feature of documentary drama: 'Free verse carries its speaker along much more readily than prose, especially when it comes to a subject which is so closely involved with contemporary events and depends so entirely on historical documents. Then, things must be transposed, heightened by language. Otherwise, it would often be likely to sound as if one were merely quoting from the documents.'[12]

Only in a few late examples of documentary drama does a preoccupation with content overrule formal considerations, a danger inherent in a genre dealing exclusively with political subject-matter, whether contemporary or historical. But, as well as their theoretical credos, the dramatic output of these playwrights testifies to a serious concern with formal problems encountered in the use of documentation.

Hochhuth's *Der Stellvertreter* was only the first in a whole series of plays to document the political and economic pressures which determined the behaviour of a recent public figure in a particular crisis: Pope Pius XII was followed by Oppenheimer, Brecht, Churchill and Trotsky.[13] Hochhuth's play – like his later works *Soldaten* (1967) and *Guerillas* (1970) – does, however, contain more fictional material than do the plays of his successors. For example, one of the leading characters in *Der Stellvertreter* is an invented priest, Riccardo, there to be a foil for the Pope. Riccardo decides to accompany a transportation of Jews to Auschwitz. Through his own martyrdom he, Riccardo, becomes the true representative:

> Und da der Papst, doch auch nur ein Mensch,
> auf Erden sogar *Gott* vertreten kann:
> so werde ... so wird doch ...
> so wird ein armer Priester ja zur Not
> auch den Papst vertreten können – *dort*,
> wo er heute stehen müsste.
>
> (*Der Stellvertreter*, p. 124)

(And since the Pope, though only a man,
can even represent *God* on earth,
then I'll ... then will ...
then a poor priest if necessary
can also represent the Pope – *there*
where he ought to be standing today.)

Hochhuth felt little in common with Kipphardt and Weiss, who each tried
to write plays with an absolute minimum of authorial interference with the
source material, and who certainly never invented any of their major
figures. With reference to two of their plays, *In der Sache J. Robert Oppenheimer*
and *Die Ermittlung*, Hochhuth went as far as rejecting for himself the
'Schlagwort vom Dokumentationstheater' (the label 'documentary
theatre')[14] and pleaded to preserve 'der Phantasie ihr Recht auch im
historischen Drama (the right of the imagination in historical drama too).[15]

Kipphardt's *Oppenheimer* uses one document as raw material: the play is
based on the three-thousand-page transcript of the 1954 hearings which
considered the atomic scientist Oppenheimer's application for security
clearance. By confining himself to one source of material relating to one
specific question – the problem of scientist versus state – Kipphardt found
the content apparently most suited to the form. Two more major
documentary dramas followed Kipphardt's example by dramatising trial
records: Weiss with *Die Ermittlung* and Hans Magnus Enzensberger with his
Das Verhör von Habana (The Havana Hearing, 1970).

The more recent examples of what might be called 'documentary collage', such as Wallraff's *Was wollt ihr denn, ihr lebt ja noch* (What do you want?
You're Still Alive, 1973), take respect for the document that one step further
where the playwright's task has become merely editorial. Wallraff, after
printing the dramatised proceedings of a committee meeting goes on to
supply in over two-thirds of the book photocopies of all the newspaper
cuttings, letters, and documents relating to the issue under discussion: the
building of a chemical plant close to a built-up area in the north of
Germany.

Weiss and Kipphardt too had felt strongly that their source-material
should speak for itself, but they did much more than merely edit the trial
records. Kipphardt, considering the bulky evidence before him, realised the
necessity to reduce it to manageable proportions. This involved certain cuts
so that he uses six witnesses instead of the actual forty and much repetition
of evidence is omitted. This selective process needs no defence, but
Kipphardt does more than merely select. In his postscript to the play he
hints at substantial changes; like Hochhuth, he stresses the historical
accuracy of his information but mentions a number of liberties that an
author may take with trial records in order to give them shape: 'Die
Freiheiten des Verfassers liegen in der Auswahl, in der Anordnung, in der

Formulierung und in der Konzentration des Stoffes.' (The author exercises his freedom in the selection, the arranging, formulating and concentration of the material.)[16] But even these quite extensive formal alterations did not achieve Kipphardt's aim and he found himself forced to go further: 'Um die Form eines sowohl strengeren als auch umfassenderen Zeitdokuments zu erreichen ... waren einige Ergänzungen und Vertiefungen erforderlich.' (In order to arrive at a more tightly-knit as well as comprehensive document of our time, some expansion and deepening was necessary.)[17] At the end of most of the play's scenes one of the leading figures has a monologue created by the playwright to add 'depth' to the play and make explicit the wider implications of the hearings. The most important of these monologues is Oppenheimer's own final statement (an obvious parallel to Brecht's *Galileo's* concluding speech). Kipphardt's claim to have written these monologues in the spirit of their speakers' known and well-documented views is difficult to substantiate. In the case of Oppenheimer himself we know that he protested against the liberties taken. In a letter to the author and a number of directors intending to produce the play, Oppenheimer wrote on 12 October 1964: 'Von Anfang an hat sich mein Einwand nicht auf den Umstand beschränkt, dass ich während des Verhörs die Rede, die Sie erfunden haben, gar nicht hielt: mein Haupteinwand ist der, dass Sie mich Dinge sagen lassen, die meine Meinung weder waren noch sind.' (From the very beginning my objection was not confined to the fact that I did not make your invented speech at the hearings: my chief objection is to your making me say things which neither were nor are my opinions.)[18] Where Kipphardt, for example, makes *his* Oppenheimer refer to his work in nuclear physics with the words: 'Wir haben die Arbeit des Teufels getan' (We did the work of the Devil),[19] the real Oppenheimer stood up and protested that he never expressed any regrets at having participated in the production of the atom bomb. In order to make his play more clear and comprehensive than the actuality it represents, Kipphardt used hardly a sentence of the original transcript, and he offers the traditional Aristotelian defence for his procedure in terms of the aesthetic and philosophical superiority of art over history: 'Die gebotene Konzentration war mit einer wortgetreuen Montage von Rede und Gegenrede nicht zu erzielen, und sie schien dem Autor im Interesse der Einheit des Stückes auch nicht wünschenswert. Er bemühte sich, die Worttreue durch Sinntreue zu ersetzen.' (The required concentration could not be achieved with the use of a montage of literal speeches and counterspeeches, nor did this seem desirable to the author in the interests of the play's unity. He attempted to stick to the spirit rather than the letter.)[20] Some critics have found Kipphardt's procedure provoking. The legitimacy of such a mongrel form is indeed questionable.[21] Kipphardt tries to explain away his play's lack of literary quality in terms of its respect for the facts, and to defend the liberties taken with those facts in terms of literary licence. There are some obvious difficulties inherent in the genre. In the process of dramatisation, documentary material necessarily undergoes a number of changes. To select and condense are the rightful prerogatives of the playwright. But in all documentary plays to date, the author's own political and moral commitments have led him to adapt the material with a personal bias. In the *Oppenheimer* play this results in a distortion of Oppenheimer's views on atomic warfare, although Kipphardt's own views on the subject are unmistakable. Similarly, Günter Grass in *Die Plebejer proben den Aufstand* (The Plebeians Rehearse the Uprising, 1966) interprets the role of Bertolt Brecht in the workers' protest march of 17 June 1953 in East Berlin, and presents a general statement of his personal beliefs rather than an objective account of Brecht's attitude towards the event. When the workers asked Brecht for his support in their fight against excessive demands for higher productivity, Brecht's political views were, according to Grass, put to a test which he failed. Brecht saw the matter differently: for him, the workers' protest was not a potential revolution but the expression of temporary conflict within a progressive socialist system. The revolution had already taken place – in 1917.

A similar tendentiousness, imposed upon the material, rather than abstracted from it, informs Weiss's *Die Ermittlung*, where we have a distillation of the proceedings of the Frankfurt Auschwitz trial based on official records and on Weiss's own notes when he attended the trial towards its end. 'Von all dem', Weiss comments in a prefatory note to the play, 'kann auf der Bühne nur ein Konzentrat der Aussage übrig bleiben. Dieses Konzentrat soll nichts anderes enthalten als Fakten, wie sie bei der Gerichtsverhandlung zur Sprache kamen.' (All that remains of this on the stage is the essence of the statement. This essence must contain nothing beyond the facts as they were brought up in the course of the trial.)[22] After having reduced the number of witnesses and the amount of testimony, Weiss added a number of statements which are blatantly tendentious. In the course of his research on Auschwitz Weiss had come across material which convinced him that some of the largest and most famous public companies in present-day Germany had worked hand in hand with the SS, profiting from the extermination camps. Weiss argues with Brecht that fascism is the ultimate manifestation of capitalism and, going beyond the trial records, he attempts to show that economic forces determined the behaviour of the defendants. One of the most frequently quoted speeches from the play is one of Weiss's own additions to the trial records:

> Wir müssen die erhabene Haltung fallen lassen
> dass uns diese Lagerwelt unverständlich ist
> Wir kannten alle die Gesellschaft
> aus der das Regime hervorgegangen war

Das solche Lager erzeugen konnte
Die Ordnung die hier galt
war uns in ihrer Anlage vertraut
deshalb konnten wir uns auch noch zurechtfinden
in ihrer letzten Konsequenz
in der der Ausbeutende in bisher unbekanntem Grad
seine Herrschaft entwickeln durfte.

(*Die Ermittlung*, pp. 78–9)

(We have to drop the superior attitude
that the world of the camps is incomprehensible to us
We all knew the society
from which the regime had emerged
The system that ruled the camps
was basically familiar to us
that's why we could go along with it
even in its ultimate manifestation
when the exploiter could
extend his tyranny to a degree previously unknown.)

In his answer to a review of the Stockholm production of the play, Weiss explained with reference to this speech: 'Ein zentraler Abschnitt des Stücks weist auf die Rolle der Gesellschaft hin, in der solche Lager entstehen können. Es wird ausgesprochen, dass es sich hier nur um die letzte Konsequenz eines Systems der Ausbeutung handelt, das von einem andern Gesichtspunkt aus schönfärberisch "Freies Unternehmertum" genannt wird.' (A central part of the play points to the role played by the society which can create such camps. I say that what we have here is nothing but the ultimate manifestation of a system of exploitation which from a different viewpoint is put forward in fine colours as 'Free Enterprise'.)[23] Weiss's play sets out to interpret the concentration camps as a natural product of capitalism, and this intention clearly defines the dramatic convention he is working within. Like so many playwrights in the post-war tradition, he uses drama as a weapon against his own society. 'Das Stück', Weiss writes elsewhere, 'entbehrt nicht der aktuellen Sprengkraft. Ein Grossteil davon behandelt die Rolle der deutschen Grossindustrie bei der Judenausrottung. Ich will den Kapitalismus brandmarken, der sich sogar als Kundschaft für Gaskammern hergibt.' (The play is not lacking in political dynamite. A major part of it deals with the role played by German heavy industry with regards to the extermination of the Jews. My intention is to expose capitalism as having sunk to trade with the gas chambers.)[24] And Weiss goes further; the contemporary relevance of *Die Ermittlung* rests on the author's challenge of his own society as well as that of the previous generation: the play is an investigation into the capitalism of Germany in the sixties. This is how the prosecution concludes one of the cantos:

Lassen Sie es uns noch einmal bedenken
dass die Nachfolger dieser Konzerne heute zu glanzvollen Abschlüssen kommen

und dass sie sich wie es heisst
in einer neuen Expansionphase befinden.   (*Die Ermittlung*, p.93)

(Let us remember once again
that the successors to these big firms win huge contracts these days
and as I hear
they are going through a new phase of expansion.)

In his notes on the play Weiss repeatedly emphasised its topicality and
demonstrated its 'Modellcharakter' (representative nature) by showing
similar forces at work all over the world: 'Die Technik der Men-
schenvernichtung geht weiter ... Die gesamte afrikanische Bevölkerung
Südafrikas lebt praktisch im Konzentrationslager ... Amerikaner lassen
sich nach Vietnam ausschiffen, um eine andere Menschenrasse anzu-
greifen, und so weiter.' (The practice of genocide continues ... The whole
African population of South Africa lives practically in concentration camps
... Americans let themselves be shipped to Vietnam to attack another race,
and so on.)[25] In his *Notizen zum dokumentarischen Theater* Weiss indicates the
main strength of the documentary play: 'Die Stärke des dokumentarischen
Theaters liegt darin, dass es aus den Fragmenten der Wirklichkeit ein
Verwendbares Muster, ein Modell der aktuellen Vorgänge zusam-
menzustellen vermag.' (The strength of documentary theatre is its ability to
fashion a serviceable model from fragments of reality, to indicate a system
underlying contemporary events.)[26] We are forcefully reminded of Frisch's
insistence in his introductory remarks to *Andorra*, warning the audience
against identifying the events of the play with just one particular set of
circumstances. He too wished to emphasise the pattern emerging from a
study of history when he insisted: 'Andorra ist der Name für ein Modell.'
(Andorra stands for a system.)[27] Frisch has repeatedly rejected
documentary theatre as an acceptable alternative to his own parable plays,
referring to it as 'jener hoffnungslosen Art von Theater, das sich Realität
durch Imitation von Realität verspricht' (that hopeless kind of drama
which fancies it will achieve realism by imitating reality).[28] One of the
playwrights Frisch implicitly rejects is Hochhuth, who has quoted *Andorra*
as an especially fine example of the kind of realism he is aiming at in *Soldaten*:
'*Andorra*, völlig frei erfunden, ist dennoch Wahrheit, ist Wirklichkeit, ist
realistische Kunst – und das strikte Gegenteil jeder Willkür. Auch die Figur
meines Bomberpiloten Dorland ist frei erfunden – frei, nicht willkürlich.'
(*Andorra*, entirely free invention, is nevertheless true, real, realistic art – and
the very opposite of arbitrariness. My figure of the bomber pilot, too, is
freely invented – freely not arbitrarily.)[29] Introducing his last documentary
play *Guerillas* (1970), Hochhuth insists on typicality as a necessary quality
of literature: 'Wenn Schopenhauer vereinfachte: die Geschichte *eines*
Bauernhofes enthalte die aller anderen – so bleibt immerhin zu überlegen,
ob nicht doch erzählenswert von einem Bauernhof nur ist, was so auf jedem

sich ereignet oder ereignen könnte.' (Schopenhauer simplified matters when he said that the history of *one* farm contained within itself the histories of all others – still one has to consider, whether the only thing worth telling of a farm is not what happens or could happen on every one of them.)[30]

Possibly critics have gone too far in placing *Andorra* and *Die Ermittlung* at the opposite ends of the spectrum of contemporary theatre and perhaps they have concentrated too exclusively on formal aspects, over-stressing the differences between parable play and documentary play.[31] Both explicitly attempt to make a general statement on society, whether or not a specific country's history is used for that statement. Authors and critics have exaggerated the aloofness from actuality of *Andorra* and the restriction to actuality of *Die Ermittlung*. There is a shared, and in the case of the documentary play an underestimated, concern to transcend the accident of history. Kipphardt makes this point especially emphatically in his postscript to the *Oppenheimer* play:

> Es ist die Absicht des Verfassers, ein abgekürztes Bild des Verfahrens zu liefern, das szenisch darstellbar ist, und das die Wahrheit nicht beschädigt. Da sein Geschäft die Bühne, nicht die Geschichtsschreibung ist, versucht er nach dem Ratschlag des Hegel, den 'Kern und Sinn' einer historischen Begebenheit aus den 'umherspielenden Zufälligkeiten und gleichgültigem Beiwerke des Geschehens' freizulegen, 'die nur relativen Umstände und Charakterzüge abzustreifen und dafür solche an die Stelle zu setzen, durch welche die Substanz der Sache klar herausscheinen kann'.

> (It is the author's intention to present a shortened version of those proceedings, a version which lends itself to being staged and which does not distort the truth. As the author's business is the stage, and not the writing of history, he endeavours to follow Hegel's advice and lay bare 'the core and significance' of an historical event by freeing it from the 'adventitious contingencies and irrelevant accessories of the event', to 'strip away the circumstances and aspects that are of merely secondary importance, and to replace them with such that allow the essence of the matter to appear in all its clarity'.)[32]

But when Kipphardt says he is following Hegel's advice in allowing 'the essence of the matter to appear in all its clarity' we must remind ourselves that it is *Kipphardt's conception* of that essence that emerges, and the same applies to Hochhuth and Weiss.

In the early seventies the movement of documentary drama appears to have exhausted itself, with its major representatives Hochhuth, Kipphardt, and Weiss having abandoned it. Among the reasons for this was a disillusionment among intellectuals with the extreme left-wing politics which had informed most of the plays. This disillusionment was nurtured by such events as the publication of Solzhenitsyn's *One Day in the Life of Ivan Denisovitch* (1964) and ten years later the same author's documentary *Gulag Archipelago*, both of which illustrate the terrifying reality of one particular

206 Drama and society

Communist regime. The general public in West Germany between 1970 and 1974 was confronted with the terrorist acts of the Baader–Meinhoff group, resulting in a fear of all forms of extremism. The trial proceedings against the Baader–Meinhoff group have not inspired a documentary play and perhaps, if one had been written, there would have been no audience for it. In 1967 Peter Weiss could not find a German theatre to produce his play on Angola *Gesang vom lusitanischen Popanz* (Song of the Lusitanian Bogey), and it was premièred in Stockholm. Hochhuth felt that it was due only to Piscator's influence and powerful position that his early plays were produced at all.[33]

Towards the end of the sixties documentary prose works appeared alongside the plays. The *Bottroper Protokolle* (Bottrop Transcripts, 1968) compiled by Erika Runge[34] are the transcripts of interviews with the inhabitants of a small mining town in north Germany, recording their reactions to the closing down of the mine on which their livelihoods depended. F. C. Delius's documentary satire *Unsere Siemens-Welt* (Our Siemens-World, 1972) takes a look at the history of the Siemens works – there is a chapter on Siemens's involvement with Auschwitz – but concentrates on an analysis of the powerful economic and political position of the company in contemporary West German society. These publications appear to indicate a greater concern with issues of very topical and specifically German interest, rather than with the broader historical and often international subjects of the plays discussed here. It remains to be seen whether this development can lead to a new form which might employ the documentary technique for valid criticism of contemporary society.

NOTES

1. Peter Weiss, 'Notizen zum dokumentarischen Theater', *Rapporte 2* (Frankfurt: Suhrkamp Verlag, 1971), pp. 98–9.
2. Rolf Hochhuth, *Der Stellvertreter* (Hamburg: Rowohlt Verlag, 1963), p. 229.
3. Weiss, 'Notizen', p. 104.
4. *Ibid.*, p. 91.
5. Erwin Piscator, *Das politische Theater*, ed. L. Hoffmann (Berlin: Henschelverlag Kunst und Gesellschaft, 1968), p. 267.
6. Hochhuth, *Stellvertreter*, p. 229.
7. Rolf Hochhuth, *Guerillas* (Hamburg: Rowohlt Verlag, 1970), p. 20.
8. Hochhuth, *Guerillas*, p. 21.
9. Rolf Hochhuth, 'Zu *Soldaten*', *Krieg und Klassenkrieg* (Hamburg: Rowohlt Verlag, 1971), p. 193.
10. Hochhuth, *Stellvertreter*, p. 229.
11. Günther Rühle, 'Versuche über eine geschlossene Gesellschaft', *Theater Heute*, 10 (1966), 9.

12. *The Storm over The Deputy. Essays and Articles about Hochhuth's Explosive Drama.* ed. Eric Bentley (New York: Grove Press, 1964), p. 53.

13. The plays in question are: H. Kipphardt, *In der Sache J. Robert Oppenheimer*; G. Grass, *Die Plebejer proben den Aufstand*; R. Hochhuth, *Soldaten*; P. Weiss, *Trotzki im Exil*.

14. Hochhuth, 'Zu *Soldaten*', p. 194.

15. *Ibid.*, p. 194.

16. Heinar Kipphardt, *In der Sache J. Robert Oppenheimer* (Frankfurt: Suhrkamp Verlag, 1964), p. 142.

17. *Ibid.*, pp. 142–3.

18. Quoted in Heinz Geiger, *Widerstand und Mitschuld* (Düsseldorf: Bertelsmann Universitätsverlag, 1973), p. 177.

19. Kipphardt, *Oppenheimer*, p. 141.

20. *Ibid.*, p. 143.

21. D. E. Zimmer points to the 'Fragwürdigkeit eines dramatischen Zwittergenres, das sich für seine mangelnden literarischen Qualitäten entschuldigt mit dem Respekt vor den Fakten ... und die Freiheiten, die es sich mit diesen Fakten dennoch nimmt, mit den Erfordernissen der Literatur rechtfertigt,' (the questionable nature of a mongrel dramatic form excusing its lack of literary merit by referring to its respect for the facts and justifying the liberties it nevertheless takes with these facts by referring to the demands of literature). Quoted in Geiger, *Widerstand*, p. 83.

22. Peter Weiss, *Die Ermittlung* (Hamburg: Rowohlt Verlag, 1969), p. 7.

23. Peter Weiss, 'Antwort auf eine Kritik zur Stockholmer Aufführung der *Ermittlung*', *Rapporte 2*, p. 47.

24. *Über Peter Weiss*, ed. Volker Canaris (Frankfurt: Suhrkamp Verlag, 1970), p. 82.

25. Weiss, 'Antwort auf eine Kritik', p. 49.

26. Weiss, 'Notizen', p. 97.

27. Max Frisch, *Stücke*, II (Frankfurt: Suhrkamp Verlag, 1966), p. 200.

28. 'Noch einmal anfangen können' Ein Gespräch mit Max Frisch (Dieter E. Zimmer), *Die Zeit*, 22 December 1967, p. 13.

29. Hochhuth, 'Zu *Soldaten*', p. 195.

30. Hochhuth, *Guerillas*, p. 20.

31. See, for example, Hellmuth Karasek's '*Die wahren Beweggründe*' and the other pieces brought together under the heading '*Dokumentartheater – und die Folgen*', in *Akzente*, 13 (1966).

32. Kipphardt, *Oppenheimer*, p. 142.

33. Hochhuth, 'Die Diskussion des Aufrufs zum Klassenkampf', *Krieg und Klassenkrieg*, p. 69.

34. *Bottroper Protokolle*, Aufgezeichnet von Erika Runge (Frankfurt: Suhrkamp Verlag, 1968).

British television drama and society in the 1970s

EDWIN EIGNER

British television drama has always seen itself in relation to society. Its hope now is that it may continue to please a nation which, confidently, almost patronisingly, it began by intending to serve and which, in its most vital years, it struggled to change. According to Shaun Sutton, the purpose of his BBC drama department is primarily to entertain. Mr Sutton has done a great deal to preserve television drama, but he would certainly not like to be understood as a man with a social mission. And at the independent companies, where the flag of drama flies much lower than at the BBC, some of the same playwrights who once frightened their subsidised competitors into a period of genuine creativity are now working almost exclusively on television series and waiting, perhaps, although with rather mixed emotions, for another Sydney Newman to come out of the West. Just now Britain badly wants an international winner of any sort, and its television drama is freely acknowledged the best in the world, certainly the most widely respected (very nearly the only respected) of British exports. One might look for a healthy arrogance among television drama people if these were not such nervous times for all institutions.

The functions which television drama first thought to fulfil were to bring the theatrical heritage to the people, and the West End to the provinces. No one doubted that theatre was good for society, and British television, committed as it was to the Reithian ideal of public-service broadcasting, saw itself largely as a means of distributing these national treasures. 'In the three pre-war years of television', writes Anthony Davis, 'the BBC transmitted 326 plays ... only 14 of ... [which] were specially written for television.'[1] And a similar emphasis prevailed after the war until the middle 1950s. During Michael Barry's years as Director of Drama, BBC television became a sort of national window into the London theatres. In the meantime, the tradition of transmitting plays presented from, or originally written for, the stage has declined, although it has been kept alive with such BBC series as 'Festival', 'Theatre 625' and, currently, 'Play of the Month', whose title would, if it were not for the fact that some months pass with no theatrical ration at all, provide an apt illustration of what has become of the tradition in forty years. ITV's prime-time contribution of stage plays adapted for television during the 1976–7 season consisted of a brief winter spurt of only three pieces, all from the twentieth century and one of these American.[2]

This decline from about two-a-week on a single channel to about one-a-month spread over three has been caused in part by the growth of other aspects of television, including, of course, the emergence of original television drama. But theatre-on-television has suffered along with original television plays from what is certainly the most frequently discussed and widely lamented development in the field of television drama – the increasing disinclination among controllers to schedule many single plays. An ex-scriptwriter for ITV affirms that:

> Over the years the hours given to drama have shrunk. I believe that the BBC's drama slots, covering all kinds of drama, have shrunk by 200 hours a year. This has particularly affected the single play ... but the companies go around pretending that the situation doesn't exist. They will tell you that far from the single play being relegated, it is uppermost in their mind and they will rattle off the names they have lined up for the autumn, all of them well-worn names, to prove that they are investing heavily in the single play.[3]

The single play has indeed been the greatest casualty of the competition between the three channels. 'Both the serials and the series have', as Raymond Williams writes, 'advantages for programme planners: a time-slot, as it is significantly called, can be filled for a run of weeks, and in their element of continuity the serial and the series encourage attachment to a given station or channel.'[4] Since the single play can provide no week-to-week continuity of plot or character or situation or, except in the broadest sense, of theme, it fails to develop much viewer loyalty. As a result, those in charge of drama have been going more and more to serials and series or – and this is a compromise worked out specifically to save the single play – to anthology series expressing some common theme. The compromise has provided less benefit for televised stage plays than for original television drama because it is harder to find plays which express a given theme than to commission them, and it will become even less of a help in the future as producers are made to understand that the themes in an anthology series had better be pretty specific if they are to provide the kind of hook for viewers which is apparently required. A programme title like 'She', which London Weekend Television used in 1977 for a short series of original plays about women, could also have worked for *Electra*, *Antony and Cleopatra*, *The Duchess of Malfi*, and *Hedda Gabler*, but the audience of the imagined series of classics would probably be as unaware of the existence of a controlling theme as were the viewers who watched all or, like the present writer, only a part of the actual series. The thematic anthology is, for reasons we shall discuss later on, an unsatisfactory solution to the problem of the decline of the single play written for television, but it certainly will not rescue the classic drama, which will be regarded as an even greater liability as the time slots fill with ongoing programmes, whose loyal viewers can be expected to resent having a favourite show pre-empted for the sake of their culture or the companies' burdensome commitment to a faded social purpose.

Another reason for the decline of stage drama on television is, undoubtedly, the feeling among television people that they have failed to bring the essence of the theatre to the television audience, that something important has almost always been lost in the transmission. Television had to go through the same experience as the cinema in discovering that it could not get away simply with presenting a moving picture of a stage production, except that television, since it is seen in the familiar environment of one's own livingroom, makes even greater demands for realism than the cinema does. Actors, like politicians, had to learn to moderate their gestures and facial expressions if they were to have any credibility within the intimate family circle. At the same time, the viewers, most of whom had been conditioned for drama by watching the cinema, required much more movement and a greater variety of setting than stage plays generally provide.

One cannot, therefore, simply televise a play from the stage or move the play from the stage into the studio. A special television production has to be mounted, and even this alteration will not necessarily make the play entirely satisfactory, for the very language of the theatrical drama is usually wrong when presented through this traditionally less formal and less stylised medium. Television dialogue, writes Arthur Swinson, 'needs a simpler, more realistic style. Neither the heroic nor the highly artificial style of theatre proves effective on television'.[5] And then the television production, since neither BBC nor the independent companies can afford more than three weeks of rehearsal time, lacks the polish, the timing and, most essentially, the *ésprit* which is achieved in the theatre through the more leisurely pace of preparation. Something else is missing: the excitement of presentation. Major drama seems to fizzle out on British television, probably again because of the rehearsal routine. This is the one respect, it seems to me, in which American television drama has the advantage. The Americans rehearse even less, I suppose, but their general blast-off-to-the-moon mentality appears to work on such occasions.

In America, unfortunately, it is now almost impossible to see televised adaptations from the stage except on the educational channels, and when drama becomes education, the game is very nearly over. BBC's major 1977 effort for the stage play, a Sunday morning Open University class in the history of the drama, has therefore to be regarded with mixed feelings. On the one hand, some of the performances of plays or parts of plays were excellent. But even if the production of *Woyzeck* may have been superior this time, I cannot help thinking that the total enterprise was in a better state in 1967 when an updated version of Büchner's drama appeared as BBC's 'Wednesday Play', and where the educational thrust, like Büchner's, was social rather than cultural. British television drama's relationship to society had already changed in the 1960s, and what we see now when we regard classic drama on television is only a ghost-like reminder of that first confident and dedicated resolve to bring the theatre and its tradition to the British people. We ought not, therefore, to be very optimistic about the ambitious BBC project to tape or film all of Shakespeare. Unmotivated by this dedicated resolve, the individual plays may lack vitality. Still, it will be good to have them for our classrooms.

'Wednesday Play' had been instituted at BBC in 1964 when Sydney Newman was Head of Drama, and the adaptation of *Woyzeck* was something of an anomaly for that series which usually specialised in contemporary drama written specifically for television. This had been one of Newman's important innovations at ITV a few years earlier when he had taken over 'Armchair Theatre'. His other major contribution was the impetus he gave this original drama towards the examination of social questions and the depiction of working-class life. 'I came to Britain at a crucial time in 1958 when the seeds of *Look Back in Anger* were beginning to flower', Newman is quoted as saying in the *Daily Express* of 5 January 1963. 'I am proud that I played some part in the recognition that the working man was a fit subject for drama, and not just a foil in a play on middle-class manners.'[6] According to Anthony Davis, Newman called for 'plays about real people in provincial towns, people who worked in factories and shops and got dirty and had the sort of problems the majority of viewers might experience. [And] he sought new writers to give him what he wanted ... adaptors virtually disappeared from the studios at Teddington.'[7] Most commentators recall this time, a period of realism and social engagement, as the most creative in the history of British television drama. Allan Prior, one of the writers, calls 1960–1 'the best original drama season ever mounted'.[8]

In the late fifties and early sixties, television drama, under the influence of the angry young men and with the impetus supplied by Newman's personality, seemed to have found a purpose in social protest, a form in the single play, and a genre in kitchen-sink realism. The purpose, or at least the too-frank avowal of it, no longer suits the mood of Britain in the 1970s, a place where it does not seem wise to take things too seriously. The single play, as we have seen, is, moreover, the victim of strong economic pressures. Thus Christopher Morahan, former Head of Plays in the BBC Drama Group is quoted as saying, 'We at the BBC want to produce plays that are seen. We're not in a minority business, and we like to have large audiences.'[9] Only the genre, realism, which came under attack from very early on, maintains something of a strange and irrelevant hold. The 1976 BAFTA award for the best single play was won by *The Bar Mitzvah Boy*, which was written in what Sean Day-Lewis calls 'the familiar [Jack] Rosenthal slice-of-life style'.[10] Rosenthal's *The Evacuees*, a semi-autobiographical piece, was an important prize-winner of the year before.

All of these developments of purpose, form, and genre are interrelated. The social commitment of television drama has certainly been modified by the economic pressures, and it can be argued that realism played its part in the demise of the single play by encouraging the development of its greatest competitor, the dramatic series. The great season of 1960–1, which television writers recall nostalgically, was the heyday of 'Armchair Theatre', but also of 'Z Cars', an uncompromisingly realistic police series. The soap-opera 'Coronation Street', which also began around this time, has never seemed comparable to the early 'Z Cars' in quality of dialogue and characterisation, but both continuing dramas are clearly developments of British television realism, as have been nearly all the popular series.

'Everybody wants the single play to go on', reports Allan Prior,[11] but he and the other realists have been able to accommodate themselves to writing the series with remarkably little difficulty. Ted Willis was one of the first to voice fear that the series might kill the single play,[12] but Willis was himself the creator of the excellent realistic police series, 'Dixon of Dock Green'.

Willis's concern was that dramatists would turn away from the single play because they could not make a living writing such works, but neither he nor the other realists should be hastily accused of selling out. Prior believes that 'the drama-series and the one-shot play are basically similar exercises. Having written both, my experience is that it is possible to treat *some* subjects as frankly and honestly inside the very best drama-series as it is inside a single play.'[13] There are, moreover, or appear to be, some advantages for the realist in the series form. The great strength of British realism has always been in the gradually unfolding depiction of credible characters. This is one of the reasons that the romance, with its emphases on plot and theme, was regarded as a minor genre in the nineteenth century and why the British short story has never been able really to compete with the novel as an art form. The dramatic series has the advantage, as the Lord Annan *Report* points out, that it provides 'actors and both new and experienced writers with an opportunity to develop characterisation'.[14]

The television dramatist John Hopkins suggests another factor which favours the dramatic series, one which only a realist can sufficiently value: 'The continuity of a series ... allows a greater freedom in the resolution of each story; the freedom not to resolve the story.'[15] And, of course, when the series is one of those principally connected by a theme rather than a set of characters, as was the case with Hopkins's own excellent set of six plays, *Fathers and Families* (January to March 1977, on BBC1) then the format can serve actually to underline the idea which the writer is trying to express. He gets juxtaposition and a cumulative effect, not to mention the benefit of two titles.

Nevertheless, Raymond Williams is concerned that when 'many television dramatists now write episodes for serials or series more often than they write single plays, they usually find themselves writing within an established formation of situation and leading characters, in what can be described as a collective but is more often a corporate dramatic enterprise'.[16] In this situation the individual vision of realism is, of course, jeopardised, and the kind of social protest which can be expected to come from a sort of committee of between-jobs writers hired by a public institution is probably limited.

Just such a committee, composed of the writers of the Lord Annan *Report on the Future of Broadcasting*, recommend that 'both the BBC and commercial broadcasters should have a duty to produce single plays, so long as good single plays are being written' (p. 329), but such a statement is not responsive to the most frequently voiced concern of the critics of the series, which is that good single plays will not continue to be written unless enough time-slots are kept open to encourage the development of new writers of the single play. BBC2 reserves portions of the 'Centre Play' series – 'Centre Play Showcase' and 'Second City Firsts' – for the single plays of young writers, but such nurseries are another instance, like the Open University series of classic drama, of television having to do self-consciously and with a special effort what it used to do naturally and as a part of its ongoing function. Some of the 'Showcase' and 'Second City' plays were worth watching, but new writers do not seem to be growing from such soil as profusely as they did when they responded to the rougher and less artificial nurture of 'Armchair Theatre' and 'Wednesday Play'. 'Ten years ago', wrote W. Stephen Gilbert in the *Observer* for 10 July 1977, 'when "The Wednesday Play" scored a 34-play season, many of the writers were learning on the job. But since the arrival of Colin Welland and Arthur Hopcraft as the last products of the Golden Age of teledrama, you can count the new TV playwrights of substance on the fingers of one hand.'

The arguments and attitudes we have been following all suggest that while the realistic dramatic series may, for better or for worse, be edging out the single play, realism is nevertheless the appropriate genre for television. Realism encourages an emphasis on characterisation, which Englishmen have always regarded as the proper business of narrative or dramatic art; it demands a dialogue of understatement, which the medium seems to require; it presents settings that do not clash violently with the livingrooms in which it is received; and when pushed to naturalism, it allows the kind of social statement television dramatists still sometimes hanker to make. At least, when the television set is a mirror to those watching it, its contents ought to seem relevant to their lives.

There remain those, however, who believe that realism has destroyed the single play, not indirectly, through the creation of the more popular realistic dramatic series, but immediately by virtue of the unimaginative, despairing single dramas its influence created. This is not a new attitude. It stems from a feeling which was voiced even before there was much original television drama in Britain, that directors and actors were settling on realism too easily and thus cutting off important possibilities for fruitful experimentation. Twenty-five years ago Jan Bussell, a television writer and producer, regretted that his medium 'seems to have been wedded to a realistic style both in its acting and in its scenery, even when presenting Shakespeare. On such a beautifully compact and small screen [Bussell was also a gifted puppeteer] there is not room for the detail of realism. But there are great opportunities for the use of dramatic symbols.' According to Bussell, 'experimental production' was 'a crying need of television'.[17] More recently, Stuart Hood has commented on how the television play 'has – broadly speaking – remained attached to the tradition of naturalistic drama and failed to show that adventurous spirit for experiment which, in the same era, has marked both film and stage'.[18]

Allan Prior writes more specifically of how this failure of originality has worked against the single play:

> British audiences, in the main, do not like a hopeless and despairing view of life, and in the main that is what the younger playwrights have been giving them. There have been, over the last two or three years [this article was published in 1971], a lot of dark-grey comedies on British television, some-times so many that they seemed to merge into one another and become a sort of strange drama series, with interchangeable characters and situations. Writers in television are influenced by other writers in television (like writers anywhere), and a fashion and style of drama developed that the play-watching public did not like.[19]

The influence, according to Arthur Swinson, came not only from John Osborne, but much more powerfully from the American television writer Paddy Chayefsky, and the trouble was that while British writers found Chayefsky's bleak world compelling, they lacked the optimistic faith in human nature by which he had transformed and redeemed his world. 'Week after week', Swinson laments, 'both channels are occupied by realis-tic little dramas .... The husbands bicker at the wives, the wives nag the husbands. Their minute failings and retreats are chronicled in agonizing detail .... This is not ... [Chayefsky's] "marvelous world of the ordinary". It is the sub-ordinary world of the ordinary.'[20] But Swinson's most severe criticism of British television realism is his attack on its social relevancy. The realistic little dramas, he asserts, are 'played out in a vacuum. The winds of change, the great forces of religion, economics, politics, the great subterranean movements of our time, the passion of sport, the fires of ambition, play little or no part in these plays.'[21]

This, of course, is a difficulty with realism. It imitates the real world as the writer perceives that world, and any comment it makes, social or otherwise, must come out of the imitation. Realism withers when idea controls character and situation, or, more frequently, the irrepressible characters of realism refuse to illustrate the ideas which the author would impose on them. They have their own souls to make. An excellent illustration of this sort of refusal was made by Evan Jones's *Rehearsal* (BBC2, 19 July 1977). Here, a propagandist lady producer of an improvised play which is in rehearsal, knits furiously like Madame Defarge and tries repeatedly to alter the course of the improvisations with stentorian interruptions; but is nevertheless unable to force the actors to make what she regards as socially responsible statements. Operating from the reality of their creative imaginations and on the bases of their own experiences, which is indeed the essential technique of realism, the actors produce a poignant *Zoo Story* instead of an instructive *Animal Farm*. It is likely, moreover, that when ideas emerge from realistic works, as indeed they sometimes do, it is as the result of a much longer study of the situation and the characters than the hurried writing of so transient a form as the television drama can afford. And this is perhaps another reason why television seems to be losing interest in social commentary, if to be socially relevant requires the abandonment of realism.

But for those who remain interested in social relevancy, what other more appropriate genres are available? Although an excellent adaptation of *The Picture of Dorian Gray* appeared on BBC1 in September 1976, serious fantasy does not seem to present itself as a real alternative. The adaptation was by John Osborne and may indicate, along with his other September 1976 contribution, a half-hour romantic piece broadcast by Yorkshire Television called *Almost a Vision*, that, twenty years after *Look Back in Anger*, Osborne, if he could find some of the old power, would like to lead British television drama in a new direction. It would, indeed, require a major voice to revitalise romance, with which, outside the nursery, the English have never really been comfortable. There is a fair amount of the occult or mysterious on British television, but the English romantic imagination has been so trivialised with regard to romance that when things go bump in the night here, one need no longer be alert for some important message.

Satire is, of course, a dangerous business when one addresses an audience of millions, for, as most satirists quickly learn, the opposite of the intended meaning is the one most likely to be received. Alan Plater's 'The Middleman', a series of satiric fantasies about a pair of operators trying to carry on business as usual in spite of the collapse of civilisation and the absence of all commodities, shows flashes of brilliance and is quite as relevant and imaginative in some of its episodes as 'Trinity Tales', his series broadcast in

1976, was pointless and elephantine. But British television usually knows enough to keep away from satire. And plays which try to make the social point directly usually fail as drama. Examples are Brian Clark's *Happy Returns* (Granada, 6 May 1977), a heavy-handed demonstration by juxtaposition of how the rich get away with their tax fiddles and how the poor do not, and Alan Plater's *Short Back and Sides* (Yorkshire, 3 May 1977), in which a successful city planner is unconvincingly converted to social responsibility.

The great development in the field of social drama during the last ten years has been the fictional documentary, a television drama which pretends to be a public-service broadcast calling the viewers' attention to some problem in society. This genre has succeeded in almost every way. Many of the plays have been considerable artistic achievements, and most have been remarkably popular. Jeremy Sandford's *Edna The Inebriate Woman*, (BBC1, 21 October 1971) had an estimated audience of 9,250,000, which was about four million better than the average of the twenty-one other dramas which Irene Shubik produced on 'Play for Today'. Sandford's *Cathy Come Home* (BBC, 1966), a powerful treatment of 'the break-up of one family by our society['s] failure to provide housing',[22] achieved another kind of success. Its tremendous impact helped create Shelter, an organisation for the homeless which has become one of Britain's best supported and most effective charitable institutions. Nor was this effect on society merely the accidental benefit of a writer whose primary desire was to produce a work of art or, like the professed desire of those who now control BBC drama, merely to entertain. Sandford was most gratified at the changes his play had brought about in the lives of the real Cathys. Thus he writes:

> I wish that there had been more change in the general situation of Britain's homeless since I wrote *Cathy*. As regards its particular effect, however, I can feel pleased. It is good to know that I have altered, if only by a very small bit, the conditions of life for others in my own society. As a result of the film and certain meetings we held in Birmingham afterwards, this town and others ceased their practice of separating three or four hundred husbands each year from their wives and children. The husbands were allowed to return back to their families in a great gushing stream. It was intensely moving. I was lucky enough to be present on this jubilant occasion, and that moment, if no other, justified in my opinion not only my writing of *Cathy* but also my own existence.[23]

The metaphor of the gushing stream to describe the reunions of the husbands and wives is perhaps unfortunate, but Sandford's tone of self-congratulation betokens a healthy confidence of social purpose which has been missing from English letters since Dickens.

The potential value of the fictional documentary is considerable and has been recognised even by critics who object to its artistic possibilities. Thus Paul Ableman writes that such drama, while it cannot provide a true artistic experience because it chains itself to superficial reality, which it is incapable therefore of transcending, has, nevertheless, 'a function, one that it performs exceedingly well':

> It is not mere chance that the very best examples of the form – works like *In Two Minds, Cathy Come Home, Edna,* or even Colin Welland's *Roll on Five O'Clock*, should all be socially conscious plays, illuminating a highly specific and perfectly clear-cut social problem. For the logical role of the fictional documentary is a social-activist one. It is an efficient instrument for exposing social evils and indicating paths of rectification. It has, in other words, an essentially propagandist function.[24]

The emergence and even the success of this genre was a natural development of British television and might even have been predicted. Although it seems experimental in its use of film, of hand-held cameras, in its preference for amateur or at least little-known actors, and in its escape from the studio, the fictionalised documentary was only a logical next step from kitchen-sink realism with a social purpose. And it was not by accident that *Cathy Come Home* was produced for 'Wednesday Play' or that one of this controversial work's first champions was Sydney Newman,[25] whose background in creative documentary was of the best, since he had worked under John Grierson on the Canadian National Film Board.[26]

Grierson, who was, of course, the great master of the film documentary after Flaherty, saw himself as an artist and a realist. All the fictionalised or dramatised documentaries which have appeared on British television were based, I believe, on principles which derive from his works and writings. His was the insistence on 'authenticity and the drama that resides in the living fact',[27] and his also was the clear-headed understanding that the maker of the creative documentary, who reveals the reality of a situation and, by his juxtaposition of details, creates an interpretation of it, has an important social responsibility[28] and must be willing, therefore, to recognise himself frankly as a propagandist. Grierson, moreover, had a canny understanding of why the creative documentary had been so successful in Britain: 'It permitted the national talent for emotional under-statement to operate in a medium not given to understatement, [and] it allowed an adventure in the arts to assume the respectability of a public service.'[29]

When documentaries became purely fictional and were shifted from the cinema to television, where understatement and realism seem to be required (or have, at least, come to be expected) and where a public-service role is taken for granted, it was bound to be both popular and effective, so popular and so effective, in fact, that it has begun to frighten some people with the thought that our masters in 1984 will be certain to find a useful social purpose for the fictional documentary. For what are the safeguards against propaganda which convinces by presenting the imaginary as the real in a medium which characteristically mixes the two by transmitting news broadcasts and dramas back-to-back? Television has recently been testing its powers and possibilities in this direction. An ITV fictional documentary called *Alternative 3* (20 June 1977) was a reverse of the 'Mercury Theater' *Invasion from Mars* hoax. Through mock interviews and investigative reporting, it established in the minds of many gullible viewers that scientists, who are supposedly disappearing all around the world, are not being drained to America but resettled on the red planet, where there *is* life after all. And if David Ambrose and Christopher Miles, the authors, failed to create as much panic as Orson Welles did in the 1930s, it may have been because, since this was, after all, only a test, the producers took the responsible precaution of alerting the newspapers. The number of viewers who were nevertheless taken in is therefore even more impressive. Television dramatists are also experimenting with 'documentaries' which are almost entirely authentic but with perhaps one strand of purely imaginary drama interwoven. An excellent example of this technique is Karl Francis's *Above Us the Sky* (BBC, 11 June 1977) which combined an account of a fictional miner dying of emphysema with films of real miners discussing the closure of their pit. If television drama makes itself indistinguishable from television news, it may be accepted as fact and thus become frighteningly powerful propaganda. But, of course, the sword cuts in both directions, and the result of the confusion may be that television news loses its credibility. The only safeguard, really, is the discretion of the companies and the producers, and the only effective guarantees at the moment are the fear of controversy and the consequent waning interest among heads of television drama groups in social action.

This play-safe attitude of the companies (or is it an attitude reflecting artistic responsibility and social maturity?) is, of course, galling to those who believe that in days when television drama was willing to be more socially active, it managed also to be more exciting in the artistic sense. A recent editorial in *The Stage and Television Today* laments the situation:

> Have we got to the stage where, if a writer's work is to be accepted, it has to be put through a sieve and the ideas taken out before his script is produced. . . . The dramatic piece, as *Cathy Come Home* showed, can be a very powerful advocate, as well as being entertaining and moving. But television drama has been, and still is, absorbed in the past and has brought forth no work where ideas could intrigue and capture the audience's imagination. . . . If television drama cannot start to find room and attract writers with ideas, then it is going to become a glossy chocolate box parade.[30]

Of all forms, the period drama seems to most television commentators the glossiest and the least capable of social relevancy. I have saved it and the serials which have developed out of it for last because, while I shall have finally to agree that television's apparent absorption in the past may be crippling to its social purpose, I nevertheless find the blanket judgement against period drama odd and strangely uninformed about the tradition of the historical novel, which the period drama has come to resemble. The writer of an article entitled 'In Flight from Reality', remarks, for instance, that all period drama on television, even that dealing with recent periods, is motivated by 'escapism pure and simple', by the desire 'not to have to face up to today's reality quite yet'.[31] My own feeling is that while the period drama and the historical television novel certainly offer the chance to escape from the social problems of today, and while there has indeed been a certain amount of mindless costume drama on television, these forms also offer an excellent opportunity of facing the problems. My belief is that, in the last few years anyway, British television drama has, more frequently than not, made use of this second opportunity and has found in it the most effective and responsible way of keeping socially relevant.

I find my position difficult to argue because to do so involves interpreting the motives of the television producers and controllers who have chosen the specific period dramas to mount and the specific historical novels to adapt, and I could indeed be interpreting unconscious motivations as well as conscious. Or I may simply be imposing a pattern where none exists. Nevertheless, it certainly appears that most of the period dramas and historical television novels are concerned with the collapse of civilisation and that, while there have been some outstanding successes with the Tudor and the late Stuart periods, the period most frequently portrayed or recalled is the recent past – the last part of the nineteenth and the first part of the twentieth centuries – an era which Englishmen frequently enough recall with nostalgia, right enough, but sometimes with anger; and sometimes less emotionally, but with a constructive desire to learn from the past.

These three attitudes towards one's grandfather's days have been pre-occupations of the serious historical novel since Sir Walter Scott popular-ised the genre with *Waverley*. His romances made a lot of money and they may, indeed, have caused some people self-distructively to look away from the realities they had been better off to face. Flaubert was probably correct to blame Scott, if blame is the right word, for both of Emma Bovary's adulteries. Scott filled lots of heads with romance. And there may even be some justice in Mark Twain's extravagant pronouncement that Sir Walter was responsible for the American Civil War. But Scott wasn't writing for bourgeois Frenchwomen with dull husbands or Southern farmers on dull plantations. In any case he never realised a profit from such readers. Few men, however, were more aware of the political problems of Scotland than Scott was, and no one ever wrote more relevantly about them.

For Dickens, who, since *Pickwick Papers*, has been the patron saint of the serial form and has naturally enough become the special darling of period drama on British television, the historical novel provided an outlet for political opinions and a means of confronting his worst social fear, the breakdown of society and the attendant collapse of those human qualities which keep us decent to one another. Of Dickens's two historical novels, the one deals with a French revolution that goes mad and the other with a London riot in which men and homes are wantonly destroyed. Dickens's audience understood pretty well what he was up to, and *A Tale of Two Cities* was more frequently criticised for the liberties the author allegedly took with history in order to prove his political point than for any escape from the contemporary scene which the costumes may have seemed to afford.

The majority of the stage adaptations presented during the 1976–7 season on BBC1's 'Play of the Month' were twentieth-century period pieces, and except perhaps for Terence Rattigan's *The Winslow Boy*, which seemed somehow the oldest play in the series, they all had to do with the end of things or with the destruction of an aged social order. The tone was set rather early in the season with a twentieth-anniversary revival of *Look Back in Anger*. The anger, somehow, had turned to petulance. Later, the production of Noël Coward's *Private Lives* was perhaps the darkest ever mounted. A somewhat cleverer *No Exit*, this version left one feeling not that the principals had lucked into a marvellous escape, or even that they had lost their one opportunity for happiness, but rather that there never had been a chance for them and they have only now come to realise it. The shrill acts of Shaw's *Heartbreak House* were separated by film clips of approaching bombers, so as to make the final all-destructive air raid last throughout the play.

The older dramas shown on 'Play of the Month' reinforced the season's theme. *London Assurance* and *The Country Wife* showed foolishly decadent societies being manipulated by its cleverer but not more valuable members. This Horner was as much a fop as were the men he cleverly cuckolded, and the play consequently lacked any sane centre. With Wycherley, as in the modern plays, we were all going together to our destruction, although some of us were perhaps enjoying ourselves along the way a bit more than others. Actually, the enjoyment did not come across as all that great. The offering from Shakespeare, of course, had to be *King Lear*, and the 'nothings' re-echoed thunderously. It was, by and large, a desperate season. Even the production of *The Winslow Boy* left one feeling not so much that England would ultimately be saved by its principles of fair play, but that it was being strangled by the political divisions and social conventions which prevented Miss Winslow and the barrister from going off and, at least, having a dirty weekend together like the more vital and optimistic couple in *Hindle Wakes*, which ITV presented.

A difference between Dickens and the BBC in their uses of historical material or old plays to portray an end of things, is that Dickens was probably trying to come to terms with a catastrophe he expected in the future, while the television people seem to be concerned with a collapse which appears already to have taken place. At their best, the adaptors and writers of the television historical drama or novel are trying, I think, to discover and examine the event so that they can understand and learn from it.

History itself, if not historical fiction, is generally regarded in Britain as a socially useful discipline, a status which, in spite of the recent Bicentennial and the phenomenal success of 'Roots', it no longer enjoys in America. I do not suppose that many people in Britain still believe with Matthew Arnold that if we study the track of the past with sufficient care we may be able to discover where in the modern forest we lost it and thus be able to get back on and progress to a confident future. But there is a hope, bolstered by the general Marxist orientation and its respect for history, that if you can discover how you got into the fix, you may be able to devise some way out. I suspect this hope accounts for some of television's preoccupation with historical drama.

The phenomenally large audiences won by the television adaptation of Galsworthy's two trilogies certainly operated to focus attention on the beginning of the present century, but it is possible that some of the success of 'The Forsyte Saga' was due to the interest I have suggested in the period when the collapse is presumed to have occurred. In any event, a great deal of television's energy, and some of its best energy, has gone into the depiction of England and Europe in the years on either side of the First World War. 'Upstairs, Downstairs', 'When the Boat Comes In', 'The Fall of Eagles', 'Edward VII' are all of this period and they all deal, sentimentally, analytically, or dramatically, with the end of the old order. The great success of the 1976 season was Jack Pulman's fine adaptation of *I, Claudius*, which treats, of course, the collapse of another empire, the one from whose example the British, from the time of Gibbon and later of Bulwer-Lytton's *The Last Days of Pompeii*, have been most ready to accept instruction.

All of the television dramas mentioned in the preceding paragraph are either series or serials, and they allow therefore for the free use of the technique which Scott established as the norm for the British historical novel, that of following the event through the character development of an individual participant. Television drama, which has roots also in Shakespeare's history plays, differs from Scott in that it is sometimes much more likely to follow the development of the king himself than to see things through the eyes of one of his anonymous advisers, and this difference is significant, for the practice of focusing on the great man himself places at least an apparent emphasis on the historical as opposed to the fictional. Nevertheless, in 'Upstairs, Downstairs', where Edward VII appears as a minor character, and in 'Edward VII', where, of course, he figures centrally, the primary emphasis is on the unfolding of character, and this is an emphasis which the serial form, whether of publication or of television transmission, does superlatively well. As the writers of the nineteenth-century serial novel discovered, characters become more real to the readers when the acquaintance is spread over a considerable period. Another obvious advantage of the serial form is that it aids in creating the illusion of time passing, an illusion which is necessary in most long novels but particularly important for historical fiction.

The serial drama has proved, therefore, and should continue to prove, a good instrument for the cultivation of a socially responsible interest in the past. It presents history more convincingly than most other forms of imaginative literature do, and the week-long pauses afford time for reflection and perhaps even discussion if the series is popular enough. Whether the historical series will be allowed to pursue its logical development and become what Balzac made of Scott, the historical novel whose period is the present, is not yet clear. The 1976–7 season featured both an ITV serial, 'Holding On', which followed the fortunes of a London family from 1903 until the time of Queen Elizabeth's coronation, and 'Jubilee', a thirteen-part BBC series reflecting British life over the past twenty-five years. But the serial has so many deep affinities with the nineteenth-century novel, which gave the form its first great popularity, that television seems to be having some difficulty prying it away from the past. Adaptations from nineteenth- and early twentieth-century fiction come very naturally. We have already mentioned the success with Galsworthy. There have been many other such ventures, including adaptations of novels by Balzac, Dickens, Hugo, Thackeray, Flaubert, Trollope, Dumas *fils*, Tolstoy, Hardy, Henry James, Bennett, George Moore, and others. But the last century fascinates not only with its fiction. The past year alone has brought series, usually with a strong Freudian colouring, on Victorian crimes, painters, scandals, and women; and it has produced serial biographies, original or adaptations, of such nineteenth-century figures as Eleanor Marx, Nurse Dorothy Pattison, and, in thirteen parts, Charles Dickens. Interest in our own century seems to be more moderate, and, certainly, modern television serial novels, either original works or adaptations from modern novels set in our own times, have been less frequent than the nineteenth-century classics. 'Roads to Freedom', of a few seasons back, was perhaps the most ambitious.

But it is not just the association with history and the affinity with nineteenth-century fiction-by-the-numbers which keeps the serial out of the present. Serial dramas, which television resisted for a number of years out of fear that they would cause a degeneration into whole evenings of 'Crossroads' and 'Coronation Streets',[32] have become the cultural element of British television drama. Thus Bill Slater, Head of Serials at BBC, is quoted as saying in an interview:

> By and large, the BBC2 serial strand has been loved and cherished just because it *is* the classic strand. When we did contemporary novels, no matter how well they were done, the audience was not at all pleased with us. The moment they had Madame Bovary back, a sigh of relief seemed to go up around the country. I am sure it would be a grave mistake to take our feet out of the classical field.[33]

The series therefore appears to have inherited the cultural role which once belonged to the adaptations of stage drama, and although the culture may be only of a middle-brow variety, it is several wrinkles above what television might be presenting – what it does present elsewhere – and, apparently, it gets through to people in a way single play drama never did. Television drama appears after all to have succeeded in its original social purpose of bringing the literary tradition (if not the dramatic, then the fictional) to the people, and it seems to have made some money at the same time. But if I am right in suspecting that the television serial can only find its maturity and fulfil its function as a social commentator by presenting novels and histories of the present period, then there is some irony in the thought that television drama's second social aim, the attempt to change Britain, should be hindered by the success of its first objective, to raise the nation's cultural tone. On the other hand, this is how the situation must have looked in the late 1950s when original, socially committed television drama was about to come into its own. Even better times could easily be just ahead.

NOTES

1. *Television: The First Forty Years* (London: Independent Television Publications, 1976), p. 73.
2. The ITV plays were *Caesar and Cleopatra*, *Hindle Wakes*, and *Cat on a Hot Tin Roof*. There were also two new productions of Harold Pinter plays on ITV during December and January, *The Collection* and *The Lovers*, but these were both originally written for television. BBC1 and BBC2 presented the following on prime time during the 1976–7 season: *London Assurance*, *Look Back in Anger*, *East Lynne*, *Private Lives*, *The Winslow Boy*, *The Country Wife*, *King Lear*, and *Heartbreak House*.
3. George Markstein interviewed in *The Stage and Television Today* (29 January 1976), p. 12.
4. *Television: Technology and Cultural Form* (London: Fontana, 1974), p. 60.
5. *Writing for Television Today* (London: Adam & Charles Black, 1963), p. 30.
6. Reprinted in Irene Shubik's *Play for Today: The Evolution of Television Drama* (London: Davis-Poynter, 1975), p. 40.
7. *Television: The First Forty Years*, p. 74.
8. 'The Role of the Television Dramatist', *Theatre Quarterly*, 1 (January–March 1971), 10.
9. 'The Single Play: A Means of Preserving and Nurturing the Creative Talent Among Writers', *The Stage and Television Today* (9 October 1975), p. 14.

10. *Daily Telegraph*, 15 September 1976, p. 3.
11. 'What is the Condition of the Single Play?', *The Stage and Television Today* (16 December 1971), p. 30.
12. 'TV and the Dramatist' [views extracted from a lecture given to the Royal Society of the Arts], *Plays and Players* (June 1965), pp. 19 and 50.
13. 'The Role of the Television Dramatist', p. 12.
14. *Report of the Committee on the Future of Broadcasting* (London: HMSO, 1977), p. 326.
15. 'TV Drama', *Plays and Players* (July 1971), p. 67.
16. *Television: Technology and Cultural Form*, p. 60.
17. *The Art of Television* (London: Faber & Faber, 1952), p. 56.
18. *A Survey of Television* (London: Heinemann, 1967), p. 144. In a similar vein Irene Shubik notes that Peter Nichols, who writes with touches of fantasy when he writes for the stage, is a thoroughgoing realist as a television dramatist. (*Play for Today: The Evolution of Television Drama*, pp. 121–2.) Shubik, a highly successful producer, believes that experimentation is necessary if television is to find its appropriate form, but she concedes that 'plots that are innovatory in technique inevitably command smaller audiences than the more conventional works'.
19. 'The Role of the Television Dramatist', p. 13.
20. *Writing for Television Today*, p. 166.
21. *Ibid.*
22. Jeremy Sandford, *Cathy Come Home* (London: Marion Boyars, 1976), p. 138.
23. *Ibid.*, p. 14.
24. 'Television Documentary Drama: *Edna* and *Sheila*: Two kinds of Truth', *Theatre Quarterly*, vol. ii, no. 7 (July–September, 1972), p. 47.
25. *Cathy Come Home*, p. 17.
26. Irene Shubik, a protégé of Newman's at ITV and BBC, calls Grierson Newman's 'mentor'. *Play for Today: The Evolution of Television Drama*, p. 40.
27. *Grierson on Documentary*, ed. Forsyth Hardy (London: Faber & Faber, 1966), p. 215.
28. *Ibid.*, pp. 148 and 151.
29. *Ibid.*, p. 18.
30. 13 January 1977, p. 20.
31. Hazel Holt in *The Stage and Television Today* (23 October 1975), p. 14.
32. This fear was partially realised when 'A Bouquet of Barbed Wire', a serial novel about an English family practising sex and ego, was followed by a sequel, 'Another Bouquet of Barbed Wire'.
33. 'Planning BBC Serials from Pops to Classics', *The Stage and Television Today* (19 February 1976).

The effects of subsidy on Western European theatre in the 1970s

JOHN ALLEN

An opportunity to take a synoptic view of the contemporary theatre in Europe has been provided by an inquiry into the effect of public subsidy on theatrical creativity that is at present being conducted by the Committee for Cultural Co-operation of the Council of Europe (1977). It is a timely moment for such an inquiry. Perhaps the greatest change that has taken place in the Western European theatre over the last three decades has been the increasing provision of governmental subsidy. It is a policy that has brought inestimable benefits to the theatre as a whole together with some dangers that an enlightened bureaucracy should be able to avoid. But few attempts have been made to take stock of the general situation.

The present survey will be concerned with the results of subsidy, not its theory. Although the provision of subsidy is common to most countries in Western Europe, its justification is not being widely argued. The Swedes and the Swiss, for example, in extensive surveys of national cultural policy,[1] have had little to say about the theory of subsidy. It is taken for granted as a 'good thing', like a national airline and participation in the Olympic Games. One continuing argument will be found in the annual reports of the Arts Council of Great Britain;[2] but for the rest we have to accept a traditional liberal view that culture is desirable and that quality cannot be wholly left to the hazards of commercial or private enterprise.

Readers may be glad of some preliminary references. The history of developing governmental involvement in the arts in the United Kingdom has been entertainingly described by Dr Janet Minihan in *The Nationalisation of Culture*.[3] An interesting discussion of certain aspects of British 'boulevard' drama can be found in J. R. S. Goodlad's *A Sociology of Popular Drama*.[4] Nearer to the subject of the present article, though covering the visual as well as the performing arts, is *The Economics of the Arts* edited by Mark Blaug.[5] The editor, though using a good deal of American material, discusses some crucial social and economic principles that are involved in the granting of subsidy, in particular the basic economic problem that 'the salary increases [of artists in subsidised theatres] are wholly cost inflationary because they are not offset by productivity gains within the arts'.[6] The gap between receipts and expenditure can only increase and there is little that can be done about it.

The beneficiaries of this situation are, anyway for the time being, the theatregoing public, which represents a serious socio-cultural problem. As a result of various surveys[7] this public can be identified fairly exactly. It is middle-class, well-educated, and financially well-to-do. It constitutes somewhere between two and ten per cent of the population with the lower figure being the more usual. People go to the theatre in couples rather than individually, more frequently when they are young and independent than in their thirties when they become increasingly involved with children, and rather more consistently, though in lesser numbers, when they are older.

It is therefore arguable that to subsidise the theatre is to subsidise the pleasures of an already moneyed and privileged class and, since there is little evidence anywhere of theatre audiences increasing, it is to emphasise existing socio-cultural class distinctions. This is a subject of considerable concern to the Council of Europe, which has initiated a number of inquiries into the problems of cultural democracy.[8]

Historically, and in most countries, the theatre has been the creation of private initiative and commercial enterprise. Certain countries such as France, Sweden and Denmark have supported for upwards of two centuries a national theatre in their capital city. In Germany, as a result of the political and social structure of the country in the eighteenth century, there has been a long tradition of state support for the theatre: in West Germany today there are some two hundred subsidised theatres and opera houses.[9] But, generally speaking, subsidy of the theatre with public money has been the exception, not the rule. It was only in the years immediately following the Second World War that most countries of Western Europe seemed tacitly to agree that the democratic and cultural principles for which the war had been fought must be secured by governmental involvement in the theatre.

During the last thirty years there has been throughout Europe a rapid growth of state subsidised theatre alongside a commercial or free-enterprise theatre. In Britain, France and Germany – and it would be more accurate to speak of London, Paris and the larger German cities – the commercial theatre is more in evidence than in Belgium, the Netherlands, and the Scandinavian countries. In mixed social-democratic and capitalist economies the commercial theatre has found a working relationship with both the government and the unions. This form of theatre is still the object of vituperative disapproval by the theatrical radicals, but the existence of more than fifty such theatres in London and Paris suggests that they are serving some kind of social function, if it is only, in the irreproachable words of Mr Goodlad, 'to reinforce the values of the middle and lower-middle classes'.[10] In many countries the commercial theatre is in receipt of some modest help from public funds; in Britain there is a kind of understanding between the two forms of theatre, the subsidised managements staging plays that are too risky or too expensive for the commercial theatres and the latter exploiting the commercial value of plays in a manner that is not possible within the subsidised system.[11]

There is a national theatre in the capital city of each of the countries with which we are dealing – London (belatedly), Paris, Brussels, Stockholm and Copenhagen. There is no national theatre or opera in Rome although there is a Rome opera and a Rome *stabile* (subsidised regional theatre). Switzerland, theatrically, is wholly decentralised. The Stadtsschouwburg is the biggest theatre in Amsterdam and houses the subsidised Nederlandse Comedie but is in no sense a national theatre. Occasionally a national theatre will house both dramatic and operatic companies, but more often there are separate houses owing to the different requirements of dramatic and lyric theatre. In Germany there is no national theatre as such since Berlin is neither the political nor the theatrical capital of the country.

National theatres are often viewed with a mixture of veneration and contempt. Their function is usually considered to be the maintenance of traditional standards. In this respect the position of artistic director is not enviable, for if he stages the classics in too orthodox a manner he is accused of fossilisation and if he is unacceptably non-conformist he will be attacked for excessive radicalism.

The main criticism directed at national theatres is on the subject of their expense. The 1977–8 budget for theatre in the Bavarian *Land* is 72m DM (about £20m). Of this sum 59m DM (£16m) has been assigned to two theatres, both in Munich, the opera and the Residenztheater.[12] (In other Bavarian cities as well as in Munich considerable subsidy is provided by the municipality.) In France, in 1975, the five national theatres received sixty-two and a half per cent of the total theatrical budget.[13] In Great Britain in 1975–6 the National Theatre, the Covent Garden Opera, the English National Opera, and the Royal Shakespeare Company received total subsidies of £8m against an allocation of £6m for over two hundred other dance and drama companies.[14] The situation is the same elsewhere. This is not the place to argue the rights and wrongs of this particular problem, but it remains a profoundly important socio-cultural issue.

Theatrical subsidy extends from national to regional theatres. In Britain there are some fifty theatres in the regions. In France there are nineteen *centres nationaux dramatiques*, in Italy eight *teatri stabili* and in Sweden eleven regional theatres. In Denmark the official regional theatres have recently been subsidised and there is a similar structure in both Dutch- and French-speaking Belgium. The situation is a little different in the Netherlands where theatres tend to be subsidised by the municipalities and the companies by the state. In the Federal Republic of Germany subsidy is entirely the responsibility of *Land* and municipality.

The establishment of a cultural democracy favours, of course, regional rather than centralised development. It is therefore not surprising that the key word in European theatrical policy is decentralisation – which is to be subtly distinguished from devolution. This concept requires that the arts be 'made available' to as large a proportion of the population as possible; and if public money is to be spent on theatrical activities it becomes a matter of economic justice as well as political expediency that the theatre should be taken to the people. This accounts not only for the development in many countries of a network of regional theatres but also for a widespread policy of touring. National theatres, as the biggest recipients of public money, should logically be the first to tour but for artistic reasons, as well as variations in regional taste, they are the most reluctant to do so. The higher the standards of production in their main theatres, the more difficult they find it to maintain these standards in ill-equipped regional theatres. Although the Swedes, for example, with impressive loyalty to the cause of touring, claim that their leading ballet company has given adequate per- formances of *Swan Lake* in school-halls with taped accompaniment, it is difficult to accept that this is a suitable environment in which to enjoy the theatrical qualities of Tchaikovsky's luscious score or Petipa's sophisticated choreography.

The mainstream theatres, faced with a shortage of stages equipped to take their major productions, are obliged to choose and shape their material to the resources that exist. It is fortunate that most national and many regional theatres have several stages – proscenium, thrust, in-the-round; large, medium, intimate. One of them is likely to be a studio theatre for experimental and less popular productions, often used in Germany for the first performance of new plays. But small does not signify poor, and it is often the productions from the studio theatres that go on tour. Many companies, however, accept touring 'dates' that are not in theatres but halls and other venues where they play to specialised audiences of children, the aged and infirm, the handicapped, a factory audience, perhaps, or a specialised audience at a conference. Thus the livelier companies do not limit themselves to touring simplified versions of their more successful productions, but try to create plays or programmes for the particular audiences they are to meet. In this way they further the general principles of decentralisation and cultural 'participation'.

Actors, traditionally, do not care for touring; but in the smaller countries such as Belgium and the Netherlands where they can usually return home after each night's performance, they do so more readily. Mainstream companies rarely tour in France; in Britain they frequently go on short tours prior to London production and even shorter tours at the end of their

London run. But in some countries touring is virtually a condition of subsidy and in Sweden there is a Riksteater that sends out a hundred and thirty tours a year, eighty of which are specially staged productions, a vast undertaking that is run from Ingmar Bergman's former film studios in Stockholm. In Norway there is a similar organisation, a former director of which has spoken of the excitement of playing the Norwegian classics to small uncultured audiences in small fishing villages sometimes lying within the Arctic circle.[15] This is to be reminded of the experiences of the Old Vic company in Britain during the war when they gave performances of *The Merchant of Venice* to mining communities in Wales for whom the experience was of a wholly new and thrilling kind.

The policy of artistic decentralisation raises some interesting problems. It is governmental policy in some countries to hand increasing responsibility for subsidising the arts to the municipalities (more often than to the regions). This involves the complex question of where a municipality gets its money from. If, as in Italy, it is from the capital, there is very little decentralisation involved. If a municipality can raise its own money as in Britain, for example, through the rates, it has a measure of independence but is subject to political pressure from the local representatives. Moreover it is an unfortunate fact, to which at least one of the Council of Europe's enquiries has drawn attention,[16] that there are few cities in Europe, outside Germany, with a coherent cultural policy. Decisions on matters concerning the arts tend to be taken in *ad hoc* fashion without reference to a broad consistent policy. Theatre directors have tumbled to this fact and have stated quite explicitly that they would far rather deal with the Arts Council of Great Britain or the Ministère de la Culture, or whoever it is that represents the theatrical bureaucracy, in spite of the grouses they nurture against such centralised authorities, than their local councillors whom they regard as parochial and uninformed. Ministerial civil servants, though perpetuating the bureaucracy, are professional, informed and disinterested. Nevertheless in most countries the relationship between the responsibilities of central and local government for funding the theatre is intricate and ill-defined. The fact of the matter is that the structuring of a bureaucratic machine that will encourage and facilitate theatrical creativity and not destroy the very vitality it is in existence to foster is one of the outstanding problems with which the European Ministers of Culture are faced.

We have already considered some of the problems raised by a policy of decentralisation and there are others of even greater complexity. There is a tendency in Britain to look on the year 1956 as the beginning of a new contemporary spirit in the theatre. It is vaguely associated with the establishment of the Royal Court Theatre as a stage for new playwrights. Something of the same importance can be attached to the year 1968.

Theatre audiences had reached a numerical peak in the early 1960s and had then begun to decline. But the revolt of the students was evidently symptomatic of a more profound malaise. There was the notorious 'tomato' revolution in Amsterdam when dissatisfied audiences pelted the stage of the leading theatre with fruit. This wave of social protest did not alter the face of Europe because it did not express itself in those political forms that perpetuate the results of revolution; but it inaugurated a period that can only be described by such words as participation, involvement, and the sharing of responsibility. The theatre shook itself and set about recapturing some of its lost audiences.

It was out of this upheaval that there grew the so-called alternative theatre. It is difficult to find a generally acceptable term for what in Britain is still referred to as the 'fringe'. The term was first used to describe the companies that provided an alternative to the main fare of the Edinburgh Festival. The Swedes use the term 'free' theatres, the Dutch 'experimental' theatres, the French 'théâtres engagés' or 'en marge', the Italians 'sperimentali' or 'teatri di base', the Germans speak of 'cellar' theatres, but all such terms are inadequate or inaccurate. Many of these companies are not particularly experimental; they are by no means all committed; they perform in attics as often as in cellars and sometimes in the streets. But they do provide, by and large, an alternative to the mainstream theatre.

In England the fringe grew out of the work of an enterprising American, Jim Haynes, who in 1968 'launched an experimental Arts Lab. in London's Drury Lane [not the theatre], providing . . . a remarkable shop-window on a new theatrical phenomenon – the underground'.[17] The term 'underground' soon gave place to the 'fringe', but the implicit social challenge was preserved in the titles of the groups – Joint Stock, a leading collective; John Bull's Puncture Repair Kit, a highly satirical title; Belt and Braces, suggestive of an attitude to work; 7:84 referring to the fact that seven per cent of the population own eighty-four per cent of the country's wealth; and so on.

Many of them are structured as co-operatives. In Sweden this is a *sine qua non* for membership of the umbrella organisation, Teater Centrum. The co-operative structure is virtually forced upon many of them through the low level of their income but the concept of the co-operative is important for two reasons: it represents an amalgamation of an economically and socially acceptable method of working and living, with the artistic concept of the group ensemble that has been a feature of the European theatre for upwards of a hundred years.

Some such companies are more concerned with methods of work than developing a body of contemporary plays. The repertoire for 1976–7 of the lively Ensemble Théâtral Mobile of Brussels consisted of Marivaux's *La double inconstance* – the recent interest of the avant-garde in Marivaux is an extraordinary phenomenon – Ibsen's *A Doll's House*, a dramatisation of *Les paysans* by Balzac, and a new Belgian play. The authorities argued that this was not a sufficiently substantial repertoire to merit an annual subsidy. The director replied that he wanted to create a collective such as that of Peter Stein in Berlin and that number of productions has nothing to do with quality of work. He wanted to rehearse each play, as is rarely done, for at least three months.

A policy of revivals on the part of the alternative theatre disappoints the directors of the mainstream theatres who suggest that they can revive Ibsen as well as, or better than impoverished fringe companies whose responsibility is rather to encourage, and offer a stage to, new and young dramatists especially those of marked originality.

It is possible criticism of the alternative theatres in certain countries that their directors are much more interested in methods of staging than in finding new plays. In England the situation is the opposite: there is no great interest in methods of staging but an astonishing outcrop of new dramatists. It is significant that the dramatists are writing for the most part in a conventional naturalistic or social-realistic convention which may be a reflection of the kind of theatre they see in front of them. But of their proliferation over the last twenty years, there can be no question. While it is impossible to explain so curious a manifestation of the creative spirit, a few comments might be relevant.

One of the most striking phenomena of the British theatre immediately following the Second World War was the emergence of a popular poetic theatre led by T. S. Eliot and Christopher Fry. At the heart of the movement was the work of E. Martin Browne at the Mercury Theatre, London, where, between 1945 and 1948 he staged plays by a remarkable number of English poets, including Anne Ridler, Ronald Duncan, Norman Nicholson, Christopher Hassall and Dorothy Sayers. But for some reason the poetic theatre did not develop. It was supplanted, in a way, by the theatre of social realism that was developed by George Devine at the Royal Court Theatre. The record of this theatre has been remarkable. Since 1956 its directors have staged some two hundred new plays by British playwrights as well as a number of revivals of the classics and the first British productions of many outstanding foreign plays. Knowledge of the existence of this theatre and its policy has been an enormous encouragement to many playwrights.[18]

The Royal Court has assumed a position midway between the mainstream theatre and the fringe. High production costs, a small auditorium and a subsidy that has not kept pace with inflation have constrained its activities. It has done no touring and so, while building up its own audiences, it has done little to advance the general policy of decentralisation. Herein lies the strength of the fringe companies which play in halls, community centres, schools, and on the streets, wherever they can collect an audience. It might well be asked whether this is to build a new public for the theatre; to which in turn the answer may be that it is a question of what is meant by a new public – a public that will go to plays at theatres? or a public that will enjoy theatrical performances, wherever they take place, as an expression of contemporary society? The alternative theatre is not seeking to create a mass audience; only sporadically does it touch a working-class audience. Finland appears to be the only country where factory workers constitute an appreciable element in an average theatre audience.[19] Some people think that a working-class audience can be won to the theatre with pieces that reflect its political commitments, but the factory-worker looks on the theatre, and in a sense needs the theatre, for the same relaxation and entertainment for which, radicals complain, the middle classes visit the theatre. The function of the theatre at large is to provide a varied fare, and plays of political and social significance are no less relevant to the middle than to the so-called working class. David Edgar's political play *Destiny* has been a popular success in the repertory of the (subsidised) Royal Shakespeare Company even though a bulk of its support came from that phenomenon of social-democratic society, the 'radical chic'. What worries theatre workers everywhere is that much of the population, irrespective of class, income or education, is finding relaxation and entertainment in television.

This discussion reinforces the problems that have been raised by a policy of decentralisation. The European theatres are faced with the necessity not only of touring but of participating in what can only be described as a vast programme in adult education that will, it is hoped, further the creation of a general cultural democracy. The means is what is widely known as 'animation', a term that is now commonly found in France, Belgium and Italy. It covers a wide variety of lectures, demonstrations, practical classes of many different kinds in which there is often close collaboration between professionals and the public. The Belgian National Theatre of Brussels, for example, during the season 1975–6, gave four hundred and forty-four performances and a hundred and eight 'animations' in Brussels, two hundred and fifty-five performances and three hundred and thirty-three 'animations' *en décentralisation*, that is to say in the provinces.[20] In March 1977 one of the companies from the Royal Shakespeare Theatre spent a month in Newcastle-on-Tyne. They not only gave evening performances in the city theatres but by day conducted a great number of classes, lectures, demonstrations and 'animations' of all kinds.

It is arguable that in many instances the directors of the subsidised theatres are not carrying out a sufficiently vigorous policy to increase the scope of their audiences. They leave it to *animations décentralisés*; but if they do not consider these cavortings to be ends in themselves, which assuredly they do not, they must consider how they can induce the participants to visit the theatre proper.

There is a second and more serious charge to be levelled against the subsidised theatres. It arises from the playwrights who have grown increasingly to resent the dominance of the director. The accusation has been specifically raised in France, but it is echoed throughout Europe. The emergence of the director as a major force in the theatre has been evident for the last hundred years. Gordon Craig has devoted some of his most eloquent polemic to substantiate his claim that the director – he uses the term 'stage manager' – is the dominating figure in the theatre and arguing that the actor should be reduced to the status of an *Übermarionette*.[21] Erwin Piscator was probably among the first directors to demonstrate openly that for him the text was merely a vehicle to be used for the projection of his own theatrical visions.[22] Historical tradition supports the integrity of the text and we may have reached a moment in history when values are to change. But the attitude of the playwrights is clear. They complain that there are few directors who will take the trouble to work on a new play and help to shape it for the stage, a belief that has been substantiated by the dramaturgs of at least two German subsidised theatres who have confessed that there are indeed directors who prefer to work on the established classic rather than the malleable 'creation'.

The question of why there are not more playwrights of distinction is a complex one. Even in Germany with its enormous subsidy to the theatre[23] there are only a handful of playwrights of European stature   Heinar Kipphardt, Thomas Bernhard, Rolf Hochhuth, Peter Handke, Martin Walser, Tankred Dorst, Günther Grass ... (Max Frisch and Friedrich Dürenmatt are Swiss). While one is assured that there are many more promising dramatists, one might be forgiven for asking when this promise is likely to be fulfilled. The repertory of the German subsidised theatres consists of about sixty per cent foreign plays and forty per cent German.[24] During the last week of March 1977, for example, the four big successes in the Residenztheater, Munich, were *Hamlet*, *Macbeth*, Tom Stoppard's *Jumpers* and Peter Shaffer's *Equus*. In Italy by way of contrast, during the season 1975–6, the professional theatre staged four hundred and forty-one plays, three hundred and fifty-one by Italian authors, and ninety by foreign authors.[25] There are no figures available for the percentage or number of foreign plays staged in England, but it must be very low indeed. Cynics, of course, will be quick to point out that this is only to confirm the notorious insularity of the English. And they will be right. At the same time it is arguable that England and France are the only European countries that are virtually self-supporting in new plays. It is to be hoped that if the European community can have little effect on the creativity of young playwrights, it will stimulate a far more vigorous interchange of scripts and facilities for translation. This point has in fact been argued energetically by a young theatrical agent in the Hague.[26] He claimed that the failure to establish an international exchange of plays of a far more vigorous kind than exists at present, is simply a question of marketing, of arranging for a more general interchange of scripts.

The argument is surely plausible. Every critic can name some half-dozen dramatists who are not without honour in their own country yet neglected in others. But is it true that theatrical taste is as variable between one country and another as we know it to be in the case of fiction? The Italians speak with respect of Leonardo Sciascia, Franco Brusarti, Diego Fabbri, Patroni Griffi, Mario Moretti, Dario Fo. Is the Italian theatrical taste so intensely chauvinistic that none of these dramatists has written plays of possible international appeal? The Swedes have a lively theatre. Why do we know so little of the plays of Kent Andersson, Allan Edwall, and Goran Eriksson? How does it come about that a country produces a Strindberg or an Ibsen and then lapses into dramatic silence? Both Dutch- and French-speaking Belgians can name their dramatists: it is difficult to believe that they have not something significant to say to the rest of Europe. And even the French, whose young people are writing plays, we are assured, in considerable numbers[27] are no longer supplying the international market to the extent that they have done in the past. No wonder the Council of Europe has seen fit to question whether theatrical subsidy is touching the mainsprings of creativity.

Creative work in the theatre, however, does not rest wholly on directors and playwrights. The actors are now beginning to assert their creative potential. Mention has been made of the growing practice of actors creating their own plays for special audiences. A number of fringe companies do so because this is the way they like to work. Their tendency, however, to dramatise existing stories or works of literature may be a tacit admission of the creative limitations of the actor. To what extent does creative potential which expresses itself in the ability to create character, to project emotion, to communicate with an audience, comprise the ability to reorganise aspects of social reality in theatrical terms? In short, is the skill of the writer implicit in that of the actor? Can the one subsume the other?

Peter Cheeseman, for many years director of the Victoria Theatre, Stoke-on-Trent, has exploited the creative potential of his actors in a succession of musical documentaries which in many cases have been researched, written and composed by members of his company. The British Theatre-In-Education movement has been firmly based on the ability of actors to work with children creatively and constructively.[28] Joint Stock, one of the leading British fringe companies, insists on the fullest possible collaboration with their playwrights.

Perhaps the most positive expression of this development is to be found in Italy. During the last few years some fifty-five co-operative companies have been established from within the mainstream theatre. The motivation is to be found in the determination of many actors to contribute to a kind of theatrical participation. They have been unwilling to accept the traditional role of the actor as an interpreter of a text within the creative structure set up by producer, director, and designer. This new attitude has been very clearly expressed by Franco Parenti of the Teatro Pier Lombardo in Milan and director of a leading co-operative. He argues that the imaginative potential of the actor is as significant for creative work in the theatre as that of the playwright.[29] Yet he recognises that even if the conceptual ability of the actor is as powerful as that of the playwright, he has a far less potent command of language and that it is through language alone that large areas of the conceptual imagination can be expressed. The actor, ultimately, is not a poet. Signor Parenti has therefore sought collaboration with a writer, and has been working with the novelist Giovanni Testori in the creation of a theatrical language that can embody the creative fantasies of the actor. The results of the collaboration are impressive: Testori's *Edipus*[30] is a monologue in which the actor speaks to the audience with a strange combination of artist, philosopher and metaphysician though in a synthesis that is theatrically riveting since before all else the experienced actor knows how to hold the attention of an audience.

This direct relationship between actor and audience has been growing over recent years. It has been clearly expressed in theatrical architecture. In many of the new theatres that have been built since the war some kind of thrust or open stage has taken the place of the former proscenium stage in order that a more direct relationship between actor and audience can be established. This new 'intimacy' is evident in the Brechtian concept of theatre which destroys former ideas about theatrical illusion. It is not without significance that a British fringe theatre group which calls itself 'Shared experience' begins its performances with the actors sitting on the edge of the stage and chatting to the audience. The practice echoes a comment that has recently been made by Michael Billington, dramatic critic of the London *Guardian* on the current New York Theatre:

> As an outsider, however, what strikes me about modern American theatre, is that the confessional monologue is more and more taking over from shared dialogue. People talk to us, the audience, rather than to each other and the theatre becomes a strange combination of analyst's couch, expiatory church confessional and protest platform.[31]

The provenance of this new found assertiveness of the actor is clearly the work of Constantin Stanislavsky, the effect of whose work on the European theatre has been profound. It is hardly surprising, with an increasing number of actors having experienced a variety of improvisatory techniques, that they should have come to discover in themselves a capacity for creativity which has led them to question their traditional role as interpreters. At the same time it seems to have been some kind of historical

accident that this newly-discovered creative potential on the part of the
actors should have coincided with a period in which the authority of
language and the power of the spoken word have been put in question.
George Steiner has analysed acutely[32] the language revolution and the new
linguistics arising from a lack of confidence in the act of literary communication. But a theatre of social realism, with its language limited to the
vernacular and its physical expressiveness to a slovenly reflection of real-life
behaviourism, is likely to be an exceedingly dull theatre failing to project an
exciting or relevant theatrical image. So it is possible to envisage that one of
the most promising developments in the contemporary European theatre
may be a new relationship between actors and playwrights, in which the
capacity and contribution of both is mutually regarded and a new creative
collaboration is established. When this is related to the policy of decentralisation and the attempts to establish a genuine cultural democracy
through forms of 'animations', a new contact between the public and the
theatre may well be in the offing. It may well be this combination of
directness of approach, relevant political comment, and considerable acta-
bility – his plays are extraordinarily interesting to stage – that accounts for
the remarkable popularity of Brecht throughout Europe.

The theatre will continue to take its own organic way whatever the critics
and the pedagogues may have to say. Marxist, Freudian, or sociological
analyses may help to explain but they cannot predict. Old and established
forms of theatre may wither or be destroyed, if their validity is in question.
The public is the final arbiter. For a hundred years the European public has
been the spectator of *rapprochements*, relationships and rejections that would
have been unthinkable in the age of the Enlightenment. They have watched
the eroding of one establishment and its replacement by another; the
destruction of frontiers between one discipline and another, and a challenge
to the validity of the work of art itself. A Ministry of Culture, with limited
funds at its disposal, has at the best restricted powers. A million pounds will
not write a *Hamlet*. All that the Minister and his civil servants can do is to
structure a bureaucracy that will fertilise and not frustrate creative work.
The point has already been made. But the Minister himself is subject to
pressures no different from those besetting the artist he is in business to
support. Every Minister will feel that the artists do not understand the
cabinet pressures to which he is subject: every artist will feel that no one
really understands the emotional pressures he is trying to encapsulate. And
in his case the final irony is that it is sudden and unexpected success that can
make him question the depths and the extent of his own creativity.

If European society stabilises itself in its present form, the theatre may
preserve something of its traditional structure. The ingredients of change,
the pressures that give rise to change, both social and artistic, are all present
in abundance. One is justified, perhaps, in suggesting that at no time in the

history of European society can there have been so many artists thinking so radically about the very nature of their work nor so many civil servants thinking sympathetically about the way in which it can be helped. It is a situation that does not lend itself to great art. But before art can be great it must be genuine. And whatever the extravagances of the entertainment industry, there are many people in the theatre, throughout Europe, returning thoughtfully to the basic ingredients of their profession.

And this within a context that sees culture not as an artefact but as a quality of living investing every aspect of society. Of all the radical ingredients that constitute the life of the artist this is perhaps the most fundamental of all, his relationship not only with his profession but with his society. In that respect the present scene gives cause for optimism.

NOTES

1. Kulturradet, *New cultural policy in Sweden* (Stockholm, 1973); *Elements pour une politique culturelle en Suisse* (Berne, 1975).
2. See especially those for 1951–2, 1952–3, 1955–6, 1961–2, 1972–3.
3. Janet Minihan, *The Nationalisation of Culture: the Development of State Subsidies to the Arts in Great Britain* (London: Hamish Hamilton, 1977). The sub-title is the more accurate description of the book's contents.
4. J. R. S. Goodlad, *A Sociology of Popular Drama* (London: Heinemann, 1977).
5. Mark Blaug, ed., *The Economics of the Arts* (London: Martin Robertson, 1976).
6. *Ibid.*, p. 18.
7. *Ibid.*, especially chapter 9. Also Augustin Girard, *Cultural Development: Experiences and Policies* (UNESCO, 1972); and Alphonse van Impe, *The Theatre and Authority* (UNESCO, 1977).
8. J. A. Simpson, *Towards Cultural Democracy* (Strasbourg: Council of Europe, 1976); and Finn Jor, *The Demystification of Culture: Animation and Creativity* (Strasbourg: Council of Europe, 1976).
9. International Theatre Institute of the Federal Republic of Germany, Bulletin on the new theatre in the F.D.R.
10. *A Sociology of Popular Drama.*
11. Conversation with the chairman of Moss Empires, London
12. Conversation with the Ministerialdirigent for the Bavarian State Ministry of Culture.
13. *Secretariat d'état à la culture: activités, 1975.*
14. Arts Council of Great Britain, *Thirty-first annual report and accounts, 1975–6.*
15. Lecture by M. Frits von der Lippe, former director of the Norwegian Riksteater.
16. Stephen Mennell, *Cultural Policy in Towns* (Strasbourg: Council of Europe, 1976).
17. Peter Ansorge, *Disrupting the Spectacle: Five Years of Experimental and Fringe Theatre in Britain* (London: Pitman, 1975).
18. Terry W. Browne, *Playwright's Theatre: the English Stage Company at the Royal Court Theatre* (London: Pitman, 1975).

19. Finland in *The Theatre in the Five Scandinavian Countries*, Norsk Teaterunion (Stockholm, 1975).

20. *Rapport sur l'activité du Théâtre National de Belgique, 1976.*

21. E. Gordon Craig, *On the Art of the Theatre* (London: Heinemann, 1911).

22. C. D. Innes, *Piscator's Political Theatre* (Cambridge University Press, 1972).

23. The total figure is in the region of one thousand million DM a year (1976).

24. For general information on the German theatre see Werner Schulze-Reimpell, *Development and Structure of the Theatre in the Federal Republic of Germany* (Cologne: Deutsche Bühnen-Verein, 1975).

25. For statistical details of the theatre in Italy see Associazione Generale Italiana dello Spettacolo, *Rilevazioni statistiche sulla stagione teatrale di prosa 1975–6.*

26. Hemmo B. Drexhage, of United Dutch Dramatists.

27. Alfred Simon, *Les diverses possibilités d'aide aux auteurs dramatiques* (privately printed, 1973).

28. J. B. Parnaby, *Actors in Schools* (London: HMSO, 1977).

29. Conversation with Franco Parenti in Milan.

30. Milan: Rizzoli, 1977. Rizzoli also publish his other plays.

31. *The Guardian*, 22 June 1977.

32. George Steiner, *Extra-Territorial* (London: Faber, 1972).

Illusion and conflict: drama in Eastern European Societies

ISTVÁN EÖRSI*

In the history of drama there are so few periods of great achievement because both tragedy and comedy depend upon sharp, clearly discernible conflicts within society. There must be sharp conflict within individuals, and between people who represent opposing tendencies, dynamically changing systems of values. And yet, precisely because the conflict in society would be so violent, there is usually a recourse to brute force. The group which has political power becomes mercilessly oppressive: it oppresses not only its opponents but also those of its own ranks who adopt positions of some independence. A paradoxical and parallel development takes place. Conflicts necessary for serious drama do in fact develop in society, but at the same time an authoritarian ethos and bureaucracy also develop to prevent the relatively unbiased portrayal of these conflicts (a *wholly* unbiased portrayal is, of course, unimaginable, since any attempt must be influenced by the individual's complex relationship with his time and society).

In support of this argument, I shall cite a study written in the late 1960s by the Hungarian sociologist András Hegedüs, who raised some problems of importance about past and present alternatives in Eastern European societies. Hegedüs was later forced into silence, partly because of his studies along these lines, and as yet I have myself not been able to arrange publication of a study which examines the consequences of such sociological analyses for the theory and practice of drama. To develop social conflicts in a play in Eastern Europe, or even to discuss the subject theoretically in a journal, calls for great delicacy; the more real the social conflicts are, the more problematic it is to talk about them.

Hegedüs's starting point is that each revolutionary epoch creates certain illusions, since it necessarily envisages the future as more beautiful than it could be made; it also tends to regard the prevailing order as being more intolerable than it actually is. These illusions are the subjective preconditions of revolution. Had Robespierre and his companions not believed that it was possible to establish a state of Reason, had Lenin and his

*Translation by Ninon Leader.

comrades not nursed illusions about world revolution, neither of those revolutions would have taken place. Hegedüs develops his argument: 'But quite soon, once the new order is established, a tragic change of role takes place time and time again: the illusions *no longer refer to the future, to a desired state of affairs, but to what has already become the reality*, and thus the illusions begin to have a radically different function. After a while they no longer encourage the fight for progress, they no longer foster new growth; rather they hinder social progress with the most primitive apologetics for existing conditions, for forms of society which have already become rigid and institutionalised.' Thus, a new development begins because 'the social groups which have a stake either in keeping up or in defying the illusions about social conditions are already formed'. I shall list a few schemes of conflict involving the theme of the changing role of these political illusions. In such conflict, both sociological and psychological, we have an important and hitherto almost untapped source of material for Eastern European drama.

(a) Illusions that were initially progressive gradually become reactionary. The hero does not recognise this, and the old content of his life-style becomes worn. Outwardly, even in his subjective convictions, he is still a revolutionary, but in reality he is defending a petrified state of affairs. He bridges the chasm by deluding himself.

(b) The hero realises the role of illusions has changed but he 'runs after his money'. Out of self-interest or love of comfort, having long since gained ruling power, he adheres to his adopted stance, which has become reactionary. This is one way to become a cynic.

(c) The hero loses his progressive illusions historically early, or perhaps he never had them. On account of this, or perhaps even because of his very perspicacity, he comes to oppose the revolutionary movement. For example, he did not believe in the prospect of world revolution in 1917, therefore he opposed the Bolsheviks. By the time it turns out that he had been right, he has already become wrong, because his decision has aligned him irretrievably with the wrong forces.

(d) The hero loses his progressive illusions early, but preserves his revolutionary stance. But the movement confronts him with its alternative – which had been justified during the civil war but gradually became more and more false – that one has to join either one side or the other. For example, during the show-trials he has to choose: either he approves of the liquidation of communists, or he himself becomes the ally of the enemy. Following precisely the order of his revolutionary stance which is now bereft of illusions, he rejects both possibilities and becomes tragically isolated.

(e) The hero cannot separate the real from the illusory elements of his revolutionary stance; when he has to renounce his illusions he renounces the real elements of his political convictions too, and in the process he renounces himself as well.

(f) The hero, in order to remain in his position, conceals the fact that he has lost his illusions. He recognises the changing role of illusions but regards it as tragic and intends to use his position to reverse the process. This intention, too, proves to be illusory. In the compromise he wears himself out, or is ground down.

I could go on endlessly listing these paradigms. But even in the above basic types, the possible combinations are infinite. For example, the self-deluding and the cynical 'revolutionaries' present a similar face to the outsider, yet they could come to oppose each other in many ways; their clash might be further complicated by the presence of a man who, because of his deep convictions and after a great deal of inner struggle, has cast off his illusions. Or, an 'illusionless' revolutionary might come face to face with a 'revolutionary with illusions'. Or, all these people might come to oppose, in their many differing ways, representatives of the younger generation who never had illusions to lose in the first place. Or, regarding it from the other side, in some members of the illusionless, apolitical, younger generation a longing might awaken for some kind of communal way of life, and this longing would clash with those actual ways of life which the changing role of illusions has created. There might be conflicts, further, between inherited illusions and reality. And if we take into account that disillusionment is a process, and that individuals on its different rungs can also clash; and if, furthermore, we consider that real and unreal ideas compound a very personal witches' brew in all of us, and that slices of the truth are distributed among mankind as haphazardly as thinner or thicker slices of bread in a Hungarian students' cafeteria, then we can get an idea of the inexhaustible number of conflicts inherent in the process of the changing role of illusions.

A salient point in Hegedüs's study is that each European socialist country has had on its agenda the 'self-criticism' of its form of socialism. This compels everyone to take a stand in a conscious or unconscious fashion, since a general self-criticism includes everyone's personal self-criticism as well. In this process of confrontation the changing role of illusions obviously demands a principal role, but this, of course, will be intertwined with other, no less essential, processes; for example, a growing sense of loneliness, the search for pretexts and loopholes, the consciously accepted mechanisation of the soul and of life-styles, and so on. Literature in our Eastern European societies and most of all our drama, will remain hopelessly provincial and apologetic as long as it is forced, in the battle of opposing interests, to avoid these and similar conflicts. Criticism cannot help in this until our drama reaches a stage when its starting point is not the closed worlds of routine ideology and routine dramaturgy, but the basic realities of our life.

REVIEW SECTION

PRODUCTION

Opening up the text:
Shakespeare's *Henry VI* plays in performance

DAVID DANIELL

The three parts of *King Henry VI*, though fully present in good texts in the First Folio, have been neglected for nearly four hundred years. Until quite recently, they were generally thought, wrongly, to be written in the order 2,3,1, by several hands. They have usually been properly dated in the early 1590s, and thus seen to stand at the beginning of Shakespeare's career — a vulnerable position which allowed Darwinian scholarship to dismiss them too easily as primitive rather than different.

Under Trevor Nunn, the Royal Shakespeare Company took a certain risk in presenting all the plays, in full Shakespearian texts. They were warned that it was economic folly, with a hint of artistic lunacy. The plays, directed by Terry Hands, opened in June 1977, and took their places in the repertory at the Royal Shakespeare Theatre, Stratford-upon-Avon, having a hundred and two performances by the end of the season. They transferred to the RSC's main London theatre, the Aldwych, in April 1978.

The RSC's policy has been an open one, allowing a team of actors on an uncluttered stage to work from inside the lines of text. The casting includes famous names like Alan Howard as King Henry, Helen Mirren as Margaret, Charlotte Cornwell as Joan, James Laurenson as the Dauphin and Cade: but the result is in fact fine ensemble playing from the huge cast. In contrast to the approach of Peter Hall and John Barton in 1963, Terry Hands has imposed no directoral thesis at all: the plays are not arranged to demonstrate anything, except the full text. The result is a quite new set of understandings of central areas of the three plays. That the RSC has done something of importance, I want to show here.

Critical and scholarly interest in the nine history plays of Shakespeare was late in starting. In particular, serious study of the *Henry VI* plays was considered eccentric until well after the Second World War. Two major studies began to turn attention towards the Tudor context of ideas of religion, history and government in which the plays were written: E. M. W. Tillyard's influential *Shakespeare's History Plays* (1944) and Lily B. Campbell's *Shakespeare's 'Histories': Mirrors of Elizabethan Policy* (1947

What might be called the Providential School of criticism followed Tillyard, seeing Shakespeare reflecting his major source, Hall's Chronicle, and Tudor doctrine exemplified in the official Homilies to be read in churches, to show that a divine plan could be seen in English history. So much is Providence overseeing affairs, the doctrine was said to run, that, though men have free will, divine order will be restored to a world made chaotic by sin; in particular, the English political world of the fifteenth century, driven into barbaric chaos as a punishment for the deposition and murder of Richard II, is now blessed by the providential reign of the Tudors. These ideas, though interesting, and pervasive in criticism of the history plays for thirty years, are now strongly challenged as having any special relevance to Shakespeare's dramas, or indeed even to Hall's Chronicle.[1]

The 1950s and 1960s saw a flurry of new editions and critical interest. The most significant event in the study of the *Henry VI* plays has been the publication of the three Arden editions by Andrew S. Cairncross, *Part Two* in 1957, *Part One* in 1962, and *Part Three* in 1964. Though W. J. Courthope had suggested, as far back as 1903,[2] that only Shakespeare had had a mind big enough to conceive these three dramas together, many wrong notions had to be cleared before Shakespeare could be firmly grasped as the sole author. Peter Alexander in 1929 gave strong grounds for Shakespearian authorship and a logical order of writing and there were three fine pieces, all in 1961,[3] which assumed Shakespearian integrity. But Cairncross had no doubts, and gave good evidence, and was far more widely read than any monograph. Now all students of Shakespeare could see that if Shakespeare was allowed to have written all fifteen acts of the three plays, twenty with *Richard III*, a host of new effects became visible. Moreover, these effects were properly Shakespearian, though they did not all quite fit with other expectations.

One of the qualities newly visible at the end of the 1960s was the complexity of the construction; the patterns of parallels, repetitions, inversions, echoes, restatements, anticipations, unwitting insights – a dialectic of all kinds of competing forces, which reverberates forwards and backwards by means of oaths, prophecies and forebodings as well as encounters, styles, settings and pacings. These presented a challenge to the interpretative imagination. Now that we no longer spoke of an irregular patchwork, but could see a grand design, much of the criticism that followed was able to re-animate the issues of Tudor context, looking now for subtler matters altogether. Excellent recent work on Shakespeare's source-material too, particularly by Bullough in 1960,[4] has given a greater confidence to those who write about Shakespeare's intentions. Furthermore, it is now understood that there was no Chronicle Play tradition: Shakespeare apparently invented the English history play. Pattern-seeking continues busily today, finding a set of conscious models for Shakespeare in the Tudor morality plays. This, conveniently to some minds, helps to form a view of King Henry as saint, even Christ, and allows fresh discussion of older topics like epic structure or the nature of kingship or, in a post-Watergate world, the morality of the State. As I write, the air of academic comment on the three plays crackles with abstract nouns: ambivalence, moral history, self-reflexion, ontology, epistemology, hermeneutics, didacticism and many more. It is something, I suppose, to find so much interest. Eight major books giving great attention to the plays, seven from the U.S.A., have appeared since 1970, and learned articles, almost all American, multiply, some more comprehensible than others. There is much esoteric discussion, though little real advance. There is an air of puzzlement. It is significant that none of these readings can have been checked against a performance.

Though the most recent academic critics have simply substituted a new restrictive orthodoxy for the old, the opportunities for a fresh look at the *Henry VI* plays have never been so open. It is greatly to the credit of Trevor Nunn, Terry Hands and their colleagues at the RSC that they have take them, just as they are, and been bound by no conventions, on an open stage.[5]

For a hundred years after his death, all Shakespeare's history plays were generally ignored by actors: being neither comedy nor tragedy, they were felt to be unworkable. Nahum Tate's rewriting of *Richard II* under the title *The Sicilian Usurper* (1680) and Colley Cibber's famous version of *Richard III* (1700) hardly count as Shakespeare.[6] From the earliest years of the eighteenth century the *Henry IV* plays had regular performances. For Garrick and for many others, most of the histories were found to yield some star parts, but always with the rider – except the *Henry VI* plays.

We have evidence of a total of about thirty nights when performances were given of bits of the three plays in various versions, usually extraordinarily barbarised, between 1600 and 1906. On 2nd, 3rd and 4th of May in that year, Frank Benson mounted all three parts at Stratford in succession with severe cuts. In 1923, Robert Atkins staged a telescoped version of all three parts on two nights at the Old Vic to mark the tercentenary of the First Folio. Performances of all three parts are noticed at the Pasadena Community Playhouse in California in 1935: I have no details of alterations.[7] Since then there have been performances of single Parts for a few nights, by the Hovenden players in London, and in America notably at the Ashland (Oregon) and San Diego Festivals.

I myself went specially down from Oxford to Birmingham in 1952 to watch the complete trilogy, which I did in acute discomfort on three over-warm evenings, my long legs jammed tightly against those most uncomfortable seats in the 'gods' at the old Birmingham Rep. The occasions were exhilarating, a combination of triumphs – of staging, by a

director 'who knew what a clear, straight thrust could mean to the production of any crowded chronicle',[8] of local initiative, 'the trilogy ... turned
by the faith of Barry Jackson, the art of Douglas Seale, and the loyalty of
forty actors and actresses, into one of the high feats of the Birmingham
Repertory Theatre',[9] and of course, of Shakespeare. There was much
colour, life, youth and enthusiasm, to which a young, predominantly under-
graduate, audience responded with delight, as if at some partisan victory.
The action, however, felt constricted, by the big triple-arched set on the
small stages of the Birmingham Rep and, later, the Old Vic in 1953. The
armies of the English and French, or of York and Lancaster, though they
established themselves with clear colours and banners, crowded each other.
And though this produced some stunning effects of close fighting, it did give
to all the scenes a sense of colourful uniformity. They were at first mounted
in the odd, but at that time orthodox, sequence, with *Part Two* first and for a
long time on its own, as the only good play, and *Part Three* later as being
worth a risk. *Part One* was an after-thought, later still: it was thought to be
'the most dangerous', containing 'a certain amount of nonsense, much
fustian and some good mixed cursing'. From *Part One*, three entire scenes,
including the Countess of Auvergne and Mortimer, were 'lopped' as 'the
feeblest passages'.[10] There were other major cuts and 'amplifications'.[11]
Eleven scenes in all, including half of act IV of *Part Three*, and a total of one
thousand six hundred lines were cut. The trilogy was cheekily topped and
tailed by having as additions the last Chorus of *Henry V* to open *Part One*,
and, most celebrated at the time, the first lines of *Richard III* to close *Part
Three*.

   Douglas Seale was invited to return to the Old Vic in the autumn of 1958,
to stage the three plays again, for fifteen performances each, as part of the
marathon presentation over five years of all the plays in the First Folio
which the Vic had undertaken. The heavy set was taken over from the
previous season's *Richard III*, with, as additions, a portcullis, a giant gnarled
oak, and 'some distant spikes'. In the words of Mary Clarke:

> The Old Vic company went at the play with almost ferocious vigour. Snarl-
> ing, spitting, choking, gasping, lumbering around in heavy armour, leaping
> off walls, over-turning tables, wielding double-edged swords, or spiked mace
> with equal ferocity, they made the battle-scenes a paradise for schoolboys.
> There were times when one felt that the entrance of one more six-foot stalwart
> in clanking, plated steel, would crash the whole thing into absurdity. Yet this
> never quite happened, and in the scenes of human anguish, which separate
> the bluster and the banging, sympathetic direction and fine playing often
> aroused in the audience an almost unwilling compassion for these medieval
> gangsters.[12]

The same recording angel mentions, a little casually, that 'Seale com-
pressed the text [of the three *Henry VI* plays] into two evenings instead of

three ... The funeral of Henry V, the scene in the Temple Garden ... and some lines about beauteous Margaret, were all that survived' of *Part One*. Even the previous favourite, *Part Two*, was reduced, and *Part Three* lost an entire act (iv). So much for the First Folio! In the early 1960s the Cambridge Marlowe Society produced for a few nights a heavily condensed version of *Parts Two* and *Three*, making a play called *Alarms and Excursions*.

In 1963 and 1964, the Royal Shakespeare Company under Peter Hall and John Barton mounted the enormously successful *The Wars of Roses*, at Stratford, then at the RSC Aldwych Theatre in London, and then at Stratford again, with all-day performances of the trilogy at the Aldwych and Stratford later, and BBC TV presentation, and world acclaim. The *Henry VI* plays had, apparently, arrived. Yet this was a cruel illusion. 'All three plays' meant, working backwards, *Richard III* as the last of the trilogy, and two *new* plays to lead up to it: the first called *Henry VI*, being extracts from *Part One* and some of the first half of *Part Two*; and the second called *Edward IV*, being a conflation of the rest of *Part Two* and much of *Part Three*. To make this happen, the twelve thousand three hundred and fifty lines of the four plays were reduced to half. Worse still, the plays were by William Shakespeare and John Barton, over one thousand four hundred lines being added, with some self-congratulation,[13] by Barton. Finally, to add insult to injury, the production values were most influenced not by English acting traditions, English history, or English scholarship, but by imposition of the bitter Iron Curtain experiences of the Polish writer, Jan Kott, who did not in fact discuss the *Henry VI* plays.

In the present RSC productions, no scenes are cut. They have been modest about one of their most striking achievements, which is that they have successfully mounted the most complete versions of these plays to be seen since Shakespeare's day.[14]

Only a big organisation can present them, it may be felt. The RSC plays to over a million people a year, and is the largest theatre company in the world. As the *Henry VI* plays got into their stride, in the summer of 1977, the company had nineteen productions playing in six theatres – though the actual size of the company has hardly increased in fifteen years, and thirty fewer actors were used than in *The Wars of the Roses*.

The young people who made a cult of David Warner's Henry VI in those plays, and his Hamlet of the same period, were responding to theatrical, and political, excitement. Now the emphases are different. From the first, Terry Hands was against cutting, and for letting the actors be what they speak, with the minimum of directorial imposition. The result is fluidity of effect, and of meaning. The empty stage allows the actors simply to come on and make their statements, and what happens is both complex in a new way and very simple to understand. This fluidity is helped by the developments in the lighting, making the Stratford theatre miles ahead of its European rivals: there is one splendid innovation of a forward-facing high row which makes a screen of light, isolating the thrust. (The 'above', a cumbersome bridge which ponderously rises and falls, may be thought to be less successful, though it does leave a clear stage.) The whole effect has a curious lightness of tone, almost a flying quality, which makes nonsense of all the assumptions held until fifteen years ago, and held with enough force to set Hall and Barton re-writing, that the patchwork scenes were impossible to follow. As *The Times* noted of these new RSC productions 'the performance continuously grips attention through its mobile control of narrative' (13 July 1977). The *Financial Times* said 'scene melts into scene, each one contrived with a masterly simplicity that announces its content at once, so that there is as much continuous action as in a football match' (14 July 1977).

Casting is from RSC resources. The sheer presence of Julian Glover's Warwick, with the York boys gambolling around him, makes massive point. Emrys James's York ties the performances with the earlier productions of the two parts of *Henry IV*, and *Henry V*. Helen Mirren plays Margaret with quicksilver variety, while allowing a tenacious quality in her to keep her steady. These three move further and further from the 'standard' readings, and they have a little distressed the old-fashioned, who see Margaret, for example, only as steely arrogance and cruelty.

The plays, however, are firmly called *King Henry VI*. There is an odd sense in which nobody seems to have appreciated that before. David Warner played Henry with passive, pathetic saintliness, likening him to Richard II, as has been done before – Hazlitt wrote a few pages on *Henry VI*, almost all of which are about Richard II. Alan Howard comes to the part at the peak of his great powers, with a stunning Henry V and an overwhelming Coriolanus in the same repertory. He brings to the trilogy the experience of playing this Henry's father, as King and as Prince before that. He brings, too, high intelligence and great personal power – not qualities usually associated with Henry VI. His speaking is superb, his playing uniformly interesting and unexpected. This is a Henry who has the capacity to be as revolutionary as Joan or Cade. Far from being a pale weakling, he can see too much, feel too much, and call on powers far beyond the rest. What he says rings with the possibility of meaning. He speaks, and then is silent, while the fierce lords clamour around him.

Theatre of this kind changes nightly, subtly but importantly. The sensation, watching, is of steady movement outward across a boundary, letting something free that has been imprisoned far too long.

PART ONE

While the house-lights are still up, Henry V's coffin, draped with his colours, and helmeted, is spotlit amid the black drapes. A harsh brass Dead March brings on the six lords in slow file out of the darkness, in rich black hoods and cloaks, black and gold shields at their shoulders. They turn and swing in single file down-stage. Those awkward opening lines are delivered in high style directly to the audience, over drum-beats, as each speaker steps forward in procession, and crosses to form up on the other side. Taunted by Gloucester across the stage, it is Winchester who first throws back his hood, and in his rage to retort pounds the coffin with his hands. The coffin remains centre-stage for the entire scene in near-darkness, lacking occasion to remove it, while the messengers cause the groupings to break and re-form down-stage. The scrambling chaos at the death of Henry V has begun.

The drapes fly out as, using the depth of the stage, to a great deal of music, light, noise and smoke, four enormous cannon are rolled forward, with the young French lords, swaggering before them, parodying the slow down-stage swing of the ancient English lords. The music has a properly hollow bravado for a scene that starts with Mars and ends with Venus, and the conceited French in their jewelled armour are presently beaten forward again in what must be the world's sketchiest skirmish. Joan la Pucelle is the first distinctive figure. Charlotte Cornwell plays her with a big smile and a well-cut mop of red hair, and in an open white calico tunic; hers is the first body not smothered in cloaks, armour, insignia, or all three. She is slim, strong and sexy, soon getting on top of the Dauphin, riding him pelvis to pelvis, leaning amorously over him, and making a strong erotic point of 'Then will I think upon a recompense.' Stuck with four huge cannon, the designer, Farrah, has had to make them do, all anachronistically, for the Tower of London, in a swift and economical scene change.

Twenty minutes in, at the end of the Tower scene, it is clear that *Part One* is being played for speed and a dark pageantry, the 'colour' including a lot of music for wind-band and percussion (out of sight) and inventive lighting. Guy Woolfenden's music, which punctuates every scenic change and underlines a great deal of emotion, is the aural partner of the lighting. There is great freedom of feeling; fast transitions develop all the time, with efficiency. The many lightly-signalled characters (seventeen named, and half a dozen extras, up to the end of the third scene) establish, even so early, kaleidoscopically-patterned parallels, doublings, placings and repetitions. The language is unexpectedly effective. The verse works with a sort of coded brevity, an easy lightness, which says much more than it appears to do on the page. If the scenes of the *Henry VI* plays are emblematic, working like a theatrical *Faerie Queene*, then in fact here they make emblems which move very fast.

David Swift makes Talbot a burly, bald, piggy man, in a big sheepskin jacket, obviously the serving front-line officer who, as an individualist, is going to get up the noses of the staff officers who visit the 'theatre of operations'.[15]

He has a cheerful, brave exuberance, and is a bonny fighter, like a wild Highlander, and much feared by the French: only witchcraft could make his bouts with La Pucelle leave him like a fallen colossus at the tail of a cannon. Across the stage, a sword-bearing Joan, supple and sexy, gives a sense of her uncanny powers and their ambiguous sources: left alone, all Talbot can do is mutter classical references. Later, Joan, in the middle of the euphoria after the victorious capture of Orleans, catches sight of the torch-flame and retreats from it in fascinated, underplayed horror. Critics are sharply divided about this; but Joan as seer is permissible, and the notion is, in fact, backed by the text: the French are at that moment developing one of their favourite themes in the presence of Joan – that they can't wait for her to be dead so that they can make her wonderful memorials (I, vi, 21–7).[16]

I want to deal later with a sequence of scenes from this part of *Part One*. Two tributes should be made here: one little one to Barrie Rutter, excellent in several parts throughout, for the tiny cameo of the soldier crying 'A Talbot! A Talbot!' at II, i, 77 – a very Shakespearian thing. The second and major one is to Alan Howard for his first entry, in the scene before the interval, which is simply astonishing. He is distinctly fourteen years old, and conveys the innocence of this child king, impotent, in spite of highest intentions, to do anything at all about the catastrophically increasing disintegration pressing all around him. He sits still on the throne while fighting breaks right across his tiny, erect body as Gloucester and Winchester rage and their common people brawl all over the Parliament House. (*The Guardian* referred to Alan Howard's 'swivel-eyed' Henry VI, who looks on like a Wimbledon spectator watching Nastase play Nastase' (14 July 1977.)

The interval is taken after III, i. The audience stumblingly explain to each other the intricacies of Yorkist and Lancastrian genealogy and what 'Plantagenet' means, as they gaze over the Avon. It is clear, by now, that this is not, as used to be said, a Talbot play; it is more Talbot v. Joan. Talbot is a rough, tough fighting figure, but he is not the only dramatic hero. Playing the text as it is, intelligently and inventively, produces rapid ensemble work, around certain conflicts. The French and English skirmish together in half-light amid the guns with much knee-work and kicking as well as clashing swords. It is also a play of adventure: Bedford and Burgundy, their backs to the audience, climb long ladders to the bridge, while on the other side, Talbot makes a monkey grab at it from the shoulders of

7A *Henry VI Part One*, act ii, scene v. In the Tower of London, Richard Plantagenet (Emrys James) hears from the dying Mortimer (the late Clem McCallin) the details of his claim to the throne

7B *Henry VI Part Two*, act iii, scene ii. Queen Margaret (Helen Mirren) pleads with the shocked King Henry (Alan Howard) not to blame Suffolk for Duke Humphrey's murder

7C *Henry VI Part Two*. 'Come, wife, let's in, and learn to govern better.' King Henry (Alan Howard), his country torn by rebellion, is lovingly comforted by his Queen (Helen Mirren)

two of his men, to surprise the comic French. These are caught in a gaggle in their nightshirts and compromising circumstances, the whole short scene showing the greatest variety of attitude, dress (or lack of it), lighting and sound.

The French, in particular, work corporately, under Joan. They are modern and ruthless, base and secretive, as the most unchivalric slaughter of Salisbury shows. He is shot by a young sniper with a big gun in the dark down front, and dies in a muddled moment on the bridge. Joan's witchcraft extending to the flow of scenes, the French are made to be active, immediate and everywhere; their feelings are powerful and instant, all qualities we shall meet again in *Part Two* and *Part Three* in the York family. So it was intelligent to make the coronation a huddled affair in the barest of light far up-stage, after a brave but flimsy show of scarlet. The English are in a threatening situation, even without Vernon and Basset quarrelling viciously in brilliant red right forward on the thrust.

The complex knot of dramatic forces at the coronation, with the news of Burgundy and the York–Somerset quarrel, makes a firmly Shakespearian scene. The child king punctures Duke Humphrey of Gloucester's wrath with the line 'What! doth my uncle Burgundy revolt?' This Henry, though young, finds his own authority rapidly. From nervously appealing to Gloucester over his shoulder when faced with Talbot, to gently making the thirty-line sermon to the two factions, Alan Howard allowed him to grow in both force and innocence at once. The King is the focus of the scene, and the clash of his worst possible solutions with his highest possible intentions makes the sort of ironic resonant effect we usually associate with later Shakespeare. Henry makes three great mistakes, sending his one devotedly loyal and disinterested follower, Talbot, away: choosing one rose, the red one, and – played here as an afterthought – splitting the command in France. Howard suggests that there might be ironies in Henry here: more, there might be something closer to home, something at the root like sheer humanity, the ordinary capacity to make crashing mistakes and not see. Howard's Henry in his new self-confidence in France suddenly sees himself as a Good King, in the delight of growing up, not because of any unique royal circumstances. Romeo in alien territory, in Capulet's rooms or far Mantua, made great mistakes for similar reasons.

Henry's errors ensure Talbot's death. I found I had mixed feelings about these scenes. The French conveniently fought whenever Talbot stopped speaking, but it did not seem odd in the general effect. The down-front scenes with Sir Thomas Lucy and York and Somerset were excellent (whenever Terry Hands makes use of the new thrust, it is successful). Lucy was emotionally lucid and strong – even though, finding him played by Jeffery Dench, who had also been so competent as Salisbury, as Edmund Mortimer and as Bedford, I expected to see a programme note which listed

the principals and then said 'All other parts played by J. Dench.' But
Talbot and John died amid clutter of all kinds, vocal, physical, theatrical,
and even directorial, being watched by no fewer than nine motionless
French. We have tended to see these scenes as the last apogee of chivalry,
and Talbot and John speak the language of it, in the text. In this performance, anything so abstract as chivalric style had been left behind. Just
as Talbot had had no place at court, and was glad to leave, so he was out of
place here, with both the older courtly rhetoric and the new French and
their guns. This Talbot spoke and fought without style at all, just as an
honest old English warrior in non-regulation battle-dress who has been left
far behind in the new perfidious world of French villainy and up-to-date
English politics. The scenes are famous, and Nashe's contemporary report
about the moving effect on 'ten thousand spectators at least, (at several
times)' might make us wonder at the possibility that the Elizabethan Talbot
went for naturalism of style, too, here.

The tableau of the dead Talbot, an anonymous English soldier, and Sir
Thomas Lucy, remain shadowed on stage while the young King Henry,
terrified of marriage, stands on the huge bridge and agrees to everything,
lost in the devious, reptilian moves to a French peace – even that Machiavel
the new Cardinal of Winchester's dazzling crimson outfit did not quite
rescue this scene, which was strongly side-lit and confusing behind the
struts of the wooden engineering.

Joan, below and alone, coming forward through the battle-ground on to a
wide front stage, offers herself to her spirits with strong body movements
and a big ugly square mouth. The 'Fiends' suddenly appear among the
darkened guns, looking like gas-masked soldiers from the French trenches
of the First World War.

Instantly on Joan's obscene down-front exit, grotesquely held by York,
far up-stage among the cannon young Margaret, in a lemon and green
gown, daintily picks her way forward through the battle-field, and is
captured by Peter McEnery's youthful, dark, handsome, careless Suffolk.
The wooing scene here rises to greater heights than one would have thought
possible: an economical duet using the whole down-stage width which
draws together almost all the serious threads of the play and yet is delicious.
It is patterned with echoes of Joan, and the Countess, of the hollow French –
Reignier, as well as being an ally of the Dauphin, is vulgar – of shallow
English victories, and of all the 'practice' around the King. The scene
makes another sudden Shakespearian point of focus. Seeing this production
I feel it is this, and not the scene with the Countess of Auvergne, which
should have had all the recent critical attention. The Petrarchan language
is made empty, and, too, that newest stage convention, the soliloquy, is
mocked, with enjoyment, by McEnery and Mirren. The scene is a delicate
tissue of falseness, yet Helen Mirren plays a humanly desirable Margaret:

her sensuous adolescent body offers the third level of eroticism in this production. First Joan, assertive and roughly available; then the Countess, trying to act out the Lady of the Castle, to be won by the Hero. Here in Margaret is slim grace, youth, and knowing, tender, sexual promise.

Her grace makes the more disgusting Joan's final ugliness. She is cursed by and curses her peasant father, whose rich country smells offend the sardonically watching Warwick and York, the latter played by Emrys James holding a white rose to his nose, his face held in profile: Charlotte Cornwell is as slippery as a toad and as tricky as a monkey, even when carried violently out. The disgust extends to the botched peace-making on French soil, where the hateful Winchester has arrived with a suddenness of appearance which marks everything on this territory. And the botching, and suddenness, and disgust apply to the new marriage arrangements imposed by Suffolk on King Henry. Played right down front in the brightest light, the scene makes young Suffolk affect his young sovereign with the sudden availability of sex. Alan Howard's Henry, already, one feels, troubled by sex, giving up his 'father's' advice, and choosing instead to listen to his handsome friend, gives point to his last, and otherwise puzzling, word in this play – 'grief'. He stops his ears to other voices. He will have none but Margaret.

The company is almost all assembled mid-stage, nobody having left since Joan's destruction, the taking of a few paces forward being used to signify the new location for King Henry in England. But the play is not quite finished. Suffolk has achieved not only the certainty of a double adultery, treason, control of the King, control of the realm, and the grotesquely lavish 'tenth' of national taxes, but also a very young, seductive and pliant mistress. Peter McEnery plays his final six-line soliloquy like a restrained tom-cat full of cream, with more than a touch of Richard Crookback addressing his beloved audience.

PART TWO

Eager audiences return, as to a family party, where the new uncles will perform. This is odd, because even a sketchy knowledge warns that there will be much deceit and bloodshed. Perhaps criticism has been over-solemn, and Shakespeare knew a thing or two about entertainment.

Now a grassy green carpet covers the stage.[17] It is unmistakably holiday in feeling. Up-stage a red rope holds back commoners who gently wave red and white roses at the audience, good-humouredly waiting on a summer day for a royal procession. The Clerk of Chatham squats reading a book. Eight, nine, ten, a dozen people assemble; they are the first thing established in the new play, in which they are going to be dominant. As the house-lights go, they greet the young King with rapture, and Alan Howard, his back to the audience, establishes astonished delight in what is happening. The English nobility march forward with him, in two files, to cheerful music, and group themselves on either side having not now mourned a dead king but knelt to kiss a young king's hand. Last comes Suffolk to present Margaret. This time, the messengers from France are a cool nobleman and a warm girl.

The young people, King and Queen, are enraptured from their first encounter. For all her old-fashioned courtly language, this Margaret expects a warmer kiss than the nervous little peck on the cheek that Henry manages. He retreats a few paces, confused by his feelings, but then comes forward again, and while Duke Humphrey begins to read the marriage-terms, Henry and Margaret gaze on each other's faces; they are eager and sensual, not attending to anything else. The point is made that like their near-contemporaries in Shakespeare, Antipholus and Luciana, or Petruchio and Katherine, like Romeo and Juliet or Bassanio and Portia, they fall in love at first sight. This is clearly going to be a different Henry and Margaret from any that have been recorded. From here until the end of *Part Three* their complex, mysterious love-affair will continue. Each sees in the other complementary qualities. Margaret, as the *Sunday Telegraph* observed, 'grows in stature until she achieves a surprising degree of dignity . . . in her final moments of middle-aged authority' (17 July 1977). This is a woman who would die for Henry, as she says. They share much more than has normally been recognised.

The listening commoners are shocked by the lack of dowry, but they manage muted cheers at the up-stage exit of the King and his Queen, and Suffolk, the cheerful music now sounding a little forced. The quarrelling nobles who now piece out their chess-moves are more numerous and full-blooded than in any scene so far. The old Duke Humphrey (Graham Crowden) is a man whose love for England comes from far back in his ancestry. Two new voices cut across the odious Winchester's drearily-reiterated attacks on Humphrey: Warwick (Julian Glover), and York (Emrys James). Glover represents an older tradition, both of character and performance; there is good decorum in giving Warwick to such a big actor, in every sense. Emrys James at first sight seems bizarre. His restless off-beat inattention, however, his neurotic focus on himself, his sudden, instantly-expressed violent reactions set him apart – that is, until his sons appear. Only when this choleric Lord is with his psychotic off-spring is reason clearly given for the casting. These Yorks are obsessed and manic; later, they giggle as they fight. *The Sunday Times* called him 'the plausible chieftain of a bloody dynasty' (17 July 1977), *The Times* 'a snarling underdog speedily on the way up' (13 July 1977) and later 'a full-blown reptilian narcissus' (14 July 1977). Now, York hangs his head and twitches almost imperceptibly. He is listening to what his peers say, but he is listening to something else inside himself. He is on his own for what is probably the first major soliloquy in Shakespeare, and at the end of the scene a new tone comes through: self-absorption. The very latest thing at the English court is self-seeking as a way of life. It was seen before in York, touched in Winchester and Somerset, fully introduced in Suffolk's speeches, responded to eagerly by Margaret and taken up by young Warwick. It is now wildly sung by York. Going for the crown is an afterthought for this man (unlike his son Richard), simply something that will give him a theatre of action big enough for his violent and immense ego and its new verbal style. Emrys James gives him the authority of the bounder or even of the psychopath. This is not the man whose chivalry and power were known throughout Europe. But does Shakespeare say it was?

The common people, meanwhile, have retreated nervously to one side away from Warwick, who, grieving the loss of his own conquests, Anjou and Maine, has stalked up-stage to control himself. The commoners act like the audience to a play-within-a-play. They rush off to follow the good Duke Humphrey when he leaves in barely-controllable rage against Winchester and Suffolk. The Nevilles point the theatrical image at Winchester's exit with 'Pride went before, Ambition follows him.'

Ruthless self-seeking is a betrayal held to the very bosom of Duke Humphrey. With the grass floor lit as a Persian carpet, Humphrey and his wife Eleanor, two long-married lovers, stand and caress at ease in the domestic shadows, telling their morning's dreams. The amorous and beautiful Eleanor (Yvonne Coulette, also the Countess of Auvergne), made a detailed parallel and contrast with Joan, the Countess, and Helen Mirren's Margaret, who each set a course of sexually enticing betrayal. The scene is beautiful; restrained, delicate, emotionally strong, it is made by two actors and an ambiguous atmosphere of low lighting. But the winner is John Hume, making money in a black hood. The conjuring episode, two scenes on, was, as it has so often been,[18] excellent, with a villainous one-toothed, totally bald Bolingbroke organising thunder in the dark. As her 'spirit' is raised, the prostrate Margery Jourdain's mittened witch-fingers claw the ground like a tortured animal – a worse than Joan is here. After the cry of 'Asnath!', she shrieks *in extremis* with tones recalling York's voice in crazy soliloquy.

In brighter sunlight on the green sward, the colourful scenes flow into each other in prettiness – there are real falcons at St Albans. But Humphrey and Winchester claw at each other with hisses down front behind the King's back; they stop as the suspicious King draws near. Like old-fashioned overgrown schoolboys, they plan to fight each other as if it were behind the fives-court after Prep. The more captivating the scene, on the pleasant grass, the darker the corruption. King, Queen, Lords and a falconer mingle: there is much merriment, and the commoners, on their narrower side of

8A *Henry VI Part Two*, act I, scene i. The young King Henry (Alan Howard) greets for the first time his young Queen, Margaret (Helen Mirren), while Suffolk (Peter McEnery) looks on

8B *Henry VI Part Three*. King Henry (Alan Howard) entails his throne to the Duke of York (Emrys James) after his death

the red ropes, show a little of that variety of experience and social range we have always so admired in the much later *Henry IV* plays. The richnesses of *Part One* have come home, and spread. It is a strikingly well-made effect.

But the people's petitions are torn up by Margaret, the 'miracle' is an oily cheat, the court is electric with plots, and the trial-by-combat is a drunken farce. Helen Mirren's spoiled brat of a young Queen makes an important point in emending I, iii, 40 to 'Away, base scullions! Suffolk, *make* them go.' This is not a dominant Frenchwoman lording it over an English court, but a child who is simply reflecting and focussing the manners of the world she lives in. This line, and Mirren's performances in the rest of these out-of-London scenes, hang together most interestingly. She is wholly impressionable, and thus most widely responsive. She gets light laughs with no more than a chagrined amusement at the lines wishing her husband could be made Pope (I, iii, 61–4). Her interest in Suffolk is easily distracted. She laughs merrily at Saunder Simpcox running, and before that she has taken young delight in aggravating the Duchess of Gloucester to make her 'ten commandments' remark at I, iii, 142 as she only just manages not to scratch the Queen's face with her ten nails. But she expresses something else altogether when at the end of II, i Buckingham brings the news of the arrest of Dame Eleanor. The stage darkens a little as he speaks, and Margaret goes to stand very close to Henry.

Alan Howard finishes that scene with a couplet that has become more pointedly uncertain as the months have gone by:

> And poise the course in Justice' equal scales,
> Whose beam stands sure, whose rightful cause prevails.

Obviously and silently objecting – the only face not laughing – at both the exposure of Simpcox and the victory of Horner, and disliking the necessity of condemning to execution the Bolingbroke conspirators, he is troubled by apparent varieties of justice: but he is simply wiped out by the powerful sounds of self-seeking all round him. In these scenes he cannot speak the new animal language of self-aggrandisement which is the latest English style, from serving-man to Cardinal, from Protector's wife to York. Yet in less than an hour of playing-time before the interval, Howard shows Henry expressing his insight into truth in a succession of strong scenes that were certainly new in drama in 1590. He is given intelligently-played surrounding scenes to which his own fuller statement of the dark side can be seen to relate. The conclusion of Eleanor's personal drama, II, iv, with five cold figures on the big bare stage, is one of the most moving of the entire sequence, leaving largely unstated feelings of grief about hurt affairs of state and tragic married love.

Henry is given, too, as opponent, a York gaining in real authority. From the beginning of II, ii, until the end of III, i, apart from that scene of the parting of Humphrey and Eleanor, York is not away from the stage. The sequence begins with the after-supper scene with the Nevilles in his garden, again excellently played. The struts holding the ropes for the open-air daylight scenes make elbow-rests for Salisbury and Warwick at ease with drinks in the softly-lit darkness, York between them urbanely telling off on his fingers his line to the crown. Warwick gets an unsatirical laugh on 'What plain proceedings is more plain than this?' The scene is open, rapid, lucid, and uncluttered, and Emrys James's powers of simple, sardonic speech are at their best – his claim is something of a quick joke. By contrast, in the following scene, when Duke Humphrey is persuaded to give up his staff, there is a very long moment of slow, puzzled anguish from Howard. Helen Mirren's reading of Margaret's first line after Humphrey has left, 'Why now is Henry king, and Margaret queen' (II, iii, 39) is original. Barbara Jefford, playing throughout the 1958 Old Vic productions as the passionate scheming she-wolf, was widely noticed at that point. It was 'her supreme moment of triumph', and on that line 'her arms stretched upward exultantly'.[19] Here, for the RSC, Helen Mirren's arms come forward, as she goes to Henry in affectionate pleasure. She is also taking pleasure, of course, in her growing political interest and power; but she is altogether removed from the older tradition of scorching the stage as a French tigress.

The long scene of the Parliament at Bury St Edmunds has the commoners, in the half-light, busily setting up the throne and benches (one is half-seen naughtily sitting in the throne for a second or two). They stay and watch at the side and back, right through the scene until the King's exit. Every word that Henry speaks, as Howard reads him, results in an exercise of the power of life or death: but he can't do properly what his father and grandfather could, dirty his hands with politics. He is simply wearied at the incessant attacks on Duke Humphrey. He tries to hold to Humphrey's innocence, out of a loving certainty of it, and so dismisses him to the murderous clutches of the whole court. He himself attempts to follow the departing Humphrey as if drawn by a rope. Called back by Margaret, who makes 'What! Will your Highness leave the Parliament?' into a genuine question, not a shrill crow of victory, Howard is seen to be shedding real tears, and speaks of his 'heart drown'd with grief,/Whose flood begins to flow within mine eyes'. His first long speech of passion, about the calf roped for slaughter, expresses some of the grief previously unspoken by Humphrey and Eleanor at *their* parting. Henry grieves too for his own special understanding.

His exit makes a closing period. It is followed by a flurry of rapid political bargaining, in which Margaret controls York and Somerset by physical warmth to them; York responds to Margaret's pressing presence, but he is too quick a thinker for her, and this *echt Politiker*, left alone to glory in his power over the audience, has suddenly achieved leave of absence, and an army.

Even so, Henry rises for a while to out-top them all in personal power. The second and third scenes of III rise steadily, from the moment of his swoon at the news of the death of Duke Humphrey. Margaret shows sudden human concern, swooping like a lover to recover him, holding his head to her bosom. But as he wakes, he spurns her, and rises, and from then on, point after point gets home to him. One can almost see the scales falling from Howard's eyes, as he backs away from both Margaret, and, separately, Suffolk. His seventeen lines beginning 'What, doth my Lord of Suffolk comfort me?' are delivered at almost full Howard power, though he attacks Suffolk from inside the news of Gloucester's death, as it were, not from the politics involved outside. (Margaret's reactions at this point I want to look at a little later.) Henry sits in paralysed horror on the throne, his cheeks puffy with unshed tears, staring ahead at the visible truth. It is the commons, of course, who make the final point, clamouring against Suffolk at the gates, and Howard's double banishment of Suffolk now has the power of some of his greatest speeches from his powerful *Henry V*. But there is more to come. The scene of the death of Winchester, only thirty-four lines long, feels intrusive after the closing of the Margaret–Suffolk parting: but only for a few seconds. The centre of the play is Henry, not Margaret. John Rhys-Davies's gross and physically powerful Winchester could not die in a bed, it must have been felt, especially Gloucester's bed, though that is what Folio states, and Quarto amplifies. Instead, he staggers across the stage, stumbling over the throne, and falls to the ground in a parody of the death of young Talbot. King Henry, wrestling with the fiend in Winchester, urgently holding his cross to his face, finds the element of darkness he has been coming to understand. Warwick, aloof and lofty, murmurs a little smugly, 'so bad a death argues a monstrous life'. Alan Howard's next line is at full power, a recognition that in this court, justice is dead: 'Forbear to judge, for we are sinners all.' The line and a half that follow after a pause, 'Close up his eyes, and draw the curtain close;/And let us all to meditation' let us down for the interval. But that great cry reverberates on, quite against the traditional 'religious and ineffectual' reading of the lines.[20] Biblical it certainly is: but that gives it the greatest authority. This is a new Henry, demonstrably here the son of his father. Convincingly, Howard has brought Henry to power, for the first time, I suspect, for nearly four centuries.

But, unlike his father, Henry has had no training in the difficult business of political casuistry, and he has declared the truth too late. Events simply sweep him away. York's triple advantage of being in Ireland, perfecting a private army, and maintaining Jack Cade's rebellion, from a distance, wins everything in the rest of this play.

The dramatic grip of the opening of iv took me by surprise. Barrie Rutter's 'Lieutenant' (i.e. pirate) gets great moral weight against Suffolk in powerful, vivid speeches. So strong was the theatrical pressure, though we had barely settled into our seats again after the interval, that the audience reaction at the end of the scene to Suffolk's head, discreetly wrapped in a black cloth, was, each time, a low murmur of horror. It is a key scene, one suddenly sees, in the preparation for Cade.

In this production, the scenes of the Jack Cade rebellion are uniformly brilliant, and beyond cavil. Each time I saw *Part Two* it was played to an international house unfamiliar with the play, twice on a matinée; yet the second half, after the interval, got the sort of concentrated, breath-holding attention usually reserved for a fine *Othello* or *Macbeth*. This was a little more understandable in the royal and court scenes later on: but the Cade scenes involve here much running about, and great activity all over the big stage. There are laughs, of course; but not many, and not of the kind which the *Henry IV* plays get. There is unease in the audience; crisp playing only adds to the sense of simply *watching* matters get worse and worse so rapidly – the scenes are played to be in a proper sense cinematic. There is a little of the circus, too; but one of the achievements of this production is to get the sense of the largeness and closeness of the catastrophe, with much senseless slaughter all over the streets, and with half London on fire. There develops, too, an alarming sense that the anarchy will begin to extend out into the audience. The first death, of the Clerk of Chatham, momentarily surprises the murderers, who are in fact simply the 'commons' who have been spectators of so much in the first half. The Staffords are more horribly butchered, their aristocratic superiority infuriating the mob. The deaths of Lord Say and his son-in-law are sickening – and suddenly the mob too has had too much of killing. Clifford wins them over with the name of Henry V, and, cynically, with scattered coins, but some of them are half won already, revolted – as are the audience – by Barrie Rutter's Dick the Butcher and his horrible bloody cleaver.[21] James Laurenson (who was a swaggering Dauphin) makes Cade a parody of the timeless revolutionary, a hint of the would-be Che Guevara about him. He is fully in command, sitting on mossy London stone directing with large gestures the destruction-of-civilisation-as-we-know-it. His supporters know the facts of history, and mock him even while they follow him. They reflect York, their ultimate master, in their opportunism, exulting at first in mad claims and murder. Like York, they are very dangerous. The point of the wider application is made with characteristic discipline in the treatment of the soldier who comes running in shouting 'Jack Cade! Jack Cade' at iv, vi, 7. He is killed instantly and startlingly for using the wrong name, and the incident is over in five seconds. His body is allowed to remain unobtrusively on stage for nearly twenty minutes, through the riotously swirling scenes of the '*Alarums.*

Matthew Goffe is slain, and all the rest' in the stage direction before scene vii, the long scene of the deaths of Lord Say and his son-in-law, the surrender to Clifford, and right through scene ix, between Queen Margaret and King Henry (of which more later). It remains as a comment on the emptying of all value which the Cade rebellion is effecting, as a weapon of the Duke of York.

Iden, called 'Eden' here, as making a point about ideal gardens which seems unnecessary, is played by Dan Meaden[22] as a bulky John Bull, killing Cade with contemptuous ease. The overlapping of the collapse of the Cade rebellion and the arrival of York and his army is painfully clear. There are suddenly too many political fronts even for the newly-strong King to fight on. He is called 'our dread liege' by Buckingham, not ironically, but the opposition is suddenly monstrous. Even the father and grandfather of this 'dread liege' would have been overtaxed by so impossible a test. Enraged, treacherous and deceitful, grimacing like a fiend, York has to pick a quarrel, which he does over Somerset's liberty, and state a reason – and he gives the incredible one that he is the real king.

All the Cade scenes had been backed by a sort of mindless banner, the vacant grin of a silly turnip-lantern face with blood running down it. Emrys James makes York's claim wear an equally silly face, it being the mischievous whim of a black opportunist. Old Clifford, he who knew and defeated the anarchy of Cade, has to grope for sense about York. 'To Bedlam with him! Is the man grown mad?' (v, i, 131). Suddenly, Henry has no power at all. The Nevilles, scenting advantage, are supporting York, and new rebellion catches fire among the youth. Animal language of childish insults, all initiated by the York father and sons, turns to fighting. James gives a crazy passion to York's reply to the royal challenge, calling Margaret 'O blood-bespotted Neapolitan, / Outcast of Naples, England's bloody scourge'. This line is widely quoted by commentators as a clue to Margaret's character, but it is said by an egomaniac in response to the first check he has received, and even if York be played otherwise, it is hard to see why Margaret is 'blood-bespotted' compared to York himself, who caused the deaths of the Talbots and their army and many innocent Englishmen in the Cade adventure. 'England's bloody scourage' is taken to link Margaret with Joan,[23] but here the link with Joan is through someone else. The York family win the battle of St Albans in swaggering triumph. There is no apparatus of battle; no guns, no barricades – just almost comic noblemen on England's green grass, as if on a cricket pitch. But the Yorks and Nevilles grin like the French, and the witchcraft of Joan is in young Richard's hunched back and withered arm.

PART THREE

The aircraft-carrier stage, as *The Guardian* called it (15 July 1977), reverts to blackness, as in the opening of *Part One*. Black-draped benches and throne are ready for Parliament, a spot illuminating the floor behind.

There is no procession. The front of the thrust is suddenly full of an excited row of black and silver Yorks and Nevilles, brilliantly top-lit with the screen of light; their individual victories at the battle of St Albans fill their mouths. The screen becomes transparent, and the big box of the empty Parliament-house, and the throne, lie before them as they turn. What more natural then but that York should advance and sit on the throne? His followers kneel close round him like figures in some parody of heaven. The lighting makes points itself – as *The Guardian* also said – varying between sudden bursts of illumination and a feeling of watching rats scurry at the end of a tunnel, with the further remark that many lights make Hands' work.

Alan Howard in a grey gown gives the King on his entry a wry humour at the sight of York's presumption. This Henry will be surprised by nothing, now. York sits squatly on the throne, his sword across his arm like a sceptre, the identical posture and prop of Jack Cade on London stone. A silly, vacant grin masks his face. Howard makes the authority of the scene belong to the King. He will not 'make a shambles of the Parliament-house'. His commands to the seated York, 'I am thy sovereign', gets the lunatic, uncaring retort 'I am thine.' It is checkmate, a reply straight from hell. There is no answer except to join the Yorks in childish argument: Warwick calls from the back of the throne, 'Be Duke of Lancaster: let him be king.' He makes one attempt to use superior reason on his own terms, and fails. He is routed in the general scramble for political advantage. Howard's 'My title's weak' aside was in later performances a steely remark from revealed truth. Henry is isolated because he can see further in to such matters, because he alone is *sane*. Emrys James's manic crowing whoop of astonishment, on realising that in entail the crown is his, tells a whole history. Henry's father and grandfather would have done otherwise, of course, prepared to blacken themselves for the sake of the throne, be lunatic if that was the game, in this monkey-house Parliament. From now on, Henry is powerless, taken about like a dog or a mascot, deserted in human terms by everyone – except his wife.

Helen Mirren, in a gown of apricot and brown and gold, is no battle-axe. If her eye flails and her voice rings, it is for love of Henry and grief for him, and her son. Conservatives find that this reading of Margaret takes some getting used to – it is certainly emancipated. Helen Mirren will grow even more in power, of course, as time passes: but she is already stronger than some critics have allowed. The point here is that she is forced into military action because she loves Henry, rather than being a fierce political, military – and foreign – female only waiting for her chance to get started. Her entry precisely at the departure of Joan in *Part One* has led to too easy an equation. The evil at that point was all round her, not only in her: in the selfish advantage of Suffolk, and in that of Winchester more deeply. In England she is hated by the court because she makes manipulating the King more difficult, because of her own manipulation by the traitorous Suffolk, and because power went to her young head. Yet she has been played, since records were made, in Queen Cambyses' vein. Power she must have, of course, when it is needed. But her strong nature must show many sides. It is limiting Shakespeare to make her the Duchess in *Alice in Wonderland*, only *fortissimo*. Margaret is much more interesting than that, and it is Helen Mirren's greatness that that is what she shows us. Here, indeed, is one of the great parts in Shakespeare. As a most unhistorical old lady she is again something new in *Richard III*: but we haven't got there yet.

On the bare stage, the only prop a little book which the serious York is reading, the demonic Richard seduces his father into abandoning his oath to Henry and going for the crown. (York's death I will deal with later.) The symbols, patterns and parallels, though less strong than in *Part One* and *Part Two*, are still at work. The head of York on an enormous pole, fully fifteen feet high, stands aside down front outside the gates of the city of York, unobtrusively lit through the next sequence of scenes, a brooding emblem over all that happens. Henry, at first central, refuses to do anything but gaze on York's head, though Margaret is cheerful and Clifford vocal. He recovers to dub Prince Edward knight. Then he is steadily pressed out of the close knot of excited Yorks and Lancastrians which surrounds the anomalous, feminine figure of Margaret in her silver gown. He sits, cross-legged and patient, at the foot of York's pole. He is still there, gently lit like the head high above him, during the fight at Towton, only moving at the start of his celebrated 'molehill' speech, when he comes slightly more to centre-stage, to sit again cross-legged on the bare floor.

This sad scene was exactly the relief from martial clashes and high-stomached words which Shakespeare clearly intended. Alan Howard brought to the soliloquy a muscular strength of thought so that there was no evidence of self-absorption. It is, of course, reprehensible that Henry can bring this mental force to the idea of being a shepherd and not to the business of being a king, and shortly, in the Scottish scene, he is going to stumble, too late, on the Yorkist secret of being a king in mind. Yet for all that, the strong world Howard creates *is* outside himself: though it is a fiction, it is not self-pitying. The son and the father, themselves speaking strongly over lamenting oboe-music, do speak, as they should, for England. At the end of the scene, the Prince, Margaret and Exeter run on as if from another play altogether. Howard makes Henry impossibly slow to move, even having difficulty in speaking Exeter's name, and rising with the crown in his hand, putting it swiftly on Margaret's head on his last lines, and then, actually ahead of them, calling both ironically, and as from a great mental distance, 'For-ward; a-way!'

The young York boys and Warwick make a meal out of taunting the dead Young Clifford, which they do with animal exuberance, Richard in particular showing a relaxed inventiveness, lightly lying against the body as if on a day-bed, but with an agile mind well ahead of anyone else. He makes his 'Let me be Duke of Clarence, George of Gloucester' line a sudden cheerful idea for a game. Everything Anton Lesser does as Richard, however, reverberates with something else, particularly hurt. Several times he is thrown across the stage before *Part Three* ends, playfully or in anger, and each time he lands awkwardly, frowning slightly at sudden pain, whether of body or of pride is not clear.

After the interval, there is a change of key. King Henry, older and quite alone, stops in his reading and walking to step elaborately over the 'brook' and stand on English soil, flashing a gleeful smile. A prisoner, and away in Scotland, his mind can see the political scene abroad with an extraordinary, visionary clarity, exactly imagining Margaret in France, now with a political sense of balance.

Balance is what the court now in London precisely lacks. Edward, like Henry, reneges on his bridal arrangement, on his own initiative this time, while his brothers edge and scheme and joke around him, until Richard is left alone, to prove in his soliloquy that he is a new voice in drama. Anton Lesser's teenage, crop-headed Richard, widely and justly praised, grins like a friendly demon-puppy, a Clockwork York. Hobbling with a great turn of speed and total courage in skirmishes, he is absolutely insane and, equally absolutely, fascinating, as Richard well knows. Critics for several decades have wondered where Richard gets his motivation from for his supposed sudden change in this act III soliloquy. Here there is no problem. He has been warped from the beginning. His brother's twisted court gives him power enough. (The scene opens with him swinging idly on the arm of the empty, tilted throne.) Edward, like his father, takes on the impossible. What if lying with the excessively proper, frosty Lady Grey means marrying her? What if a similar challenge similarly impeccably argued meant, for his father, seizing the throne? What if for Richard it means killing all his kin? He knows he can smile, and murder while he smiles. He is already far too clever to be caught on the wrong side.

The scene at the French court is refreshing: no 'crazy, miserly Lewis XI of France' here,[24] but a shrewd father-figure and his bony daughter, who with Margaret, Oxford, and later Warwick sit on a row of high-backed blue and black thrones right down front, in front of the top-lighting 'screen'. Margaret is convincing with her reference to 'Henry, sole possessor of my love'. She gets a big delighted laugh on her move across at III, iii, 199, saying, musically, 'Warwick!', like a society hostess, and playing the rest of the little speech of welcome to him with contented irony; she's not entirely convinced, but she is grateful.

The play resumes its English setting. Like a long game of chess, the permutations of position have to be worked out as the board steadily empties of pieces. After the French scene the play suddenly feels quite new again: gone are the crowds, even for the battles. Incessant self-justification is mouthed at the audience from side-changing or dying nobility. Warwick, in Lancastrian red, stands behind King Edward's throne and pushes him sprawling off. The royal coat of arms turns blood red, or deathly pale. Clarence is seduced back to Edward exactly as Joan took Burgundy, except that fewer people are present. The few glimpses of the King show him old and wise as prisoner, wearing a new weariness in understanding. When he is at liberty and King again in act IV, scenes vi and vii, he is a little dotty too, especially in joining together the Lords of Clarence and Warwick, the two turn-coats, like an uncle with naughty children as he makes them joint Protectors. He is suitably able to bless the child Richmond, of course.

The figures revolve in smaller and smaller circles, even the awkward bridge, which appears again for Coventry walls, giving no relief at all. Warwick dies grandly on the bare stage, the nearest to old-fashioned Shakespearian voicing that we have heard. Before Tewkesbury, Helen Mirren gives Margaret's long stirring speeches to her followers, not to an army but to two men and a boy while the spaces of the quite empty stage swim away into dusk. Terry Hands, I'm told, wanted the bleak ending to *Part Three* to look like the view through the wrong end of a telescope, and he succeeds. The great Battle of Tewkesbury is fought in weary slow-motion by six people. F. P. Wilson pointed out 'how few are the lay figures, and how sharply the chief characters are placed before us,[25] in *Part Three*. Even the chief characters are few and small in this high vacancy. What a helpful contrast this is to the Victorian performances of history plays with their hundreds of extras.

The last three scenes move forward, fast, into something new yet again. This play has unexpected powers of surprise, accelerating and making oblique its subject-matter. Helen Mirren's demands for death on the killing of Prince Edward, again quite without high baroque style, and all the more powerful for that, are almost dwarfed by the simple business of Richard's exit and his line 'The Tower! The Tower! I'll root them out.' She crouches, crawling like an animal, but pathetic. The wildest animal has left, sideways, down front. He leaves a sense of his absence behind him which is nearly visible. Edward's comment a little later is Absurdist: 'He's sudden, if a thing comes in his head.'

Under the eave of a big trap down front, Henry appears; old, crouched, reading, wearing only a dirty white robe, chained and gyved. Richard slowly pushes up another trap door in the steel grating, to join him, laughing. It is all brightly bottom-lit and side-lit. Alan Howard gives Henry an all-knowing courage and weird simplicity, not playing the saint at all, though he dies in a crucified position, blood streaming from his side. Richard's thirty-two-line soliloquy is made squatting beside the body; and as he brightly chatters about himself and develops his plans, his dagger strikes the steel bars between his legs, with a regular, punctuating ringing. He rolls sideways as the trap closes down on the falling Henry – and he is two paces from his infant nephew in the final court scene.

'Sound drums and trumpets!' calls King Edward at the end of the play. The familiar martial bray begins. Everyone reaches for his weapon, and turns to look up at the musicians. The cue is silently corrected to livelier music. In the half-light, the court begins clumsily to try to remember the steps of a dance. Richard watches from behind the throne.

In *Part One* that sequence of scenes which begins in ii, ii, uniquely played here in full, calls for special attention. Act ii scene ii is a curious, slack, short triple-decker, containing, apparently at random, Salisbury's funeral procession, gossip about 'the Dauphin and his trull', and the mysterious summons to meet the Countess of Auvergne. Terry Hands makes the scene drop steadily in pitch: Talbot stretches full-length on the ground to gossip, and receives the banter of Bedford and Burgundy with easy amusement. In scene iii, the Countess appears before the top-light screen. She is full of high dreams about her role, expressing a witchcraft derived entirely from fantasy, and making a clear point about the power of such folly to shape events which throws light into most corners of the three plays. Talbot scores a victory over bewitchment with warm humour and strong physical presence, teaching the lady a little elementary metaphysics, too. Physical pleasure takes over on the promise of wine and cates; Talbot's words 'nor other satisfaction do I crave' are played for erotic effect, against the lines. The earlier drop in pitch, an unwinding effect, has happened again. Talbot restores to earth the over-reaching fantasy. There are rich patterns of association here. Though the two scenes are little more than sketches, they contain not individual 'character-development', nor great poetic music, but human encounters in a quickly-placed context. The two 'downward' scenes, in parallel, relate not only structurally, together, and to many parts of the three plays, but also emblematically, thematically, psychologically – even physiologically, in a sense: Talbot returns things to a human frame.

There is immediate contrast in the two following scenes, which both end in death, and both wind feelings upwards. The Temple Garden scene, II, iv, is very well done. Two files of young men, echoing the quarrels of the first scene, march briskly in, in mid-point of a dispute, presently breaking off white or red roses from a harshly metallic bush. Itself metallic, controlled and clashing, the scene elevates the love-imagery of the Rose into high fantasy, with the power to 'drink blood', 'send a thousand souls to death and deadly night'. By contrast with the two scenes before, these encounters are inhuman, even anti-human – distances are kept and everyone is rigidly upright. It is all that the previous scenes were – symbolic, emblematic and so on – but this time meaning strife and death: Richard Plantagenet is the initiator of it. The next scene (v) has been so universally cut, or cut up, that it was a surprise to see it. The dying Edmund Mortimer tells why he has been, as the Countess wished at first to place Talbot, 'in loathsome sequestration'. He raises in Richard his already high pride. At the moment of death, Richard calls Mortimer's ambition 'mean' – that is, below him: and in the following scene his bustling envy and brutal politicking make the first success in his campaign to revenge his father. He is created Duke of York, on the heels of a brawl which removes power from the child King, demeans Parliament, ensures the ultimate violent deaths of everyone present, and acts out over England the quarrel begun near a rose-bush in the Temple Garden.

The four scenes are framed by the contrasting funeral exits of Salisbury and Mortimer: one recalls this in another play too, at another time, when York suddenly brings Mortimer to life again, in the murderous capering figure of Jack Cade. Such links multiply as one watches, given the chance to see what was written.

A sequence of a quite different kind was allowed to develop in *Part Two*, across the interval. Helen Mirren's Margaret, though involved with Suffolk, did not make him the centre of her existence; she was therefore more interesting. Her one attempt at political machination, in agreeing to the fall of Duke Humphrey, is controlled for his own ends by Suffolk (see I, iii, 87–100). Her condoning Humphrey's murder is a terrible mistake, as her reaction to the King's swoon shows. This adds new significance to her powerful long speeches in III, ii about her voyage to England. Her lines have been taken as a Lady-Macbeth-like attempt to distract the King from Suffolk. Helen Mirren, completely shut out by Henry's shock as he sits paralysed, makes them come from a longing for the restoration in him of the power of attention as she crouches and moves around Henry. Her famous parting scene with Suffolk is subtly changed in tone, now suggestive of two people whose hearts are not *quite* in what they do, and who very slightly over-play. Margaret fell for the dashing Suffolk – as what young girl wouldn't? – but he is devious and a schemer. This couple both know how to end an affair, he by hyperbole, she by brave dismissal – 'Go; speak not to

me; even now be gone./O! go not yet . . . (III, ii, 351–2). But she is not totally
consumed even by having his head in her lap, and when Vaux comes past
with news that Winchester is dying, she is alert and interested, and thinks of
the King (twice), and has to call her mind back to the courtier at her knees.

She did not know, of course, that ending the affair meant Suffolk's death
at the hands of lawless men. Nor did King Henry know at his 'forbear to
judge' cry that York's reaching arm would set other lawless men murdering
their way from Kent to the palace. When they next meet in IV, iv, Henry and
Margaret are both grieving. She holds Suffolk's head to her breast in its
cloth: he fears his people's deaths and sends Lord Say, as he suspects, to his
assassination. Henry is gentle with Margaret, and she with him. She is
saying, in effect, 'bear with me, I'll get over it', in an almost Chekhovian
way. The first of two moving moments, raising both of them to higher
stature, now occurs.

> *King.* How, madam! Still lamenting Suffolk's death?
> I fear me, love, if that I had been dead,
> Thou wouldest not have mourn'd so much for me.
>
> (IV, iv, 21–3)

Alan Howard says it gently. Helen Mirren's reply startles him, in her
sudden strong truth of feeling as she quietly replies,

> *Queen.* My love; I should not mourn, but die for thee.

We hear no more of Suffolk. Four terrible Cade scenes follow, ending with
the collapse of the rebellion. In IV, ix Margaret enters again, silent, but
attentive to the King. He dismisses the rebels, and receives at once the news
of York's arrival with a large army. He makes quick and accurate decisions,
and issues commands, even managing an ironic touch in reference to York
(lines 43–4). He sits alone on the only property, Cade's mossy London
stone. Margaret comes across and perches there with him. They share their
bewilderment and momentary despair in silence. The King rouses himself
and says, again quietly, 'Come, wife, let's in, and learn to govern better . . .'
Helen Mirren turns to him, her arm around him for a moment, her face to
his. Then they leave in silent, mutual comfort.

Though things have much advanced, this sets the same tone on what
went before and what now follows as did the scene of the Countess and
Talbot. In human encounter, these two, King and Queen, touch a norm.
Against that, York, as he did before, seems mad. As before, the grounding
touch is followed by the death of the deluded Mortimer (Cade) and the
vicious strident quarrelling of York, white rose against red, with Somerset
again the key figure. This time it will end in real fighting.

My third special scene is that of the death of York, early in *Part Three*. On
a totally bare black stage Emrys James staggers in, and spits his soliloquy
until a quartet of figures, Margaret, Clifford, Northumberland and Prince

Edward, stand coolly around him, at a distance. The sensation throughout the long and painful episode that follows is of bodies coming closer to the ground together, and falling, until the final killing is like a nest of vipers. Margaret's insults to York and his boys are physical, not political: they come from close in. Much of this scene at Seale's 1958 Old Vic production had York trapped in his own castle behind a portcullis: there is great gain now from bare boards and a passion.

For long stretches of this scene Emrys James kneels in feebleness and shock, calling out pity and terror, with Rutland's blood smearing his face and closing one eye, the hastily-torn paper tied with Margaret's black ribbon to make a lopsided crown and he himself silent but collapsing from within like a slowly-dying leviathan. His 'she-wolf of France' speech starts quietly. York's wildness has brought him to this: it is impossible for him to accept it, and he spits his venom on Margaret in the artificial rhetoric of his formally constructed invective. It is his last weapon, and he intends all that he says to hurt.

But his projected foul feeling comes back in to him as he weeps, and his long series of sobs, with his attempts to wipe the napkin clear of Rutland's blood, with his tears, are as disturbing a thing as one can see. When, at line 164, he says 'There, take the crown', he grabs Margaret's reaching hand and pulls her down, so that, horrified, she is caught, her legs apart, half under him as he falls forward. Crouching Clifford leans across from the far side to stab him. Margaret plunges her sword into York's side even while he is almost lying in her lap, and holds the moment after very still. It is her first, and only, killing. Northumberland crouches alongside. The group is tightly connected, on the ground. There is nothing else but space, except that a hooded figure, far off, has watched it all, and will report to Edward and Richard.

A performance of this kind, which allows a very small group of actors working together on a big bare stage to develop suppleness of suggestion, constantly widening the aperture, as it were, of the lens through which we see the events, shows that the pain of this play is not the similarity of events, as Dr Johnson seemed to imply, but the awful possibility of too many differences. Anyone can now do anything to anyone, it seems. The spectator is made to concentrate on a physical landscape with fewer and fewer figures, who go wearily through fewer and fewer possibilities: but the mental landscape is without any boundaries at all, and this enervated world is violent in its fantasies.

Having watched these three plays several times, I am not aware of the 'Tudor myth' at all, nor of any Providential process, come to that. Playing the text as it is, as Hands and his company have done, produces Shakespearian richness everywhere. The plays move in and out of different planes of experience. They flow continually across all kinds of style and event. The trilogy is tragic, but not in the Eastern-bloc political way Jan Kott meant. The tragedy is that at every level humanity is betrayed. The power of the barons, the politics of the committee-room, the ambivalence of love, or the unforeseeable mix of the crowd do not relate even to a certain period of history: the centre is not the 'aspiring and relentless' Margaret, as Court-hope called her, nor a saintly king, nor even the obsessed Machiavellian, persuasive York and his would-be Tamburlaine, Cade.

What we see is neither the nineteenth-century notion of 'character' nor the twentieth-century insistence on themes. The Shakespearian elements that are familiar to us are all there, but in disconcertingly unfamiliar proportions. Shakespeare appears to have used his material, about equal and warring forces, to work ideas of the conflicts of a group rather than single personalities, conflicts not even so much of the state as of the family; and to move with a swift and splendid pace. What we find in performances like these is a surprising lightness of touch in the writing: the verse, so long condemned, seems to ask to be spoken; the events want to be understood by the instincts rather than the mind.

The centre of the trilogy is a human group, warm or crafty, full of love or pride, eaten by ambition or destruction, swayed by fantasy or insight. This is like the Shakespeare we have always known. His full presence in these plays – so very powerfully original, here at the start of his writing life – has been denied us until now.

NOTES

1. Robert Ornstein, *A Kingdom for a Stage*, (Cambridge, Mass: Harvard University Press, 1972) especially chapter 1.
2. W. J. Courthope, *A History of English Poetry*, 6 vols (London: Macmillan, 1895–1910), IV, appendix, especially p. 463. It is to be noted that earlier critics in Germany, and Charles Knight in his edition of Shakespeare in 1842, ascribed the three plays to Shakespeare.
3. J. P. Brockbank, 'The Frame of Disorder – *Henry VI*', *Early Shakespeare* (Stratford-upon-Avon Studies 3, ed J. R. Brown and B. Harris; London: Edward Arnold, 1961); M. M. Reese, *The Cease of Majesty*, (London: Edward Arnold, 1961); A. P. Rossiter, 'Ambivalence: the Dialectic of the Histories', *Angel with Horns* (London: Longmans, 1961).
4. Geoffrey Bullough, *Narrative and Dramatic Sources of Shakespeare*, 8 vols (London: Routledge & Kegan Paul, 1964–75), III, 1–217.
5. British theatre critics record many different, often opposing, explanations of what the plays in these performances are 'about', which is a good sign.
6. Tate creates a good king with a loving wife: his wholesale rewriting is aimed to place Richard 'in the Love and Compassion of the Audience', his 'Conduct . . . sufficiently excus'd by the Malignancy of his Fortune.' *Shakespeare: the Critical Heritage*, ed. Brian Vickers, (London: Routledge & Kegan Paul, 1974), I, 324.

Cibber's mangled version was acted until far into the twentieth century, 'some of its melodramatic lines being retained in Laurence Olivier's film of 1956'. Michael Jamieson, 'Shakespeare in the Theatre', *Shakespeare: Select Bibliographical Guides*, (Oxford University Press, 1973), p. 36.

7. A. C. Sprague, *Shakespeare's Histories: Plays for the Stage*, (London: Society for Theatre Research, 1964), gives a convenient brief summary; somewhat amplified in the Stage History sections of Dover Wilson's New Cambridge editions of *Part One* and *Part Three*, (Cambridge University Press, 1952).

8. Sprague, *Shakespeare's Histories*, 112.

9. J. C. Trewin, *The Birmingham Repertory Theatre, 1913–1963*, (Barrie & Rockliff, 1963), 149.

10. *Ibid.*, p. 143.

11. Sally Beauman, 'Past Productions' in *Royal Shakespeare Theatre: Henry 6* (Souvenir programme, Stratford-upon-Avon, 1977). Incidentally, this booklet is one of the most stimulating and intelligent companions to the plays that I have come across.

12. Mary Clarke, *Shakespeare at the Old Vic* (London: The Old Vic Trust & Hamish Hamilton, 1958; pages not numbered).

13. John Barton, in collaboration with Peter Hall, *The Wars of the Roses*, (London: BBC Publications, 1970), pp. xvi, xxv.

14. There is an ironic footnote in Barton's book. 'Evidence of the risks a large popular theatre takes if it tries to present the *Henry VI*'s is provided by the experience of the Shakespeare Festival Theatre at Stratford, Ontario. It planned to present the cycle of the three parts of *Henry VI* and *Richard III* in its 1966/67 season, condensing the plays in the same way as the Royal Shakespeare Company, and using the RSC's version. In 1966 it played our *Henry VI*, but had to abandon the project of giving *Edward IV* in 1967, as public response was disappointing.' (Barton, *The Wars of the Roses*, p. xvi). Stratford Ontario might possibly have scored a notable 'first', and made money too, had they gone for Shakespeare's three plays.

15. *The Times* in 1906 noted that Benson played Talbot as 'a rugged dog of war, bent in the shoulders, and all but shuffling in his walk, lean, grim and graceless'.

16. All references are to the Arden editions.

17. The green carpet is also, of course, by an old tradition dating from Shakespeare's time the stage-setting for tragedy. *The Dublin Theatrical Observer* for 6 March 1821 observed of the opening of *Love in a Village* at the new Theatre Royal, 'Upon entering the Theatre, we were somewhat surprised at seeing the stage covered with a green cloth, and naturally imagined that the performance had from some unforeseen cause been changed to a tragedy . . .'

18. Sprague, *Shakespeare's Histories*, p. 116.

19. Clarke, *Shakespeare at the Old Vic*.

20. See for example A. S. Cairncross's footnote at III, iii, 33, in his Arden edition.

21. Mary Clarke reports on the 1958 Old Vic production that the Cade scenes got all out of hand, with everyone working up his comic bit-part for all it was worth. 'Cade himself was obliterated in the hurly-burly and it is doubtful if anyone in the audience had any idea of what was going on.'

22. Dan Meaden gets what we might call the Jeffery Dench Award for the Most

Frequent Appearances, as in the trilogy he appears as Falstaff, Woodville, Sheriff, Mayor, Whitmore, Iden, and Hastings.

23. See A. S. Cairncross's footnote at v, i, 118, in his Arden edition.
24. Clarke, *Shakespeare at the Old Vic.*
25. F. P. Wilson, *Shakespearian and other studies*, (Oxford University Press, 1969), p. 17.

I want to record here my warmest thanks to Alan Howard, Helen Mirren and Ian Judge of the Royal Shakespeare Company, and to Richard Proudfoot of King's College London, each of whom gave time generously to talk with me at length about these plays. The opinions I have expressed above are, of course, my own.

English Drama, edited by Marie Axton and Raymond Williams
and Judith Weil's *Christopher Marlowe*
reviewed by NIGEL ALEXANDER

The bibliography of the books and essays of Muriel C. Bradbrook, which concludes the handsome volume of essays in her honour,[1] is itself an interesting record of the history and progress of English scholarship during the past forty years. The interest in *Elizabethan Stage Conditions*, an essay which won the Harness Prize in 1931, proved to be the foundation for a lifetime's investigation into the themes, conventions, and conditions of the Elizabethan and Jacobean theatre. *Themes and Conventions of Elizabethan Tragedy* (1935) was followed the next year by *The School of Night*. If we no longer believe everything that we read in these books it is in many cases because the author herself has advanced beyond them. They still, however, pose a number of fundamental questions which it has been the business of scholarship and criticism to investigate. The core of Professor Bradbrook's own work has been the double study *Shakespeare and Elizabethan Poetry* (1951) and *The Rise of the Common Player* (1962). These are an examination of Shakespeare's relation to the literary tradition and the theatrical conditions of his time. It is in this field that the most spectacular advances of scholarship have been made. Anyone turning to an examination of these problems now has a whole range of information at his command which was certainly not available in 1931. Vital works of reference such as G. E. Bentley's *Jacobean and Caroline Stage*, Glynne Wickham's *Early English Stages* or Geoffrey Bullough's *Narrative and Dramatic Sources of Shakespeare* have appeared or are nearly complete. All of the known documents relating to Shakespeare's life have been reproduced in photo-facsimile in Samuel Schoenbaum's *William Shakespeare: A Documentary Life*. Even more essential documents have been put within the reach of the student by the publication of R. A. Foakes's admirable facsimile of *The Henslowe Papers*. We are indebted to the work of such historians of the theatre as Nagler, Southern, Hosley and Hodges for a much more accurate understanding of the playhouses themselves while a book like Sydney Anglo's *Spectacle, Pageantry and Early Tudor Policy* provides an excellent link between what the art historians have taught us about the nature of Renaissance myth and emblem and the political and practical realities of court performances or

popular shows. Work of a more controversial but equally important kind
has been done by Frances Yates in drawing our attention to the nice
speculations of philosophers interested in hermeticism, alchemy and magic
or to that remarkable phenomenon which she called the Rosicrucian
Enlightenment.

The advancement of criticism has always depended upon the most exact
scholarship coupled with the ability to speculate and form new hypotheses
to explain or re-interpret familiar phenomena. Professor Bradbrook has
contributed her share to both activities and it is pleasant to find listed here
those articles which will long continue to be placed in the hands of generations of students: 'No room at the top: Spenser's pursuit of Fame'
Elizabethan Poetry (1960), 'Marlowe's Dr Faustus and the Eldritch tradition'
Essays on Shakespeare and Elizabethan Drama in honour of Hardin Craig (1962),
'Shakespeare's Primitive Art' *Proceedings of the British Academy* LI (1965) and
'*The Comedy of Timon*: a reveling play of the Inner Temple' *Renaissance Drama*
IX (1966).

It is this tradition that Marie Axton and Raymond Williams have set out
to continue and develop in the volume of essays that they have collected in
Muriel Bradbrook's honour. As Raymond Williams writes in his introduction: 'The problems of English dramatic forms and their development
are of outstanding importance both in the history of all English writing and
in the history of world writing.' It is also vital that: 'its emphasis is
historical, both in the simple sense that its chapters range from mediaeval
drama down to our own, and in the more specific sense that the problems of
form, however strictly and locally defined, are normally considered in
relation to specific historical circumstances, whether social, dramatic or
theatrical'. The book is therefore an extremely ambitious one in that it sets
out to be a 'conscious pointer' towards the necessarily collaborative work
that will have to be done for the making of a history of the development of
English dramatic form. It is, however, exactly a measure of the work that
has been done during the past forty years that such a project now seems a
possibility instead of a desirable improbability. It is certainly a remarkable
fact that there is, at the moment, no history of the development of English
drama that can be put with any confidence in the hands of a student. The
volumes of the Oxford History of English Literature which were to have
undertaken the task have been plagued by delay and the first part that has
appeared seems distinctly lacking in many of the elements which Raymond
Williams feels necessary for such a history. The second part, which has been
undertaken by Samuel Schoenbaum, may well reform these matters
altogether. *The Revels History of Drama in English* which was clearly designed
to provide some answer to the kind of comprehensive history required
has clearly suffered from lack of the general editorial direction which was
once such an outstanding feature of the *Revels* series and, despite some excel-

lent sections, the unevenness of the contributions can only leave the reader perplexed and lacking the guidance which he deserves from such a history. It is evident that collaboration of this kind is not the answer and in many ways the most satisfactory of histories, at least of the Elizabethan drama, is the volume by Christopher Ricks in the Sphere *History of English Literature*.

The quality of this particular endeavour is demonstrated early on in Richard Axton's 'Folk play in Tudor Interludes'. The inclusion of 'folk' in any academic title usually induces an immense depression in the reader since it is normally an excuse for every kind of inaccuracy and the wildest speculation. Yet the existence of folk drama has to be accounted for and interpreted if any history of the drama is even to be attempted. Axton's first two pages inspire confidence by providing an exact critique of this problem and a just and generous assessment of the work of his predecessors in the field. His thesis that 'In the best interludes folk play was sub-text rather than text' is evidently by its nature difficult to prove but in concentrating upon the contemporary significance of the interludes rather than vague ideas of 'pagan survival' Axton is able to show how the deeply ambivalent attitude of the folk play towards 'normal' order provoked an equally ambivalent response from the authorities to such plays which eventually resulted in their suppression.

Not, of course, that this suppression could eliminate the ambivalent attitude towards authority. It interestingly enough makes its re-appearance in the English history play which is here studied in an admirable article by Anne Barton and which has also been the subject of considerable attention in Emrys Jones's *The Origins of Shakespeare*.[2] It is a good example of the necessary collaborative endeavour of scholarship that this book, one of the best recently published on Shakespeare, and Anne Barton's 'He that plays the king' should be complementary in material and in attitude. It is also the virtue of this book that a discussion of the Tudor Interlude should also immediately open questions about the later drama. The strength of these articles lies in the relationships which the reader is forced to perceive as he progresses through the book – relationships which are the more convincing as they come from the reader's attention to specific historical circumstances rather than general editorial directives about 'influences'.

The centre of Axton's argument about the nature of 'folk' elements is the study of *Calisto and Melebea* (printed by John Rastell c. 1529) which was based upon the notorious Spanish novel *La Celestina*. This, 'the work of a sceptical Jew and cramful of vicious life', could, in the right kind of dramatic version, have transformed the English theatre years before Kyd, Marlowe and Shakespeare finally restored tragedy to the stage. It was, however, within the pious discipline of the Thomas More circle that the English adaptation was made and

> The English interlude is not a translation but a free adaptation, using only
> four acts-worth of the story, enough, that is, for about an hour-and-a-half, 'in
> maner of an enterlude'. From the turbulence of the novel the English poet
> selected only what was susceptible to his received notions of dramatic form
> and subject. The result is a comic-satiric wooing play which has some
> interesting affinities with the Middle English *Interludium* and *Dame Sirith* and
> which is also a temptation-and-fall morality. His story ends at the point where
> Melebea gives her girdle to Celestina to take to Calisto, and his play con-
> cludes with a scene (not in the Spanish) of Melebea's contrition for a sin not
> carnally committed and with her father's forgiveness. The English omits
> altogether the tragedy and the violence: Celestina stabbed in a quarrel with
> Calisto's servants, Calisto's brains dashed out falling from a ladder,
> Melebea's eloquent leap from the tower of her father's house. Whether or not
> the audience is expected to supply the sequel is an intriguing question.
>
> (p. 14)

Confronted with Spanish riches which he was unable to handle the English
dramatist reverts to the elements which he can turn into a folk wooing play.
Yet he has already imported into the English drama the elements from
Spain that will eventually transform the tradition and eventually bring
about a revolution on the English stage that will cause Ben Jonson, who
idolised the classics and revered his friend this side of idolatry, to call forth
Aeschylus, Sophocles and Euripides as the only possible comparison for the
tragedy of Shakespeare. It is an exact demonstration of how a particular
play looks both before and after. It contains elements which clearly go back
to a time of 'folk' drama where the history is obscure and the evidence
scanty and it looks forward to the more sophisticated drama of a later time.
It is precisely this combination of 'folk' and 'romance' with Renaissance
sophistication that Emrys Jones has argued is the most powerful element in
Shakespeare's own plays. It is evident that what Richard Axton has
touched on in his article is of major importance for the history of English
drama. The expansion of these suggestions will be awaited with interest.

No less interesting or important is Marie Axton's discussion of 'The
Tudor Mask and Elizabethan court drama'. She demonstrates most convincingly that the Tudor mask cannot be encompassed by the definitions
proposed by Stephen Orgel for the Jacobean. This would, of course, fit
exactly with Professor Wickham's thesis that *The Masque of Blackness* represents an entirely different stage tradition and, despite Jonson's use of
neo-platonic imagery, is a move away from the emblematic drama
presented in such structures as the Globe towards a theatre which was
attempting realistic or naturalistic settings. It is again instructive that
Professor Williams's own article in this book should be an examination of
the long English resistance to the kind of naturalistic theatre which the
stage conditions of a proscenium arch seem to require.

The mask conventions of the Tudors were, it is argued, methods of portraying a divided self. Henry VIII, who paid for his own masks, was thus able to represent, not idealisations of the prince, but different aspects of the man. Elizabeth, who did not spend much on her own court entertainments but had, in general, her masks presented to her by her nobles and lawyers of the Inns of Court, had different aspects of her personality and state emphasised for her in the entertainments at Kenilworth or *The Lady of May* before she herself imposed her own pattern on her subjects and they acquiesced in the cult of Cynthia. The influence on literature is obviously immense since the same kind of presentation of competing aspects of the personality, including destructive ones, are dramatised by Spenser in *Belphoebe* or by Lyly in *Endimion.* The history of the mask in these reigns is therefore, according to Marie Axton, a dramatisation by Henry himself of the conflicting elements of his own nature and the political events which encompassed the King's service to Queen Katherine, the proposed marriage of his sister Mary to Charles of Castile, her actual marriage to Louis of France, and her sudden and secret marriage, after Louis's death, to the King's friend and companion in his jousts and revels, Henry Brandon, Duke of Suffolk. Possibly even more important is the conflict between Henry's public loyalty to Katherine and his irrepressible wish for a male heir which was embodied in the first mask danced by Anne Boleyn at court in 1522. It is here argued that, although the figure of Ardent Desire dressed in flame coloured taffeta accurately reflected the King's wishes, Henry was himself circumspect enough to be one of the lords dressed in blue and gold who beseiged the court ladies and finally obtained their consent to dance.

In Elizabeth's reign

> A struggle for maistry between the queen and her male subjects in Parliament and the Privy Council is reflected in several of the entertainments offered to Elizabeth in the first decade of her reign. Gray's Inn staged an entertainment in 1565; before the dancing began Juno triumphed over Diana in debate. The queen turned to the Spanish Ambassador and remarked, 'This is all against me.' Elizabeth was a guest at a marriage in 1566; in the mask penned by a gentleman of Lincoln's Inn, Diana was described as a hearty red-faced athlete, and the golden apple of Beauty was bestowed, not on the queen, but on the bride, who had fulfilled her proper destiny of marriage. This harsh critical version of the judgement of Paris stands in stark contrast both to the pageant offered to the queen's mother, Anne, on the day of her coronation in 1533 and to Peele's later graceful tribute to the aging Elizabeth in the *Araygnement of Paris.*   (p. 34)

It is evident, therefore, that it can reasonably be established that 'The cult of Cynthia or Diana was not imposed; it was a hard won personal triumph, not firmly established until the 1580s.' This view deserves to be considered along with the account by Frances Yates of the Accession Day tilts in *Astraea.* The iconography of the Tudor court is at last beginning to be interpreted and understood.

With two such important and interesting articles it is plain that the book deserves its place in every scholar's library. The reader will be rewarded with other excellent articles but it is the nature of so ambitious an endeavour that there should be problems. One of these is the subject of alchemy which is not, as yet, sufficiently studied nor its influence in the period properly appreciated. In 'Comic form in Ben Jonson' Leo Salingar argues that the dominant metaphor in both *The Alchemist* and *Volpone* is the idea of alchemy. It is argued that this gives Jonson 'the release he apparently needed for both sides of his personality at once, the rational and the fantastic'. Salingar argues that:

> Treated as a 'unifying symbol', alchemy fitted in with Jonson's admiration for the classical satirists and for the humanism of More and Erasmus; at the same time, it enabled him to carry further his ambition to adapt some of the basic forms of Old Comedy to the Elizabethan stage. He made of it the image of a latter-day world-upside-down, a counter-Utopia. (p. 52)

This seems to me to be unquestionably a valuable insight and an impressive extension of Salingar's own recent and valuable book on comedy. In this particular article, however, it cannot be said that this important case has been demonstrated or proved. We are given interesting parallels with Aristophanes but when it comes to the crucial matter – Volpone's invocation 'O, thou son of SOL' – where it is evident that the language of alchemy is being used there is no real follow-up. The case, once stated, is more or less assumed without any production of the evidence or the vital comparison that is surely necessary between the alchemical terms used in both plays. Nor is there any consideration, as there surely should be, of the relationship between the language of alchemy in these plays and the neoplatonic, number symbolic and alchemical masks. The original pioneering work done by D. J. Gordon in his fascinating articles in the *Journal of the Warburg and Courtauld Institutes* (volumes VI, VII and XII) should surely be carried on and one can only regret that here an opportunity has been missed for doing so. The contrast between the alchemy of the plays and the alchemical transformations of the masks again presents a revealing insight into the two sides of Jonson's own nature distinguished by Mr Salingar. One has the impression of a distinguished scholar here keeping to a deadline rather than writing at his best. It is to be hoped that he will return to the subject at a later date.

The Tempest was performed the year after *The Alchemist* but that seems to have had no effect whatsoever on John Northam's reading of the play in his comparison of *The Tempest*, *Waiting for Godot* and *Rosmersholm* in 'Waiting for Prospero'. The importance of the relationship between *The Alchemist* and *The Tempest* has already been pointed out by Frances Yates. Unfortunately she has done so in a book (*Shakespeare's Last Plays: A New Approach*) which is certainly not amongst her best books and indeed, in some ways, obscures the implications of her work on Giordano Bruno and on the Rosicrucian Enlightenment. Northam sees that 'The skeleton of *The Tempest* is the triad, Prospero, Ariel, Caliban' but he does not continue to observe that the whole play appears to work in triads and that this is only one among many groupings such as Prospero, Ferdinand, Miranda; Stephano, Trinculo, Caliban; Alonzo, Antonio, Sebastian; nor that Caliban is distinctly referred to as 'earth' while Ariel appears as fire, air and, perhaps most dramatically, as water in the remarkable stage direction '*Enter Ariel disguised as a water nymph*' which appears to serve no other dramatic function except to bring on water in its proper order before earth. Prospero's project clearly moves from the second hour, the number of chaos, to its triumphant conclusion at the sixth, the hour of the completion of creation. As Caliban proclaims his freedom Prospero's 'new man', Ferdinand, enters bearing the logs which will fuel the fire of the project – a project which surely includes the philosopher's stone since at least Michael Maier thought that coral was the 'stone'. Mr Northam could hardly be expected to be aware of all of these points since they are currently buried in an unpublished but important thesis but he might have seen, since he singles it out specially, that the mask celebrates precisely the kind of 'Chemical Wedding' described by Johann Valentin Andreae. It is surely of significance for his thesis since it seems apparent that Beckett at least had grasped the point and that although the philosopher's stone is certainly not discovered in *Waiting for Godot* a transformation is worked, as it is in *The Tempest*, upon the audience.

New directions are certainly pointed out in Richard Luckett's essay on English dramatic operas and Howard Erskine Hill's account of Gay's drama. A history of the development of English dramatic form must surely include an account of the development of English music, its relation with the drama and the kind of English opera that was produced as a result of the nature of the court mask, whether Tudor or Jacobean. The supercession of this form by Italian opera had what are arguably disastrous consequences for English song and English music. This is a field which requires unusual competence on the part of a critic and it is a regrettable fact of the economics of publishing that musical examples, which are after all essential to an understanding of the matter, should be so prohibitively expensive that they are virtually impossible to include.

The book does, I believe, fulfil its ambition. It does point the way towards the kind of history of English dramatic forms that is desperately needed. It is perhaps still astonishing that at this time it can only point the way. It shows very clearly the kind of area in which work must be done but it is hard to see how, in present conditions, that work is going to be done. One of the significant omissions from the book is George Chapman – he occurs only as the title of a British Council pamphlet on which Muriel Bradbrook is currently engaged. At a time when the university presses of Oxford and Cambridge are again venturing on highly expensive and competing editions of Shakespeare is it not reasonable to ask where is the standard modern edition of Chapman, of Middleton, of Ford? That the task is not impossible has surely been shown by the edition of Massinger recently edited by Professor Philip Edwards. It is time, surely, to reverse the damage done by the triumph of the bibliography of Bowers which gave us a number of unusable editions of very dubious value and to concentrate upon establishing the literary and social connections of these works. The book demonstrates how much fundamental, elementary and essential work remains to be done. If the glory of present-day English scholarship is some of the major works referred to at the beginning of this review then its shame is not merely what Housman called the 'sloth and distaste for thinking which are the common inheritance of humanity' but also his more serious charge, 'sheer ignorance of facts'. It is to the credit of the editors and authors of this book that they have done a little to illuminate our darkness.

It is axiomatic that a history of English dramatic form should include an account of the way in which an individual dramatist develops his own manner of organising perception for his audience – an organisation which must encompass what is now called both 'construction' and 'style'. It is precisely this organisation of perception which is the subject of Judith Weil's intensely interesting, intelligent and most perceptive book.[3] It is still true, however, that the present lack of any adequate vocabulary to describe the structuring of perception for the stage (and the clumsiness of that phrase bears adequate testimony to the difficulties involved) involves her in laying much more weight on phrases such as 'style' or 'ironic style' than they will really bear. Her basic thesis, however, can be, and has been, much more simply stated

> Few playwrights have been as willing as Marlowe was to obscure disaster in the offing, to postpone the resolution of ambiguities. Few have disguised self-deception so well or exposed it so belatedly. We might expect that Marlowe would have been anxious to guide the judgement of his audience. We probably do *not* expect that he would have sought to suspend our judgements and let them go straying through the dark.   (pp. 7–8)

Anton Chekhov continually pointed out to his editor, whom he was vainly trying to educate in the nature of literature, that a dramatic author could not afford to be the judge of his characters – it was up to the audience or a jury to judge them. Successful plays which are still played three or four hundred years after they were first written usually contain material which allows for all kinds of different judgements on the part of the spectators. It is moralistic literary criticism – from the first and in some ways the worst of literary critics, Aristotle, on – that has insisted on a 'solution' to problems

which are permanent, intractable and generally insoluble except in terms of
an individual compromise with the harsh facts.

We need not, therefore, identify Marlowe either with Faustus or Barabas
since when 'they celebrate their wisdom they are actually praising their
folly'. Judith Weil is, in fact, locating Marlowe as part of that long tradition
of the praise of folly which evidently includes Erasmus and More and also,
according to Richard Cody in his difficult but essential *Landscape of the Mind*,
is the central driving force of Shakespeare's comedies. The thesis is sustained by an interpretation of some of the best lines Marlowe ever wrote

> O, thou art fairer than the evening's air,
> Clad in the beauty of a thousand stars.

Marlowe, it is pointed out, was alluding to the encomium on divine wisdom
in *Wisdom* 7

> For she is the brightness of the euerlasting light, the vndefiled mirroure of the
> maiestie of God and the image of his goodnes. For she is more beautiful than
> the sunne, and is aboue all the order of the starres, and the light is not to be
> compared vnto her.
>
> For night cometh upon it, but wickednes cannot ouercome wisdome.

This is the most impressive support for the argument which occurs earlier in
the book that

> Through the allusions which occur in all of his plays, Marlowe reveals an
> abiding preoccupation with wisdom. We can discern, behind his mistaken
> praisers of wisdom, the shadow of that lady who praised herself in the books of
> Proverbs and Wisdom as the bride of God and the mother of all creation. The
> Church Fathers chose to replace this mediating Wisdom figure with the
> second person of the Trinity, Christ. Nevertheless, she preserved a feminine
> identity congenial to Erasmus and to such Christian poets as Dante, Spenser,
> and Donne.   (p. 10)

What we are now being offered is a poet and playwright who is much more
self aware and self mocking than in any previous account. It is the test of
criticism that it should explain clearly to us what we have known all along.
By that test it is evident that the book is a triumphal success. It has long
been evident that the 'historical' version of Christopher Marlowe as found
in the Baines document or other evidence – including the evidence of his
murder at Deptford – is part of a contemporary distortion and caricature.
This caricature, Judith Weil suggests, was one which Marlowe himself
invited and even enjoyed. The central concern of the plays is a wisdom
beyond that kind of distortion and caricature. This wisdom may be associated with the divine wisdom of the Bible but it is also used by Marlowe to
appeal, across the gulf of time and circumstance, to audiences undreamed
of. What we are at last given in this book is a dramatist capable of
constructing a *Tamburlaine* which can hold an audience fixed at the

National Theatre in the brilliant production of 1977. The brilliance of the production lay in recognising the brilliance of the dramatist and in following and supporting the structure that he had designed to support his actors.

The importance of this book lies in the fact that its central thesis will survive disagreement. It is not essential to accept Mrs Weil's own final estimate of characters like Edward II, Barabas, or Faustus in order to agree with her that the turning point of these plays is indeed about the nature of 'true wisdom'. Where exactly that is to be found, and how it is to be expressed remains, as always, a matter for the audience which – as Mrs Weil has already pointed out – Marlowe was quite content to leave in a state of suspended judgement. What we are offered is a playwright who was interested in divine wisdom and created characters who, as praisers of their own folly, are inevitably doomed to destruction.

The difficulty is that the folly that they praise may also turn out to be wisdom. The shadowy figure whom Mrs Weil locates behind the plays is, we must agree, certainly there but her nature is perhaps less certain than is dreamt of in the philosophy of the book of Wisdom. The tragic flaw is, therefore, that Mrs Weil herself appears to believe in a version of the literary tragic flaw which, concocted from the interpretation or misinterpretation of Aristotle, is the one critical doctrine which is sure to be the death of tragedy. The paradox of the book is that Mrs Weil appears to wish to get rid of that most persuasive of literary critics, Lewis Carroll's Duchess whose refrain of 'and the moral of that is' has been effectively echoed throughout the history of criticism, and yet continues to act like her. The trouble is that to the critic the moral appears fixed. It is the perception of the dramatist that, for his audience, the moral may move. It is that perception which continues to make the immoral morals of Christopher Marlowe most moving, in every sense of that term, from his time until our own. It does seem fair to say that we are not yet out of hell and it is questionable if we should believe in the experimental nature of the religions and moralities which claim to be able to release us. Christopher Marlowe seems an admirable recorder of that hell known as human existence.

NOTES

1. *English Drama: Forms and Development. Essays in Honour of Muriel Clara Bradbrook* ed. Marie Axton and Raymond Williams (Cambridge University Press, 1977).
2. Oxford University Press, 1977.
3. *Christopher Marlowe: Merlin's Prophet* by Judith Weil (Cambridge University Press, 1977).

List of books and articles referred to

Sydney Anglo, *Spectacle, Pageantry and Early Tudor Policy* (Oxford: Clarendon Press, 1969)

G. E. Bentley, *The Jacobean and Caroline Stage*, 5 vols. (Oxford: Clarendon Press, 1941–56)

M. C. Bradbrook, *Shakespeare and Elizabethan Poetry* (London: Chatto & Windus, 1951)

The Rise of the Common Player (London: Chatto & Windus, 1962)

Geoffrey Bullough, *Narrative and Dramatic Sources of Shakespeare*, 8 vols. (London: Routledge & Kegan Paul, 1957–75)

R. J. Cody, *The Landscape of the Mind: Pastoralism and Platonic Theory in Tasso's 'Aminta' and Shakespeare's Early Comedies* (Oxford: Clarendon Press, 1969)

R. A. Foakes and R. T. Rickert (eds.), *Henslowe's Diary* (Cambridge University Press, 1961)

R. A. Foakes (ed.), *The Henslowe Papers*, 2 vols. (London: The Scolar Press, 1977)

C. Walter Hodges, *The Globe Restored* (London: Ernest Benn, 1973)

Richard Hosley, 'Shakespeare's Use of the Gallery over the Stage', *Shakespeare Survey 10* (1957)

'The Discovery-space in Shakespeare's Globe', *Shakespeare Survey 12* (1959)

'Was there a Music-room in Shakespeare's Globe?', *Shakespeare Survey 13* (1960)

'The Gallery over the Stage in the Public Playhouse of Shakespeare's Time', *Shakespeare Quarterly*, 14 (1963)

'The Origins of the Shakespearian Playhouse', *Shakespeare Quarterly*, 15 (1964)

A. M. Nagler, *Shakespeare's Stage* trans. Ralph Manheim (New Haven: Yale University Press, 1958)

S. Schoenbaum, *William Shakespeare: A Documentary Life* (Oxford: Clarendon Press in association with the Scolar Press, 1975)

Richard Southern, *The Seven Ages of the Theatre* (London: Faber, 1962)

The Staging of Plays Before Shakespeare (London: Faber, 1973)

Glynne Wickham, *Early English Stages, 1300–1600* (London: Routledge & Kegan Paul, 1959)

Frances Yates, *The Rosicrucian Enlightenment* (London: Routledge & Kegan Paul, 1972)

Shakespeare's Last Plays: A New Approach (London: Routledge & Kegan Paul, 1975)

L. C. Knights's *Drama and Society in the Age of Jonson*

a retrospective review by NICHOLAS GRENE

Drama and Society in the Age of Jonson, reprinted now without revision or alteration,[1] just forty years after its first publication, is in many ways identifiably a period piece. There is the pervasive influence which L. C. Knights acknowledges in his historical section of R. H. Tawney's *Religion and the Rise of Capitalism*; or, on the literary critical side, there is the inspiration which he draws from T. S. Eliot's essays on the Elizabethan dramatists. We find a characteristically Leavisite exclusiveness in his canon of major literature: Middleton, for example, is discredited to accentuate the unique greatness of Jonson. 'We should do well, I think, to reserve the description "great comedy" for plays of the quality of *Volpone* and *The Alchemist* – where we can find them' (p. 269). Above all, the bold claims for the central importance of literature in the understanding of a society mark it as a book of its time. 'If this book establishes anything it should be that the reactions of a genuine poet to his environment form a criticism of society at least as important as the keenest analysis in purely economic terms' (p. 175). The whole design of *Drama and Society*, with its survey of the social and economic history of the Renaissance set beside the literary criticism of the drama of Jonson and his contemporaries, is aimed at validating this claim. Great plays are not to be reduced to social documents illustrating patterns of historical change; rather they form the most profound expression of these patterns which we possess.

Although Knights's book has been enormously influential, particularly in the study of Jonson, it is doubtful if many scholars or literary critics working in the field of Renaissance drama would express this point of view quite so directly today. Criticism has tended to move away from the study of the specific social attitudes represented by the plays towards the elucidation of their themes and structure. Brian Gibbons, for example, in his book on *Jacobean City Comedy*, suggested that Knights might have overstressed contemporary economic and social issues and pointed out that the playwrights inherited from the Middle Ages 'a stylised, Complaint-derived account of the lamentable evils of "nowadays"'.[2] Alexander Leggatt, also, in a broader study of the same field, stressed the range of experimentation with the form and within this generic context analysed the major comedies of Jonson which Knights saw as a unique expression of the 'reactions of a great poet to his environment'.[3] Jonson criticism since the war has been very largely concerned with the analysis of formal technique. A whole series of studies by F. L. Townsend, A. H. Sackton, John J. Enck, E. B. Partridge, and Jonas Barish,[4] has been devoted to the exploration of Jonson's linguistic and dramatic skills and the way in which they contribute to the achievement of the comedies.

Yet Knights's conservative and moral Jonson reproaching his society for the ideals they were rapidly abandoning is still very much the orthodox critical view. Brian Gibbons, even while expressing his reservations about Knights's approach, indicated a substantial area of agreement:

> It is certainly not the aim of this study to assert that there is no relation between the form and mood of Jacobean City Comedy and the Jacobean moral and social world; merely that the plays do not present in any useful sense 'a keen analysis in economic terms' [Knights]; nor may they be rashly cited as evidence of actual conditions at the time. What they present is a keen analysis in moral terms first and last.[5]

One of the most illuminating studies of Jonson's style, E. B. Partridge's *The Broken Compass*, reads almost like a systematic expansion of the ideas implicit in Knights's commentary on particular passages of *Volpone* and *The Alchemist*. Where Knights pinpoints in the speeches of Sir Epicure Mammon 'the typical inflation containing within itself the destructive irony' (pp. 207–8), Partridge remarks in the style of *The Alchemist* 'that peculiar combination of the sublime and the low, the glamorous and the sordid which creates the violated grandeur and extravagant bathos characteristic of Jonson's plays'.[6] The deliberate exploitation of stylistic indecorum makes it possible for Jonson's audience to contrast the traditional ideals represented by classical allusion and religious imagery with the petty and corrupt interests with which they are now associated. Other areas of Jonsonian criticism have contributed to this viewpoint. Alan Dessen's study of morality play structure in Jonson's comedies accentuated the traditionalism of his moral attitude.[7] Several critics of the masques, of whom the most outstanding is Stephen Orgel,[8] have confirmed the picture of Jonson as the highest of high Tory idealists.

There has always been a danger that, with this increasing emphasis on Jonson the doctrinaire moralist, our sense of the comedian may be diminished if not completely eclipsed. Jonson's avowed aim, as a good neo-classicist, was to 'mix profit with pleasure', but an undue stress on the moral profit to be gained from his comedies may taint our appreciation of their pleasures. Knights allows that there is a double reaction to the great comic speeches of Volpone and Mammon, a primary enjoyment of their grotesque splendours, as well as a simultaneous implied criticism. Yet his book concentrates entirely upon the major comedies of Jonson in which the tone of satire is strongest, and gives no attention to works such as *Epicoene* or *Bartholomew Fair* in which the comedy is less obviously controlled by a satiric viewpoint. It is perhaps significant that these latter two plays are in prose, for Knights is mainly interested in Jonson's dramatic verse, and by implication belittles prose as an artistic medium. Jonas Barish in *Ben Jonson and the Language of Prose Comedy* revealed just how mistaken this attitude was, with a brilliant analysis of the virtuoso skills which Jonson displayed in prose. Barish has also contested the image of the consistently moralist Jonson. Instead he traces a graph of Jonson's development as a comedian away from the asperities of the comical satires towards a more genial and permissive comedy of which *Bartholomew Fair* is the final achievement.[9]

Bartholomew Fair, in fact, has become a regular battleground for those who want to maintain Jonson's anarchic comic exuberance against the school of moralist Jonsonians who to some extent derive from Knights. Barish suggests that here Jonson has at last abdicated his role as moral authority and 'with this play, in which reformers are reformed by the fools, confesses his own frailty and his own flesh and blood'.[10] Ian Donaldson very interestingly aligns *Bartholomew Fair* with the tradition of festive comedy and sees in it a fantastic and therapeutic image of the world upside-down.[11] But the moralists have fought back. Alan Dessen sees *Bartholomew Fair* as 'Jonson's most ambitious attempt at a panoramic treatment of both the cause and effects of society's diseases, contamination and impurity.[12] The image of 'justice in the stocks' which Donaldson and Barish interpret as a comic celebration of anarchy can equally be read as a sombre indictment of the failure of authority within the society of the time.

It is surely remarkable that Knights never once mentions *Bartholomew Fair* throughout the whole of *Drama and Society*. In his later essay on Jonson for the Pelican Guide to English Literature, he suggests that it belongs with *Epicoene* in 'the category of stage entertainments' in which 'the fun is divorced from any rich significance'.[13] Yet *Bartholomew Fair*, in the circumstances of its performance if in nothing else, is one of the most striking illustrations of the relation between drama and society in the Renaissance period. It was first produced on 31 October 1614 before a public audience at the Hope Theatre, and the following night before King James and his court. For the public performance Jonson wrote an Induction which provides us with one of the most vivid glimpses we have of the inside of a Jacobean playhouse and the relation of a popular comedian to his audience. For the court production a Prologue and Epilogue addressed to the King were substituted, suggesting the attitude Jonson expected his monarch to adopt towards this comic image of his kingdom. *Bartholomew Fair* may not be as directly concerned with contemporary political and social issues as *The*

Devil is an Ass, a play which Knights studies in some detail, but it is the most systematic image of the whole of his society which Jonson ever attempted.

A commonplace of past Jonson criticism was the sprawling plotlessness of *Bartholomew Fair* as contrasted with the disciplined construction of *The Alchemist* or *Volpone*. This view was challenged by Freda Townsend, and since then the play's structure has been defended by a number of different critics, most outstandingly by Richard Levin.[14] The play has its own principles of organisation, it is now often argued, which were mis-understood by those trying to apply classical criteria of dramatic unity. One of these principles appears to be the attempt to give a deliberate cross-section of the classes within the social community. The groups of fairgoers who assemble in the first act of the play are carefully distinguished in their relative social positions. There is what we might call the Littlewit group – the proctor, his wife Win, her mother Dame Purecraft, and the zealous Rabbi Busy. Purecraft and Busy are from the dissident Puritan lower-middle classes: Busy was a baker until he gave up his profession for full-time preaching. John Littlewit and his wife are keen that the aristocratic Win-wife should marry Purecraft, because for them it would mean a step up in the world.

> *Littlewit.* ... Win and I both wish you well ... Win would fain have a fine young father i' law with a feather, that her mother might hood it and chain it with Mistress Overdo.   (I, iii) 15

Mistress Overdo in her French hood and chain, with her husband the Justice, are in a social group just above that of the Littlewits. Mistress Overdo's brother Cokes is 'an esquire of Harrow', and Overdo himself is a justice of the peace in the pettiest sessions of the land, the court of Pie-powders. Grace Wellborn is, as her name suggests, of a higher rank than the Overdos but, like so many aristocratic wards of court in the period, she is being forced to marry an imbecile relative of her guardian – in this case the foolish Cokes. Finally there are Tom Quarlous and Ned Winwife, the traditional impecunious young men of good family out to restore their fortunes by mercenary marriage or otherwise.

Jonson draws our attention to these class-groupings only to show them disintegrate under the impact of the fair. If we think of each of the groups as a social molecule, then the action of the play after the visitors appear at the fair consists of a steady break-down of each molecule into its constituent atoms. Characters drop away in ones and twos from their original parties until every single individual is isolated from his or her normal social company. This pattern of dispersal is accompanied by the gradual elimi-nation of the outward and visible signs of the characters' rank or status. Bartholomew Cokes is stripped of his two purses, his hat, his sword and his cloak, and by the final scene is reduced to his shirt-sleeves. 'Off, off, ye lendings' might be the cut-purses' motto. There is an equivalent significance in the use of the women's clothes. The culmination of the play's movement towards dispersal comes in act IV where the several women characters are left alone without their normal male protectors. Both Win Littlewit and Mistress Overdo are pressed into the service of the pimps. Win now gains the terms of equality she sought for her mother – 'to hood it and chain it with Mistress Overdo' – but it is in the ironic shape of the common uniform of the whore. Alice the professional objects vehemently to the competition represented by these amateur ladies: 'The poor common whores can ha' no traffic for the privy rich ones; your caps and hoods of velvet calls away our customers and lick the fat from us' (IV, v). It is typical of the levelling quality of the fair that what began as the token of Mistress Overdo's superior social standing – her 'justice-hood' to borrow Wasp's pun – makes her in the end no more than a higher-grade whore, a twelve-penny 'velvet-woman'. The progress towards anarchy in the play is pervasive, and the whole system of society with its complicated structure of shibboleths is subverted.

What is more, Jonson does not limit himself to a cross-section of London life. Bartholomew Fair was a great national institution with people coming into the capital for the Horse Fair, the Cloth Fair, and the Lord Mayor's show. This explains the presence in the play of Northern, a clothier from the North of England, and Puppy, a western wrestler, who is to perform before the Lord Mayor. When, however, we add to these two, Whit the Irish bawd, Bristle who is Welsh, and Haggis who might at least conjecturally be Scots, it is clear that Jonson is assembling comic delegates from the various parts of the kingdom of Great Britain. As the representative trio Fluellen, Captain Jamy, and Captain MacMorris assist at the national victory of Agincourt, so the provincials in *Bartholomew Fair* contribute to the image of the national holiday. The play appears to be a parody version of the Tudor and Stuart concept of the union of the nations, so strongly emphasised for obvious reasons by James I of England and VI of Scotland. If in the earlier acts of the play we are watching the usual sort of city comedy, with its close but limited view of the world of London, as the action develops it seems as though the whole country is being sucked into the maelstrom of the national fair at Smithfield. What Jonson is presenting to his London audience and to his monarch is a view of their society, James's kingdom, in the process of reduction to a mass of crooks and fools, pimps and whores, drunkards and madmen. To say the least it would seem an odd dish to set before the King.

Are there not, indeed, signs that the King may have been offered his own image as part of this grotesque view of his kingdom? It seems tempting to note similarities between Overdo's great anti-smoking speech and the King's own *Counterblast to Tobacco*. Zeal-of-the-Land Busy fulminates against the uncleanness of pig; James I's dislike of pork was sufficiently

well-known to warrant allusion in Jonson's court masques.[16] And yet as Ian
Donaldson sensibly argues, 'it would seem unlikely that in a play dedicated
to the king and designed (partly at least) for a royal occasion Jonson would
have held James up to derision'.[17] One would certainly think not, in view of
the lesson he had learned from *Eastwood Ho*, and the succession of fulsome
eulogies of James contained in his masques. Jonson covers himself by the
terms of his Prologue:

> Your Majesty is welcome to a Fair;
> Such place, such men, such language and such ware,
> You must expect ...

He invokes the monarch's sense of decorum in watching what follows so
that where there might be resemblances between the comic characters and
the King's own person, these would only serve to make the characters
funnier, not derogate from the dignity of the King. Or as Jonson told his
public audience in the Induction the play is designed 'to delight all, and to
offend none; provided they have either the wit or the honesty to think well of
themselves'.

Both Ian Donaldson and William Blissett have stressed the idea of the
monarch's presence in the audience as an ultimate frame for the play's
image of disorder. In the court Epilogue, Donaldson argues, 'the final
appeal to the king re-affirms ... with something of the effect of the entry of
the main masque after the anarchy of an anti-masque, the existence of a real
and workable social order with James at its head'.[18] Blissett echoes this
view: 'the presence of the court itself must, if it can, serve as its own masque
to dispel the antimasque'.[19] By this analogy, *Bartholomew Fair*, with all its
anarchic comic licence, may still be reconciled with the concept of an
authoritarian Jonson upholding the social order which the comedy so
spectacularly disintegrates. Yet it would surely be perverse to over-
emphasise the similarity between the intricate and extended image of
disorder presented by *Bartholomew Fair* and the fairly perfunctory piece of
comic business which is all the anti-masque amounts to in most cases. If the
comedy implies a stable and secure social standpoint in its audience, it
certainly does not celebrate that social stability as the mask does.

Bartholomew Fair is a fascinating test-case in that it raises most strikingly
issues about the relation of comedy to the society in which it is performed.
For L. C. Knights, presumably, it is 'divorced from any rich significance'
because it does not clearly affirm, as *Volpone* or *The Alchemist* do, the highest
moral ideals of the period. Yet its attempt at a comprehensive and fully-
balanced anatomy of the range of Jacobean society could surely be said to
be richly significant. The audience in the Hope Theatre were invited to
observe what was no doubt familiar to them, and yet to watch it from a
vantage-point of comic detachment. The comedy is a distorting mirror in

which the audience can comfort themselves that this is not what they really look like, and yet recognise that it is their image that they see. The fair, in which abnormal behaviour is traditionally sanctioned as normal is an especially powerful vehicle for this dual vision of comedy. By its nature it implies a holiday dispensation from the rules of sobriety and order, a period of exceptional licence. And yet there is a sense in which we accept, if only temporarily, that the fair is an appropriate metaphor for man's condition as a creature of meaningless appetite and equally meaningless aggression, whose only redeeming feature, if it might be called that, is a mad and undirected vitality. The simultaneity of this comprehensive and authentic vision of chaos with its distancing and qualifying norm of order gives us in *Bartholomew Fair* not just an enjoyable 'stage entertainment' but a deeply satisfying comedy.

There is perhaps a final irony, that L. C. Knights in claiming a central importance for great drama in the understanding of a society may have to some extent limited our appreciation of that drama's greatness. His book certainly inspired some of the best and most illuminating studies of Jonson of the last forty years. Re-reading his work now, with a sense of the trivial professionalism of so much modern criticism, we may well admire his authentic commitment to literature and to the significance of literary criticism. Yet his insistence on the moral function of literature and the location of its meaning in the social and economic issues of its time narrowed the criteria of judgement to the exclusion of such an excellent dramatist as Middleton, and even of some of the great plays of Jonson himself. One of the main achievements of Renaissance drama studies since 1937 has been to make us aware of just how complicated the relation between drama and society can be, and nowhere more so than in that area in which they apparently interact most closely and directly, the satiric social comedies of the Jacobean period.

NOTES

1. London: Methuen 1977
2. *Jacobean City Comedy* (London: Hart-Davis, 1968), p. 29.
3. *Citizen Comedy in the Age of Shakespeare* (University of Toronto Press, 1973).
4. *Apologie for Bartholomew Fayre* (New York: MLAA, 1947); *Rhetoric as a Dramatic Language in Ben Jonson* (New York: Columbia University Press, 1948); *Jonson and the Comic Truth* (Madison: Wisconsin University Press, 1957); *The Broken Compass* (London: Chatto & Windus, 1958); *Ben Jonson and the Language of Prose Comedy* (Cambridge, Mass.: Harvard University Press, 1960).
5. *Jacobean City Comedy*, p. 29.
6. *The Broken Compass*, p. 135.
7. *Jonson's Moral Comedy* (Evanston, Ill.: North-western University Press, 1971).

8. See Orgel's two excellent books, *The Jonsonian Masque* (Cambridge, Mass.: Harvard University Press, 1965), and *The Illusion of Power* (Los Angeles and Berkeley: University of California Press, 1975).

9. See also his article 'Feasting and Judging in Jonsonian Comedy', *Renaissance Drama*, 5 n.s. (1972) 3–35.

10. *Language of Prose Comedy*, p. 238.

11. *The World Upside-Down* (Oxford: Clarendon Press, 1970), Chapter 3.

12. *Jonson's Moral Comedy*, p. 218.

13. 'Ben Jonson, Dramatist' in *The Age of Shakespeare*, Pelican Guide to English Literature vol. II, ed. Borris Ford (Harmondsworth, 1969), p. 314.

14. See his book *The Multiple Plot in English Renaissance Drama* (University of Chicago Press, 1971), chapter 6.

15. Quotations from *Bartholomew Fair* are taken from the Yale Ben Jonson edition, ed. Eugene Waith (New Haven and London: Yale University Press, 1963).

16. Other resemblances between Overdo and James are pointed out by William Blissett in 'Your Majesty is Welcome to a Fair' in *The Elizabethan Theatre IV*, ed. G. R. Hibbard (London: Macmillan, 1974), pp. 80–105.

17. *The World Upside-Down*, pp. 72–3.

18. *Ibid.*, p. 72.

19. 'Your Majesty is Welcome to a Fair', p. 105.

Ronald Gray's *Ibsen – a dissenting view*

reviewed by JAMES MCFARLANE

An exquisite irony attends the way in which the challenge to received opinion – already heralded in the title of Ronald Gray's new and provocative study[1] and spelled out in its opening paragraphs – becomes in its concluding phrases a mission as compulsively Ibsenist in the intensity of its dedication as anything examined in its pages. The standard received view of Ibsen, Gray claims, awards him a stature totally undeserved, passes over in silence the more obvious ineptitudes of his dramatic method, discovers profound significance in symbols which in essence are little more than empty and portentous devices, and insists on 'poetic' merit for what to any dispassionate observer is the bleakest prosiness. Beginning his book with a declaration that 'there is still a large body of opinion unconvinced by the reputation Ibsen has gained as the greatest dramatist of the last hundred years, as the modern Aeschylus, Shakespeare or Racine', Gray finally winds up his case with an urgent call for resolute action to halt this juggernaut of unsubstantiated and hyperbolic adulation: 'The case for Ibsen as a poet has still to be made. There is no more foundation for it than there is for the value placed on his plays on other grounds. But the juggernaut has been rolling for a good many years now, and is likely to go on by its own inertia indefinitely. Only deliberate effort will reverse the movement' (p. 212).

The charge sheet which Gray draws up in the course of his inquiry makes a formidable indictment and would, if even only the half of it could be made to stick in the court of public opinion, impose drastic revision on our present assessments. Actually, not everything is wholly negative; but where Gray does award approval, it is carefully selective and designed in the main to acknowledge a limited kind of journeyman skill – a skill which, Gray is nevertheless quick to add, 'need no more conduce to good drama than the skill of a first-rate joiner need lead to fine furniture' (p. 21). Thus he allows himself phrases appreciative of Ibsen's 'carefully devised theatrical moments, . . . pace, climaxes, dramatic thrust and counter-thrust, surprise, revelations, reversals and repeated excitements' (p. 83); an approving word for the exemplary design of his stage sets (p. 3); a nod in the direction of his use of 'ingenious contrivance' (p. 35), of his expert handling of exposition (p. 43) – admissions which in sum testify to little more than a competent constructional and fabricational talent. Under different rubrics, there is also admiration for Ibsen's 'intense individualism' (p. 1), for his 'passionate concern', for the ferocity and dynamism of his spirit, and for the way in which, as never before, he 'combined modernity and social problems with such determination' (p. 2). But nobody must think that these things serve as any real defence against the more crucial charges which Gray announces his intention of bringing in the course of his investigation: 'The question whether Ibsen can be accounted a great dramatist who, for all that, had next to no power of characterisation, manipulated his characters as he pleased and allowed his plots to dictate to them, did not differentiate essentially between their forms of speech, or create any genuine poetry out of his prose, who built his plays on the model of ordinary popular successes and thumping melodramas, and repeatedly used essentially the same themes, is not answered by saying that in his very passion he aroused a livelier debate, stimulated more audiences to take action, than any other dramatist' (p. 25).

In these phrases all is foreshadowed. Not only do they usefully catalogue the main heads by which Gray marshals his indictments, but they also in themselves embody some of the exuberance, betray something of the polemical delight, the ready provocativeness which Gray brings to the conduct of his case. Selected and anthologised, his more extravagant comments would make a *Schimpflexikon* comparable in depreciatory intent (though, one hastens to add, not in silliness) with any of those compiled by William Archer from the critical furore of the Nineties.

Take a look, he bids us, at those Ibsenist characters: at the many, of whom Hjalmar in *The Wild Duck* is but one (though the supreme) example, 'for whom it is hard to find a more charitable name than "booby"' (p. 102); at 'the crudity introduced' into *A Doll's House* 'by the caricaturing of Helmer' (p. 55); at the naive, excessively black and white characterisation in *Ghosts* (p. 83); at the improbabilities in *Rosmersholm*, where Rebecca's account of her motives will not bear examination (p. 120), and where Rosmer 'strains one's suspension of disbelief to the uttermost' (p. 121); at the conventionally drawn, one-dimensional characters in *Hedda Gabler* which are 'like grotesques in the rigidity of their personalities', creatures who (here as elsewhere in Ibsen) speak and act 'more to further the climax intended by Ibsen than in realisation of their own characters' (p. 141), and all this in a play where convincing characterisation and realistic probability are sacrificed to the desire for startling curtain falls.

Consider also the absurd implausibility of the plots and the creaking motivation of the action: how these plots so often require either a totally wide-eyed innocence or else a double-dyed villainy before they even begin to operate (p. 31); how many of the characters are so crudely manipulated that an immediate end is put to any serious pretensions (p. 105); how, for example, *John Gabriel Borkman* – a play in which 'all the characters are either embittered or ruthless or naive and even rather silly' (p. 174) – displays 'a vacuity in the action, an arbitrariness in the sequence of events', in consequence of which 'the play does not hold together, its premises are too vague, its conclusion too inconsequential. No major dramatist ever provided a theme so indistinct' (p. 182). As for those lauded symbols, they are unrelievedly crass: 'All the evidence of the later plays goes to show that the symbols are useless additions, attempts at giving greater portentousness, distractions ...' (p. 153); they are, in their suggestivity, 'more fortuitous than poetic' (p. 207), mere 'false buttresses' (p. 209). Moreover, and accompanying all this, there is a regular descent into melodrama: in *An Enemy of the People* the full chord of Victorian melodrama is struck (p. 97); *Hedda Gabler*, too, is reminiscent of Victorian melodrama (p. 143); the final words of *Little Eyolf* are 'orotund melodrama' (p. 173); and many things that might, in Gray's estimate, have been both tragic and real are doggedly turned into melodrama and heroics.

The nadir is reached with the last plays: *Little Eyolf*, *John Gabriel Borkman*, and *When We Dead Awaken*. They merely document the sad collapse of Ibsen's powers: 'As plays, they fail in coherence, dramatic movement, psychological insight, even in ordinary perceptiveness about human behaviour. The increasingly crude caricatures and comic treatment indicate a lack of self-possession, a need to assert strongly where no real strength was felt' (p. 198). Appropriately, the last scene of Ibsen's last drama stands as 'a slapdash end to his career as a dramatist' (p. 198).

Finally, in a separate appendix, Gray looks at the quality of Ibsen's language, at the claims made on behalf of its 'poetry', and is distinctly unimpressed. Cautious enough to admit the danger of pronouncing too dogmatically on Ibsen's use of language without having oneself a good command of Norwegian, he nevertheless makes very clear the lack of conviction he feels at the arguments of those critics who, like Francis Fergusson, Inga-Stina Ewbank and John Northam, have argued on behalf of the 'poetry' of Ibsen's prose. Unless the case can be made more convincing than it has up till now, he concludes, 'the presumption that a dramatist crude in so many other ways would be unlikely to achieve great heights in language must be allowed to stand' (p. 223).

Gray is conscious that, in taking the line he does, he speaks not for himself alone but for an identifiable (if not always in the past conspicuously vocal) body of opinion. Among those on his side, he instances F. R. Leavis and the *Scrutiny* critics (who remarkably and evidently intentionally withheld their published interest), together with Lawrence, Yeats, Synge, Eliot and (a little incongruously?) Mary McCarthy and John Weightman. On the other side there is an admission that Ibsen has been admired not only by many critics but also by 'dramatists from Shaw to Osborne'. This has resulted in a deep cleavage of opinion. (Perhaps in view of the later discussion of the nature of Ibsen's 'poetic' language, it might have prevented the argument from seeming too obviously slanted at this stage if some indication had also been given that among Ibsen's most devoted and articulate admirers were not only dramatists of problematic realism like Shaw and Osborne but also dramatists of the persuasion of Maeterlinck and Pirandello, as well as novelists like Joyce and Forster, and poets like Hofmannsthal, Pound, Rilke and Auden.) But that there *is* a body of opinion that shares Gray's views is undeniable; that it has traditionally found expression either in polite though eloquent disregard (as with Leavis) or in brief dismissive phrases (as with Eliot) makes it all the more welcome that Gray should now put it with all the forcefulness and passionate conviction of which he is known to be capable. He brings to the task a brisk impiety and a spirited iconoclastic zeal which the continuing debate requires from time to time if a merely stultifying cosiness or a regressive in-breeding is to be prevented from totally taking over. At the very least this book raises legitimate doubts about a whole range of matters relating to Ibsen's achievement which will now have to be squarely faced and – thanks to his forthright definition of them – can now be vigorously debated.

But although his case is an important one, and passionately, entertainingly and courteously presented, its substance is deeply flawed. Texts which everybody agrees – no matter to which side of 'the cleavage' they may belong – merit the closest and most sustained attention are too often given hasty and insensitive reading. Easy fun is frequently allowed to win over sober truth. (The feigned innocence, for example, with which he dresses Irene, on her first reported appearance in *When We Dead Awaken*, like some Miss World contestant, supposing that it must be 'a strange but integral part of Ibsen's purpose . . . to introduce them [Irene and the Sister of Mercy] as humorously as possible, by making Rubek imagine that the figure he saw walking about the grounds at night was wearing a bathing costume' (p. 188) is unworthy of Gray's high intent. 'Badedragt' in this context *must* of course be thought of as some kind of enveloping 'bathing wrap' in order to match the actual appearance of Irene a few moments later 'dressed in fine creamy-white cashmere . . . her dress floorlength, falling about her body in long regular folds'. His fun with Irene's swansdown hood (p. 195) in the same chapter is equally contrived.) The rhetoric of the book is not always fully under control, though in mitigation it must be said that some of the more extravagantly adulatory books in existence (like F. L. Lucas's) are well calculated to drive a passionately heretical mind like Ronald Gray's to intemperate expression. Finally, one becomes aware of a habit in Gray of earnestly and elaborately setting up selected Aunt Sallies, the knocking down of which achieves little but to diminish the persuasiveness of his case in general.

Instances of careless reading range from things which, though intrinsically of small significance, are nevertheless disturbing as indications of a general level of inattention, dangerous when it is Ibsen one is reading (such as his habit of referring to Torvald Helmer, Nora's husband in *A Doll's House*, as 'Helmer Torvald'), up to a more serious kind of misreading – serious because the 'evidence' obtained from it starts a whole chain of progressively larger and increasingly denigratory generalisations. It is a process which goes something like this: first one draws attention, on sturdy, commonsense, naturalistic premisses, to alleged implausibilities in the plot, for which our derision is then solicited ('What we are asked to believe is ...'). This is then used as evidence to prove a degree of naivety or gullibility or at least unsubtlety in the characters which is technically culpable; this is then deployed to highlight a more pervasive fault in the wider *œuvre*, until, finally, the end product is a sweepingly dismissive comment about some aspect or other of Ibsen's general competence. If however, as happens not infrequently in Gray's account, the initial reading of the text reveals itself as defective in significant details, the consequences in logic for the concatenating argument are then dire.

Gray's discussion of *The Wild Duck* can perhaps be taken as typical. First comes the alleged implausibility, with the attendant scorn:

> There is a complex situation to be divulged: first, that fourteen years ago Werle senior has had a child, Hedvig, by his former housekeeper, Gina, and has arranged for the mother to marry Hjalmar, whom he has set up in business as a professional photographer.... We are asked to believe that after Werle discovered Gina's pregnancy he first dismissed her from her job as his housekeeper, then arranged matters so that Hjalmar took up lodgings in her mother's house, and finally waited until Hjalmar not only fell in love with Gina but married her before her pregnancy became obvious to him – and then failed to notice that she gave birth rather soon after their marriage (p. 100).

This, Gray declares, so strains our credulity that the only way we can reconcile ourselves to it is to assume that old Werle is here ready to gamble on very long odds, and that Hjalmar is so naive and unintelligent as to be dismissed as 'a booby'. Thereupon the inference is widened to take in 'Ibsen's characters' in general; and finally it takes off in fanciful and audacious flight:

> But such simple-mindedness and gullibility are too frequent a feature of Ibsen's characters for one not to feel that the sheer technical difficulties have prevented the portrayal of characters possessing more subtle qualities, or else that Ibsen was little interested in the real complexities of behaviour. (p. 102).

But Gray's point of departure, his account of the initial dramatic situation out of which this last and somewhat breathtaking allegation is born, is not only distortingly crude; it is so wrong in its significant detail as to seem almost wilfully perverse. Werle did *not* make Gina pregnant whilst she was still a servant in his house and before dismissing her; there were not even at that time any illicit relations between them, though Werle did pester her, and his wife was suspicious. Gina left his employ of her own accord and went back to her mother's long before there was any hanky-panky; only after a lapse of some time, during which Werle's wife died and Gina finally yielded to her mother's sordid promptings, did Werle 'have his way' with her, by which time it was altogether possible that Hjalmar (following his father's imprisonment and the abandonment of his own studies) had already taken up lodgings in Gina's mother's house. One does not even have to dig particularly hard for this information, as is occasionally necessary in Ibsen; most of it is there openly displayed. In response to Hjalmar's direct question as to whether there was anything between her and old Werle when she was in service there, Gina lays it all on the line:

> It's not true. Not then, there wasn't. Mr Werle pestered me plenty, that I will say. And his wife thought there was something in it. What a fuss she kicked up! She just went for me, played merry hell, she did. So I left. . . . Then I went home. And my mother . . . she wasn't quite what you thought she was, Hjalmar. She kept on at me, about one thing and another . . . Because Werle was a widower by then. . . . Well, you might as well know it. He wouldn't be satisfied till he'd had his way.[2]

Moreover, it is left entirely open how long the relationship between Werle and Gina had been going on before Gina discovered she was pregnant, and it is entirely possible that Hjalmar and Gina were moving towards marriage already by this time. Gina herself later hints that what Werle was really hoping for in subsidising their marriage was the chance 'to come and go as he liked'. Old Werle himself defends his subventions to Hjalmar on grounds of conscience, as making up in some way for what the Ekdals have had to suffer and which he was fortunate enough to escape; and he denies a lot of the stories current about himself as the inventions of his embittered wife's lying tongue during her lifetime, and of Gregers's since. However all this may be, it does not require to be 'proved'; and it would in any case have been totally contrary to Ibsen's purpose to have given everything here an obvious clarity. Indeed the whole question of Hedvig's paternity, and of Werle's real motives – selfish or possibly altruistic – is deliberately kept ambiguous and imprecise as part of a whole lattice of inter-related dramatic impulses. To think that one can define Ibsen's expository intentions in the reductive terms Gray uses – that Werle *has had* a child and then arranged to marry off the mother – is to impose a crudity on the play which is wholly alien to it. So it appears that the events surrounding Gina's pregnancy are not so crudely improbable after all, and that consequently Hjalmar is not just the simple booby which those events seemed to make of him; and so on, down the line.

A second example. Gray repeatedly reproaches Ibsen for creating characters who – perhaps in obedience to some abstract Hegelian 'dialectic' – implausibly 'swing from one extreme to another'. Krogstad, Mrs Alving, Stockmann, and Rosmer are all accused of showing this distinctive and unhappy feature – a feature which Gray, predictably generalising, claims 'is distinctive of many other of Ibsen's characters'. This he then follows with another boldly speculative notion about the pattern of Ibsen's mind:

> Ibsen's characters generally move by these extreme swings, but that does not help the feeling that the construction of the plays is made so much the easier by such idiosyncrasy. The frequency with which these labile – though not therefore incredible – characters appear in central roles not only makes them inwardly resemble each other but suggests a limitation in Ibsen's capacity to imagine firmer wills. (p. 117)

Gray's discussion of Krogstad, in *A Doll's House*, shows the patterning of this line of argument. First: define Krogstad as 'a villain of the deepest dye' (p. 50); contrast the alleged villainy of the Krogstad of act I with the reformed character of act III; deplore the sudden volte-face, but shake a sad head at the recognition that this is nevertheless a common fault 'even (in) Ibsen's principal characters' (p. 50), and in indicating how all this adds up to a 'near-melodramatic situation', pay a nicely calculated back-handed compliment by saying that here 'Ibsen is using melodrama without being naively committed to it' (pp. 49–50). But to see Krogstad as a stock villain straight out of Victorian melodrama is to offer a grotesquely insensitive reading of the part. 'Bad' he may be, but essentially like one of those 'méchants animaux' of the standard phrase: 'Quand on les attaque, ils se défendent.' Granted he has faltered in the past – Helmer, with predictably self-righteous exaggeration calls it 'forgery', though in the circumstances it can hardly have been seriously criminal – and has been made to pay for it with his job. Now, a widower with children, he is on the long slow haul of trying to rehabilitate himself, to re-establish himself in a career, to regain respectability. 'Bad' he may also be in the stock way that all moneylenders are deemed 'bad', yet there is evidence in the text that nevertheless his interest charges are not exorbitant, that he has sought nothing but the agreed repayments in the past, and that his methods have never before held any taint of 'blackmail'. He has been content to collect what was owing to him without ever seeking to make improper use of what he knows about Nora's forgery. Only when he is quite outrageously sacked from his job at the whim of the new manager, apparently because the latter cannot bear being addressed in the familiar 'du' form by his one-time student friend – what would our 'wrongful dismissal' procedures today think of this one? – and thus finds his entire career, his children's future, his family's existence destroyed at one cruel and arbitrary stroke does he vigorously react to defend himself and his position. True, he allows his fury and his sense of contempt for Helmer to provoke him into wild talk of ousting Helmer from the managership; but even this is based on an assessment of Helmer's character which the entire subsequent course of the play goes on to legitimise. Given the indefensible way he is 'kicked off the ladder', his bitterness is understandable, and his fight to keep his job excusable. Menace certainly attends his appearances in the Helmer household; but it is much more defensive in its vehemence, much more provoked, than anything that could be called stock 'Victorian villainy'. Everything in the text invites a view of him as a man wary of life, suspicious of treachery, ruthless perhaps in his determination to defend his legitimate interests, but fundamentally of generous impulses. There is *no* volte-face between some supposed Mark I and Mark II Krogstad; and everything that is made to follow from it in Gray's argument – the melodrama, the swings from one extreme to another, the inability on Ibsen's part to 'imagine firmer wills' – thus loses much of its warrant. Once again the alleged 'crudity' stems from what one can only think of as a pre-determined and prejudiced reading of the play by a mind already made up.

A third (and, for reasons of space, final) example. Central to Gray's assessment of *John Gabriel Borkman* is the view that the Erhart element is arbitrary and does not contribute significantly to the play: 'Ibsen tacks on the sections of the play dealing with Erhart without concern for any general unity. Erhart is said by his mother to have a great mission in life (for what end, she does not say) ...' (p. 179). That any qualified reader can remain unaware that Erhart's 'mission' is to act as his mother's agent in revenging herself on Borkman, to rehabilitate the name and the fortunes of the Borkman family, and in so doing to consign John Gabriel to oblivion is nothing less than astonishing; and to fail to notice that his mother obsessively goes on and on about this mission of Erhart, what his first duty is, what *she* has determined he will dedicate his life to, shows an almost wilful myopia. Indeed Erhart is not only totally central to Mrs Borkman's embittered purposes, but he is also the one person in the play to whom practically all the other characters turn for the fulfilment of their designs: Ella as a source of comfort in her last dying days; John Gabriel as an associate in his last bid for commercial power; and Mrs Wilton for sexual gratification. Situated as he is at the intersection of so many desires, drives and aspirations, Erhart – it can be powerfully argued – could hardly be more centrally placed.

The same reluctance to respond to the play's perfectly clear indications attends Gray's rather querulous summary of the situation as it related to Borkman, Ella and Hinkel. He complains that the whole business of the letters remains wantonly obscure, and summarises the events in terms that seem deliberately calculated to obfuscate the meaning; he then uses the opportunity to allege 'exaggeration and mystery together with, once again, a complete absence of clues to the real circumstances, ... an undesirable gap in our knowledge' (p. 177). Yet all the clues are surely there, open and accessible: the ambitious Borkman was promised to Ella; he threw her over in favour of her twin sister Gunhild in order to leave the field free for Hinkel, who in consideration of this arranged a bank directorship for him; Hinkel pressed his suit diligently with the now available Ella, who nevertheless repeatedly turned down his advances, believing Borkman to be responsible for his lack of success with Ella; Hinkel betrayed his friend, sold him down the river by publishing private and confidential correspondence which had passed between them and which obviously revealed to the world Borkman's fraudulent business plans. But when Gray summarises these events, the account is in terms that build in an exasperated puzzlement that is difficult to explain:

> It would have been a simple enough matter, here, for Ibsen to have let [Borkman] attribute [his downfall] to some unlucky slump, some unpredicted change in market values. What Borkman alleges is more obscure, and less easy to understand as a cause of financial failure. It was through no mistake or mischance that he fell, Borkman says; it was rather due to the publication by his friend Hinkel of certain letters of Borkman's about whose contents nothing is revealed. There is no intimation of how these letters could have damaged Borkman's reputation so severely, no hint of why he himself is so outraged. His reaction is out of all proportion to the bare statement that the letters were published: we are left merely speculating why he accuses Hinkel, on these grounds, of 'the most infamous crime a man can be guilty of'.... The sacrifice of Ella to Hinkel is rather fanciful: only such a complete egotist as Borkman could imagine that a woman could be switched from one man to another, or that Hinkel could expect to gain anything from such a bargain. (p. 177).

If this is the kind of understanding one brings to the text, if one wants to re-design the play so that some simple stock-market slump sends Borkman to prison, and write out, or ignore, the complex interplay of business ethics, power seeking, love and marriage at work here, then it is not surprising that one should wish to conclude that the play 'seems vague and unorientated' (p. 178).

(In parentheses, Gray has a few moments of legitimate fun with the phrase which Borkman uses of Hinkel: that he is 'infected and poisoned in every fibre with the morals of the higher rascality'. This, Gray rightly says, is 'a phrase mysterious enough in itself and which Ibsen declined to explain, when asked about it by William Archer' (p. 177). But one should know that the fun has to be more at Archer's expense, as translator, than Ibsen's, and incidentally for reasons which few people are better qualified to appreciate than Gray himself with his close familiarity with nineteenth-century

German philosophy. If the Norwegian phrase in question – 'forgiftet og forpestet af overskurkens moral' is put into literal German, its overtones are more immediately audible: 'vergiftet und verpestet von Über-schurkenmoral'. This much more obviously than any English phrase brings in all the intended harmonics from the Nietzschean concepts of 'Über-mensch' and 'Herrenmoral'; the reference, contrived though at first sight it may appear – and indeed absurd when put too literally into English – is entirely consistent with the speech and thought patterns of a Borkman who, elsewhere in the play, speaks of himself with Nietzschean self-satisfaction as an 'undtagelsesmenneske', an 'Ausnahmemensch'. And who, being Ibsen, would not groan at the thought of explaining all *this* to the earnest Archer?)

In themselves, and separated out from their wider context in the book as a whole, these and other individual aberrations may seem to be defensible as momentary slips of attention. I fear their significance goes deeper. I see them as representative features of a critical approach to Ibsen which – beginning with a genuine distaste for many aspects of Ibsen's work – is betrayed by its initial antipathy or, if less intense than that, by an im-patience with what are believed to be the extravagant claims made by certain commentators on Ibsen's behalf, into a succession of false recog-nitions, misinterpretations and prejudiced readings which a careful and reasonably responsive reading of the textual evidence does not substantiate. One knows well how easy it is to make even the greatest works of literary (and, even more so, operatic) art seem ridiculous by deliberately hostile paraphrase of the plot; how easy it is, too, to subject the dramatic events to a kind of sane man's, no-nonsense scrutiny whereby any quotidian plausi-bility they may claim to have is exposed as plain absurdity. How is it, Gray asks, that Captain Alving's debauched living could have been kept con-cealed so long: 'Did his nose never change colour or his breath smell?' (p. 68). Or, he suggests, is it not unfortunate for the play as a whole that Stockmann's outburst in act III 'is enough to alienate from him the sym-pathy that a more realistic liberal might attract...' (p. 88). And think of all the fuss we'd have been spared if only old Werle had had roast duck for dinner that time: 'What was old Werle doing, sending a duck with two slugs in its body and a damaged neck as a pet for Hedvig? Presumably he shot it in order to eat it' (p. 106). It is a critical policy which invites hilarious speculation as to how, for example, the plot of *King Lear* might lend itself to this kind of reductive treatment.

When however Gray moves in to counter-attack the claims made on behalf of Ibsen the 'poet', the more knockabout arguments of the body of his book shift into another gear, and the discussion takes on a different order of significance. At the very least, there emerges from his discussion of this aspect of the work a recognition of the urgent need for clarifying not only our terms but also our critical expectations.

Once again however there is a bit of unnecessary and maladroit pleading to be cleared out of the way first. Early in the book (pp. 23–4), Gray refers to a much quoted letter of May 1883 from Ibsen to Lucie Wolf; he does so in the following terms: 'As he [Ibsen] declared ... in a letter, "I myself during the last seven or eight years have scarcely written a single line [of poetry], but have exclusively devoted myself to the incomparably harder task of writing poetry in straightforward, realistic, everyday language," and some have been convinced by this, though "writing poetry" was not exactly what Ibsen said (see p. 214 below).' In his concluding appendix, Gray once more returns to this question, re-quotes the phrase about the 'very much more difficult art of writing poetry in straightforward, realistic, everyday language', and then goes on to argue that 'the translation of his words can be misleading' (p. 214). The difficulty, he indicates, lies with the Norwegian verb *at digte* which, like the German *dichten*, 'need not imply anything remotely like poetry but rather a certain literary quality above the ordinary level. ... Ibsen's sentence in his letter could have been rendered almost as well with "writing in straightforward, realistic everyday language"' (p. 214). Failure to understand the essential meaning of *digte* has thus, in Gray's view, sadly misled many of his English interpreters into 'a lot of attempts at showing Ibsen truly wearing vine-leaves in his hair'; for, he adds, to say '"writing poetry" seems to introduce an element of deliberate paradox ...' (p. 214).

Indeed it does. But *who* among Ibsen's interpreters has failed to understand this meaning of *digte*? And *who* has introduced the phrase 'writing poetry' into the English translation, quoted here, of Ibsen's letter? Gray does not give any source for the translation he himself uses; but a quick check of the more obvious sources he might have used shows none of them using the phrase 'writing poetry' at this point: *Ibsen's Letters and Speeches*, ed. Evert Sprinchorn, p. 218,[3] Michael Meyer, *Ibsen*, p. 535,[4] and *The Oxford Ibsen*, v, p. 439 all have simply 'the art of writing ...'; and Inga-Stina Ewbank (*Ibsen Year Book*, II, pp. 6off), with whom Gray particularly joins issue, not only carefully formulates it as 'the far more difficult art of writing (*at digte*) in a plain realistic everyday language', but also goes on to draw attention to the ambiguities in 'that untranslatable word "digte"'. The particular door that Gray is here pushing at so hard is in fact wide open. He himself in the preface admits to his sometimes having made his own translations for use in the book 'in the interest of bringing out some particular point'; it is unfortunate for the rigour of his argument in general if this happens to be one of those occasions.

Once this point has been cleared away, there is nevertheless a hard central core of substance in much of what Gray writes about current attempts to define the 'poetry' of these last twelve 'realistic' plays of Ibsen. There is no doubt that the choice of the term 'poetry' for the enriched meaning that informs the dramatic mode – whether 'realistic', 'symbolic' or whatever – bedevils the debate; even the conveniently specialist denotations of the term *poésie du théâtre*, which at least provides a constant reminder that we are using the notion of 'poetry' in a very particular sense, is not always sufficient to discourage the application of familiar methodologies of rhetoric where their deployment is clearly out of place. (One thing that does not really need labouring among Ibsen critics is that if you claim to find 'poetry' in the prose dialogue, you are not issuing a general invitation to see it emulating Shakespearian dramatic verse.) If – to adapt an older and in these days wholly non-trendy definition from I. A. Richards – one were to postulate that drama is a mode of communication, and that *what* it communicates and *how* this is communicated and the value of what is communicated is then the legitimate business of criticism, provision is made for a suitable framework of reference for such elements inherent in drama as visual imagery, physical movement and gesture and the semantics of situation; but to take all which is extra to the sum of the referential meanings of the verbal utterances and call it 'poetry' is, though legitimate enough, nevertheless at the risk of inviting a set of stock responses to the term which are obstructive of true understanding.

Drama continues, as it always has done, to mount raids on the inarticulate; but, in the modern age particularly, it is largely with weapons of inarticulation. Conspicuously evident today is a reduced dependence on the purely unsupported resources of words, a progressive preoccupation with the understated, the throw-away, the tangential, the inconsequential, a penetration into areas of human experience into which simple verbalisation cannot by itself enter. As Pinter said in 1960: 'A character on the stage who can present no convincing argument or information as to his past experience, his present behaviour or his aspirations nor give a comprehensive analysis of his motives is as legitimate and as worthy of attention as one who, alarmingly, can do all these things. The more acute the experience the less articulate its expression.'[5] It is a line of thinking that goes straight back to the final moments of *Ghosts*, to a created situation where conventional language has been almost completely pared away, where words fail and speech becomes an idiot's babble and a mother's cry of pain and irresolution and where, in the overall interdependence of parts in the dramatic mode, the role of verbalisation is reduced almost to vanishing point. That this can result in an extremely powerful mode of communication is undeniable; that it succeeds in communicating things incommunicable by any other means seems at least arguable; but that we continue to denote as 'poetry' the particular mode by which such communication is achieved, though doubtless in itself defensible, seems sadly imprudent. Yet always, as a subdued accompaniment to these arguments, there are the cautionary revelations of Roy Fuller's poem 'Ibsen', where a first confident contempt for the symbols – 'ridiculous . . . they clump across the stage as obvious as wigs' – is arrested by a maturer realisation of what can be found enfolded deep within 'crude interpretation', whereby

> . . . all the high stiff collars and the ledgers
> Shine out with their own intense interior meaning:
>   The names like fiords, the
>   Chorus of doctors, take
>   Their place in consummate verse.[6]

NOTES

1. *Ibsen – a dissenting view. A study of the last twelve plays* (Cambridge University Press, 1977).
2. *Ibsen*, ed. and trans. James Walter McFarlane, 8 vols (Oxford University Press, 1960–77), VI, 203.
3. New York: Hill and Wang, 1964.
4. Harmondsworth: Penguin, 1974.
5. Programme note for the production of *The Room* and *The Dumb Waiter* at the Royal Court Theatre on 8 March 1960. Reprinted in Martin Esslin, *Pinter: A Study of his Plays* (London: Eyre Methuen, 1973), p. 40.
6. Reprinted in James McFarlane, *Henrik Ibsen*, Penguin Critical Anthologies (Harmondsworth, 1970), p. 272.

Ronald Gray will be commenting on James McFarlane's review in volume 2 of 'Themes in Drama'.

Index

Index